C1

D1651911

DONE THIS DAY

OLIVER CRAWFORD

Done this Day

The European Idea in Action

Rupert Hart-Davis   London   1970

© Oliver Crawford 1970
First published 1970

Rupert Hart-Davis Ltd
3 Upper James Street
Golden Square, London W1

Printed in Great Britain by
C. Tinling & Co. Ltd
London and Prescot

SBN: 246 63883 4

FOR PAULINE GALLICO
BECAUSE SHE HAS HER OWN BOOKS
TO GIVE THE WORLD
YET HELD THEM BACK
TO HELP THIS BOOK FORWARD

'That our principle, however baffled or delayed, will finally triumph, I do not permit myself to doubt. Men will pass away—die politically and naturally; but the principle will live, and live forever. Organizations rallied around that principle may, by their own dereliction, go to pieces, thereby losing all their time and labor; but the principle will remain, and will reproduce another, and another, till the triumph will come.'

Abraham Lincoln, Speeches in Kansas, Dec 1-5, 1859

ACKNOWLEDGEMENTS

One of the greatest pleasures in writing a book is the opportunity to say thank you to those who helped. Yet it grieves me that some who helped most in London, Bruges, Brussels, Luxembourg, Strasbourg and elsewhere did so on strict condition of anonymity because of their official status. Some names are in the text, more not—to all my warmest thanks.

I am, however, honoured to be able to thank here Sir Geoffrey de Freitas for his support and generosity in writing the Foreword. With him, it is a pleasure to thank Mr R. J. Jarrett of London, and in Strasbourg Mr Hugh Beesley, now Secretary to the Committee of Ministers of the Council of Europe, whose help has been quite invaluable at all stages in checking facts: he is of course responsible for no expressions of opinion except those given under his own name.

I wish also to thank Mr Francis Pagan for his hard work and good judgement in seeing the book through the press (including selection of the illustrations) together with his present and former colleagues at Rupert Hart-Davis Ltd, particularly Mr John Knowler, who first saw its possibilities.

Among my friends in London I am most happy to thank Mr and Mrs George Denwood, and Mr and Mrs Zoltan Frankl of Hampstead; and it is a great personal pleasure for me to thank that noted translator of Balzac, my aunt, Miss Marian Ayton Crawford of Limavady, Northern Ireland; Mr and Mrs Harold Moss of Weybridge, Surrey; and Mr and Mrs Harry and Margaret Challoner of Brixham, Devon. In Canada, I similarly wish to thank Professor and Mrs Lewis, of Lakehead University, Port Arthur, Ontario, who suggested the title of the book.

Here in Jerusalem, it is my special pleasure to thank, among others, Mr Elias H. Bullata of the Gloria Hotel, the Old City; Dr Meron Medzini; Brother Atanaz of the Franciscan Order; Miss Batsheva Herman; Mr and Mrs Zoltan and Shoshana Schwartz; Dr Daniel Sperber, and Mr Khalil Ibrahim el Masri. Finally, I wish to pay homage to those writers, speakers, and men of action—living and dead—who have fought so hard for the European Idea.

O.C.

Acknowledgements

Thanks are due to the following for permission to quote from published works:

Curtis Brown Ltd and Coward McCann Inc. (*The Coming Caesars* by Amoury de Riencourt); Manhattan Publishing Company (*Towards a European Parliament*, by Kenneth Lindsay); The Bodley Head (*Europe Will Not Wait*, by Anthony Nutting); Hutchinson & Co. (*Towards the United States of Europe*, by R. W. G. Mackay); George Allen & Unwin (*Speaking European*, by Horsfall Carter); McGraw-Hill Book Company (*International Politics*, by Frederick L. Schuman); Stevens and Sons (*The Council of Europe*, by Dr A. H. Robertson and *Important*, by Noel Salter); Pall Mall Press (*Europe Against de Gaulle*, by John Pinder); Louisiana State University Press (*The Path to European Union*, by Professor Hans Schmitt); William Kimber and Doubleday & Co. (*Armageddon*, by Leon Uris); New York University Press (*The Struggle to Unite Europe*, by Arnold J. Zurcher); Houghton Mifflin Company (*The Human Use of Human Beings*, by Norbert Wiener); Reader's Digest ('Dante, Poet of Hope', by Ernest Hauser); Hamish Hamilton and Harper & Row (*Profiles in Courage*, by John F. Kennedy); and The Selden Society (*The Yearbooks of Edward II*, by F. W. Maitland).

CONTENTS

Foreword by Sir Geoffrey de Freitas, PC, KCMG, MP   *page* xi

Author's Note   xiv

1 'No one can wish the ship to sink'   5

2 'What one man has imagined, another man can make'   34

3 'Wherewith will you unite men?'   75

4 'Something more than common'   120

5 'Citizen of Novara'   155

6 'Look at the map'   189

7 'Consider the What, consider more the How'   239

8 'Whither we are tending'   267

9 'The union of theory and practice'   304

10 'Let us be quite sober'   346

Appendix: Charts showing the deposit of ratifications of Council
            of Europe Conventions and Agreements   389

Index   394

A*

PLATES

Winston Churchill and Edouard Herriot   *facing page* 84

Jean Monnet   85
Robert Schuman

Ernest Bevin and George C. Marshall   116
Ernest Bevin signs the Marshall aid agreement

The signature page of the Statute of the Council of Europe   117

Member states of the Council of Europe   244
Organisation of the Council of Europe

The House of Europe, Strasbourg   245
Young visitors to the Consultative Assembly

Professor Henri Brugmans and R. W. G. Mackay   276
Sir Geoffrey de Freitas presiding at a meeting of the
    Consultative Assembly

The 'Human Rights Building' at Strasbourg   277
A meeting of the European Commission of Human Rights

FOREWORD

by The Right Honourable Sir Geoffrey de Freitas KCMG MP

This book is about 'The European Idea in Action'. I have been asked to write the foreword because I have spent the last three years as President of the Consultative Assembly of the Council of Europe. I shall not discuss the history and philosophy of 'The European Idea' which are so well presented by Mr Crawford. Instead I shall concentrate on one aspect of the 'Action'—our Assembly.

When democratic Europe is united its essential democracy will have come from the democratic nature of the Assembly. The Council of Europe was the first international organisation to have an assembly of Members of Parliament. Not only was this Assembly to be consulted by Governments, but it was to include Members of Opposition parties. Looking back over the last 20 years it is difficult to exaggerate the importance of the Consultative Assembly. There have been the big debates. Nearly every political development in Europe has grown from an idea first discussed in the Assembly in Strasbourg.

Then there has been the practice of Members of Parliament working together as Europeans rather than as British or French, or as Christian Democrats or Socialists. By a fortunate decision taken at the beginning, members of the Assembly sit in neither national delegations nor party groups. Instead they sit as Europeans in the alphabetical order of their surnames. Among these Europeans who have been members of the Assembly are postwar Prime Ministers from three of the four big countries: Chaban-Delmas, Churchill, Douglas-Home, Kiesinger, Macmillan, Mollet and Pflimlin.

This list does not include Prime Ministers who have come as guests to take part in our debates. All the present Prime Ministers of the four big countries have spoken in the Assembly, either as Members or visitors. It is a unique Assembly. Nowhere else can these Prime Ministers be questioned in public by Members of Parliament from other countries. The most widely reported speech of recent years was that of Mr Harold Wilson in our Assembly in January 1967. It was at the beginning of Britain's second attempt to enter the Community. Except by the Gaullists he was well received. In fact the Assembly has consistently supported the enlargement of the Community and the admission of Britain, Denmark, Ireland and Norway.

After President de Gaulle's veto in 1963 the Assembly, instead of indulging in tedious repetition of its arguments for expansion, spent more time in discussing its role as the only European forum of debate. From this came its increasing interest in how Europe looked from the world outside. U Thant spoke to us in 1966 and reminded us of our wealth and of our responsibilities to the developing countries. Speaking as Secretary General of a world organisation he begged us not to sink back into prosperous European 'provincialism'. It may turn out that the years of waiting for the expansion of the Community were not wasted, because we had time to look at ourselves from outside. It could be that as a result the enlarged Community will be able to look outwards and see its world role more clearly than if it had had only its own internal problems to consider. The colonial powers may have hauled down their flags, but they cannot avoid their responsibility to those to whom they offered their institutions, their culture and, above all, their language.

Strasbourg was chosen as the seat of the Council of Europe because a Germanic city in France provided the best atmosphere for a reconciliation which immediatly after the war was most important to the future of Europe.

Those who created our Assembly forbade the discussion of national defence. This has enabled neutral countries to join the Council of Europe as full members. My successor is a Swiss. Finland is now the only country with parliamentary democracy which is not a member and she co-operates in many technical conventions.

Under prodding from the Assembly, the Committee of Ministers and the Secretariat have, in recent years, worked for technical co-operation with the European countries which do not have our system of parliamentary democracy. After all, Poland and Spain are both European countries and we are the Council of Europe. There are an ever-increasing number of environmental problems such as polluted air and polluted water, which do not distinguish between people who live under different political systems.

But however much co-operation there may be between the Council of Europe and the authoritarian countries, they could never be full members. Our Assembly is of members of democratically elected parliaments, a substantial minority of whom are politically opposed to their Governments. We would not sit in our Assembly with 'parliamentarians' from Poland or Spain. We might invite Ministers from these countries to take part in our debates. They represent governments. But our parliamentarians are chosen by secret ballot by their own people. Even the Greek military regime had the grace to recognise this by announcing within a few days of the *coup d'état* in 1967 that they would not send a delegation to our Assembly.

Many see the development of European unity in terms of a conflict between democracy and bureaucracy. Thanks to the founding fathers, who insisted on a parliamentary assembly, to my predecessors from Paul-Henri Spaak to Pierre Pflimlin, the democratic basis of any unified Europe is assured. Governments and international commissions are necessary, but the business of international government is far too important to be left to Ministers or international civil servants. There must be parliamentary control.

Mr Crawford tells us what there is to achieve, what has been achieved and how it has been achieved. Unlike many scholarly writers on contemporary politics he does not ignore the 'how'. In fact one of his chapters begins with a quotation from Goethe: 'Consider the What, consider more the How'.

Mr Crawford has given a great deal to this book. It is profound and extremely interesting.

House of Commons   *Geoffrey de Freitas*
11 November 1969

Author's Note

THERE IS a belief in many circles that the European Idea is today the monopoly of the European Economic Community and its related organisations. There is a belief in other circles that the ideal guardianship of the European Idea is today the monopoly of the Council of Europe, and all it represents. Each view is only partially true. The emphasis of this book is to suggest there are aspects of the work of the Council of Europe in Strasbourg which tell us more about the real meaning—the real challenge—of the European Idea than is yet accepted or even realised, just as there are also aspects of the European Community in Brussels whose real meaning have not yet been unequivocably expressed to the public. This book is thus a selective commentary with a purpose. It should be made clear this book is deliberately partisan and uncompromisingly federalist.

Its method is to look at a different aspect of the European Idea in each chapter.

Thus in Chapter One we look at the European Idea in terms of the origin of the Council of Europe.

In Chapter Two we look at the early struggles of the Council of Europe, and the creation of the European Coal and Steel Community.

In Chapter Three we look at two of the Council of Europe's Conventions or European Treaties—the Convention on Human Rights and the European Social Charter.

In Chapters Four and Five we look at the European Idea as expressed through the creation and evolution of all the Conventions of the Council.

In Chapter Six we look by contrast at Brussels, and examine the underlying purpose of the European Economic Community, and its interpretation of the European Idea as revealed solely in its own documents addressed to the general public. And we examine seven propositions which attempt to express a possible ground of common agreement for all concerned with the creation of a true union of Europe.

In Chapter Seven we consider the relevance for these seven propositions of what has happened more recently in Strasbourg, and we examine the European Idea as expressed in a single public speech by the Secretary General of the Council of Europe, introducing the Council's Intergovernmental Work Programme.

In Chapter Eight we look at the way this same Programme of Work was introduced—not to the public—but privately to Governments.

In Chapter Nine we examine the Programme itself, its claim to represent a turning point in the evolution of the Council of Europe, and its relevance to the future pattern of European unification.

In Chapter Ten we look at the power-relationship between the Council of Europe and the European Community, some aspects of the federalist question, and the meaning of these in terms of the seven propositions introduced in Chapter Six.

We have come to a point today where public understanding and enthusiasm for the European cause is being crippled by the necessity to get done what we can today by the expedient of avoiding proper discussion of the principle at stake. It is even felt by some that we shall continue to gain most by saying least. Yet the price we pay for these tactical advances is public puzzlement, suspicion, uninformed hostility—and even more often, at the other extreme, indifference. In the long run it is public opinion that carries the day. An argument cannot be won unless it is opened. Conviction cannot grow unless counter-convictions have been faced in open controversy. The conviction that unites the very diverse chapters of this book is that for us in Europe the European Idea is the most creative idea of our century, and its logical imperative is that we must combine our experience, our energies, our ability and our faith towards one single aim—the eventual creation of a European Federal Government for all Europe and in perpetuity.

The writer's own attitude is probably best expressed in these lines by John Bunyan, from his *Author's Apology for his Book.*

> *When at the first I took my book in hand*
> *Thus for to write, I did not understand*
> *That I at all should make a little book*
> *In such a mode; nay, I had undertook*
> *To make another, which when almost done*
> *Before I was aware, I this begun...*
> *Well, when I had thus put mine ends together*
> *I show'd them others that I might see whether*
> *They would condemn them, or them justify...*
> *And some said, 'Let them live'; some, 'Let them die';*
> *Some said, 'John, print it'; others said, 'Not so';*
> *Some said, 'It might do good'; others said, 'No'.*
> *   Now I was in a strait, and did not see*
> *What was the best thing to be done by me;*
> *At last I thought, since you are thus divided,*
> *I print it will, and so the case decided.*

OLIVER CRAWFORD

Jerusalem
1969

CHAPTER ONE

'No One Can Wish The Ship To Sink'

'In a storm at sea no one can wish the ship to sink, and yet not infrequently all go down together because too many will direct and no single mind can be allowed to control.'   ABRAHAM LINCOLN, 1861

THE EUROPEAN IDEA is simple in essentials, complicated in application, and for us in Europe will prove the decisive event of our century. To come straight to the heart of the matter, a truly united Europe must imply the necessity for a Government of Europe. Furthermore a Government of Europe implies the necessity for an unbroken succession of individual men in whom responsibility centres in turn as we, the people of Europe, wish, permit, and decide. It is a universal truth that a Government which can neither act nor endure is not a Government in which its citizens can have confidence, either for themselves or for their children and coming generations. It is also true that a Government which does not respect the individual is not a Government which the individual can permanently respect.

We are today in Europe in a perplexed mood. Our problem is the unification of Europe, and yet because we recognise only partially the implications of this problem we fear to recognise its remedy. For the solution of this problem is its replacement by a greater: that of the governing of Europe. For all of us concerned with the creation and character of a viable and enduring union of Europe this is a question not only of administrative, parliamentary and governmental mechanics, but of the morality of modes of power.

Our present necessity to establish new systems of European responsibility, whose integrity at every level must depend on the combined strength of conscience in individual minds, is the most subtle and demand-ing challenge that can face any evolving society—weighted as it is with uttermost consequences for good and for evil. The vision and capacity for action of any one generation is necessarily always limited, but not necessarily the responsibility resting on that generation. And yet it is on us today in Europe that the responsibility rests for unifying Europe, and it rests on all of us. We shall go down damned in the eyes of coming genera-tions if we do not succeed in creating a Government of Europe. While we shall certainly go down damned if we do it wrong, we shall go down damned unutterably if from fear of doing it wrong we turn aside. Dare we forget that for evil to triumph 'it is necessary only for good men to stand still'?

Our problem—our necessity—and also our hope—is so to construct a Government of Europe that the door to reasonable progress is always open as far as we, the people, indicate, and the door to tyranny always, unalterably and implacably bolted, barred and everlastingly locked.

The European Idea implies a united Europe responsible for all her own actions. Responsibility must centre somewhere. Sober though we must be at the prospect of all-European responsibility eventually centring in an unbroken succession of individual minds, we can also draw reassurance from the fact that—at least in a democratic society—no single mind ever carries total responsibility totally alone. If this happens democracy dies and there is tyranny. In all government of which free and upright men and women may feel proud there is always around every single mind a circle of other minds, each of whom is again individual and alone—to the extent that there again an aspect of responsibility centres—and it is on this combination of individual conscience and collective capacity that all depends. This is true not only at the top but also at the bottom—and at every level of responsibility in between as well. And the final responsi-bility, the only total responsibility, though it may centre temporarily in an individual, is nevertheless the permanent and inalienable property of the people. It can be nowhere else. In a united Europe, this means with *all* the people of our Continent. A Federal Government of Europe can be created and maintained only by the combined ability, action and example of very, very many men and women—and only a Federal Government can itself be a full and final proof and guarantor of the unity of Europe. Would we wish it any other way? For we are contemplating not a small matter but a matter without precedent—a Federal Government not merely of part of Europe at some time in the foreseeable future, but of all Europe and in perpetuity. We have today in Europe a European ship of state to build. We are destined to embark upon it whether we like it or not, and whether it be seaworthy or faulty and leaking. And we must soberly face the fact that a ship that has not been built to sail through storms will sooner or later infallibly sink.

Let us listen at once to the European Idea as reflected in the private conversation of a very distinguished Dutch federalist with the ribbon of the French Legion of Honour in his button-hole, talking off the record during a fast and tortuously difficult drive from near Hyde Park to London Airport; the car meanwhile dodging in and out of traffic in an attempt to reach London Airport in time to catch the plane to Brussels. The speaker was on his way back to the College of Europe in Bruges (which has done so much to shape the minds and warm the attitudes of post-graduate Europeans) and those who know him will already have recognised him— Professor Henri Brugmans, Rector of the College of Europe, and holder of the Charlemagne Prize (awarded annually by the City of Aachen for services to European Unity, and whose recipients include Churchill, de Gasperi, Hallstein, Monnet, Luns). Professor Brugmans, distinguished historian of European civilisation that he is, will perhaps forgive us for eavesdropping on how the history of European unification itself sounded at the time of this conversation—spring 1966—and he would not ask us to edit out that very confusion characteristic of the European Idea in our time.

'...That meeting last night, it was difficult, wasn't it?...Yes, I always stay at St Ermins...that meeting was razor's edge—however, I think the right things will happen now, in spite of what was said. It's on the move now in the right minds. The self-dissolving committee, however, is something we haven't yet invented, have we?...Yes, I have an idea of what we decided: there's a clear timetable and a clear deadline on when we next meet. It will coincide, of course, with some speeches I have to make around Rome, but never mind...Now tell me, what about the election? The question interesting us is what will happen to Heath if the Conservatives lose. Of course, if the leadership passes to Maudling...What part of London are we in now? That must still be re-building after bomb-damage. Look at those houses—and those windows—mullooned, you call it?...Aha, *mullioned*! I always think they are such an extraordinary attempt to combine art with architecture...That reminds me, that other meeting in Oxford was also most useful, Professor Kitzinger was there, and let me see, who else besides...The gigantic strength of the Community is of course a dominant fact and when it comes to correlating that with the Convention of the Council of Europe...You know about the Belgian schools case? There is this case now before the European Court of Human Rights·in Strasbourg asking for a definitive judgement on these Belgian schools giving...Yes, it was brought by the French-speaking minority in Belgium...It is disgraceful to use the Court like this, but there it is—they demand a judgement giving them the right to maintain independent schools where their children will be taught to speak French, not Flemish...I tell you the region is entirely Flemish...If the decision from Strasbourg supports them, and if the Belgian Government supports the Strasbourg decision, the result could well be civil war. The local Flemish population will not stand for it...Yes, perhaps conflict can be evaded, but a decision like that would run counter to the whole Belgian compromise so long established on this...If not civil war, then certainly civil discord, and that can flare into civil war overnight. Once crowds get out on the streets, once stones start to fly, once the first person gets killed...Now here is this minority, they feel themselves socially superior, they teach the same to their children, they are trying by high and low means to maintain intact their exclusiveness, they want to go on living in a ghetto. Certainly the right to education is written into the Convention, that parents can choose it—certainly Belgium has signed the Convention, but if it is enforced the consequences can only be irretrievably damaging. Civil war, I said. It would be most dangerous of all for us to blandly deny that it is—I say it is—possible, unless properly managed. Force will be needed if those schools are to be defended. Just look what's happening all the time now on civil rights in America. Would you defend those schools with force, now would you?...I do not know if I would...I grant the right of parents to choose the education of their children, but when it comes to this...And here it is, this, right on top of us now, without warning. The case should never have been brought. It should have been stopped before it started. Now it has started and cannot be stopped. At least I think it cannot. The point it raises is clear: *should Europe be governed by judges or by politicians?* That is what we are beginning to decide right now, precisely by how we deal exactly with cases like this. And no one knows it is already happening. Well, should matters like this be determined solely by judges, should they? —matters that are political, utterly practical, matters that can have literally the gravest consequences? Belgium has signed the Convention, and the Convention is now invoked in Belgium, and against the wishes of the Belgian government. If the Court in Strasbourg decides one way, and the Belgian government decides the other way, that it cannot enforce the ruling of the Court, that it says, 'No, we have not the strength to enforce this even if we wished'—why, what then? Why, as night follows day, civil discord, civil strife, permanent damage to the social fabric no matter who wins, endless ill-will, and possibly—I say possibly—immediate bloodshed—completely suddenly...Our only hope is some legal loop-hole can be found so that schools are not permitted to become a cancer in Society, and yet somehow the Court maintains its integrity, until the rights it defends can be properly defended. Just contemplate the consequences either way for our struggle towards integration. It is such a big battle we have on our hands. Like that meeting right here last night at St Ermins. So very small, you see, it was, but a part of the big thing—and did you see, the whole thing there turns on nothing more than how—exactly *how*—we succeed in creating a larger committee but in the new form we now must have. Now we have a committee like that in Denmark, we've done it in Germany, here I think also it should be all right...We shall see, anyway—so much depends on what that man writes in his report...I would admit that parents do have the right to choose their children's education—and this is only on languages, how about *religion*?—but to do that in Belgium where it strikes at the entire root of the politics of the region...It's different in Finland, mark you—there the Swedes can have their Swedish schools as much as they like because they are not disturbing the social peace, are not perpetuating—not even starting—ill-will and social schism...We must find a legal loop-hole now for the sake of the future—Aha, this is the airport? Well now, if only we are in *time*...'

This conversation, and the winding, tangled, hemmed-in and then finally accelerating drive to the airport during which it took place, is an authentic account of what happened: in its detours and its urgency, in its cryptically labyrinthine complexity—and yet also in its unquenchable simplicity of hope—it is itself symbolic of the European Idea. During this book the reader will doubtless observe the same characteristics at work—but they are in the coming chapters at least not glossed over, but accepted as inevitable characteristics of the theme of this book and of our time. For the purpose of this book is not to suggest that the eventual achievement of a European union and a federal European Government will be easy—but that it will be difficult; not to suggest that progress towards this aim will make crises less likely—but on the contrary, that it will make them more probable; not to suggest that the simplicity of our aim allows us to consider only the obvious but that on the contrary it must force our attention towards the complex, the subtle, the elusively powerful currents of our time. It is not to suggest that we are now living through times that try our souls, but on the contrary, that perhaps we do not allow our times in Europe to try our souls *enough*, and that if—for all our unwillingness and natural hesitancy—such times should come, we can and must today make certain that when they come they will at least try our souls *for the right reasons*.

Both the simplicity and also the complexity of the European Idea have been inherent in it from its beginning. The most dramatic expression of the European Idea within living memory was, of course, during the war years. When this 'cradle of the human spirit' we call Europe was still covered with a cloak soaking in blood, Churchill calmly wrote to the War Cabinet '...I look forward to a United States of Europe...' In 1943 he said publicly on the radio:

> 'One can imagine that under a world organisation embodying or representing the United Nations there should come into being a Council of Europe...We must try...to make this Council of Europe into a really effective league, with all the strongest forces woven into its texture, with a High Court to adjust disputes, and with armed forces, national or international or both, held ready to enforce these decisions and to prevent renewed aggression and the preparation of future wars...This Council, when created, must eventually embrace the whole of Europe, and all the main branches of the European family must some day be partners in it.'

And the same Churchill, now in opposition, called from Zurich in 1946 for what he named 'the sovereign remedy—a remedy which would, as if by a miracle, transform the whole scene and would in a few years make all Europe, or the greater part of it, as free and happy as Switzerland is today. We must build a kind of United States of Europe.'

And in 1949, on the 5 May in St James's Palace in London, the first step towards this expressed aim of a United States of Europe was taken when representatives of Belgium, Britain, Denmark, France, Holland, Ireland, Italy, Luxembourg, Sweden and Norway put the signatures of their people to the Convention establishing the first European organisation of all—the Council of Europe in Strasbourg. And as with this and all subsequent Conventions of the Council of Europe, the date was preceded by the words *'Done this day...'*—which explains the title of this book.

1949 was a year in which political facts of life included a Soviet Russia steadily closing its fist on all Europe east of the Elbe; an America still influenced by Roosevelt's myth of cheery good partnership between giant global powers; and a China enduring revolution. 1949 found Europe nervously sheltering from the menace of Russian armies under America's monopoly of atomic holocaust, and struggling to adjust its political habits to a new grouping called the Brussels Pact and its military habits to a new grouping of armies called the North Atlantic Treaty Organisation. It was the year America watched excitedly on television as waiters uncorked champagne bottles at the Waldorf-Astoria to honour the election of Thomas Dewey as President, only to wake up next morning and find Harry Truman's will to trust in himself and persevere had prevailed. It was the year when generals whispered ominously about the moral virtues of preventive nuclear war 'before they have it too'. It was the year of that centuries-awaited hope, a Council of Europe—yet neither the organisation nor the idea were to evolve as was then expected. As Amaury de Riencourt puts it in his book *The Coming Caesars*, 'Those who establish enduring institutions have only a dim perception of the historical implications of their own doings.'

We shall see in coming chapters how very true this is, but if historians of the twenty-first century really want to disentangle the who-caused-what of the unification of Europe, they will have to look behind the words of statesmen and the facts in newspapers. They will have to seek events recorded only in the personal memories and correspondence of the time. They will have to find some record of the many quietly decisive meetings held by little groups of three, five or seven people at a time—meetings which mounted pressure that moved Governments. What historians will find is that these groups were not made up of Heads of State or Government, nor of people of any normally acknowledged status, but of almost unidentified people who came spontaneously together to form those small groups which certainly always exist in history, but rarely change events decisively. The historians will have to explain how it was that from the actions of these few people, and only shortly after the Second World War, there emerged in Europe new methods, purposes, and principles.

Let us trace this evolution *backwards*, from events to their preceding causes. When the Convention creating the Council of Europe was signed in St James's Palace, a memory then still vivid was the day when Churchill, still in opposition, marched on Downing Street in the name of Europe—and successfully. That day has been recorded for us by Kenneth Lindsay:

'It was an unusually bright and sunny morning when members of the British delegation (from the Congress of the Hague) met in Mr Winston Churchill's room at the House of Commons. I remember some of those present—Sir Arthur Salter (now Lord Salter), Robert Boothby, Lady Violet Bonham-Carter (daughter of Lord Asquith) and a leading Liberal, Mr R. W. G. Mackay, Labour, and well-known later at Strasbourg for his proposals to create 'a European authority with limited funtions and real powers', and others. 'Good morning' said Mr Churchill, 'are we all here, all parties represented? It is a beautiful morning, let us march on Downing Street. *Have we a flag?*' So, led by a long cigar and to the consternation of the police, we crossed Whitehall and soon found ourselves opposite Mr Attlee and Mr Bevin and their officials. Our case was stated with moderation and modesty; an agreed communiqué was published. The British later agreed to send an official delegation to a five-Power committee convened by the Consultative Council of the Brussels Treaty Organisation and which met under the chairmanship of M. Herriot, on November 26, 1948...As is well known, the first meeting of the Consultative Assembly took place in the martyr University of Strasbourg, on August 3rd, 1949. I retell this story solely to illustrate the possibilities of a pressure-group, operating first on five and then on ten national parliaments.'

Behind this effect was the cause—for the memory vivid in the minds of those who marched on Downing Street was that of the Hague Congress of May 1948. In all accounts of the Congress there is a strongly personal note of pride as if the participants felt that what they had done was new, needed, notable. Kenneth Lindsay called it 'a spontaneous uprising of eight hundred free men and women gathered at the Hague under the leadership of Mr Churchill to create the European Movement and dramatize European unity'.

Anthony Nutting wrote of 'a veritable galaxy of European political talent, including Churchill, who was made *President d'Honneur*, de Gasperi, Reynaud, Bidault, Schuman, Spaak, Blum, de Madariaga, van Zeeland, Ramadier and Monnet...all the 750 representatives of European politics, industry and literature who went to the Hague were as one in their aim of promoting the concept of European unity. All were agreed that the first step towards this goal should be the creation of a European parliamentary assembly. Accordingly a proposal was made to the five Brussels Treaty powers that the Brussels Treaty should become the nucleus for further action towards European integration and that a European Parliamentary Assembly should be set up without delay...'

R. W. G. Mackay, in his posthumously published *Towards the United States of Europe*, placed the Hague Congress in global perspective: 'The basic idea of a united Europe, as expressed in the Hague Conference of 1948, was that by uniting Europe would become a powerful force for peace in the world, that it would ensure its economic independence and social progress; and that in making a European community Europe would become an equal partner with the United States...' And Mackay quoted Benjamin Franklin in 1758: 'Everybody cries: a union is absolutely necessary; but when it comes to the manner and form of the union their weak noddles are perfectly distracted.'

There has never yet been a noddle not at some time distracted. As we trace these themes backwards, we can perhaps clear our own heads by considering the following passage from Horsfall Carter's *Speaking European*:

'It is necessary first to clear our minds about federalism, to define and circumscribe the concept. Mr Roy Pryce, himself a federalist, in *The Political Future of the European Community*, has performed a useful service in bringing down to earth the glib patter about establishing a European Government, a 'United States of Europe'—implying transfer of power to an overriding and omnicompetent central authority—with which we have not seldom been regaled by Continental zealots and the small number of professional federalists in Britain. As he reminds us, the basic principle of federalism is, on the contrary, a *division of powers*, i.e. within a given society: 'a method of organising power in such a way that those matters which can be dealt with at the local level are so treated; and those which must be treated as matters of common concern are dealt with by an organ of government which acts for the unit as a whole'. We can indeed agree with Mr Pryce that traditional political terminology is inapplicable to the Community phenomenon and also that for us in Britain, in particular, there is a wall of prejudice, a 'thought-barrier to be broken down'. If then, federalist fancies can be dismissed...'

'If' indeed, as the Spartans replied to Philip of Macedon. For the progress of the European Idea, both in these present times, and in the years we are tracing backwards, shows that today's fancy can become tomorrow's fact. Mr Carter, however, is not alone in perhaps underestimating the

historical forces at work in the European Idea—as recently as 1958
Frederick L. Schuman, Woodrow Wilson Professor of Government at
Williams College in the United States, felt able to reduce the entire
struggle to unite Europe to the following compressed tabulation, and
this in a book of seven hundred pages—his *International Politics:*

EUROPEAN UNION OF FEDERALISTS (EUF). Founded 1946, at a meeting in
Luxembourg of delegates from various federalist groups. Leaders
include Henri Frenay, Henri Brugmans, Alexandre Marc, J. Keith
Kilby, Denis de Rougemont. Program: a European Federal Constituent Assembly to frame a pact of Federal Union.

EUROPEAN MOVEMENT. Founded at an unofficial 'Congress of the
Hague', May, 1948. Honorary Presidents: Winston Churchill, Leon
Blum, Alcide de Gasperi, Paul-Henri Spaak. Journal: *Europe Today
and Tomorrow.* Its educational and propaganda activities led to the
establishment of:

THE COUNCIL OF EUROPE. Statute signed in London, May 5, 1949, by
10 Foreign Ministers. Unlike other groups here listed, this is a public
international organisation, but is not a European Federation, as some
of its supporters hoped it would be, since its organs at Strasbourg have
no legislative, executive or judicial powers...

Advocates of a regional federation of democracies thus achieved a
European intergovernmental organisation, albeit not a federation.
Prospects of an actual federation of Europe, or of the Atlantic Demo-
cracies, or of the British Commonwealth, Western Europe and the
Americas were not promising in the 1950's, despite advocacy of
European integration by Dwight D. Eisenhower and other distin-
guished Americans and despite the establishment and growth of
NATO, the adoption of the Schuman Plan, and other steps towards
unity...

It is difficult to understand the power of the European Idea unless we
realise that from the federalist viewpoint, the question of European unity
is not just like other questions, and its difficulties are not to be judged as if
on the same scale as ordinary difficulties in ordinary politics. It is fundamentally distinguished from them by its potential for the future, which
is unimaginably great. Hence on the federalist side we find throughout
the whole history of the European Idea a grim dedication which can be
devastating to those who encounter it unawares. It is thus always a shock
for those who are not committed federalists, and who have taken their
position for what they believe most genuine and admirable motives, to

find that when they are weighed in federalist scales they are not merely found wanting, but silently treated as opponents.

This can be illustrated by a story. Certain friends and colleagues in what we may call a tight inner circle of those who had long proved their deep commitment to a federal Europe, were heard one evening enquiring about the orientation of a Prime Minister. The occasion was a private dinner in an inn between Strasbourg and the Vosges. As the night drew on and the wine circled the key question was re-phrased. And there was a thoughtful pause before the quietly damning reply, 'Non, ce n'est pas un frère.'

Which was to say, no, his allegiance does not rise high enough to be valued as truly European; it is always to something less than Europe. That answer, given by one who knew, was so damning that little discussion followed. The power and prestige and motive of that Prime Minister had been noted and surveyed, and his name added to the list of men holding temporary power who ranked as opponents to be out-manoeuvred, nothing more.

Having now glanced at some of the attitudes provoked by the European Idea, let us consider more closely the meaning of the Congress of the Hague. A tiny turmoil in a tea-cup, or a turning-point in Europe's destiny—which was it? If it really was, as Kenneth Lindsay says, a 'spontaneous uprising', it needs explaining.

Dr A. H. Robertson, in his book *The Council of Europe*, gives the following breakdown of 'delegates from sixteen countries...Austria 12, Belgium 18, Britain 140, Denmark 32, Ireland 5, France 185, Germany 51, Greece 18, Italy 57, Lichtenstein 3, Luxembourg 8, the Netherlands 59, Norway 12, Saar 5, Sweden 19, Switzerland 39.' And there were also observers, some of whom were refugees, from Bulgaria, Canada, Czechoslovakia, Finland, Hungary, Poland, Roumania, Spain, U.S.A. and Yugoslavia.

If we look at what these delegates agreed, we shall find it so formidable that to understand the forces which produced this agreement, we shall have to look not just at the years before the Congress but the centuries. For the delegates adopted a series of political resolutions which make remarkable reading in the context of events today, and have been summarised by Dr Robertson as follows:

1. No attempt to reconstruct Europe upon the basis of rigidly divided national sovereignty can prove successful.
2. The nations of Europe must create an economic and political union in

order to assure security, economic independence and social progress; and for this purpose they must agree to merge certain of their sovereign rights.

3. A European Consultative Assembly, whose members should be nominated by the Parliaments of the participating nations, must be convened forthwith.

4. The European Union or Federation should be open to all democratic European nations which undertake to respect fundamental human rights.

5. A European Court of Human Rights backed with adequate sanctions should be established to adjudicate in cases of alleged violation of these rights.

6. The creation of a United Europe must be regarded as an essential step towards the creation of a United World.

And backing these resolutions was the following 'Message to Europeans':

We desire a united Europe, throughout whose area the free movement of persons, ideas and goods is restored;

We desire a Charter of Human Rights guaranteeing liberty of thought, assembly and expression as well as the right to form a political opposition;

We desire a Court of Justice with adequate sanctions for the implementation of this Charter;

We desire a European Assembly where the live forces of all our nations shall be represented;

And pledge ourselves in our home and in public, in our political and religious life, in our professional and trade union circles, to give our fullest support to all persons and governments working for this lofty cause, which offers the last chance of peace and the one promise of a great future for this generation and those that will succeed it.

This was in 1948, only three years after the war, and it was thus that the phoenix of the European Idea arose even out of its fires—reborn of ashes, but with brilliant plumage. To understand how this rebirth was possible we have to consult the founding fathers of the European Idea, and as Denis de Rougemont has shown us in his *Twenty-One Centuries of Europe*, and Henri Brugmans in his *History of European Civilisation*, they form an astounding genealogy. These two men themselves, as we have seen, took part in the first post-war groupings of federalists noted by Professor Schuman. It was from Montreux that a first appeal was made for the summoning of a Parliament of Europe. This was preceded by Churchill's Zurich speech of September 1946, and this in turn was preceded by the Hertenstein Declaration which laid down the guiding principles expressed in the later Message to Europeans already quoted

Even during the war, Resistance leaders from nine European countries were meeting together secretly and repeatedly in Geneva. Of the war they said 'this anarchy must be ended by the creation of a Federal Europe among the peoples of Europe...' Of the world they said 'Peace in Europe is the keystone of world peace.' These were the same years in which Roosevelt was anticipating a future world governed in peace by a 'gentlemen's agreement' between the Caesars who would govern the giant powers; the same years in which Count Coudenhove-Kalergi was ceaselessly active also in the United States and seeking to convince America's future leaders of the necessity for a united Europe; and the same years in which Churchill's thoughts were already being polarised along the European wavelength.

And even shortly before the war we see the plumage of the phoenix, close to the flames though it was. Briand and Stresemann had made their great effort to unify the energies of France and Germany, and failed— yet Briand, even though seeing all was for the moment lost, that war must come and might destroy the European soul, nevertheless wrote his famous Memorandum to the Governments and people of Europe. Any- one who enters the Library of the Council of Europe in Strasbourg can read Briand's Memorandum, and it is surely the place to read it today. And in a private conversation in Berlin, Stresemann sat down wearily with Hungarian film producer Gabriel Pascal and his wife Pauline (later Gallico) and said; 'Our only hope is Pan-Europa; all other ways lead to war'. Thus the German *Reichskanzler*, though even only among friends, nevertheless saw and held to the one great hope—and voiced it. And Stresemann was in turn using the earlier words of Count Coudenhove-Kalergi, who had proclaimed the necessity of what he called Pan-Europa as early as 1924. He in turn was merely putting into contemporary terms what so many men before him had insisted on saying in an unbroken chain, regardless of the century in which they found themselves. Nietzsche, Saint-Simon, Jeremy Bentham with his 'Plan for Perpetual Peace', Fourier, Proudhon—who said in 1868, 'the twentieth century will see the beginning of an age of federations in which humanity will begin another purgatory lasting a thousand years', Mazzini, who said 'if you want to know the future of Europe, look at the map', Garibaldi, Heine, Lamartine, Mickiewicz. These names are just a few: the line goes back and back, each in turn catching up this great rolling globe of a *completed* Idea from the past, and throwing it forward again for the future to hold. Among them, Victor Hugo, who was the first man ever to speak of a 'United States of Europe', and did

so only because provoked to sudden spontaneous fury on the benches
of the French National Assembly in the midnight hours:

> '...the first nation in the world has produced three revolutions, as
> the gods of Homer took three steps. These three revolutions are one,
> and it is not a local revolution but the revolution of humanity—after
> long trials, this revolution gave birth in France to the Republic...
> The people of France have carved out of indestructible granite, and
> placed right in the centre of a continent full of monarchies, the
> foundation stone of the immense edifice of the future, which will
> be known some day as the *United States of Europe*.'
>
> *M. de Montalembert.* 'The United States of Europe! That's going too
> far—Hugo is mad.'
>
> *M. Mole.* 'The United States of Europe—what an idea! What folly.'
>
> *M. Quentin-Bauchard.* 'These poets!'

When Victor Hugo died there was found among his manuscripts a
scrap of paper, and scribbled on it words so powerful and lasting they
were inscribed in his memory on the wall of the room in Paris where he
died in 1885:

'I represent a party which does not yet exist: *Civilisation*. This party will
make the twentieth century. There will issue from it, first, the United
States of Europe, and then the United States of the World.'

Nevertheless even Hugo had been doing no more than catching up
that same great globe of an Idea already thrown forward to him out of
the past, and by men who had long preceded him—the Abbé de Saint-
Pierre with his *Project of Perpetual Peace* in 1712—Anarchasis Cloots with
his *Plan for Universal Peace* presented to the French Revolutionary Convention—William Penn with his *Essay on the Present and Future in
Europe* in 1692—Amon Comenius with his *Universal Dream* in 1645—
Sully with his *Grand Design* in 1638—Emeric Cruce with his *Nouveau
Cygne* in 1623—and before all these by Pope Pius the Second who wrote
to Mahomet the Second, 'Now, it is in Europe itself, that is to say in our
own fatherland, in our own house, that we are being attacked and
killed'; and by George Podiebrad, King of Bohemia, who in 1542
called in his projected *Treaty of Alliance* for an Assembly, a Court of
Justice, a framework of international rules for the legal settlement of
disputes, a common armed force, and a common budget. These, of
course, imply a European Government—and as Denis de Rougemont
pointed out, King Podiebrad of sixteenth-century Bohemia was already
more truly modern in his political concepts than President de Gaulle.
Indeed, we could go even further back—back to Dante and his *De*

Monarchia in 1306, back to Pierre Dubois and his *European Tribunal* in 1305.

But perhaps that is far enough to demonstrate the continuity of thought on the union of Europe, and the honourable genealogy of an Idea which has occupied men's minds for over seven hundred years. And as de Rougemont constantly repeats, every time the Idea has been reborn, there has been a repeated call for four things—first, and always first, a spiritual community supported by a legal framework and thus for a judicial tribunal above the states; second, an Assembly or Council of Europe; third, a determination to improve the prosperity of all through common economic action; and last, and always last, a common army. We can here well recall that image used by Mihail Babits in his *History of European Literature*, when he speaks of ideas calling from peak to peak across great gulfs of time and space in that dimension where lives the true continuity of European thought—and in this continuity there has always been the image of a concert of Europe. It is an inevitable product of our European temperament at work through the centuries—always seeing, dreaming, speaking, acting, suffering and daring in response always to these same crags, inlets, seas, plateaux, plains and cities which are our inheritance; a temperament diverse as crops and trees, solid as roots and rocks; a temperament always inherently creative and imaginative, a temperament whose history includes the worlds of Prometheus, Icarus and Faust, and whose true future is today only beginning.

Before we now look forward to the purpose, power, and policy of the first years of the Council of Europe that followed the Congress of the Hague, let us pause to notice one or two aspects of the European Idea as then expressed.

First, let us pick out one word from what Mackay states to have been the basic conviction expressed at the Hague Congress—that by uniting, Europe would become 'a powerful force for peace in the world; that it would ensure its economic and social progress; and that in making a European community Europe would become an equal partner with the United States.'

The word is *community*. It is worth noting, for in 1948 this single word had not yet achieved its present significance as a word consciously re-minted into a new coinage of political courage, a new currency of political concepts. Mackay was writing after the event, for the Congress of the Hague preceded both the Council of Europe and the full Community method—but it is of interest from the point of view of semantics, cybernetics, political science, social evolution or anything else, to speculate on the causes at work in history when any single new word suddenly emerges to fulfil a need, express an aim, and sometimes in itself to become a political force.

Second, let us remember that the Hague Congress knew its purpose. 'All were agreed that the first steps should be the creation of a European Parliamentary Assembly.' Yet this was agreed by no more than, shall we say, a round thousand of men and women so actively committed to their aim that they gave time, money and energy to act together—and this with such effect that this single determined thousand succeeded in goading ten national Governments until they did create the first European parliamentary assembly in history, thereby inserting into the accepted politics of Europe a new, unknown quantity. The aim was to be a European Community, the method was to be action through a European Assembly—and included in the equation was to be another quantity also, the force of public opinion.

Public opinion—it was the key to European unification in 1948, as it is today. It was intended by the pioneers at the Hague Congress that their projected European assembly should act as a swift, decisive catalyst. It was to reform into new and increasingly dynamic combinations those many elements of latent public opinion that wished for a new and united Europe. Public opinion unexpressed can evolve only slowly, but once given *a way of hearing itself speak*, it can come to command events with surprising speed—and it was the hope of the thousand at the Hague that a European assembly designed to speak for millions would at once spark a chain-reaction of creative public opinion and creative governmental action. The moment of critical energy-change, the splitting of the political atom and its re-shaping in a fusion process, was to be precisely the creation of the assembly. And the analogy is close—split the atom and we have hitherto undreamed-of energy, said the physicists; create a European assembly and we have hitherto undreamed-of possibilities for creating a new Europe, said the European political alchemists. They were nearly right. And they nearly succeeded, for their own Congress of the Hague was itself a creative fusion that today still astonishes us in its extraordinary mobilisation of human energies—though in fact it should not, for it is, after all, our own present arbitrary method of sealing off talent into non-communicating and fragmentary groupings that will tomorrow seem extraordinary, and the Congress of the Hague was doing no more than outline in advance the future European norm. It succeeded in creating the Council of Europe—but the Council of Europe did not succeed in creating the catalytic flash-point that would change all. We shall now see why—for as the pioneers at the Hague were soon to learn, purpose alone is not enough. It must always be supported by adequate enabling power if it is to be transformed into successful policy, and even then policy cannot succeed without the support of public opinion. If policy is king, public opinion is queen.

Although the thinking of the Congress of the Hague was a new element in politics, it still had to grapple with old elements. Principal among these was the thinking of national Governments, and in particular the thinking of Ernest Bevin, British Foreign Secretary—a man soon to be seriously ill from overwork and not, it must be stressed, a man without vision. Bevin had said he hoped for the day when he could walk into Victoria Station and simply ask for a ticket to anywhere in Europe and get it at once without fuss, delay, formalities or passport, and it was this same Bevin in whose overburdened hands now lay the fate of the projected European parliamentary assembly.

We need not here go into the labyrinthine back-stage comings and goings that took place between Whitehall and all the other Governments suddenly confronted with what must have appeared a nightmare—for they faced not only a peremptory demand for a new, unprecedented, uncontrollable and unpredictable style in politics, but a demand apparently backed by public opinion. Terrifying it must have been for those enormous hierarchies of Cabinets, Ministries, Parliaments, Civil Service Secretariats and national parties, all clanking comfortably round in nineteenth-century systems of power, at nineteenth-century speeds. We can imagine their feelings at the thought of what must have appeared to them (how could they know better?) as a steel, shining monstrosity of political machinery somehow being foisted on them by men and women the British Government were pleased to label quickly as 'amateurs'. We should perhaps not blame them too much for wanting to cripple a machinery they did not understand, did not want, and from which they could not hope to profit in ordinary terms of personal, party or sectional power or prestige. For it was clear that this proposed European parliamentary assembly was not at all intended to accommodate their own comfortable and accustomed purposes—and looking at it from the other side, we should try to remember that these were men of honesty, goodwill and ability; they had all recently endured a global war; they had no factual grounds yet to understand there could be more advanced modes of politics than their own—or that even among their own contemporaries there could be men and women with wider purposes than their own. Least of all had they reason to understand that these inspired and admittedly amateur creators of a united Europe were not innovators but

B

the true traditionalists, and were doing no more than trying to guide Europe home again to where she has always truly belonged. How were the pioneers to explain, even tactfully, that Europe's need was to find new ways of creating new conditions for new creative leadership?

We do need to examine exactly, however, that power which these same men and Governments did finally confer on what came to be called the Council of Europe. Battle was joined on the drafting of the Statute or Convention creating the Council, and though most of the men then in power had no motive to assist its creation, some had motive to destroy. Some of them did try to kill any possibility of a European parliamentary assembly—and yet, even entrenched as these men were in fortresses of power, nevertheless they failed to measure the hope of Europe sufficiently to destroy it. It is the shame of Europe that they tried.

The evolution of any future Council of Europe now depended on the powers to be written into its founding Statute, and the pioneers of the Hague, having succeeded in commanding the earnest attention of the Governments, now endured that inevitable first consequence of success— shock-wave and counter-revolution. The pioneers wanted an assembly genuinely and effectively speaking for all the people. Bevin's riposte was to offer a conventional round-table conference of Ministers under strictly limited national instructions, meeting only occasionally, agreed on no purpose and armed with no powers. He is believed to have said of the proposed Consultative Assembly 'I don't like it. If you open that Pandora's box, you will find it full of Trojan horses'—a muddled myth indeed, for we all know who was left prisoner in Pandora's box after its lid had been slammed shut—Hope herself—and we also all know who succeeded in taking the city of Troy, and how.

One giant weapon in the hands of the Governments was therefore used—their negative power to permit the least possible. It was used ruthlessly. We are all today still enduring its consequences, for we are still seeking to establish that true European assembly advocated so clearly and unequivocally in 1948, and denied. For the final Statute establishing the Council of Europe was a hybrid—the pioneers got their Consultative Assembly shorn of power (or so it seemed); the Governments got their Committee of Ministers, soon to be shorn of prestige for more than a decade by its failure to lead and by its use of the same giant weapon of permitting the least possible. There was, however, at first still some hope—for everything now depended on whether the Consultative Assembly and the Committee of Ministers could learn to work in harmony, on whether either would gain dominance, and on whether this dominance would be used positively or negatively.

The pessimists among the pioneers deplored an Assembly without teeth. They thought in terms of immediate purpose, immediate power, immediate policy, and an immediate mobilisation of public opinion across all Europe. They could not but be disappointed.

The optimists among the pioneers pointed to the centuries Europe had endured without ever once achieving an Assembly to speak for all her people—and they pointed to the powers inherent in a first precedent, for this was the first Council of Europe in history.

A British Parliamentary account is given by Anthony Nutting in his book *Europe Will Not Wait*, written in 1960 shortly after his resignation from the Eden Conservative Government over Suez.

> 'The briefest glance at the Statute of the Council of Europe shows now how much had been conceded to the British and other anti-federalist views. The Assembly was completely subordinated to the Committee of Ministers, who controlled its budget and secretariat, decided on new members and appointments and on any member state's representation and financial contribution. The Assembly was only allowed to appoint its own officers and committees, decide its own rules of procedure and dates of meetings. Though permitted to debate matters pertaining to European unity, any question relating to defence was taboo. Even in the economic, social and cultural spheres that were open to it the Statute rules that the Assembly's agenda must have 'regard to the work of other European inter-governmental organisations'. In other words, no interference...Finally, any recommendation it might see fit to make could not be made direct to member governments but had to be submitted to the Committee of Ministers where the rule of unanimity applied and where one dissenting vote could stultify any further action. Small wonder the European federalists, having asked for a magic carpet, felt they had been forced to settle for a straitjacket. Nevertheless, the Council of Europe was all that they had to work from, and so...'

We shall see in the course of this book that a great deal was subsequently to grow from those two words 'and so', and that it is today growing in unexpectedly dramatic ways. This is also the moment to introduce an argument that will run through this book, for while the Statute was the first Convention of the Council it has since been followed by many more Conventions, and no matter how justifiably any Convention of the Council of Europe may be criticised, the fact remains that it exists as an agreed and binding legal document on the European level, signed by Governments on our behalf. Its existence is itself a form of pressure

by precedent; it can have cumulative effect, it has a self-contained power
of survival; it can ultimately lead to consequences not at first predictable.
All this is especially true of the first Convention of all, the Statute of the
Council, and before we rip the Statute to pieces because it did not prove
an immediate passport to the promised land, let us try to maintain a
positive attitude. Let us first see what the Governments did agree in its
Preamble. They decribed themselves as:

> Convinced that the pursuit of peace based upon justice and international
> co-operation is vital for the preservation of human society and civilisa-
> tion;
>   Reaffirming their devotion to the spiritual and moral values which
> are the common heritage of their peoples and the true source of indi-
> vidual freedom, political liberty and the rule of law, principles which
> form the basis of all genuine democracy;
>   Believing that, for the maintenance and further realisation of these
> ideals and in the interests of economic and social progress, there is
> need of a closer unity between all like-minded countries of Europe;
>   Considering that, to respond to this need and to the expressed aspira-
> tions of their peoples in this regard, it is necessary forthwith to create an
> organisation which will bring European States into closer association;
>   Have in consequence decided to set up a Council of Europe consisting
> of a Committee representative of Governments and of a Consultative
> Assembly.

This is worth learning by heart for it is uncompromisingly ideological in
the democratic sense, and its principles are a matter of uttermost importance not only in Western Europe today, but for Eastern Europe tomorrow.
With that said, let us now see how the Statute defined the purpose of the
Council of Europe:

> The aim of the Council of Europe is to achieve a greater unity between
> its members for the purpose of safeguarding and realising the ideals
> and principles which are their common heritage and facilitating their
> economic and social progress...This aim will be pursued through the
> organs of the Council by discussion of questions of common concern
> and by agreements and common action in economic, social, cultural,
> scientific, legal and administrative matters and in the maintenance and
> further realisation of human rights and fundamental freedoms...

And finally, let us notice the necessary sting in the tail—as Portugal,
Spain, Yugoslavia and other countries are today acutely aware, for it
bars them from membership of the Council of Europe:

> Every member of the Council of Europe must accept the principles of the rule of law and of the enjoyment by all persons within its jurisdiction of human rights and fundamental freedoms, and collaborate sincerely and effectively in the realisation of the aims of the Council...

Before we come to the criticisms of the Statute, let us ask ourselves whether we could say anything as meaningful as the forty-six words just quoted—remembering as we do that the challenge in 1949 was to crack a centuries-old crust of political habit, to jolt millions out of inertia, and to launch a movement designed to change the history of the world. 'Because of the inertia of human thought', wrote John F. Kennedy, 'nations, like individuals, change their ideas slowly.'

This being true, the replacement of inertia by momentum is seldom achieved overnight—and real momentum needs a long slow acceleration to gather real power. Those who by 1949 had goaded the Governments at least this far still had a great deal to do and in a great hurry—while their own momentum was already slowing down. They had been already forced to abandon many hopes. Yet they had also gained much. Just how much we can see by comparing an official statement, issued after the signing of the Statute in St James's Palace, with a rather different statement issued only recently by the Secretariat of the Council of Europe.

First, the Governmental statement, outlining the organs of the Council as they were at first agreed:

> The main feature of the Statute is the establishment of a Committee of Ministers and of a Consultative Assembly, which together will form the Council of Europe. Of these two bodies, the Committee of Ministers will provide for the development of co-operation between governments, while the Consultative Assembly will provide a means through which the aspirations of the European peoples may be formulated and expressed, the governments thus being kept continually in touch with European public opinion.

And second, the Council of Europe's own understated description of itself, issued through the Secretariat, valid today, yet scarcely even hinting at the spirit informing the facts:

> The Council of Europe is a complex body; eighteen Foreign Ministers meeting twelve times a year—ten times at Deputy level, twice at least at full Ministerial level; one hundred and forty-seven parliamentarians and one hundred and forty-seven substitutes who meet for some thirty days a year; and finally five hundred and fifty civil servants, who, under the authority of the Secretary General, work together three hundred

and sixty-five days a year to solve the complicated problems arising from a Europe criss-crossed by frontiers.

This bare description anticipates our story—for in 1949 attention was focussed far more on the Council of Europe as a means, as the Governmental statement had said, of formulating and expressing the aspirations of Europe and of European public opinion. Let us therefore turn the question at once the other way and ask: how did the Council of Europe and the attitude of Governments themselves then appear to public opinion—and in particular, what appeared to be the Council's own purpose, power and policy at this most brave of beginnings?

It is certainly true that the ominous implications of the way the Council of Europe was constructed escaped public notice. Bevin's policy had been subtle. He had reason to feel that though the Pandora's box of the European ideal had been opened, he had nevertheless made certain it would close very soon. Yet this was not yet apparent: from outside the Council appeared an organisation consecrated and blessed by Governments for its work towards European unity. The Preamble of the Statute spoke only of European unity—was it not mere cavilling to see a distinction between unity and *union*? The thousands of men and women who thronged Place Kleber in Strasbourg to hear Churchill, Ole Kraft, Henri Brugmans and others speak to them as the first Session of the Consultative Assembly opened would not have broken into tumultuous cheering if they had felt that the men looking down on their upturned faces were not genuinely determined upon their declared purpose. And the purpose was very clear: the creation of the Council of Europe was to be a first decisive step towards European unification; others would follow, and then all would be on the move.

But the power of the Council of Europe? It cannot be said there was certainty in the public mind. Certainly there were as yet no powers anywhere explicitly defined for the Council. Yet did this matter when already again a 'galaxy of talent' was assembling as it had done at the Hague, and when the power of the Council of Europe would presumably come to manifest actively through their personality and leadership? These men would presumably succeed in developing policy—and the public waited to be told, a public ready and willing to cheer again if only given the occasion and the leadership.

We shall in the next chapter examine how it was that the public did not cheer, how it was that the purpose of the Council of Europe became blunted, its power apparently negligible, and its policy at first no policy

—and above all how the European Idea as then presented through the Council of Europe was forced to twist and turn and seek expression in quite unexpected ways. It is undeniable that if the construction of the Council had been different, then the European Idea would have been manifested differently through it, history would have chosen different turnings, and our present understanding of all the immensely more complex facts now surrounding the European Idea would be fundamentally different from what it is today. There are lessons for us now in what happened then—and we shall conclude this first chapter with some examples of themes which will be running through this whole book, and which are chosen for the light they cast on the deeper nature of the European Idea itself.

First, the effects of the Council of Europe's faulty construction, stemming as they did from the Statute. We have already seen some of its damaging effects—the Statute created an Assembly with power only to recommend, and a Committee of Ministers with power to decide only when unanimous. It was this entrenched power of veto that lead swiftly to deadlock between the Committee of Ministers and the Consultative Assembly—for not only could the Committee either ignore the Assembly or directly veto it, but any single Government could itself paralyse the Committee, and therefore all other Governments represented in the Committee, and therefore also the Assembly, by its own national veto. This veto was swift, secret, and could be used without explanation either to the Consultative Assembly, national parliaments, or European public opinion. From the beginning the balance was thus weighted against momentum, in favour of inertia. And as we shall see in the next chapter, the result was at first that the Assembly was reduced and degraded to public impotence, and the private power of the Committee of Ministers was used in ways which were scarcely consistent with the long-term public good.

As Kenneth Lindsay has sharply pointed out, Montesquieu's doctrine of the separation of legislative, executive and judicial powers was not merely expressed in the Statute, but carried to an excess whereby the Assembly certainly, and soon the Council of Europe as a whole, did appear to have no powers worth attention. Mr Lindsay labels it the 'inflexible' Statute, and speaks of relations between the Assembly and the Ministers freezing quickly into 'a cold war'. And it is true that the prevailing mood in public speeches from Parliamentarians in the Assembly was shot with streaks of bitterness and fury. But where was the real weakness in the design of the Council, and was it beyond remedy? One fundamental weakness, certainly, was that the Council of Europe was not designed for speedy communication between its several parts; or between itself and other comparable organisations of power; or between itself and public opinion. The consequences of this weakness over the years have been serious. And we shall in later chapters come again and again to this word 'communication'—it is an argument of this book that one of the severest problems facing Europe today is contained in what we may call the 'communication-spectrum'. Here to some extent an understanding of cybernetics can be most helpful in any consideration of the European Idea—for as Norbert Wiener has dramatically shown us in 'The Human Use of Human Being' (*Cybernetics and Society*), communication or the flow, pattern and character of information is itself a way of talking about how power actually works—what it is. Political power in particular can often be most quickly and simply examined by asking solely what information is travelling where, how, why, in what form, at what speed, and with what effects—and we shall in chapters seven to nine see that even with an imperfect structure there can nevertheless be remedies.

Nevertheless, the first effect of this weakness was deadlock. The Committee of Ministers lacked political will to act, the Assembly lacked political power to act. But was the deadlock as complete as it then appeared? To judge from the mood of members of the Assembly, it was complete. Of the mood of the Ministers, the less said the better, but as we shall see, the bitterness and fury of the members marooned in the Assembly swung obsessively round one fact—that they were being deliberately denied opportunity to do what they had come to Strasbourg to do as a clear duty, which was to step at once into the role of Europe's first, genuine and effective parliament. Their speeches and actions take the form of what we can call genuinely righteous historical anger. The Ministers were thought to be cold-bloodedly and deliberately denying the Assembly its right to act on behalf of the people of Europe and past and future modes of purpose, power, policy and principle clashed in savage words—and the confrontation was epic in the Greek sense, with the best men suffering the sharpest pain.

A letter to the London *Times* of 15 January 1951 signed by R. W. G. Mackay and Sir David Maxwell-Fyfe (later Lord Kilmuir) will give us an immediate preview of what this deadlock came to mean. Both were pioneers in Strasbourg, and their letter was in support of what came to be known as the Mackay Protocol, aimed at revising the Statute of the Council of Europe. The Protocol was not adopted, the letter is on the surface now a record only of failure and difficulty—yet it nevertheless contained some seeds for the future, and is an example also of the blunted weapons with which the pioneers of that time had to work and for which they deserve our respect today.

'Sir,   *15 January 1951*

Shortage of space is, no doubt, responsible for scant attention being paid by the British Press to the Protocol for amending the Statute of the Council of Europe, which was described at some length by Monsieur Spaak, as Chairman of the Assembly, at a Press Conference in Brussels on Monday last. In view of the great significance of the proposals as a compromise solution to much sterile argument, and their potential significance to future British policy, we should be grateful for space to make a brief explanation of them...The Protocol, if adopted, will provide something more than co-operation at Governmental level, as exists at present in, for instance, the Council of the Organisation for European Economic Co-operation, but something less than the kind of supra-national authority which has always been opposed by the British Government. We believe that the difficulties of the Council of Europe have been increased by the transfer—both by its critics and its friends—of the terminology of different centuries and circumstances. We therefore ask you to let us describe the essence of the procedure put forward by the Committee.

'This is that no powers should be ceded in advance to the Council of Europe. It is only when all Governments have agreed that a concrete proposal is a proper subject of united action that powers will be given to carry that proposal into effect. The normal pattern of working would be that the Assembly should devote itself to evolving practical and detailed measures instead of merely to resolutions. When a measure comes to the Committee of Ministers the Governments through their representatives would say whether in their view this was a subject for united action or not. If they took the view that it was, then they would evolve the highest common factor of agreement and undertake to give effect thereto. So far as the Council of Europe is concerned the Committee of Ministers would be in a position analogous to that of a second chamber. So far as the Governments are concerned, it would be a permanent treaty-making machinery in which complete liberty of action and the requirements of unanimity would be preserved. Nevertheless, both Committee and Governments would be rightly subject to the pressure of informed European opinion on the desirability of the united action proposed.

'The other aspect is to remove some of the duplication in international agencies by letting an executive authority of the Council of

B*

Europe responsible to both the Committee of Ministers and the Assembly take care of those organisations which already exist under the O.E.E.C. convention. In the future the same authority would also take care of other international organisations created by the procedure outlined above. Defence would no longer be removed from the scope of the Council of Europe. It is not suggested, of course, that this Protocol is incapable of further amendment and improvement. But it does, at least, provide the possibility of the emergence of that political authority 'with limited functions but real powers' which is the unanimous aim of the Assembly. Nor should it be necessary to stress the relevance of these proposals to present-day defence problems and the appointment of General Eisenhower (as the Supreme Commander of Nato). It is plain enough that the closer integration of Europe is coming inevitably owing to the needs of defence; that is beyond argument. The old dilemmas are disappearing; all that remains is the choice for this country whether we are to have a European authority created by Western Europe itself, under the guidance of Great Britain, or whether we are to have one imposed from outside...'

This Protocol was rejected. Direct legislative power was not concentrated in the Council of Europe and this for reasons we shall see in the next chapter. The Statute remained unchanged, and this could persuade us that it thereby created an unworkable mechanism. It is most important not to believe this. The deadlock between Ministers and Assembly was real, but it was also limited—for it blocked action along one particular line of communication only—that leading from voters in each country to their member of Parliament, from their member to initiatives in the Assembly of the Council, from initiatives in the Assembly to the approval of the Committee of Ministers, from the approval of the Committee of Ministers to agreed common action by national Governments directly affecting the people, and so back to the voter. This desirable full circle of action was certainly broken, and deliberately. The first purposes of the Council of Europe were to this extent checked—for the Assembly lacked power to impose policy in the name of public opinion. Yet it was only *immediate* policy that was checked.

What was not checked was a parallel circuit of communication at a higher and unexpected level, leading in time to the evolution of principles and methods for very *long-term* action at the trans-European level. The potential for this action was implicit in the working of the Statute from the beginning, it was seized immediately, it has continued

ever since. In spite of the weaknesses of the Statute there was nevertheless more concealed in it than subsequent criticism would at first concede—
much that must today be defended as fruitful, and developed for the
future. Thus while the weakness of the Statute was a despair to those
men most concerned for immediate action—men forced by parliamentary
circumstances to plan always within the normal parliamentary span of
three, five, or at the most seven years—its strength was on the contrary
of great importance to certain other men whose inclination was to look
far ahead. These were the men whose temperament combined both a
power to be interested in the horizon of the far and only dimly perceptible future, and an equal power to choose at once among the possibilities open to them of what could indeed be 'done this day' and then
to act. These were the men who designed the Conventions of the Council
of Europe, and their work is a major theme of this book.

And just as we have already quoted the Mackay Protocol in anticipation
of the difficulties ahead in these early years of the Council, let us now
notice a completely contrasting and unexpected forerunner of some of
its achievements also yet to come—the European Convention on Human
Rights and Fundamental Freedoms, created by the Council of Europe
within the first two years of its life. Just as the letter to *The Times* in
defence of the Protocol dealt not only with purpose, power, and policy
but also with the fourth factor—public opinion—so we must again keep
all these four factors in mind as we look at the Convention. The letter
politely insisted on the importance of public opinion—and we must
today insist on it even more in relation to all aspects of the European
Idea. As Abraham Lincoln said over a century ago, 'with public sentiment
nothing can fail; without it nothing can succeed. Consequently he who
moulds public sentiment goes deeper than he who enacts statutes or
pronounces decisions. He makes statutes and decisions possible or impossible to be executed.' And again: 'A universal feeling, whether well
or ill-founded, cannot safely be disregarded.' And again: 'No policy
that does not rest upon philosophical public opinion can be permanently
maintained.' And again: 'Any policy to be permanent must have public
opinion at the bottom—something in accordance with the human mind
as it is.'

The Convention on Human Rights was signed on 4 November 1950—
just two months before the letter to *The Times*. When we think of Human
Rights we tend to think immediately by association of Thomas Paine
and his *Rights of Man*—Thomas Paine, that man of surprising shrewdness,
arrogance, enlightenment and common sense. Although the Strasbourg
Convention was directly concerned at this time only with Western

Europe, Paine's spirit must have rejoiced in its European proof that men were again free to insist in speech, writing, and political action that individuals have human rights by reason solely of their existence—or as Descartes might have said: 'I am, *therefore* I have rights.' We shall look more closely at the Convention in Chapter Three, but we can here at once take the position that its importance is fundamental to the entire European Idea—for in a free and democratic society it is the attitude of the individual to human rights that in the long run determines our forms of government, and it is only in our perpetual defence of human rights that we can find our perpetual protection against tyranny.

Furthermore, any written definition of human rights automatically starts a chain of moral logic which, if not broken, ultimately leads to the clear obligation to create a form of Government able to defend these rights and to pass them on enhanced to succeeding generations. Human rights cannot become an enduring force in the human mind until they have been defined in writing, which is what the Strasbourg Convention did—and its importance today is increased by the fact that its writing has *preceded* the writing of a European Constitution. We can well apply with gratitude these words by Lincoln to the conduct of those many men and women who struggled so hard in the first years of the Council of Europe to create our European Declaration of Human Rights:

'All honour to Jefferson', said Lincoln in 1858, 'to the man, who, in the concrete pressure of a struggle for national independence by a single people, had the coolness, foresight and capacity to introduce into a merely revolutionary document an abstract truth, applicable to all men and all times, and so to embalm it there that today and in all coming days it shall be a rebuke and a stumbling-block to the very harbingers of reappearing tyranny and oppression.'

The relevance of this today will become apparent by a passage from John Pinder's book *Europe against de Gaulle*, discussing the future federal reconstruction of the European political system, and with it we come again full circle to the opening idea of this book—the necessity for a European Government:

'If such a recasting of the structure of power is contemplated and not unlikely to be undertaken, it is necessary to consider the principles according to which this power should be used; the view of man as a political and social being on which the Community's laws are to be based. For as soon as a Community disposes of a preponderance of physical power—a certain stage in the development of an integrated Defence Community is the watershed—its treatment of its citizens becomes of paramount importance to them. The principles by which such treatment is to be guided are usually enshrined in constitutions in a declaration of rights. In Strasbourg, the Strasbourg Declaration of Human Rights lies ready to hand. It should be part of the constitution of a European Political Community, with fully effective means for its enforcement in all countries that become full members.'

Which, bluntly put, means that if our human rights are to be a reality they must if necessary be defended by force, which may mean bloodshed. It is necessary to think about this, because when all is going well we are not usually tempted to think about our human rights—but when all is going badly, it is usually then too late to start thinking. These matters are thus deeply sobering. They arise out of even this first preliminary survey of the founding and early years of the Council of Europe, and while in subsequent chapters we shall look more closely at questions here so far merely indicated, this chapter must conclude on a note at least as sober as the quotation set at its head. We can do this by quoting Lincoln once again—this time his final expression of attitude on the inter-relation of principles and force. In his last public address before his assassination he said:

'Important principles may and must be inflexible.'

The European Idea is itself a principle—and furthermore, like all principles it is itself both the child and father of both imagination and action. Not one of us can yet say what will happen when the actions of a Federal Government for all Europe eventually become part of the fabric of our daily lives—or what will become possible when we learn to welcome as common sense that the destiny of a truly and democratic Europe must eventually be entrusted to an unbroken succession of single minds as a process designed to continue in perpetuity. Yet we are today already building a European ship of state and it must be done and done well, for 'no one can wish the ship to sink'. A ship that is not seaworthy cannot sail through storms.

CHAPTER TWO

'What One Man Has Imagined'

'What one man has imagined, another man can make.'　　　　JULES VERNE

THE EUROPEAN IDEA is the product of the combined imagination of many people, but as an ideal it will require the combined action of many more people before it becomes the European Fact. And while in Chapter One we looked at the family tree of the European Idea, the founding of the Council of Europe, its early difficulties—and then at two examples: one of deadlock (between the Committee of Ministers and the Consultative Assembly), the other of breakthrough (the European Convention of Human Rights), in this chapter we shall look at events at a different level, and see why the imagination behind the European Idea continued to encounter both deadlock and success, and also a perpetual conflict between methods old and new. It is not for nothing that within the Council of Europe—within the ensemble of buildings which face across a boulevard on the outskirts of Strasbourg to the Orangerie designed by Napoleon for Josephine and which collectively carries the name 'The House of Europe'—there stands today the bust of the man who was first in our century to imagine a Council of Europe—Winston Churchill.

Yet it is worth also recalling that it took imagination on the part of other men (notably Lord Gladwyn) to propose that the Council of Europe should be created in *Strasbourg*. For at that time it was possible that the city chosen as host for the Council would eventually evolve into the federal capital of Europe. For this reason national capitals had then to be excluded, and while this ruled out important cities like the Hague, London, Paris, Brussels or Rome, a city of a certain dignity, history and convenience was needed. The Council had to be built in a hurry. There was no time to clear, for example, the Metz triangle and build a city of capital importance from bare earth. A city was needed with houses for a Secretariat, hotels for delegates, and extensive municipal resources—and not only had the city to be chosen, it had to possess a natural frame, a hinterland of people in a region itself worthy of capital importance.

We shall discuss this question of regionalism in coming chapters, so it is as well to realise it has been interwoven with the European Idea from the beginning, and is even more so today. Yet we are most of us so accustomed from childhood to seeing Europe as a jigsaw of coloured pieces on the map, that we are scarcely accustomed to thinking of Europe first in terms of people and therefore regions—each with its living character. When Mazzini said 'if you want to know the future of Europe look at the map', we can scarcely believe he meant the map of mutable nation-states, but rather the map of hamlets, villages and cities; the map of mountains, fjords, rivers, lakes; the map of wheatfields and orchards, farms and factories. This is the map of Europe which makes us aware visually of those groups of people we call minorities, and it is this map we need if we are to visualise Europe as she really is, a Europe of organic parts and living regions. When Strasbourg came to be considered as the possible home for the Council of Europe it was thus necessary to consider also the region in which Strasbourg lies—Alsace.

Not only has Alsace a strong character of her own, she has an in-dividual power to influence strongly both those who grow up as her children and those who come to her as friends. Alsace is neither French nor German; Alsace is Alsace—never quite sure whether one of the squares in Strasbourg is the *Place de la République* or *Kaisersplatz;* and with her memory scarred even today by the forcible recruitment in war of her youth—first for one side, then the other. Alsace flanks the second richest river in Europe, the Rhine, yet has been denied until today that wealth which should accrue from her rich valley soil between Vosges and Black Forest, from her ample water-power and her own hard-working hands. Always the first to be the battlefield, always last to be at peace, knowing her own mind very well, though not always able to speak it to others, forced to speak her own dialect and so appar-ently retreat into the provincial psychology of a stubbornly individual enclave—placed strategically at one of the great geographical cross-roads of Europe, Alsace seemed a worthy and almost inevitable home for a Council of Europe.

Alsace and her city of Strasbourg have always exercised a magic on certain men. 'At nine o'clock in the morning', said Alexandre Dumas, 'I stood before the Cathedral of Strasbourg. It was the most beautiful sight I have yet seen on my journey. It had an effect I shall not try to describe, but which I joyfully advertise to my readers as the eighth wonder of the world.'

'The city is pleasing', said Theophile Gautier, 'because of its pic-turesque physiognomy, and the small yet singular details and accent which reflect the neighbouring countries and are to be found along frontiers.'

'Strasbourg', said the Marquis de Pezay, 'that campaigning-ground of the first rank—possessing the highest of our spires, and the most beautiful women of the Kingdom. If you wish to see women with the finest figures, svelte, you must go to Strasbourg—it is there you must be to see elegant legs; it is in Strasbourg that on the pavements of the streets there step delicate and well-poised feet.'

'Strasbourg', said Mozart, 'can scarcely pass from my mind! You can scarcely believe in what honour they hold me here, or how they love me. The people say that everything goes so nobly with me, that I am myself so equable, so agreeable, and that I conduct myself so well—here everyone knows me.'

'The Rhine', said Victor Hugo, 'seems to be also symbolic. In its descent, in its course, in the regions it traverses, it is, one might well say, the image of the very civilisation which it has already served so well, and which it will yet serve further.'

'How beautiful is the spring this year', said Paul Claudel, 'and how sweet to see in the mist the Eternal Angel of Strasbourg emerging and coming forward like a betrothed!'

And Hugo again, 'I saw Chartres. I saw Antwerp. It was Strasbourg that I needed.'

And Goethe, whom Strasbourg marked and whose words marked Strasbourg, and whose youthful statue now stands outside the University at the start of the boulevard that leads to the Council of Europe, and who said of the spire of Strasbourg Cathedral, the tallest in Europe, that it was the *Himmel anstrebende Turm*—the 'Heaven-aspiring spire'. These are merely glimpses of Alsace and her city of Strasbourg, a city in whose museum is the oldest stained-glass representation of a human face known to the world—a face also divine, an eleventh century Head of Christ.

While we have Alsace in mind as a region, and Strasbourg as her city, let us take further this question of an eventual capital for Europe, for within ten years of the founding of the Council of Europe in Strasbourg

it became an issue in practical politics. The growth of European organisations had by then expanded to include the use of national capitals as
their hosts, and it seemed reasonable to attempt centralising them all in
one city, thereby creating at least a provisional capital of Europe. The
candidates were Brussels, the home of the European Economic Community; Luxembourg, home of the European Coal and Steel Community;
and Strasbourg, home of the Council of Europe. Each city engaged
architects, commissioned by hopeful city fathers to draw blueprints of
how they visualised the capital of Europe. The stakes for each region
were high, the competition intense. And even though the evolution of
integration-politics at that time enabled each of the three governments
sponsoring each of the three cities to veto each of the others, thus producing deadlock, nevertheless a decision was at least attempted; and anyone today who wishes to ponder those blueprints and see the finest
professional opinions on how a capital of Europe can be built, may do so.

This is the problem that faced the architects of Canberra, Washington
D.C., New Delhi, Ottawa, Brazilia—the great federal capitals of the
world. And even though this anticipates our story, this issue should be
here introduced, for it is today in Europe still unsolved. We do not know
today whether eventually Strasbourg, or Brussels—or perhaps by the
turn of the century, Vienna or some other quite unexpected city or
region, will in fact evolve into the real and permanent capital of Europe.
And as we look at the blueprints—at these meticulously drafted exercises in political imagination which came very close to success, we
realise suddenly we are looking at what could have been a disastrous
second-best. For we are looking at most carefully measured plans for
heliports and avenues; ministerial and governmental blocks; executive,
legislative and judiciary buildings; underground excavations and clover-
leaf flyovers; the overhead towers of a Radio Europe, and immensely
complex facilities for communication, printing, translation, transport,
accommodation and recreation—we are looking at plans for a single all-
inclusive capital designed as the political seat of a European Government
itself presumably expected to govern in that style and mode anticipated
in the city-planning of the architects.

It nearly happened. If it had, we would today be already accustomed
to having *all* organisations connected with the unification of Europe
centralised in one place, and our thinking would already be very different.
Perhaps the fact it did not happen was a setback. Perhaps it was a blessing.
Either way, we have at least been given time to consider more deeply
what is involved, and to examine issues which are likely to become
matters of intense public discussion.

First, should a truly united Europe have a single all-centralising capital? Or should we avoid centralism and instead adopt different cities, and therefore regions, for different functions? A financial capital? London springs to mind. An educational capital—why not Florence? Why not polycentricism rather than centralism, with individual cities and regions evolving gradually into centres for law, science, art, for separate branches of industry and agriculture, for scientific research, space exploration, military defence? How do we create and maintain a golden synthesis between the strengthening forces of centralism and simplification, and the enriching forces of widely diverse aspiration and emulation? Where indeed should be the hub of the wheel, where its rim?

What is decided for cities determines the destiny of regions and their population—and what is decided for regions determines the destiny of cities. The matter is not academic: it is today more difficult and more important than it was in the founding years of the Council of Europe, for there are today greater and more complex pressures. Unlike America, Europe was settled so long ago we do not remember how it began, and whereas in America, settlers in Nebraska, Illinois, or Kansas had a free hand to shape the institutions and character of their society as they wished, to settle as they felt inclined, in Europe we are not so free. Americans sometimes forget this when they blithely lecture Europeans on what they must do. Goethe said: 'consider the What, consider more the How', and to many today in Europe the challenge is not the 'What' at all but much more the 'How'. Sometimes that 'How' is much determined by regional memories and when we consider regions in Europe we must consider them with care—for our European character and reactions are entangled with thickets of folk-memory, sturdy with many centuries of growth—thickets where the roots of briars are entangled with the roots of roses. Since he who would uproot the briar must reckon with losing the rose, it can be most unwise to consider action in any region in Europe without also considering the accumulated memories of that region. Hence the relevance today of the Alsace example—where a city, a region, and a great institution together form a living and evolving unit.

All this has developed over the years from a few suave words in the Statute of the Council of Europe, saying simply that the seat of the Council shall be the city of Strasbourg. Let us now look more closely at this Statute, not only as a document but as a perplexing challenge to the parliamentarians of the Council of Europe.

Foremost among these was Churchill—second only to him, Paul-Henri Spaak. As Foreign Minister of Belgium, Spaak was expected to be the first Chairman of the Council of Europe's Committee of Ministers, but when in August 1949 the Belgian Government fell and Spaak was succeeded by van Zeeland, the way opened for him to act instead in the Consultative Assembly of the Council. The election of the Assembly's first president was held up to enable Spaak to be first approached, then elected, and it was his example that in these first years gave form, function and personality to a position defined under the Statute in only sparse terms.

It was under Spaak's leadership therefore that the first full Session of the Consultative Assembly was held on 10 August, 1949. As with everything else about the Council at its first beginning, the human problem was to create a harmonious synthesis of the ability and experience so richly available—to reconcile, rejuvenate and galvanise the best from among the many parliamentary traditions available at choice to the Assembly. And yet soon this Belgian Socialist, renowned already for his entanglements with his own King Leopold, was—as Kenneth Lindsay puts it—to find himself forced to behave in the Council of Europe more like the Speaker of the House of Commons in the days of England's first Queen Elizabeth than as the dynamic 'Mr Europe' he was later to become. 'All rising to great place', says Bacon, 'is by a winding stair'—the dazzling turbulence of Spaak's career is perhaps an example of what Bacon may have meant. For Spaak was soon in conflict with that very Committee of Ministers over whom he had so nearly presided, and the first aim of the Assembly over which he did preside became not to lead Europe, not to speak for Europe, but first of all merely to make this possible. For the design of the Statute prevented, the attitudes of the Ministers circumvented, and if the European Idea was not to die then conflict had to come.

Yet not all the feeling of the Assembly is to be found in the official documents. Every gathering of people has its own aura of memories, emotions, ideas and aims—especially in politics. It was a question at this first Session of the Assembly what kind of group personality it would acquire, and how it would evolve a working code of conduct and effective good manners. How soon would it acquire a collective *sub*conscious character of its own, thereby expressing the collective attitude of all Western Europe for the first time in history? This was a question close to Churchill's heart: his speeches in 1949 were nearly all designed to enhance the Assembly's parliamentary character and carefully establish procedures for the long-term future. Nor can this have been easy.

Perhaps the closest example we can find of any previous Assembly with so high an aim is the French Assembly of 1792, when French citizenship was conferred on Paine, Bentham, Priestley, David Williams, Madison Clootz, Pestalozzi, George Washington and others, and when Paine could tell Danton that by means of her Constitution yet to be written, France should become the orator of Europe, that 'she must speak for other nations who cannot yet speak for themselves. She must put thoughts into their minds and arguments into their mouths.' Debate in the Assembly raged between Girondistes and Montagnards over the political expediency of declaring a code of Human Rights, and it cannot have been easy when these and other questions recurred again almost in the same words a century and a half later; but now in an Assembly whose members were drawn not from one but twelve nations, and this in a Europe still divided by the Iron Curtain, yet so soon to enter the space age.

As we have seen, the founding Member States of the Council of Europe were Belgium, Denmark, France, Ireland, Italy, Luxembourg, the Netherlands, Norway, Sweden and the United Kingdom. In August 1949 Greece and Turkey joined—to be followed in 1950 by Iceland, and then (largely on Churchill's initiative) by the Saar and the Federal Republic of Germany. In the Committee of Ministers each country was represented by its Foreign Minister—and in the Consultative Assembly by Parliamentarians directly elected in their own countries, and thereafter selected for Strasbourg by procedures individually chosen by each country. Even in this first Session of the Assembly, no country sent less than three representatives, thus always permitting the three traditional party groups of Right, Left, and Centre each to have a voice. An important ideological exception was that no Communist reached a seat in the Assembly. On the other hand, no country sent more than eighteen representatives, and those who respect consistency before all else may well shake their heads at the mathematics involved. As Professor Schmitt emphasises in his book *The Path to European Union*, 'One Luxembourger sat for each 100,000 of his fellow citizens, while the ratio was closer to one to 3,000,000 in the case of Germany, France, and the United Kingdom.' Thus not merely the mathematical ratio of representation, but the voting balances of countries and also of parties in an Assembly containing Liberals, Socialists, and Conservatives now beginning to vote for the first time ever in trans-European alignments—all these were inconsistent, conforming as yet to no norm.

Nobody cared. Certainly not the governments. They knew very well the Assembly was merely consultative and could legally be ignored. Nor did the Members of the Assembly care. They were not going to quibble as long as they got to Strasbourg. Nor did public opinion care, for what the public wanted to know was what the Council of Europe was going to do.

When the individual representatives arrived in Strasbourg they found they must each make adjustments in parliamentary custom no matter where they came from. British Members of Parliament found themselves each allotted a personal desk in the curving banked rows of desks that make up the Hemicycle in which the Assembly meets—as is the custom in Continental parliaments. Members from Oslo, Paris, Rome or the Hague found themselves on the other hand required to speak, not from a superb rostrum facing the Assembly but with unaccustomed familiarity from their own desks, surrounded by their colleagues as in the British House of Commons. And it was on the initiative of the Secretary General designate, Jacques-Camille Paris, that members found themselves seated not in party or national order, but alphabetically. Professor Schmitt, quoting Kenneth Lindsay, reminds us of the shock when 'Winston Churchill sat, possibly for the first time, next to Labourite Hugh Dalton. Former Greek Premier Constantin Tsaldaris rubbed elbows with his compatriot Evangelos Tsirinokis whom he had once put in jail.' When later the Consultative Assembly produced its child—the European Parliament of the six Common Market countries which also meets in the Hemicycle of the Council of Europe—this method was smoothly superseded (as Jacques-Camille Paris had himself hoped) by seating members in their natural trans-European party blocs. These and other purely procedural techniques and innovations are among the greatest achievements of the Consultative Assembly.

The seating of members was only one of the more visible achievements. For it was necessary also to establish harmonious working procedures within the Assembly, whose pattern could mirror the best of European parliamentary practice and influence all future sessions. It was essential to break down national habits that were constricting, and combine those that were constructive. This had to be done in an Assembly lacking power at the start to decide even its own Agenda, and yet where every act was a precedent. An influence had to spread outwards from the presiding officers of the Assembly to all members on the floor, through the first primitive Committee structures within the Assembly and outwards through all the Committees and Directorates of the Secretariat, and from the Council of Europe as a whole further still, to Press, to public, and always—and this was at first the all-justifying hope—by a spark-jump of reaction and feeling back from the public to the Assembly. And it did spread—and in spite of the difficulties, reverses, and plain defeats which prevented the Assembly becoming fully what it hoped, an unexpected function began to emerge. Then, as even more today, the Consultative Assembly of the Council of Europe proved itself from the start a perpetual political research laboratory, nearly always several years in advance of its time, and concerned always in the widest, highest sense with the future of *all* Europe.

Yet in 1949 and 1950 Bevin's Pandora policy was beginning to work well. Not if he could help it was anything worthwhile to be achieved by this political hybrid foisted on him. He would perhaps have preferred to call it a hydra, a many-headed thing, speaking many tongues—and the obstacles he had constructed in London for its future containment had been clever. Then, as now, defence was a most powerful factor in all political equations relating to European unification. Since the Brussels Pact and the North Atlantic Treaty Organisation had already been created to control military affairs, it was possible to argue plausibly that a Council of Europe Assembly simply did not need authority to discuss the armies, air-fleets, navies or nuclear strike-capacity of the people of Europe—to say nothing of bacteriological or chemical warfare. The Statute thus explicitly forbade discussion of military defence, and does to this day—and to this extent the Assembly's right of free public utterance was most seriously damaged, as was intended.

It was also essential that no matter what the Assembly demanded, no Government should be under obligation to act. If the highest hope of the Assembly—united Governmental action towards the union of Europe—was to be kept firmly locked inside the Pandora's box, then a limbo had to be constructed round the Assembly, a penumbra of official nothingness permitting the Committee of Ministers and national governments to act in strict obedience to the Statute by merely saying to the Assembly: 'Yes, we hear you', and never more—like Poe's raven, hearing every question, yet answering always the same.

And this happened. Unless the Committee of Ministers said 'yes' unanimously the Assembly could get no action. The Assembly could do nothing to coerce the Ministers, though it did later develop a capacity to shame them. Under the Statute the Assembly had no weapon save its powers of public utterance—a dilemma Spaak must have pondered as he sat looming above the Assembly through debate after debate. From Bevin's point of view, and that of many other people like him in high places in all the Member-Governments from whom he drew support, it was a clever trap.

The more the assembled parliamentarians in Strasbourg realised they were in a trap, the more they came on occasion to reveal symptoms we should expect. What is remarkable is that, even caught as it was, the Assembly did not lie down, kick feebly and then suddenly die in a political parody of Pavlovian frustration.

Why did it not die? What was it in the spirit of these parliamentarians that kept their Assembly alive?

Anthony Nutting and others have said it would have been better if it had died—that its wisest course would have been to place blame publicly where blame belonged and do so by committing deliberate public suicide. A boycott was advocated. It was even suggested that members of the Assembly should pick up their credentials and encamp somewhere else, hoping thereby to win for themselves those powers they were denied under the Statute.

Yet they did not, and here begins a paradox. Briefly stated, it is that the Assembly of the Council of Europe in its earlier years seldom had power to command events continuously, yet always had power to start events in motion at their very beginnings—and also, curiously, a second power of resuming influence over these same events at a much later stage. Thus the Assembly launched initiatives, watched them make their way or not in the brute political world—as happened with the Common Market —and then when the same initiatives returned home as it were to Strasbourg, again re-launched them in new and appropriate forms. The process tended to be cyclic, running often to a rhythm of three or five or seven years, and there have thus been very few initiatives relevant to the European future in which it does not later come to be seen that the Assembly, and indeed the whole Council, has previously had a hand,

This, of course, was not anticipated in the beginning, least of all by Bevin. Some of the causes of this elusive phenomenon are given by Professor Schmitt:

'...the Council of Europe realised only a modest share of the hopes voiced at the Hague. Its feeble powers were assumed to reside in the Committee of Ministers. Composed of one member from each country, once again most commonly the foreign minister who was spending more and more time "on the road" it alone could initiate decisions. The language which conferred this authority was tortured at that; it merely bade them "consider the action required to further the aims of the Council of Europe, including the conclusion of conventions...and the adoption by governments of a common policy with regard to particular matters."

'This nebulous phraseology was further diluted by the next paragraph:

"In *appropriate* cases the conclusions of the committee *may* take the
form of recommendations, and the committee may request governments of members to inform it of the action taken by them with
regard to such recommendations."

'Thus the Committee of Ministers *might* recommend decisions, which
no one need take seriously. Since this was plainly a waste of time, it
developed very little initiative. In the words of one indignant observer,
it was "not really in any sense a responsible body...not an organ at all.
Whatever happened at the Council of Europe after it became settled in
Strasbourg originated in the Consultative Assembly...It could not
render decisions, but it could and did bring forth a wealth of ideas...
Economic integration, military integration, and political integration,
generalizations and particulars, might succeed or founder in the years to
come, but they received their first airing at the *Maison d'Europe* in the
Alsation capital. The inter-governmental pattern of European co-
operation had been broken..." '

In many problems of European unification it is not merely important
to see where the powers of initiative lie, but often surprisingly difficult.
Here at least it is clear: it was in the Consultative Assembly and not in
the Committee of Ministers. Yet at the time it was hard to see—for while
we usually feel the negative at once, it sometimes takes eyes to see the
positive. A stumbling-block can feel agonisingly big, a pin-point of light
at the end of a tunnel can seem miserably small and far off, and while
stumbling over the one we can lose sight of the other. Thus during the
two turbulent years of Spaak's presidency of the Consultative Assembly
it was the originating power within the Assembly that gave the Council
of Europe its life, and it was the Committee of Ministers that was felt
to be the immediate and immovable stumbling-block—and all this
because of the Statute. Yet before we condemn the Statute totally, it
may be as well to amplify the argument introduced in Chapter One—
that the value of an agreed political document, legal text, convention
or declaration lies not in its stultifying effects but in its permissive and
creative effects. The importance of the Statute of the Council of Europe
is *not* that it was imperfect, but that year after year it *did* permit unexpected events to happen. This may seem an unappreciative attitude
towards those many parliamentarians who struggled so hard in the early
years against the imperfections of the Statute but it is not meant to be so;
it is intended rather to place on record a new aspect of the real value of
their struggles—for today we can begin to see it better.

These struggles revolved around two ideas then destined to shape our thinking in subtle indirect ways for decades. Behind the private pressure and public uproar to reform the Statute was an inner evolution which inspired all subsequent thinking on the future structure of any European Union—thinking which in the early years revolved round the two words: '*Federalist*' and '*Functionalist*'.

Let us have a closer look, first, at two aspects of the *federalist* approach.

Psychologically, it is an inclination to change the structure of power in Europe not by approaching peripheral problems directly, but by approaching the central problem directly—and this in very careful and gradual stages.

Politically, it means a determination to keep moving always one step nearer to the creation of an irrevocable system of Federal Government for Europe—and again, let it be repeated, not instantly or overnight but by careful and gradual stages.

On the other hand, the *functionalist* approach, psychologically, is an inclination to change the structure of power in Europe not by approaching the central problem at all, but by approaching peripheral problems either separately or in groups, in the hope thereby of so changing events that thereafter a direct approach on the central problem may become either much easier, or even unnecessary.

Politically, the functionalist approach may or may not include a determination towards a Federal Government—the option can be left open, the real aim never defined.

And the word 'Government' itself—meaning a Government of Europe—was even in these first years considered almost as sensitive and indelicate as it is today—even though it was and is the first premise of federalist thinking and can be summed up, now as then, in the simple phrase—No Federal Government, No Europe. We can place these early years of the Council of Europe in a sharp perspective by recalling that, even as recently as 1962, Lord Gladwyn's Common Market Campaign in Britain took care never to define its position on the word 'Government' in the *European* sense—though it was an issue repeatedly and rightly raised for public discussion by Anti-Marketeers, as of course is happening today.

At the first Session of the Consultative Assembly, when the Committee of Ministers still controlled the Assembly's Agenda, Item Four on that Agenda was: 'Consideration of any necessary *changes in the political structure of Europe* to achieve a greater unity between the Members of the Council of Europe and to make effective European co-operation in the various spheres specified in Article 1 of the Statute'.

Item Four was referred to a Committee of the Assembly whose members included Dalton, Mackay, Macmillan and Spaak, whose *rapporteur* was Guy Mollet and whose Chairman was Bidault. The Committee had also before it no less than twenty-four separate proposals tabled by Members in the Assembly. They included the following and each reveals the same federalist psychology and approach:

1. A Motion presented by Mr Mackay proposing *inter alia* that there should be established a 'European Democratic Federation' and that a Commission should be set up to draft a 'Constitution for a political union of Western Europe'.

2. A Motion by M. Cassimatis and others recommending to the Committee of Ministers *'the creation of a European political authority with limited functions and real powers'*.

3. A Motion by Messrs Macmillan, Maxwell-Fyfe, Boothby, Ross and Eccles proposing *inter alia* the convening of a conference to decide what executive powers should be conferred on the Committee of Ministers.

4. A Motion of M. van der Goes van Naters 'to examine the creation of a co-ordinated administration of economic and technical organisations on a supra-national plane under the continuous control of the peoples' representatives'.

5. A Motion by MM. Maurice Schumann, Bidault and others calling for 'the creation of a *European Political Authority with limited aims but real powers'*.

6. An Amendment of the Statute proposed by Mr Macmillan and providing that 'The Committee of Ministers shall be an *executive authority with supra-national powers'*.

The ensuing parliamentary action led to the Assembly instructing its Committee to prepare for the next Session in 1950 'definite recommendations concerning the modifications in the political structure of the Member States which it considers desirable with a view to closer unity'. Even more significant, the Assembly adopted unanimously an amendment tabled by Mr Mackay and seconded by M. André Philip, containing the Federalist phrase already used above and from that moment on destined to become a foundation stone in federalist thinking:

> ...the Assembly considers that the aim and goal of the Council of Europe is the creation of a *European Political Authority with limited functions but real powers.*

This formula is Federalist in the sense that it could, for example, be applied to the Canadian, United States and West German Governments—which certainly have real powers, whose functions are limited under law, and whose authority one can no doubt indeed describe as both political and acceptable. Though there are important differences, advantages and disadvantages in all three governmental systems, any European application of this federalist formula is likely to be different again. Nevertheless the formula stands. Let us now see how this form of words first evolved in Strasbourg and gained acceptance.

The most revealing account is by Mr Noel Salter, at that time secretary to Mr Mackay and later to become Clerk-Assistant of the Assembly of Western European Union. Not only is it exact, it suggests the very gestures and tone of voice in Council of Europe politics at that time:

'The origin of the actual phrase is the following. The leaders of the Federalist group in the Assembly used to meet each day near the University building, either in the upper portion of the restaurant of the Pension Eliza, Place Brant, or in the offices of Mr Mackay above. At a meeting held in the restaurant on August 12, 1949, there was lengthy discussion of the right form of words to rally the majority of the Assembly behind an effective programme of action. Some were in favour of going back to the Federalist amendment adopted at the Hague Congress the year before, calling for "the transfer and merger of sovereignty". Then a French representative, M. de Felice, proposed the phrase in question. It was at once acclaimed: and from then onwards the major effort of the Federalist group was to achieve a massive vote in favour of this text by the Assembly before the end of the first Session. The opening shot of the campaign was on August 17, when several of the Federalist group, including M. Cassimatis and Mr Mackay, tabled a motion using the phrase, which was referred back to the General Affairs Committee. The *rapporteur*, M. Guy Mollet, however, did not wish to accept it, in order to keep in step with the leaders of the U.K. Labour Delegation (Morrison and Dalton). It was therefore omitted from the report as tabled in the Assembly. Meanwhile the Federalist group had been lobbying actively, and their secretary obtained eighty signatures for the motion. When M. Mollet's report came before the Assembly on Monday, Sept 5, Mr Mackay therefore tabled a formal amendment. In spite of the eighty signatures there was considerable doubt as to whether the U.K. and Scandinavian Representatives would vote for the text. However, in the early part of the afternoon, Mr Macmillan quoted from a Memorandum which Mr Churchill (who had by then left Strasbourg) had written in October 1942, which in the middle of the war had stated: "I look forward to a United States of Europe." This helped to create a favourable atmosphere, and in the event, when M. Spaak put the amendment to the

Assembly at 17.30 hours, it was adopted unanimously. By so doing, it defined a goal which has still to be achieved.'

Yet at the time men were more hopeful. As Spaak said, 'I came to Strasbourg convinced of the need for a United States of Europe. I am leaving it with the certitude that union is possible.'

Yet the certitude crumpled. The opposition of the Committee of Ministers was immovable. The federalist drive was halted, and thrown back. And since action and reaction are often equal and opposite also in emotions, enthusiasm in the Assembly was followed by depression. *Reculer pour mieux sauter* was the most cheerful cry now to be heard. A protest boycott of the Council of Europe by the entire membership of the Consultative Assembly? It is understandable this was considered as a remedy, and indicates the bitterness.

Yet that did not happen either. It is safe to say today that those men and women who perhaps from sheer intuition refused to abandon the Council of Europe, and who clung to what must have appeared a compromise of doubtful courage because there was nothing else to cling to, have been proved right. As Professor Schmitt says: '...among the political experiments of the decade, the Council of Europe, rather than the Brussels Pact and Nato, alone held the germ of development. The events of 1950 were to bear this out.'

Among the events of 1950 was the following statement agreed by the Assembly, firm but nevertheless defensive:

The Assembly:

1. Solemnly declares that the purpose of a closer European union—to be achieved by strengthening its political and economic independence through the realisation of the economic, social and cultural aims of the Council of Europe—is to enable a democratic Europe to carry out its mission as a permanent factor making for peace and unity in the world.

2. Declares that the achievement of European union should not entail any weakening of the existing links between certain Member States of the Council of Europe and the overseas territories or countries. On the contrary, the active participation of these countries and territories is particularly necessary to the progress of European union.

3. Repeating its declaration of September 1949, vigorously reaffirms that it considers the aim of the Council to be the creation of a *European political authority with limited functions but real powers*.

4. Considers that, advancing beyond mere theoretical discussion, the pursuit of this last aim should be based on the following principles:

(a) Closer co-operation must be established between existing Euro-

pean organisations. At the same time, the rules governing their operation must be made more flexible;

(b) Effective European *parliamentary* supervision must be exercised
over the actions of inter-governmental organisations;

(c) Since the Council of Europe appears to be the organisation best
qualified to supply the general framework within which such a policy
might be put into effect, its *authority must be strengthened and its organs
must be enabled to assume their increased responsibility.*

If this is read as referring to the Council of Europe alone, it certainly
documents the evolution of the Assembly and the impression is firm.
But if it is read in the knowledge that these principles were agreed one
month *after* Robert Schuman's electrifying press conference of 9 May
1950, proposing what was to become the European Coal and Steel
Community, it reads differently—it is defensive. And this for the understandable reason that until the 9 May the Council of Europe had been
not merely the first organisation dedicated to European unity but the
only one. It had therefore held a monopoly on hope. After the 9 May
the Council of Europe was forced to compete for the hopes—and therefore the energies—of all concerned with European unity, and to this
extent the price of progress was increased difficulty, just as it is today.

Thus when at 4.30 that afternoon in May 1950 Robert Schuman,
Foreign Minister of France, announced to a startled world his 'limited
but decisive plan', the spotlight of Press and public opinion swung
instantly from the politics of the European Assembly in Strasbourg westwards to Paris. Here was a plan already formed, already quietly on the
move in the minds of many men. As Schuman spoke, attention focussed
on the enormous area of industrial politics, on miners in the Borinage,
steel barons like Thyssen, homes where steel-workers lived in the Ruhr,
the Saar, and Lorraine—on the network of mines, railways, waterways,
factories, forges and foundries that roar and flame along the lower Rhine
and outwards for a hundred miles along each bank. '*We propose to pool,*'
said Robert Schuman, '*all our industries of coal and steel.*' And yet, even
before the Press and public opinion had caught their breath, the spotlight
then swung immediately back again to the Hemicycle in the Council of
Europe, where the same Churchill who had mobilised millions of men
to hammer tyranny to pieces, arose in the Assembly and demanded that
the Governments and people of Western Europe pool their entire military
strength in a single European army.

As we all know today, the European Coal and Steel Community was
created precisely as proposed by Schuman, while at the time of writing

not only is the European army still to come, but NATO itself is in disarray and the complexities of integrating European nuclear defence are a nightmare. Yet this is not enough to prove that Robert Schuman was walking the only right way, or that Winston Churchill was fundamentally wrong. Both Schuman and Churchill presumably hoped both plans would proceed together, each helping the other. We shall now see why this did not happen, and what it meant for the Council of Europe and the evolution of the European Idea.

One reason is that sometimes it is the largest plans that turn on the smallest detail—just as a giant gantry a hundred feet high and capable of hoisting a locomotive must nevertheless turn on ball-bearings the size of marbles. The man who proved a master at combining a plan of giant imagination with a meticulous and intricate engineering of detail was the man behind Schuman—Jean Monnet. What is astonishing is that as far back as the war years Monnet had already outlined his plan to Spaak in Washington; a plan which Spaak told Anthony Nutting was 'in every detail' the same as the plan Robert Schuman was now presenting in the name of a far-sighted France. This Protean force of will, this long-term determination, supple yet unyielding, and capable of taking many forms without changing in essentials, is to be encountered more than once in the chronicle of European unification. Also to be encountered is the problem—and a particularly European problem—of distinguishing between inner, hidden, long-term motives, and outer, visible, short-term motives.

One visible motive in Monnet's plan was to eliminate the perennial French fear of an uncontrolled resurgence of Germany. The Nazi cancer had been cauterised, certainly, but a full healing of the wound thereby left deep within the heart of Europe was not possible—any genuinely healthy re-unification of Germany was then still unthinkable. At stake was the future of the three Western Zones of Occupation. The Saar also was still under Allied authority, and here especially the French dared not release their grip unless they gained something as good or better. Hitler had started from nothing and ended with autobahns, guns, armies, fleets, dive-bombers and the finest panzer divisions in Europe. The inherent strength of German industry had conquered Europe: it was in the essential interest of France that German steel should never again be used to forge a solely German sword.

Europe in 1950 faced also the Communist menace. Russian divisions were on the Elbe. Whenever the two strands of military power and industrial power are intertwined, they form a powerful conductor for the electric pulse of political ideology, and there was therefore in Monnet's plan to fuse the French and German industries of coal and steel a powerful military, political, and ideological attraction for France. Once German industry merged with the French, it would not only cease to be in Germany's power to attack France or even merely turn against her, but both would be strengthened against the East. The attraction of a European Coal and Steel Community for France was to this extent both immediate and visible.

A second immediately visible motive in Monnet's plan was to provide a safe outlet for understandable emotions on the German side of the Rhine. The West Germans wished above all to escape from Allied control of their own industry. Their impulse was to welcome anything tending in that direction, and if they could not get there by one way they would presumably get there by another. Yet they could not at this time expect independent control of their industry, and when the Monnet plan carefully offered them a *shared* responsibility for both German and French industry joined together, their support became inevitable.

Yet success can sometimes be too successful. Among the French was a realistic fear that the very success of the Monnet plan might create an industrial Community that could become no more than an enlarged but now legitimate field for German domination. Was the German eagle to be released into a larger cage but with the French cock now also within the cage? The very logic of Monnet's more visible motives forced the French to look in the next direction he had himself in mind—across the English Channel.

The British were known to be pragmatic, to respect facts. In French eyes, was it not reasonable to expect the British to welcome the immense cash profits that would flow to the coal-fields of Newcastle and the Midlands, the steel-mills of Rhondda Valley and Ebbw Vale? Would not the British, like the French, welcome this device to grant Germany the strength of peace while denying her the sinews of war? Would the British not see that their own industrial might would not only be their own insurance against German hegemony within the industrial Community, but against French hegemony also for that matter? Would the British not see that this proposed pooling of coal and steel was to be no cartel or monopoly—that on the contrary, restrictions, tariffs, quotas, exchange controls, were all to go? Would the British not see that wages, prices, shares, competition and demand, were all to continue to operate according to accepted economic laws, but now within a healthily enlarged market?

What the British saw was that if the pooling of coal and steel was to succeed, there would have to be a control at the top able to transcend the traditional authority of national Governments and parliaments. In

his declaration of 9 May 1950 Schuman had explicitly said the Coal
and Steel Community was designed to assist the creation of a European
Federation—and the British saw at once this must eventually mean
acceptance of majority decisions. The British, so democratic at home, were
not ready to be democratic in any wider European sense, even in the
strictly limited field of coal and steel alone. The British refusal to counten-
ance the democratic principle in an international endeavour was at this
time still resolute: they could not yet see it was to prove the only realistic
way.

Thus, just as in the drafting of the Statute of the Council of Europe, so
now with the creation of the Coal and Steel Community, a fundamentally
emotional pre-judging of the issue in Britain made any real judgement
impossible. Yet elsewhere those motives outwardly apparent in the
Monnet plan were still powerful and attractive. The French Government
was pushing his plan steadily forward: of one mind with them were
Belgium and Luxembourg, both strategically situated in the heart of
the coal and steel country—and Italy also. Only the Dutch held back,
stipulating that they wanted a careful look at the project with the other
proposed partners, and could not make promises in advance. This was
cautious but considered fair: they were therefore in on the negotiations
from the beginning.

The British party reaction to this challenge is reminiscent of the old
distinction between pessimist and optimist: the pessimist sees a glass half
empty, the optimist sees it half full. The British Labour Government
saw the Monnet plan merely as a radical re-shaping of British sovereignty,
which it certainly was. Some at least among the British Conservatives
and Labour back-benchers saw it as an enlarging of loyalties, an opportunity for leadership, a chance to go in with a cheer—notably Mr Edward
Heath, in a maiden speech to the House of Commons of remarkable
prescience and courage. But the British Labour Government, just as it
had jibbed at the thought of granting real powers to the Council of
Europe, now refused to take part in the negotiations on the European
Coal and Steel Community—even the Foreign Office observer present
at the opening of negotiations was soon recalled. A fair account of attitudes
at the time is given by Mackay in his comment on the key debate in the
House of Commons:

'Sir Stafford Cripps gave the reasons for the government's refusal to
participate. He pointed out that as the coal production of Great
Britain was twice as much as that of the other countries invited, the
matter was of considerable concern to this country. But his main

objection was that, while Britain was prepared to join some European organisations, she was not prepared to participate in them without knowing the details of the proposals to which she would be committed. He gave as an illustration the negotiations with the European Payments Union when the Convention which created it set out in detail its functions, its powers, the obligations of members, and the way in which it was to operate...Sir Stafford Cripps, referring to the method of negotiating the European Payments Union, said: "This negotiation is, I think typical of what can be accomplished by a freely negotiated agreement between governments. I am perfectly certain that if in this case some supra-national body had attempted to impose upon us by a majority vote some payments scheme without any prior discussion between governments, it could only have resulted in a complete failure, and in our having to leave the organisation".'

And Mackay continued:

'It the British Government had approached the Council of Europe on these lines...that method of negotiation could easily have been applied, but when the amendment of the Statute was proposed to give effect to a proposal on those lines, the British Government still refused to co-operate. The Dutch went to the conference on the Schuman Plan but reserved their rights with regard to being bound to consider any kind of a political federation for Western Europe. In the debate, Sir Winston Churchill suggested that the British Government might take the same attitude, and of course, they could easily have been present at the conference, taken part in the negotiations, and, following the lines outlined by Sir Stafford Cripps in his speech, only accepted the proposals when satisfied that the draft Treaty for the Community was satisfactory for them. It is difficult to acquit the British Govern-ment of the charges of hypocrisy and perfidy that have been laid against them in regard to their policy in Europe over the post-war years; for, in spite of all their protests about their interest in Europe, in fact they have refused to take advantage of any opportunity offered for any real and effective integration of Western Europe.'

For these reasons—and certainly also because the Labour Government was deeply introspective over its own social revolution, including the nationalisation of coal and steel—Britain opted out. Just as Bevin had said of the Council of Europe, 'I don't like it', so now he said of the European Coal and Steel Community, 'I won't have it'. He would doubtless not have said this, or been able to carry the Cabinet with him,

C

if there had not been short-term advantages in his attitude. While it is perhaps too much to expect a Cabinet under pressure to be primarily concerned with hypothetical penalties which may only later have to be paid by their whole people, it does seem fair to suggest that if a British will to act had carried her forward into merely exploratory talks, and if there she had realised the causes, character and mechanics of the political method proposed, she would have been granted far-reaching safeguards: to say nothing of the cumulative powers later to be exercised by virtue of being a founder-member of the Community. Her choice was to act boldly or to abdicate: it was a choice to be repeatedly forced on Britain in subsequent years.

It is also fair to say that if Britain had been a founder-member of the Coal and Steel Community she would probably later have been a founder member of the European Economic Community and Euratom. If Britain had thus kept in step with other countries, and had herself helped to keep the pace of all quickening together—if Britain had together with them gradually adjusted her economy, currency and monetary policy to the enormous market opening out to her, she would have had elbow-room to demonstrate what her people could truly do. The difficulties then were considerable—but in the years since their scale has steadily increased. If Britain had been inside from the beginning not merely would she have been spared the incessant economic crises which have plagued her in recent years, but the whole present history of Western Europe would have been decisively different. 'He who knows most', said Dante, 'grieves most for wasted time.'

Thus, while Britain stood back, the Monnet plan went forward. Belgium, Luxembourg, Holland, France, Germany and Italy began joint planning in Paris in June 1950. By March 1951 they were agreed, and by August 1952 the European Coal and Steel Community, with its provisional seat in Luxembourg and its High Authority headed by Jean Monnet, was in being.

These are the facts, but so far we have been following them only on the surface. The inner long-term motives were deeply hidden and to grasp them we must focus on Monnet himself. Here is how Professor Schmitt introduces him:

'Monnet was the son of a Cognac merchant. Born to wealth, he was also born to adventure, and he left school at the age of sixteen to begin a spectacular career as salesman of the family product on both sides of the Atlantic. During the First World War, he was a member of various economic missions to Britain. He so impressed his hosts that they subsequently recommended him, then scarcely thirty-one, to become Assistant Secretary General of the League of Nations. He left this disheartening employment after only two years and returned to the House of Monnet, which was then in straits about as dire as the League, and succeeded in curing its ills with greater effect and dispatch.

Between 1925 and 1940, Monnet's economic and financial talents were put to work on a bewildering variety of tasks. He reorganised the finances of Poland and Rumania, acted as adviser to Chiang Kai Shek, and liquidated the affairs of 'match king' Ivar Kreuger. Upon the renewed outbreak of war, he became chairman of the Anglo-French Co-ordinating Committee and was the author of Winston Churchill's famous proposal to unite the British and French Commonwealths for the duration.

After the fall of France, Monnet went to America, where he contributed his experience and optimism to the shaping of Roosevelt's victory program. He was appointed to public office for the first time in 1945, when he became Commissioner under the Plan for the Reconstruction of Key Industries, usually known as the Monnet Plan. His achievements were there impressive: by 1965 French overall industrial production had risen to twice what it was in 1938. Nevertheless, the world owes Monnet a far greater debt for the development of another plan, a plan which was to bear the name of Robert Schuman.'

It was Jean Monnet who said to the National Press Club in Washington on 30 April 1952, 'Nous ne coalisons pas les états, nous unissons les hommes'; and at Aachen when receiving the Charlemagne Prize for European Unity on 17 May 1953: 'Today peace depends not only on treaties or promises. It depends essentially on the creation of conditions which, if they do not change the nature of men, at least guide their behaviour towards each other in a peaceful direction. That is one of the essential consequences of the transformation of Europe which is the object of our Community...Faire l'Europe, c'est faire la paix.'

These words hint at what was soon to become clearer: Monnet's long-term motive in proposing, carrying through and then running the European Coal and Steel Community was to create a force that would serve the future of Europe by acting immediately on the imagination of men—there to flash and spark and create new currents of thought, deriving its electric energy both from the prime force of first example, and also by the application of a method people could see for themselves actually succeeded.

Monnet's method is what is now known throughout Europe as the 'Community method'—so arranging things that the separate best interests of each partner gradually fuse until the common best interest of all partners together becomes visible; that decisions can be harmoniously taken by majority vote and harmoniously executed; that minorities are not alienated but on the contrary that the principles of one person, one vote—of the rule of law—of the equal rights of all individuals, are preserved and enhanced. This was the ideal at which the method aimed, and from the beginning it demanded an enlargement of loyalties in both theory and practice, and a new all-or-nothing attitude of genuine responsibility towards Europe that either exists or does not. It drew its justification from the fact that already in Europe the best interests of each country were indissolubly bound up with the best interests of her neighbours, and that in fact *all* faced the same choice—act together, or abdicate separately and ignominiously.

Ordinary methods, however, normally have only ordinary success. The secret of the Community method was that it superseded the ordinary. In order to succeed, the new Community had to do better than merely improve on what had existed before it. A mere rationalisation of methods of co-operation *between* Governments was not enough, for that was still the ordinary method and likely to be limited to ordinary dimensions of success. What was needed for success in a new dimension was somehow to liberate, co-ordinate and synchronise new human, psychological and political energies which, once created, could be released and applied industrially, socially, politically, even ethically. Yet where was this energy to come from? The ordinary and accustomed sources had been mined for a century.

What Jean Monnet did was to take a new look at an old truth—at something we have long known to be true whether in chemistry, physics, politics, literature, psychology or philosophy—the truth that when new compounds are created by combining formerly separate elements, the total energy available through the new compound may be greater than the sum total of energy formerly available through the component elements separately. It is thus unwise to view the Community method merely in terms of its mechanisms, and better to judge it by its success in creating a new form of political life. The spirit, feeling, thought and action of men is more than mechanical, and thus while Monnet appeared to be constructing primarily a great machine the machine in fact was secondary. His primary aim was to use the machine to demonstrate that a higher *European* consciousness, purpose, identity and capacity also existed. This had been precisely the purpose of the Congress of the Hague

in 1948, and of the founders of the Council of Europe—but their machine
had proved only partly effective and Monnet was now seeking the same
aim by a method that was to prove a revolution in politics.

Monnet saw the possibility of so combining the formerly separated
coal and steel industries of national economies into a composite whole
working not only on new principles, *but also capable of generating sufficient
energy to drive itself.* As a machine, it was to be a first working model of
the new political dynamo Europe would eventually have to learn to
create and manage. It is a safe mechanical rule that the fewer moving
parts a machine has, the greater is likely to be its efficiency, reliability
and often its strength, and the moving parts of Monnet's first prototype
model were therefore: an industrial Court of Justice; an executive High
Authority to initiate proposals and execute them when approved;
a Council of Ministers to approve, reject or modify those proposals;
a partly autonomous financial structure based on an industrial levy; and a
Parliamentary Assembly with considerable powers, not over the Ministers,
but over the High Authority. Monnet's ultimate aim was to demonstrate
that the principles from which this first model derived its success, would,
when greatly improved and extended, be capable of application to the
problem of governing a unified and democratic Europe.

Monnet's method for achieving his Community was itself adopted in
direct reaction to the Council of Europe. For while the Consultative
Assembly of the Council had also been a genuinely original first prototype of what would be needed, the Council's Committee of Ministers
was not, and it was precisely the deadlock in Strasbourg between the
Ministers and the Assembly that compelled Monnet to force his own plan
through by methods deliberately designed to avoid the difficulties
afflicting the Council of Europe. When Churchill called for a European
Army in the Assembly of the Council of Europe he was speaking as a
former Prime Minister now in opposition, and the forum was appropriate; when the Coal and Steel Community was launched from Paris,
Monnet was exploiting the fact that already it had the support of a
Government in power, and again the setting was appropriate. What was
different was the method of preparation.

Monnet's aim was to seek strategic surprise from the start at the
governmental level—and this in the strictly limited realm of one group
of industries only. To gain the support of a Government he had to have
the support of one key man in power, and he found the man in Robert
Schuman, Foreign Minister of France. But the plan had already been
prepared in detail in Monnet's own Paris office before Schuman knew of
it at all, and even after it had been privately unveiled to Schuman and

Schuman had agreed to commit himself, even then the two men continued to work in secret.

The plan was kept secret until Schuman had gained the support of the French Cabinet, thereafter of the French Government as a whole, then of other Cabinets and other Governments in other countries, and finally of as many influential people as possible in key positions right across Western Europe. Not until after massive secret support had been guaranteed did Schuman reveal the plan at his Paris press conference, and by then it already had sufficient strength and momentum to withstand the concerted attack of its many predictable opponents. Neither strategy, tactics nor timing were ordinary: their success was masterly.

In the Assembly of the Council of Europe, as we have seen, the thinking at this time had begun as strictly federalist, but was wilting in the face of frosty opposition by the Committee of Ministers—this inspired principally by Britain. What were needed were the warm winds of success, the momentum of the Monnet plan provided them. Its master-aim, as we have seen, was to contribute dynamically towards a European Union or a United States of Europe, and yet its apparent aim appeared no more than a shrewdly limited functionalism. And it is worth noting that in a technical sense the entire Coal and Steel Community was the implementation of merely one particular Recommendation out of many previously adopted by the Consultative Assembly of the Council of Europe: to this extent it was itself yet another example of what the Assembly could potentially become. For only in Strasbourg could the idea achieve expression in *a single agreed parliamentary text at the European level*. Only in Strasbourg could it be publicly debated as it deserved —indeed, when later the Social Democrats in Bonn protested there had been inadequate debate in the Bundestag, the West German Government retorted that there had on the contrary already been ample opportunity— in Strasbourg. And yet it was also only *outside* Strasbourg that the Monnet plan could achieve its greatest triumph by overcoming its greatest difficulty: that of proving it could succeed. For it lacked the benefit of predecessors. It was the first of its kind, and thereby distinguished for always from all subsequent plans later derived from it. No one in advance could prove from facts either that it must inevitably fail—or even that it might possibly succeed. Just as the Council of Europe had done, it had to force the future by facing the unknown: there could be no certainty in its beginning—only that intense speculation that accompanies every first great hope.

Hence the shock of its success—success that could be defined in hard terms of tonnages of steel, workers' pay-packets, stockbrokers' graphs. The very speed and power of this success was to change, as Monnet intended, the actual categories of thought in the minds of the *'classe politique'*—that surprisingly small number of people who (except when we all go to the polls) do in fact control effective power in Europe. It was the attitudes of these key people Monnet was determined to change, and the process began with the first political acceptance of his plan. In Strasbourg the effect on political emotions and thinking was immediate.

The Assembly—baulked in its direct federalist drive—was now invigorated as never before by this break through in the single yet precisely defined key sector of heavy industry. It was invigorated also by Churchill's simultaneous call for a European Army—another precisely defined key sector. If integration could be achieved with coal and steel, if a start could be made with armies, then need success be limited to soldiers and steel-mills? The Assembly proposed parallel authorities for roads, railways, rivers, canals, ports and airways—and especially an authority for what is today called *L'Europe verte*—the Europe of agriculture and green fields. The new ways opening up seemed clear. What Europe needed were European authorities for industry, agriculture, transport, defence—indeed, it seemed that a great and indispensable truth was at last making headway: the truth that when what needs to be done can no longer be done at the national level, then it can and must be done at the European level. And yet it was not proving easy. 'We are not making a machine, we are growing a plant', Churchill had said of the Council of Europe—yet now the plant seemed to be branching wildly in all directions, while none too secure at the roots. In contemporary speeches, private letters, public press, radio and television commentary and throughout this entire human hubbub a debate was beginning which would affect the future of Europe and of the world, and with it the lives of hundreds of millions of people. A bewildering array of facts, arguments, counter-arguments, proposals, methods, principles, strategies and tactics developed in public and in private, in Strasbourg, Luxembourg, Paris, Brussels, London, Dublin...It was already almost impossible for any single person involved to have the time to be fully informed even on the essential. This was true not only of individuals, but of levels of thinking: whether sectional, party-political, governmental, institutional or integrationist. The tension of their contrasts was still too great: the subtlety of their connections was still too new. History was on the move in Europe, but Europe was still blindfold.

In the Consultative Assembly of the Council of Europe, debate still focussed on the issue of federalism versus functionalism, and the possible permutations of both. In his *Speaking European*, Horsfall Carter approaches this debate as follows:

> 'It may be appropriate here to say a few words about this cult of federalism—in relation to the objective of European unity—since the term 'federal' was bandied about so freely in the first years of the Council of Europe—and it was to be one of the issues in the great debate of 1961-3 as to whether Britain should or should not join the European Economic Community. A strong group of Representatives, mainly from France, Italy and the Benelux countries, believed passionately in the necessity for creating a European organisation with real powers, involving the transfer of a certain degree of sovereignty to a central authority. And they found a convenient term in federalism, federal union. Those who took the opposite view—the great majority of the British, Scandinavian and Irish members—were thinking in terms of an ever-greater measure of inter-governmental co-operation, resulting in progressively closer integration of member states in different spheres but without any abdication of national sovereignty. They came to be known as the functionalists.'

Thus in August 1950, only shortly after the call for a European Army and a European Coal and Steel Community, the Assembly adopted two Recommendations advocating what were now to be called Specialised Authorities. They were to be created within the framework of the Council of Europe, they were to embrace political, economic, social, legal, and cultural fields. Above all, they should not be obligatory on all member States of the Council, but should be optional—each country being able to choose whether or not it wished to accede to any one of the Specialised Authorities. Their creation would have meant amendment of the Statute of the Council: an appropriate Protocol to the Statute was therefore also proposed.

The policy here beginning to evolve was two-fold. On the one hand, the Council of Europe was to have defined political powers, which were even to extend to certain sectors of foreign policy. On the other hand, there were to be the several Specialised Authorities, each probably joined by only certain groupings of Member States—and yet all within the framework of the Council of Europe. That framework was now clearly envisaged as including the European Army, the Coal and Steel Community, and whatever more might be created. Simultaneously came the struggle by R. W. G. Mackay to use this upsurge of enthusiasm to gain for the Council of Europe that *fundamental* revision of the Statute which would transform the Council indeed into his 'European Authority with limited functions but real powers'. This led to what came to be known as the Mackay Protocol and we have in Chapter One already looked at the despairing letter to *The Times* in which Mackay and Sir David Maxwell-Fyfe attempted to carry with them British opinion in support of the Protocol. It failed, because no means had yet been devised of breaking the deadlock between the Assembly and the Council of Europe's Committee of Ministers. And the deadlock was hardening: a number of the Ministers themselves and their governments were now coming under complex pressures. For the Coal and Steel Community had already outmanoeuvred them: the added combination of a European Army and a reformed Council of Europe might well lead to consequences previously unimaginable.

In November 1950, a group of Italian representatives in the Assembly brought forward what came to be called the La Malfa Proposals. These were provoked by the fact that the Consultative Assembly was not even being consulted by Governments and lacked—as it does to this day—any statutory right whatsoever to request and receive information from Governments. Under the La Malfa Proposals it would become a statutory obligation on each Government to inform, not the Assembly, but the Committee of Ministers of 'any project or proposal with European implications it might in future adopt', and it was expected that the Ministers would in turn pass the information down to the Assembly. This looks mere common sense, except that the text spoke not of decisions —but of 'projects or proposals'. It would have thus given the Assembly that decisive power fundamental to any real application of the European Idea—the right of information—and enabled the Assembly to speak for public and parliamentary opinion *before* final decisions had been made by the traditional method of inter-governmental conversations at Ministerial and Departmental level. To Governments this kind of common sense appeared not only radical but dangerous—it was not only new but could be effective. It had to be resisted, but it could no longer be resisted outright with an immediate rejection and it was clear to the Ministers that if the La Malfa Proposals and the Mackay Protocol should somehow both succeed together, the combined effect must clearly be a complete change in the structure of the Council of Europe, thus indeed enabling quite unpredictable advances in the application of the European Idea across Western Europe.

The Committee of Ministers of the Council of Europe therefore appointed a Committee on the Revision of the Statute, made up of Senior Officials, and under instructions to consider the Mackay Protocol, the La Malfa Proposals, and also other related Recommendations from the

Assembly. The Committee worked until early 1951, and reported back to the Ministers. What the Ministers approved of their work was passed down to the Assembly in the following form.

The Ministers agreed that 'the Council of Europe may take the initiative in instituting negotiations between Members with a view to the creation of European Specialised Authorities'. The Ministers approved also a number of Statutory Texts or declarations of intention relating to interpretation of the Statute but not requiring its amendment—these referred to the admission of new Member States, the procedure for the conclusion of Conventions, the establishment of a Joint Committee for communication between the Ministers and the Assembly, and relations with other inter-governmental organisations. In September 1951 there followed a further Statutory Text on the procedure for Partial Agreements—that is to say, agreements which would be binding on Member States in groups only as they chose—and relating not only to the Specialised Authorities, but other matters also. We shall see in later chapters that the procedure on Conventions and the procedure for Partial Agreements were to become decisive to the whole evolution of the Council, but at this time they were seen as little more than a most useful loop-hole in the paralysing unanimity rule of the Committee of Ministers themselves. The Assembly was, of course, still forbidden to discuss military matters, and with the sole exception that a campaign in the Assembly by, among others, Sir Winston Churchill and Mr Harold Macmillan succeeded in gaining for the Assembly power to decide its own Agenda, all revision of the Statute was blocked. The Committee of Ministers had thus been forced to a subtly plausible yielding of much that was secondary: on the essential, however, they had yielded nothing.

Nevertheless, the pressure of opinion in the Assembly remained high and the flow of Recommendations continued. The new power of initiative on Specialised Authorities was used at once in the form of renewed demands for a European Authority for Agriculture, a Postal Union, a Raw Materials and Purchasing Board, an Association of European Air Lines, and a body for Inland Transport. As an example of its very broad spectrum of interests, it should be noticed that even at this time when the whole structure and vocation of the Council of Europe was in question, one Recommendation—which attracted no notice at all at the time—took the trouble to spell out the desirability of a European policy in social affairs.

The radical pressure was also increasing: in December 1951 a new version of the Mackay Protocol was debated. This time it was no longer a proposal to revise the existing Statute, but to sweep the board clean and adopt a new Statute. The unanimity rule of the Committee of Ministers was to be retained in principle while undermined in practice; the Council of Europe was to incorporate both the economic organisation of the OEEC in Paris and the defence structure of the Brussels Treaty Organisation. The new draft Statute gathered up in a now coherent form all the better proposals made in the Assembly during the preceding three years of intensive activity, and as a document was formidable.

It may well be asked why, when even partial reform had already been denied by the Ministers, the Assembly should now advocate complete reform? It was known in advance this would be blocked by a joint Scandinavian and British veto in the Committee of Ministers. Nevertheless the Assembly went ahead—and it is a measure of the banked-up fires of bitterness in the Assembly that it went ahead solely to place on record before the eyes of the world what it believed must be done. And the predicted failure came. Again progress was blocked, but the bitterness was soon to explode and when the explosion came, it came in a form not anticipated even by the one man most personally concerned—for on 11 December 1951 Paul-Henri Spaak unexpectedly, uncompromisingly, and in a storm of eloquent and embittered anger, resigned from the Presidency of the Consultative Assembly.

To see why, we must look at the global scene. The Statute of the Council forbade discussion of defence, but it could scarcely be read as forbidding discussion of the *political* aspects of defence, and when earlier Churchill had called in the Assembly for a European Army, he had done so against the background of a world where on the other side of Asia North Korean Communist armies were swarming southwards in blitzkrieg. American emergency scraps and tatters of battalions, thrown in piecemeal by General MacArthur from Japan as the only method of slowing the Communist rush, were being cut to pieces. Their remnants were being forced back and back, scarcely hoping to hold even a bridgehead. In September 1950, America's Secretary of State, Dean Acheson, had been forced to say that West Germany must at once arm ten divisions. He proposed to balance this long-feared German rearmament by maintaining American armies in Europe. General Eisenhower was to go to Paris as Supreme Commander of NATO. While in Paris the Monnet plan was going forward, while in Strasbourg the future of Europe was the object of incessant attention, elsewhere the globe was in paroxysm.

Nevertheless, very few people wanted a West German national army. Yet the French dared not refuse the American commitment of land troops to Europe, while the Americans would not commit them unless the West

Germans were armed. In the Soviet Zone of Germany there were already a hundred thousand men equipped with tanks, guns, and planes. Under these pressures the European-minded members of the French Cabinet began to feel the force of Churchill's imagination, and turned more readily to his concept of a European Army. Very much in their minds was the fact Churchill might soon again be Prime Minister of Britain. On 25 October 1950 the French Prime Minister, René Pleven, therefore presented to the French National Assembly a plan for a European Defence Community. And more than that: the declared policy of the French Government was now to be *the creation, for the purpose of common defence, of a European Army linked to the political institutions of a united Europe*. There was to be a *complete merger of men and equipment under a European political and military authority*.

The French Assembly enthusiastically responded by voting 345 to 225 in favour of the European Defence Community concept, while on 8 November 1950, Heinrich von Brentano defended the decision to take up arms in a speech notable for its insistence that peace is defensible only when military strength is complemented by high social security and lack of want. In reply to the Social Democrat opposition in the Bundestag, he said:

'In order to preserve peace and maintain the freedom of the democratic peoples of Europe and the world my friends are ready and determined to support the idea, not of a national army, but of a united European army of free and equal democratic peoples under joint European leadership and democratic control. In voting for Mr Churchill's resolution we desire, though Germany has not yet freedom of action, to make it clear that we feel ourselves just as much under an obligation to defend freedom and justice as the representatives of the other European peoples.

'...We really cannot thrust our hands into our pockets and expect others to defend us on the Elbe, and perhaps on the Oder-Neisse line tomorrow.

'...A certain amount of astonishment has been expressed here that the Federal Government should regard the recent declaration of the French Premier, Monsieur Pleven, as a valuable step towards the integration of Europe. The truth is, of course, that none of us entirely approved of it, and it was certainly criticised. In particular I regret that the French Government should have attempted to link up the Schuman Plan with the possibility of establishing such a European

army, since to do so might well tend to create the impression that there
was an intention to exercise pressure on the course of the negotiations. On the other hand I feel it would be wrong to stress merely
the negative side of the declaration, because there are passages which
express just what we too desire: for example, its conclusion: "France
had already decided to do her share manfully in the efforts to establish
a joint defence within the framework of the Atlantic Community.
Today she takes the initiative with a constructive proposal to
establish a United Europe. Europe must not forget the lessons of the
Second World War, and at a time when Europe is beginning to
renew its forces it must be so organised that its strength can never
be used but to serve the defence of international security and the cause
of peace."

'When I read this passage I must agree with the Federal Government that here we have a real and valuable contribution to the
integration of Europe...'

We can here recall that private remark recorded by Anthony Nutting in
Europe Will Not Wait, when Chancellor Adenauer said to him: '...the
Germans are highly emotional, especially the younger generation. They
see in the concept of Europe a new ideal and a new hope for their divided
country. If this fails we shall lose the chance of escaping from the old ways
of German nationalism, which have brought so much suffering to all
Europe, including Germany herself.'

Let us continue with the British view of what then happened, for
Mr Nutting goes on:

'Although there were doubts in the Pentagon as to the military efficiency
of a European Army, once these were overcome and General Eisenhower had become a fervent convert to the idea, the EDC concept
found a ready support in the US. For some time the American Government and parliamentary opinion had been showing signs of impatience
over the failure of Europe to unite. Much of this was due to an
unrealistic tendency to oversimplify the problems created by the historical and traditional divisions of Europe. "If we could create a United
States, why can't they? After all, they are the same stock as the people of
America. Why should we help those that won't even help themselves
by the single act of uniting for recovery?'
'The Coal and Steel Community did a little to abate this criticism, but
for a nation which had suddenly awakened to the mortal dangers of
Communist military power it lacked the dynamic appeal of the idea
of a united European defence force. The European Army was something

that Americans understood and could fervently believe in. Not only
did it seem to provide the way around French objections to a German
national army and so make certain of a German defence contribution,
but it could be an essential and significant step towards the creation
of a united Western Europe.

'Only the British Labour Government disliked the whole idea and
rejected out of hand any possibility of Great Britain joining a European Army—again on the grounds of the supra-national element of its
constitution...'

But why was this? Why yet again—as with the Council of Europe, as
with the European Coal and Steel Community—did Britain prove not
merely the obstacle, but the saboteur and naysayer? How was it that
British leaders could be satisfied with always doing not quite enough?
Why did they not have the political courage to attempt doing that little
bit extra which would have been historically decisive?

A very short answer is perhaps that men in all parties in Britain had not
yet recognised the facts, for these facts were not clear to the public, they
were not yet a daily reality in British life, and these men were therefore
not under the one pressure they would have had to respect—*electoral*
pressure.

A longer and more detailed view from the inside, supported among
others by Mr Nutting, is that Bevin—burdened with sickness and soon
to die—had always been forced to commit his most formidable energies
primarily to the defence in Cabinet of Britain's pro-American policy. It
could be that towards the end his energies were sapped not by anti-
European voices but by the voices of anti-Americanism. Just as Emil
Ludwig has explained in a light-hearted way the downfall of Mark
Antony in Egypt by a simple muddling of priorities between his awareness of Cleopatra and his knowledge of the advancing legions of
Octavian—for she was visible, they were not—so perhaps we can accept
that Bevin's wrongness on Europe was the price Britain paid for his equal
rightness on America. The price was heavy. Britain was repeatedly
offered the leadership of Europe on a silver platter, repeatedly knocked
it to the ground, and is today being forced to stoop before she can even
attempt to pick it up again. Though no one at the time could have
known it, the European Army whose creation would have shaped the
whole political evolution of our present time, may have been doomed
from that secret moment when Bevin must have first acknowledged to
himself that, even if he wished, he no longer had strength to win his
battle in Cabinet. It is certainly possible that real responsibility for this

and even his earlier European failures does lie more with the covert little-Englanders in the Cabinet than we can yet know, cloaked as the explanations are by secrecy.

When Bevin died he was succeeded as Foreign Secretary by Herbert Morrison, who did now send a British observer to the negotiations on a European Defence Community between France, Germany, Italy and Benelux. Yet when on 14 September 1951, the Foreign Ministers of America, Britain and France together declared in Washington their support for the 'European Continental Community', the best Morrison could do was explain laconically that 'while Britain could not merge her forces in the proposed European Army, she favoured the project whole-heartedly and wished to be associated with it as closely as possible at all stages of its political and military development'. This curiously naive affirmation of whole-hearted non-participation was typical of the phrases in vogue during these years when London was perpetually trying to have everything both ways—phrases which inspired no confidence anywhere, except presumably in London.

More to the point was a text adopted by the Consultative Assembly in Strasbourg, calling for 'the rapid conclusion of an Agreement between those Member States who are so disposed to institute a political authority, subject to the democratic control of a Parliamentary Assembly. The competence of this Authority shall be limited to those fields of defence and foreign affairs in which the joint exercise of sovereignty is rendered necessary by the organisation of a European Army, and its use within the framework of the Atlantic Pact.'

This was more to the point because it illuminated some of the real quantities then at work in the equations governing European unification, quantities and equations very close to those we are again using today. Nevertheless, though the quantities were becoming clearer, the formula for solving the equations had then not yet been found and even the possibility of finding an immediate working-formula was soon to be destroyed. Yet not immediately, for when in October the Labour Government fell in Britain, and Churchill was again Prime Minister and Eden Foreign Secretary, it did suddenly seem there was a flash of hope—that the fundamental British attitude towards European unifica-tion might indeed improve at this, the utterly last moment. Yet this was not to be, and instead a tragedy began. Again it began from Britain.

At the Autumn Session of the Assembly in November 1951, Sir David Maxwell-Fyfe, speaking for the new Conservative Government before European parliamentary and public opinion in the Assembly, and at a time when British attitudes towards the Council of Europe, the Coal and

Steel Community, the projected Defence Community, and beyond that eventually a Political Community, were *all* in question, did his best to sieve through the chaff of British equivocation and hold up some few grains of truthful intention. After promising that a Permanent Delegation would be appointed to the Coal and Steel Community after its Treaty had been ratified, and welcoming the Defence Community, he said:

> 'I cannot promise that our eventual association with the E.D.C. will amount to full and unconditional participation because this is a matter which must be left for inter-governmental discussion elsewhere. But I can assure you of our determination that no genuine methods shall fail for lack of thorough examination which one gives to the needs of trusted comrades...In direct reply to questioning from the Press he insisted: It is quite wrong to suggest that what I said was any closing of the door by Great Britain...I made it plain that there is no refusal on the part of Great Britain...'

The Assembly understandably heaved a collective sigh of relief, for there was hope, and hope can always grow. It was not allowed to grow for long. Within hours the ticker-tapes in Strasbourg were clattering with news from Rome, news of what was, as Sir David Maxwell-Fyfe was himself to write in 1964, *'the one single act which, above all others, destroyed our name on the Continent'*. For Eden in Rome, after a quiet talk with Eisenhower, had repudiated his colleagues in Strasbourg by announcing 'emphatically and without qualification that Great Britain would not participate in a European Defence Community'.

These few words destroyed intricate military, economic and political planning across all Western Europe, already designed to shape the future for decades. In Strasbourg they coincided with a final attempt to gain support for a genuine European executive, expressed by M Pierre-Henri Teitgen as an Amendment to the Statute, and carried by his eloquence on a vote in the Assembly. Yet it was known to be no use, and these exactly balanced counter-pressures were no longer endurable for one man at least who saw what they meant—Paul-Henri Spaak. For clearly, while on the one hand it was essential to reform the Council of Europe, guard its character of representing the wider European ideal, and enable it to act effectively with real powers as the framework through which all advances towards unification could be co-ordinated and correlated, and while this was the best way, Britain would not permit it. With this admitted, it became clearly essential to press forward with limited integration by a few nations in precise spheres—economics, defence, and thereafter politics at the high level of common purposes, merged powers, and agreed policies. Britain at least could not prevent this—what was galling was that she would not reach out her hand to help and her help was needed. A small Europe would be a sad second-best, yet it was this that Britain was forcing the Continental countries to choose. Very well, and so be it, and let it at least be done decisively—this was the mood behind Spaak's resignation.

Thus the ticker-tapes were soon clattering again, with the news of this resignation, which was indeed a turning-point. It is judged by Horsfall Carter as follows, beginning with what he describes as 'the explosive speech' of the President of the Assembly, Paul-Henri Spaak, who pronounced the Assembly to be 'dying of moderation':

'Obviously nettled by some of the remarks of the British speakers in this final debate—and only too conscious of the impossible situation in which the hybrid Council had been placed from the beginning— M Spaak weighed in to support vigorously the Teitgen amendment. Granted, he said, that it was a waste of time to serve up again to the Committee of Ministers suggestions for increasing the Assembly's powers, nevertheless, now that Britain's position of "external association" had been made abundantly clear, why should not the representatives of those States that were serious about political union, the six participants in the Coal and Steel Community and sponsors of the Paris plan for a European Defence Community, go ahead and establish that European continental community of which the Ministers had spoken at Washington, with supra-national authority and all?...The Council as a whole could be content to fulfil a function of co-ordination and as a forum for discussion. M Spaak's resignation marked the end of a chapter. The Council of Europe lived on in a state of suspended animation, but all the stuffing had been taken out of it. And every one of the institutions which were to form the pieces of the European jigsaw in the years to come took root elsewhere: not merely the Coal and Steel Community, the Defence Community, which never materialised as such but was replaced by the expedient of Western European Union, the European Economic Community and Euratom, but also other bodies which came to shelter under the O.E.E.C., the European Conference of Ministers of Transport, the European Conference of Ministers of Agriculture and so on...'

Whether or not we agree this was the virtual death of the Council of Europe we can certainly agree it was the end of a chapter. Yet Spaak's resignation was also more, for it marked the beginning of an era. It was the first resignation ever to take place in the name of Europe; it marked

complexity, tension and a turning-point, and it signalled a decisive change
in the evolution of the Council of Europe—an evolution which, as we
shall see in coming chapters, was to develop surprising forms.

Nevertheless, at the time there was little that could be done. What did
bravely follow was a British initiative by Anthony Nutting, who
assembled out of nowhere a plan to be named, ironically, the Eden Plan.
It was strikingly simple. It provided only that the Council of Europe
should in future contain within itself the similar, smaller, overlapping
and interlocking systems of the European Coal and Steel Community,
the European Defence Community, and any further subsequent European organisations—whether of the smaller Europe, or of the wider. And
in March 1952 all Member Governments of the Council of Europe
received from Mr Eden a document so sensible and helpful on the surface,
and yet in truth so weighted with a heavy-handed lateness that it must
have aroused in some of them at least that bitter feeling described by
Johnson in his Dedication to Lord Chesterfield, whose help also came so
late it could but hurt the more: 'had it been early, it had been kind; but
it has been delayed till I am indifferent and cannot enjoy it...'

For Eden's Memorandum read as follows:

The movement for unity in Europe, which led to the creation of the
Council of Europe, is now flowing along two main streams: the Atlantic
Community, a wide association of States which, without formal
surrender of sovereignty, is achieving increasing unity of purpose
and action through the machinery of the North Atlantic Organisation,
and the European Community, a smaller group of States which is
moving towards political federation by the progressive establishment
of organisations exercising supra-national powers in limited fields. The
Council of Europe seems to be in danger of becoming stranded between
these two streams.

   In an attempt to acquire limited authority but real powers the Assembly has produced a draft new Statute of the Council of Europe, which
will be on the agenda at the next session of the Committee of Ministers.
This transforms what is now a purely consultative body into a quasi-
federal institution with legislative and executive powers and the right
to be consulted by Member Governments on certain matters within
its competence. If the new Statute were adopted this would undoubtedly make things very difficult for the United Kingdom.

   In Mr Eden's view, a more promising future for the Council of
Europe would lie in remodelling of the organisation so that its organs
could serve as the institutions of the European Coal and Steel

Community, the European Defence Community and any future organisations of the same structure and membership. The advantage would be:

(a) The Council of Europe would be given valuable work to do;

(b) The duplication of European bodies would be avoided;

(c) The European Coal and Steel Community and the European Defence Community would be provided with ready-made machinery.

...Mr Eden is confident that a satisfactory 'two-tier' formula could be evolved which would enable the Council of Europe to continue its work as an organisation for intergovernmental co-operation in Western Europe. On occasions the Committee of Ministers and the Assembly could meet on a six-Power basis to transact business connected with the Coal and Steel Community, the Defence Community and any future organisations of the same type and membership. At the same time both the Committee of Ministers and the Assembly would continue to meet on a fifteen-Power basis as at present for the purposes defined in Article 1 of the Statute. In particular, the present practice of receiving and discussing reports from the OEEC should be maintained. The full Council would also discuss questions relating to the European Community which were of general interest to Western Europe.

One year earlier this might have succeeded. That would have been three months before the signing of the Treaty establishing the European Coal and Steel Community, and with a powerful and prolonged political determination behind the Eden Plan, it is possible it could have led to the creation of real, organic and steadily growing links between the Council of Europe and other Community organisations—this at the Parliamentary, Ministerial and Secretariat levels. A formula of increasing association could perhaps have evolved—the British initiative was not too little but it was too late, and the problem of creating this formula remains unsolved even today, when the issues at stake are far more significant in their implications than they were in 1952. We shall look at this more closely in the later chapters of this book—for while the Eden Memorandum here given was not the first mention of the problem, it was the first time that a Government had accorded it proper dignity by precise definition and it is important to realise we are here facing a problem that has not disappeared just because it was not solved at the first attempt. It has grown larger, and year by year its roots have thrust steadily deeper, becoming ever more tangled.

In Strasbourg itself, in that Assembly so politely described by Mr Eden as 'making things very difficult for the United Kingdom', the mood among the federalists soon became one of merciless clairvoyance—

merciless because based on bitter experience. Federalist leaders across all Western Europe came to the harsh but truthful view that no matter how attractive any new British scheme might now sound, the British Government had already proved its unreliability by its refusal to commit troops to an integrated and permanent European Army. This was no longer an argument about institutions, no longer a disagreement on policies. It was now that most dangerous and damnable question of all, that question which should never be necessary, that question which destroys confidence the instant it is asked, that question which the entire European Idea aims to render obsolete—the question of good faith and good intention between political partners.

This was the dividing of the ways, for the EDC plan was going well, and already leading smoothly to the next milepost along the Community and federalist road—the drafting of a Statute for a European *Political* Community. Yet the road was to become quickly stony—for while Britain's refusal to commit troops led to her own compromise political plan being rejected, and while that rejection enabled the federalists to maintain their position of principle unblemished, yet they in turn now found their own plan for a Defence Community rejected, and this for the very reason they had failed to maintain any bridge at all with Britain. Britain would have balanced Germany—with Britain no longer present, fear of Germany grew—and the plan for a European Army was rejected in what had appeared to be the least likely place, that very National Assembly in Paris which had enthusiastically voted to launch what they would soon be voting to destroy.

It is a sadly dramatic story which has left its mark on all involved. At one point the Americans under John Foster Dulles intervened with a plain threat to deprive Europe of American security appropriations if the EDC was not ratified—a threat to the tune of billions of dollars. The text of the now agreed draft Treaty lay unread in the lockers and filing-cabinets and pigeon-holes of probably nearly a hundred French deputies. In Paris a sudden anti-German grouping arose both on extreme Right and extreme Left. 'Provocation to Russia...', 'Sabotage of French sovereignty...', thus the chorus rose. '...this monstrous Treaty', said de Gaulle, '...yes, Britain too is demanding that we join E.D.C., though nothing in the world would induce her to join it herself. Abandon your soldiers to others, lose your sovereignty, lose your Dominions— that's fine for Paris but not for London...And why? Because we are the Continent, the "unhappy Continent" as Churchill has already called us... No doubt there will be a few British soldiers in Germany and a few observers attached to EDC...Very pleasant indeed to be the guests of honour at the banquet of a society to which you pay no dues!' And Churchill himself marred the image of what he had himself imagined, and cast a long shadow across the European Army by unexpectedly proposing a direct approach to Russia, a sudden 'summit'. In Italy the Socialist opponents of Alcide de Gasperi used Churchill's action adroitly and de Gasperi lost his majority. Everywhere were signs of earthquake: the confused and traumatic struggling ceased only when on 30 August, 1954, the European Defence Community was voted down in the French National Assembly by 319 votes to 264.

Down with the Defence Community went all hopes of the draft Political Community, and together with the undecided role of the Council of Europe, these three together left a tangled complex of intertwining problems, not one of which would wither away into oblivion just because it had not been solved, and each of which would instead thrive on defeat and become larger with each succeeding year to come. This was indeed the year of the big and complex defeat, and yet it was also a year of tiny beginnings, also destined to grow larger in both positive and unexpected ways.

It now seemed—with nearly all the cards now played yet no one the winner—that Paul-Henri Spaak's resignation nearly three years earlier had been prompted not by pique but by perception, by a flash of appallingly vivid insight, all the more powerful because perhaps not fully conscious. It was one of the first public proofs that the process of European integration was already becoming as much a road of self-sacrifice and heart-wrenching decisions as of happy self-fulfilment or heart-warming advance. As before, so now again—the best men felt the worst pain, but now the pain was sharper. For there are moments in politics when the entire subconscious memory of a man—if subjected to sufficiently sudden, intense and complex pressures—can convulse to produce the instantly right answer without the man himself having time to know consciously how or why it is right, or what may be the consequences. In those circumstances, in that place and at that time, it must have seemed the only course open to Spaak, that he should resign. We cannot be wholly sorry. For the Council of Europe it was a moment of solitary and individual splendour in the midst of a sadly tangled tale. 'What one man has imagined, another man can make'—but it is not always made at once, nor always in the way first imagined.

Thus in Strasbourg the Committee of Ministers astoundingly found themselves imagining the creation of a coherent 'Programme of Work' for the Council of Europe, and aiming specifically at making the work of the Council real to European public opinion. In London, Eden at last succeeded with a make-do European military structure that created some links at least between the Six and Britain, established a framework through which West German armed forces could contribute to NATO, and came into existence under the name of Western European Union. Yet these were tiny: their progress for many years was to be negligible in quality and weak in quantity compared with what *could* have been possible.

And when we remember that the highest aim is also always the hardest, it is today perhaps worth recording these human episodes which came at the beginning of the process of European unification—a process today immensely more complex, difficult, and hard to carry through to lasting success. They are worth recording because we have today a European ship of state to build, launch and navigate, and a ship that is not seaworthy cannot sail through storms.

CHAPTER THREE

'Wherewith Will You Unite Men?'

'In this indeed is the strength of a great moral idea, that it unites people into the strongest union, that it is not measured by immediate advantage, but it guides the future of men ... Wherewith will you unite men for the attainment of your civic ideas if you have no foundation of a primary great moral idea?'

FYODOR DOSTOEVSKY*

THE EUROPEAN IDEA is subject to surprising reverses. In the previous chapter we saw how with the death of the European Defence Community, the collapse of a draft European Political Community, and the defensive and desperate concentration of federalist energies around the European Coal and Steel Community, a whole political generation in Europe lost its chance forever of real action at the European Parliamentary and Ministerial level. Their bitterness continues today, and so does the damage done to Europe.

In this chapter we shall look at an aspect of the European Idea strikingly different in character, strategy and method. For though the European Idea is subject to surprising reverses, it has also a built-in capacity for surprising successes. We shall now look at two of these successes, one achieved swiftly within two years of the creation of the Council of Europe, the other very slowly, laboriously, and in no less than twelve years. We are in fact picking up for closer examination themes already mentioned in Chapters One and Two—Human Rights and Social Rights—this chapter is thus less a study of institutional politics than a study of what happens in the European Idea when ethical, moral and

* From his reply to Gradovsky's attack on his speech at the unveiling of the Pushkin Statue in Moscow (*The Journal of an Author*, August 1880: translated by S. Koteliansky and J. Middleton Murry).

social principles seek expression in politics through the action of a number of individually very different men and women acting in concert. Our examples are two Conventions created by the Council of Europe— the European Convention on Human Rights and Fundamental Free- doms, and the European Social Charter.

The European Convention for the Protection of Human Rights and Fundamental Freedoms was signed at Rome on the 4 November 1950. We are here not merely at the heart of the matter—the federalist necessity —but at the very life and pulse within that heart: human rights them- selves. In 1856—twenty-four years before Dostoevsky spoke in Moscow— Abraham Lincoln said in Chicago:

> 'Public opinion, on any subject, always has a "central idea", from which all its minor thoughts radiate. The "central idea" in our public opinion at the beginning was, and until recently has continued to be, "the equality of men". And although it has always submitted patiently to whatever of inequality there seemed to be as a matter of actual necessity, its constant working has been a steady progress towards the practical equality of all men. The late presidential election was a struggle by one party to discard that "central idea" and to substitute for it the opposite idea that slavery is right in the abstract, the working of which as a "central idea" may be the perpetuity of human slavery and its extension to all countries and colors.'

If we put these two ideas side by side—if we accept that public opinion on any subject does have a single central idea from which all lesser thoughts radiate and that men can be united only on the basis of a primary, great moral idea, and if we now ask what is going to happen in Europe in decades to come, we must come to the conclusion that no matter what may be the course of events the central idea in our European public mind from which all thought and action must radiate must become the *maintenance, defence and extension of human rights for every European citizen.*

Whatever aspects of the European Idea-in-Action we consider— whether the creation of a legal framework throughout Europe, the writing of a European Constitution, or even the extension of aspects of European unification towards Governments and peoples now communist or dictatorial—we must always come back to this central question of human rights. It is hard to avoid the conclusion that before the pre- eminence of human rights can achieve enduring forms of acceptable political expression at the European level, we are likely to have to face a succession of crises. And if at some place and at some time and in some form as yet unpredictable, a crisis should come in which human rights are a subject of controversy and conflict, and yet *action* in regard to human rights is simultaneously regarded as being too controversial and tending merely to increase conflict, then we shall be facing a crisis in which equivocation on essentials may in the long run prove to have been the most dangerous and damaging attitude of all. As we touch human rights, so in the end we touch all else.

In the understanding, therefore, that we are considering a question certainly as old as Greece, certainly as new as the united Europe we seek to achieve, let us now look at the human rights and fundamental liberties which were agreed in Strasbourg in 1950 and supplemented by protocols in years since. In the Preamble to the Convention the signatory Governments agreed that those Fundamental Freedoms 'which are the foundation of justice and peace in the world...are best maintained' not merely by a 'common understanding and observance of the Human Rights upon which they depend' but also by an *'effective political democracy'*. They described themselves as being Governments of 'European countries which are like-minded and have a common heritage of political traditions, ideals, freedom and the rule of law' and as being 'resolved to take the first steps for the collective enforcement of certain Rights'—these rights being based in particular on the Universal Declaration of Human Rights by the General Assembly of the United Nations on 10 December 1948.

As agreed in Strasbourg, and in the context of eventual and expected European union, these Rights and Freedoms include the following:

ARTICLE TWO.
Everyone's *right to life* shall be protected by law.
ARTICLE THREE.
No one shall be subjected to *torture* or to inhuman or degrading treatment or punishment.
ARTICLE FOUR.
No one shall be held in *slavery or servitude*...No one shall be required to perform forced or compulsory labour.
ARTICLE FIVE.
Everyone has the *right to liberty and security of person*...Everyone who is arrested shall be informed promptly, in a language which he understands, of the reasons for his arrest and of any charge against him... Everyone arrested...shall be brought promptly before a judge...and shall be entitled to trial within a reasonable time or to release pending trial...Everyone who is deprived of his liberty...shall be entitled to take

proceedings by which the lawfulness of his detention shall be decided speedily by a court…Everyone who has been the victim of arrest or detention in contravention of the provisions of this Article shall have an enforceable right to compensation.

ARTICLE SIX.

In the determination of his civil rights and obligations or of any criminal charge against him, everyone is entitled to a *fair and public hearing* within a reasonable time by an independent and impartial tribunal…Everyone charged with a criminal offence shall be *presumed innocent until proved guilty* according to law. Everyone charged with a criminal offence has the following minimum rights: to be informed promptly…of the accusation…to have adequate time and facilities for the preparation of his defence…to defend himself in person or through legal assistance of his own choosing or…to be given it free when the interests of justice so require…to examine or have examined witnesses against him…to have the free assistance of an interpreter.

ARTICLE SEVEN.

No one shall be held guilty of any criminal offence on account of any act or omission which did not constitute a criminal offence under national or international law at the time when it was committed.

ARTICLE EIGHT.

Everyone has the right to respect for his *private and family life, his home and his correspondence.*

ARTICLE NINE.

Everyone has the *right to freedom of thought, conscience and religion;* this right includes freedom to change his religion or belief, and freedom, either alone or in community with others and in public or private, to manifest his religion or belief, in worship, teaching, practice and observation.

ARTICLE TEN.

Everyone has the *right to freedom of expression.* This right shall include freedom to hold opinions and to receive and impart information and ideas without interference by public authority and regardless of frontiers. This Article shall not prevent States from requiring the licensing of broadcasting, television or cinema enterprises.

ARTICLE ELEVEN.

Everyone has the *right to freedom of peaceful assembly* and to freedom of association with others, including the right to form and to join trade unions for the protection of his interests…

ARTICLE TWELVE.

Men and women of marriageable age have the *right to marry* and to found a family…

ARTICLE THIRTEEN.
Everyone whose rights and freedoms as set forth in this Convention
are violated shall have an *effective remedy* before a national authority
notwithstanding that the violation has been committed by persons
acting in an official capacity.

ARTICLE FOURTEEN.
The enjoyment of the rights and freedoms set forth in this Convention
shall be *secured without discrimination on any ground such as sex, race,
colour, language, religion, political or other opinion, national or social origin,
association with a national minority, property, birth or other status.*

And, of utmost importance concerning the enforcement of these rights
by the special *European Court of Human Rights* also established by the
Convention:

ARTICLE FIFTY-TWO.
The judgement of the Court *shall be final.*

ARTICLE FIFTY-THREE.
The High Contracting Parties (i.e. Governments) *undertake to abide*
by the decision of the Court in any case to which they are parties.

ARTICLE FIFTY-FOUR.
The judgement of the Court shall be transmitted to the Committee
of Ministers which shall *supervise its execution.*

ARTICLE FIFTY-FIVE.
The Court shall draw up its own rules and shall determine its own procedure.

The First Protocol to the Convention, signed on 21 March 1952, added
three further rights—included largely on the initiative of the Consultative Assembly:

(a) THE RIGHT OF PROPERTY
Every natural or legal person is entitled to the peaceful enjoyment of
his possessions. No one shall be deprived of his possessions except in
the public interest, and subject to the conditions provided for by law
and by the general principles of international law. The preceding
provision shall not, however, in any way infringe the right of a State
to enforce such laws as it deems necessary to control the use of property
in accordance with the general interest or to secure the payment of
taxes, other contributions or penalties.

(b) THE RIGHT TO EDUCATION.
No person shall be denied the right to education. In the exercise of any

functions which it assumes in relation to education and to teaching, *the State shall respect the rights of parents* to ensure such education and teaching in conformity with their own religious and philosophical convictions.

(c) FREE ELECTIONS.

The High Contracting Parties undertake to hold *free elections at reasonable intervals by secret ballot*, under conditions which will ensure the free expression of the opinion of the people in the choice of the legislature.

And the Fourth Protocol to the Convention, signed on 16 September 1963, included the following:

ARTICLE ONE.

No one shall be deprived of his liberty merely on the ground of inability to fulfil a contractual obligation.

ARTICLE TWO.

Everyone lawfully within the territory of a State shall, within that territory, have the *right to liberty of movement* and freedom to choose his residence...Everyone shall be free to leave any country including his own...

ARTICLE THREE.

No one shall be expelled, by means either of an individual or of a collective measure, from the territory of the State in which he is a national...No one shall be deprived of the right to enter the territory of the State of which he is a national....

ARTICLE FOUR.

Collective expulsion of aliens is prohibited.

As well as the European Court of Human Rights, the Convention established a Commission to decide whether cases are admissible. No case can be accepted unless all normal legal resources within Member States have already been exhausted. If the case is accepted, then the Commission attempts to achieve a friendly settlement, but if it fails, then the case is reported to the Committee of Ministers of the Council of Europe who rule whether there has been a violation of the Convention, and if so, what is to be done. Here, for once, the Committee of Ministers rule by a *two-thirds majority* and their decisions are binding. If the case is then passed to the Court, the Court also has power to rule upon it—directly, and finally. That is to say, the European Court of Human Rights in Strasbourg has an authority recognised under treaty as final by all Governments who have accepted its jurisdiction. The qualification is important: the Court does not automatically have jurisdiction over all eighteen Member States of the Council of Europe, but only those which acknowledge it. This principle of optional jurisdiction had to be conceded to enable the Court to be created at all—it was a very necessary and fruitful compromise. Furthermore—and we have here an innovation which is the first of its kind in the world—the Commission can accept cases both from Governments and from *individual private citizens*. This last right is called the *right of individual petition* and is fundamental in that it allows the individual citizen of any Member State of the Council of Europe which has explicitly accepted this right, to appeal in the last resort not to his own Government at all, but directly to the Council of Europe in Strasbourg. Again the qualification is important: acceptance of the right of individual petition is optional for Governments.

We thus have three distinct stages possible in each Member State— first, to have signed the Convention but not ratified (today still the position of France); second, to have ratified but not to have accepted the right of individual petition; and third to have ratified and accepted the right of individual petition and the jurisdiction of the Court (as is today the position of Great Britain). While it will take perhaps decades before every Member State has accepted the Convention to the final third stage, nevertheless its principles are here to stay, and to grow. Americans who might jump to the conclusion that we are here watching the seedling growth of an effective European Supreme Court designed eventually to fit into the structure of a Federal Europe would in fact be right to see the essential so fast: this is precisely what it is.

Nevertheless, since the rights listed by the Convention are by no means yet complete, or fully defined either in theory or in practice, it may be thought they are merely ideal expressions and of concern only to lawyers working far above our public view in a rarefied legal stratosphere. This cannot be so: they concern us all—we have behind us the experience of both Nazism and Fascism as they were in their heyday of virulence; we have with us today regimes on the Right that display varying degrees of dictatorship, regimes on the Left displaying varying degrees of Communism. It is not for nothing that Leon Uris, in his novel *Armageddon* devoted precisely to the confrontation of these two evils across Europe at the end of the '39-'45 war, makes his American General Hanson say '...we must face up to it. Our land has grown a magnificent liberty tree and its fruit is the richest ideal of the human soul. But, we cannot go on for ever merely eating the fruit of the liberty tree or it will die. We must begin to plant some seeds.' Yet even American liberty grew from seeds first brought from Europe, and the European Convention,

Commission and Court of Human Rights in Strasbourg is our own contemporary response to the same ideal, our own replanting of the same seeds.

And since the entry into force of the Convention (on 3 September 1953 after the deposit of the tenth instrument of ratification) the Court of Human Rights has grown to be a Court of established position, increasing respect and widening influence. Both in relation to Governments (as happened with the United Kingdom over Cyprus) and in relation to individuals (as happened in the Lawless, de Becker and other cases) its radius of action is increasing. The Human Rights Building in Strasbourg is today still the *first and only building in the world dedicated solely to the protection of human rights.* At its inauguration in September 1965, M. Polys Modinos, Deputy Secretary General of the Council of Europe, described it as taking its place 'with the Peace Palace at the Hague, the Palais des Nations at Geneva, and the other seats of fellowship at New York, Brussels and Luxembourg—all erected after murderous wars as confessions of our guilt and our repentance and also as monuments to that victory of good over evil, of justice over injustice, of which the Parthenon remains the eternal symbol. Just as from the darkness of the catacombs our basilicas and cathedrals emerged triumphant, so from our faith in our destinies and our hopes in our future has this new temple of justice arisen.' He defined the dominant principles of the Convention as being to 'recognise at the same time the rights of the individual and the obligations of the community, to ensure respect for human beings, to lay down the limits of the power of the State, to entrust to international authorities the task of supervising the observance of contractual obligations, to guarantee to one and all the enjoyment of the freedoms which are essential to the preservation of democracy...'

M. Modinos is very much an authentic voice of the Council of Europe. He continued, with a passionate precision appropriate to the problems of Europe today:

'Shaped by the great spiritual forces of our time, the Convention bears the stamp of universality. Its lesson is that there are not two forms of justice, one for individuals, another for States. Individuals and States must comply with the same moral laws. Nor are there two ethics, one national and one international, for Justice cannot hold more than one set of scales.

'Here, in particular, the words of Montesquieu will ring out: 'If I had something of value to my country but of detriment to Europe and mankind, I would regard it as a crime.'

'...The work already achieved—the five or six volumes of case-law which make a new contribution to international law—is proof that the preparatory stage is long past...there are now, in Europe, fifteen countries which have agreed to submit the operation of their national institutions to joint international supervision...Thus Europe, which succeeded in destroying itself without dying, now reveals itself today capable of making man's dignity his *raison d'être*...'

Speaking in Athens the same year, in his own land, and in words to be rendered so very soon all the more powerful by the shocking extent to which Greek politics were to lapse from Greek principle, M. Modinos said of the Convention:

'...You may be surprised to hear that the Commission and the Court which sit at Strasbourg have authority to request amendments in the legislature, and even in the constitutions, of States which are parties to the Convention, as well as power to intervene in matters hitherto considered as essentially within the national jurisdiction of States. '...this Convention has made it possible for individuals to appeal to an international body; this is a great innovation...we must not forget that what matters is the principle that the individual is an end in himself...when we speak of democracy and human rights, let us not lose sight of the fact that everything depends on the importance and meaning we attach to these terms...When all is said and done, in this City of Athens, where democracy was born, I cannot find any ideal but democracy to offer you...in this Greece, where humanism was born, I turn my thoughts towards man, who remains the measure of all things, in good and in evil, as we may see from his victories, and from his defeats too—man, who in fact, is only worth what his heart is able to receive and to give...'

What this comes to is that we have in the Convention on Human Rights three elements: an *ideal* steadfastly maintained as a standard and principle of conduct, a *mechanism* evolving to make action towards that ideal increasingly possible, and the two together combining in direct defence of the individual. That is a powerfully creative trilogy—and while it may in time become so powerful that it does itself create problems, it is also so designed that it is mechanically and morally unable to avoid confrontation with those problems that may come to be imposed upon it. The Trumanesque acceptance that 'the buck stops here' will in time necessarily become a basic axiom in the Human Rights Building in Strasbourg—as was the intention of the framers of the Convention. And if crisis should come, and if the buck should not stop there, then a great trust will have been betrayed.

It is the very size of the issues implicit in any honest observance of the Convention that has already also resulted in its most notorious non-ratification—that of the very country on whose soil the Council of Europe stands—France. The same France that between the wars drove Marcel Pagnol to write *Topaz* (a play significantly re-staged recently in Paris), has today consistently refused this ratification. When we consider French attitudes on defending her police system from interference; on problems of Church, government, and education; on Indo-China, Algeria and the vicious activities of the OAS in France herself, we can well understand why. There is a cruel logic in it all, especially when we recall the article in the European Convention of Human Rights on torture. Yet this is the same France whose Constituent Assembly in 1789 adopted the French Declaration of the Rights of Man, and whose Constitution of the Fourth Republic in 1946 said:

> On the morrow of the victory of the free peoples over the regimes that attempted to enslave and degrade the human person, *the French people proclaim once more that every human being, without distinction of race, religion or belief, possesses inalienable and sacred rights.* It solemnly re-affirms the rights and freedoms of man and of the citizen consecrated by the Declaration of Rights of 1789 and the fundamental principles recognised by the laws of the Republic.

Yet this is the same France whose Constitution of the Fifth Republic in 1958 quietly pigeon-holed its high ideal in the following subtly retrogressive formula:

> The French people solemnly proclaim their attachment to the Rights of Man and to the *principles of national sovereignty* as defined in the Declaration of 1789, confirmed and extended by the Preamble to the Constitution of 1946.

And yet again (as a sharp correspondence in *Le Figaro* proved) there are Frenchmen alive to this question of conscience posed to their state by the existence of the Strasbourg Convention on Human Rights. We must therefore patiently hope that sooner or later a French Government will discover itself able to sign its name with honour to the Convention. When that happens we shall all be able to cheer, for it will signal a profound change in the attitude of the French state to the future shaping of a morally viable united Europe.

This also brings us to the constitutional question in European unifica-

Two illustrious fathers of the European movement: Winston Churchill turns to address Edouard Herriot

Two great Frenchmen of the pre-de Gaulle period: Jean Monnet (ABOVE) and
Robert Schuman (BELOW)

tion—for it is a problem whether a political Constitution is most widely
based on structural precedent or defined principle. Even the Soviet Union
Constitution of 1936 does not feel able to avoid paying a circumspect lip-
service to the 'Fundamental Rights and Duties of Citizens'. And the
American Declaration of Independence of 1776 was, of course, the first
to put first things unforgettably first by phrasing Human Rights in words
known by heart by millions:

> We hold these truths to be self-evident: That all men are created equal;
> that they are endowed by their Creator with certain inalienable rights;
> that among these are life, liberty, and the pursuit of happiness; that to
> secure these rights, governments are instituted among men, deriving
> their just powers from the consent of the governed; that whenever any
> form of government becomes destructive of these ends it is the right
> of the people to alter or to abolish it and to institute a new government,
> laying its foundation on such principles, and organising its powers in
> such form as to them shall seem most likely to effect their safety and
> happiness.

The Italian Constitution of 1947 says:

> The Republic acknowledges and guarantees the inviolable rights of
> man both as an individual and in the social organisations where his
> personality is developed...All citizens have equal social rank and are
> equal before the law without distinction.

The Basic Law of the Federal Republic of Germany of 1949 says:

> 1. The dignity of man shall be inviolable. To respect and protect it
> shall be the duty of all state authority.
> 2. The German people therefore acknowledges inviolable and inalien-
> able human rights as the basis of every human community, of peace
> and justice in the world.

These statements of principle are all by suggestion leading us to face the
inexorably approaching challenge and necessity of agreeing on a European
Constitution—a challenge already anticipated in Chapter One with the
brief suggestion that the true importance of the Strasbourg Convention
on Human Rights is concealed in the fact that it has *preceded* the writing
of a European Constitution. It is not yet widely known that varying drafts
of this Constitution already exist—that already most of the thinking is
done, and awaits only opportunity to become potentially the most
impressive political creation of our century. Even the lukewarm,
politically unsuccessful, tactically suspect and mechanically incomplete

D

Draft Treaty presented by the French Government itself to the Fouché Committee in 1961—even though it attempted no more than a formalisation of a Union between Governments and could not command federalist respect—even this went so far as to say:

> The High Contracting Parties (i.e. Governments),
>
> Convinced that *an organisation of Europe on the basis of freedom* which respects its diversity will enable their civilisation further to spread and develop, *will protect their common heritage against the threats* to which it may be subject, and will thus contribute to the maintenance of peaceful relations in the world;
>
> Determined to safeguard together the *dignity, liberty and basic equality of all men*, whatever their condition, race or religion, and to help bring about a better world where the reign of these values will be definitively assured;
>
> Reaffirming their attachment to the principles of *democracy, the rights of man, and justice in all fields of social life.*
>
> Desirous of welcoming amongst them other European countries prepared to accept the same *responsibilities and the same obligations...*
>
> Determined...to give the union of their peoples a statutory character ...have agreed upon...The Union of the European Peoples...

Sooner or later we shall in Europe have to decide this question of human rights definitively. Our own times are aware of the tensions involved. They have included both the building of the Berlin Wall—that monumental affront to human rights—and the Papal Encyclical *Pacem in Terris* of Pope John XXIII—that majestic appeal for human rights. And even though the Strasbourg Convention of Human Rights is only at the beginning of its full evolution, it has already achieved what was not achieved by the League of Nations, and not even mentioned in the Atlantic Charter of 1941, the United Nations Declaration of 1942, the Moscow Declaration of 1943, or the Yalta Agreement of 1945. It is today having direct effect on those signatory countries whose legal system recognises the Convention as having force of law. Germany, Belgium, the Netherlands and other countries are already yielding examples of cases where the Convention is applied as *municipal* law. And legal structures at the *national* level are beginning to reflect its influence—as when Norway amended her Constitution to allow Jesuit Fathers into Norway (1956); when Belgium amended Article 123 of its Penal Code (1961); when Austria amended its Code of Criminal Procedure (1963). The provisions of the Convention were reflected in the constitution of seventeen newly independent states in Africa, mostly former French colonies; while the list of British Commonwealth countries influenced by the Convention is formidable.

'The important thing is to know, not what instruments guarantee the rights, but the nature of the rights themselves. To the civil and political rights attaching to the individual as a person and as a citizen must be added—not opposed—economic and social rights which protect professional freedom and govern the conditions of life in society. The first require the State, in the exercise of its political functions, to respect man's fundamental freedoms; the State shall protect the life of its nationals, it shall guarantee their equality before the law, it shall consult them on the choice of the legislature...Economic and social rights, on the other hand, entail onerous obligations. They compel the State to guarantee to its citizens the effective exercise of their rights with regard to work, hours of work, safe and healthy working conditions, remuneration, rest, holidays, occupational training and social and medical assistance...Young people will ask themselves this question: What are civil and political rights without economic and social rights? What is freedom without somewhere to live, what is family protection without work, what is the right to education without the means to acquire it? Let us make no mistake about it; no right must give place to another, no freedom be sacrificed for another: if the right is a genuine right and the freedom a fundamental freedom, then they must combine to form our ideal, which is democracy. And since "civilisation"—a human river impelled by spiritual forces—moves constantly forward, these rights evolve, develop and are transformed. No union between European States, whether in the form of a federation, a confederation or a community, would be conceivable without respect for human rights, an essential condition for the functioning of democratic regimes.' These, again, are the words of M. Modinos.

Just as at one time the proudest words in an earlier Europe were 'civis Romanus sum', so we are tending towards a time in which the proudest words of our new Europe will be 'civis Europae sum'—'I am a citizen of Europe'. Some day this will be a reality to Europeans, expressing in daily life the ethos of a political structure and of an active legal concept. This is already today the aim towards which the legal evolution of European unification is quietly designed to bring us. And as we see, the questions do not change: for they are the questions always posed by the challenge of achieving and maintaining human rights—questions of good and evil in society; of the rights of the individual man and woman in relation to political authority and of the obligations of political authority towards the individual; of the perpetually complex balances that must be maintained between political, social, civil and economic rights—and above all, the fact that a multiplicity of rights once defined implies the creation of a single authority to defend them.

'What is man that Thou art mindful of him...?' This we cannot answer in the Psalmist's language, but in our twentieth century it makes sense to say: *man is a level of consciousness*—both as an individual, and as a society. In the scale of ascending consciousness from the animal upwards there is a region in the spectrum we recognise as man, and when among the expressions of man's aspiration and action we find human rights *defined*, *enjoyed*, *defended* and *evolving*, then we know we have reached a peak in man, a high point on the scale of recorded consciousness. And it is a peak from which, once reached, it is dangerous for us to descend—as Dr Robertson put it, quoting C. W. Jenks:

'In the last analysis, there is no answer to Lincoln; it is no more possible internationally than nationally for a society to endure permanently half slave and half free. The experience from 1935 to 1945 was sufficient to show that the denial of human rights in any one area involves consequences that may affect the whole world...'

The European Convention of Human Rights is for us in Europe today so far our highest achievement, our best defence. Yet the very existence of the Convention of Human Rights already confronts us with the question: need human rights, while *defined* only in principle, be *defended* in action? And if yes, then once they begin to be defended through an increasingly complex framework of successive *action*, need they thereafter be defended in *principle*? And if yes, how? If we accept the words *'civis Europae sum'* as the legal concept towards which we aim; if we understand this as including both human rights and the necessity of their perpetual defence; if we relate this to the present process of European unification; if we project all this into the future against the entire map of Europe and regard what we see with the utmost honesty, it becomes difficult not to admit that the several hundred millions of us who today inhabit Europe are already entering an era which may well first manifest itself in the form of a series of successive and increasingly complex crises.

Let us now look at the European Social Charter, which took seven years merely to draft. Social standards in politics are hard to define positively: social evils very easy. It is hard to know what was meant by the United Nations experts who defined social welfare as 'organised activity that aims towards a mutual adjustment of individuals and their social environment'—whereas we instantly recognise William Blake's 'dark Satanic mills'. As R. W. G. Mackay was careful to indicate in his *Towards a*

United States of Europe, 'the proper starting-point for any Convention is to consider the specific needs which have to be met'—and for those in the Council of Europe concerned with social justice the first specific objective was merely to achieve an agreed text outlining, even if only theoretically, what social rights *ought to be*. Behind them was the entire social history of Europe; in front the entire social need of Europe; and while in 1950 there was a multitude of partial texts and palimpsests accumulated through centuries, there existed not one single agreed text that could be adopted as valid for all Europe, not one text sufficiently definitive to serve even as a foundation.

Today when politics for millions is necessarily reduced so often to a glance at a headline on the newstands, or a flicker-flash of snap comment on television, it may perhaps be worthwhile to consider the difficulties involved in creating the European Social Charter. Its evolution, its eventual emergence into operation, and the fact that its real history is yet to come in years ahead, are in some ways typical of many other initiatives also stemming from the European Idea—an idea itself so big that sometimes an entire decade is no more than a breathing-space between advances. The European Idea has a time-scale of its own to which we are only today becoming accustomed: the creation of the European Social Charter is a good example. And the fact should here be introduced that at this present time of writing there are over sixty Conventions of the Council of Europe—some big, some small, all quietly on the move, everyone of them an agreed legal text approved by all the Member-States of the Council of Europe, and each being slowly ratified each year by an increasing number of those States. As we shall see in Chapter Five, it will not be many years before there are a hundred. And the European Social Charter is such an illustrative and large-scale example of the compound difficulties encountered in varying degrees in the making of every one of the Council's Conventions, that it is for this reason also worth careful examination.

As we saw at the end of Chapter Two, the European Social Charter formally originated on 7 December 1951 in an Assembly Recommendation calling for the adoption by the then fifteen Member-States of the Council of Europe of a common social policy. By 1961 it had resulted in an agreed draft European Social Charter, by 1965 in a Charter operative in five countries, and by 1970 in a Charter which at this present time of writing is already operative in Denmark, the Federal Republic of Germany, Austria, Cyprus, the Republic of Ireland, Italy, Norway, Sweden, and the United Kingdom.

As we shall now see, an extraordinary network of influences went into its making, and continue today to determine its present and future development. Those members of the Consultative Assembly who in 1950 sought to weave even the first strands of this network had to begin first in the Committees of the Assembly, then carry their draft through debate in the full Assembly to a successful vote, then gain the approval of a unanimous Committee of Ministers—which meant the approval of the Government of every Member-State of the Council of Europe—and then gain a still unknown number of parliamentary ratifications in Member-countries until the necessary number had been achieved to permit the Charter to be born and so begin its practical life in the world of real problems and real people. Yet the powers open to these members of the Assembly were no more than to initiate successive texts, lobby for support, use the Committees of the Assembly for private groundwork and bargaining, the Hemicycle of the Assembly for public debate, the Secretariat of the Council for the immensely difficult work in depth—and to hope that these would all so combine that in the end not only would an agreed text emerge to express the social conscience of Europe, but that it would progressively quicken it for the future.

Let us follow their progress, step by step—remembering that this is what the European Idea really means—immensely complicated work by many men and women, here reduced to a shorthand where a sentence can mean months of this work, and a paragraph a span of activity extending across Europe.

1. The *Assembly* Recommendation of 7 December 1950 called for the adoption by Member States of a common policy in social matters and *listed a number of topics* which should form the object of such a common policy.

2. The *Committee of Ministers* of the Council of Europe then told the Secretariat to write a memorandum on the entire question, listing those *actions* the Council could properly undertake.

3. The Committee of Ministers also sent a memorandum in the name of the Council of Europe to all *Member-Governments*, while also asking the Assembly to give another expression of its collective view.

4. On 17 January 1953, the Assembly decided that since the draft then under discussion for a European *Political* Community (see Chapter Two) proposed creating also a European Economic and Social Charter, this idea should be supported.

5. In May 1953, the *Secretariat* produced a memorandum saying: 'This task is of such importance that it justifies expression in the form of a European Social Charter. This Social Charter, together with the Conven-

tion on Human Rights and Fundamental Liberties, should together constitute a solemn proclamation by the European States, of the spiritual
values which are the basis of Western Civilisation. The *principles* written
into the Social Charter would thus serve as guides for the future action
of the Council of Europe towards social progress and a broad unity
between its members.'

6. In September 1953, the *Assembly* adopted an Opinion very similar
to the Secretariat's text of four months earlier, except in the last few words
where the Assembly carefully attempted to pre-empt strategic ground in
preparation for battles to come. We shall see in the course of this chapter
how far the Assembly succeeded. 'The Assembly recognises, first of all,
the principle that a European (Social) Charter should be worked out. This
Charter should define the social objectives of the Council of Europe and
should serve as a guide to all future action by the Council in the social
field. It should constitute, within the field of social policy, a complement
to the Convention for the safeguard of Human Rights and Fundamental
Liberties. This Charter should be worked out in common with this
Assembly, *whose mission should be to define its principles.*'

Nearly three years have already been needed to start all the organs of
the Council into action—Assembly, Secretariat, Ministers—and to co-
ordinate their activity with all else simultaneously happening in Europe.
Yet even with all this already on the move, there is so far not yet even a
preliminary draft Charter ready.

7. 20 May 1954. The *Committee of Ministers* announced it would entrust
preparation of the Social Charter to an *Inter-Governmental Committee of
Experts* called into action for this special purpose. This had in fact been
already created just before, under the title of the Permanent Governmental Sub-Committee—and it is here, in the Special Message of the
Ministers explaining the situation, that we find documented almost that
first official suggestion that the Council of Europe should have a coherent
Work-Programme—a suggestion thus emerging into print simultaneously with the breakdown of the European Defence and Political
Communities.

8. 28 May 1954. The Assembly reiterated its conviction of the necessity
for a European Social Charter.

9. The *Standing* Committee of the Assembly—the Committee which
represents the Assembly when it is not in Session—ordered the Social
Committee of the Assembly to draft its own separate and independent
version of the Social Charter—and thus to work parallel with the governmental Committee of Experts, acting under the instructions of the
Ministers.

10. 23 October 1954. The *Social* Committee of the Assembly presented a preliminary report in the Assembly, thus making its progress public, and was told to submit a full draft Social Charter at the Assembly's next Session.

11. The *Social* Committee of the Assembly, now working under severe pressure, therefore created a special working task force or Sub-Committee to write the Assembly version of the Social Charter. In particular it picked up the thinking of a United Nations text of 5 February 1952 on economic, social and cultural rights. By now the European Political Community had been sunk beyond salvaging, but out of the flotsam the Sub-Committee also picked up the proposal first published on 10 March 1953 for a European Economic and Social Council *all in one*—which was not quite the same as the European Economic and Social Charter earlier mentioned. In this salvage attempt the Sub-Committee was acting on the assumption that just because a good thing cannot be achieved in one way, that is no argument it should not be attempted in another. And although the Sub-Committee was bound to report publicly to the Assembly, this when skilfully handled did become an advantage—for it could argue its case most powerfully by public speeches in the Assembly.

12. At the same time, the *Social* Committee of the Assembly therefore also created a *second special working task force*—this time to work indeed on a European Economic and Social *Council*. It was a hybrid task force; composed partly of members of the Social Affairs Committee and partly of members of the Economic Committee of the Assembly.

13. Also at the same time, the *Inter-Governmental Committee of Experts* was continuing its hard work—but under direct instructions from the *Committee of Ministers*, and *incommunicado* from the Assembly, the press, and public opinion.

14. One year later—and this was not slow work but very fast—the Social Committee of the Assembly produced a complete draft European Social Charter (October 1955). It was complementary to the Convention on Human Rights, and most deliberately in harmony with the two draft Conventions now in existence at the United Nations—one on political and civil rights; one on economic, social and cultural rights. Again the Social Committee argued that a European Economic and Social Council should be created. However, in public debate in the Assembly, this draft Social Charter met strong attack from the Assembly's own *Economic* Committee. The Assembly therefore told both its Social and Economic Committees to try again—and produce an agreed draft for the next Session of the Assembly.

15. 23 January 1956. The Economic Committee of the Assembly

produced its own independent text—the two Committees having met, fought, and failed to agree—their sharpest conflict being over methods essential to make the working of the Charter effective. This text dropped once and for all the idea of a European Economic and Social Council. Instead, it offered the Assembly a new idea—a *Tripartite Conference* to be organised both by the Council of Europe and the *International Labour Organisation* in Geneva—the ILO having always been in close touch with the Council, though never formally connected.

16. 9 March 1956. The *Social* Committee of the Assembly examined the text of the *Economic* Committee and found its changes radical. It agreed that the idea of a combined European Economic and Social Council was at that time hopeless. Yet it was also in trouble itself as a Committee. In the key vote inside the Committee, six members were for its own proposed draft, none were against—but there were nine abstentions. Thus no matter how powerful the merits of what the Committee might officially allow to go forward in its name to the Assembly, it could command only minority support and would be crippled before it even started.

17. *The Chairman of the Social Committee therefore resigned*—Monsieur Fernand Dehousse, Belgian Senator and later Minister of Education. But almost immediately after his resignation (in May 1956) he was elected President of the full Consultative Assembly of the Council of Europe— and though he had resigned in desperation, certainly, it was also with good humour. He recommended drily that his successor in the Social Committee should represent a different view from his own—but not too different, that he should in fact be a member from the 'cold temperate zone'. Into his place stepped M. Per Haekkerup, later Foreign Minister of Denmark.

18. When the Social *and* Economic Committees of the Assembly finally presented their report together to the Assembly, their draft did not resolve the conflicts—as had been hoped—but merely expressed them. Nor could the Assembly resolve the issues—the issues were too large. The Assembly therefore referred the entire matter, disagreements and all, to the Committee of Ministers. This was a proof neither of spinelessness nor intransigence, for the difficulties were not only real, they were unprecedented. The drafting of a European Social Charter had never before been attempted in history, and its creation was now proving a test not only of political courage—but of stubborn political perseverance.

Nearly six full years have now been needed merely to bring the difficulties to the surface. Let us now look at what the draft Charter actually

D*

proposed, and see in which political and social dimensions its real difficulties
were to be found. A most lucid and objective account, as always, is
that given by Dr A. H. Robertson, who says of this draft now causing
so much trouble:

'A further draft was produced in April 1956. This provided for rather
less extensive rights for the workers than the earlier draft—it was therefore considered retrograde by some and more realistic by others; it also
proposed the convocation of an Economic and Social Conference on
an *ad hoc* basis (i.e. as and when required) instead of as a permanent
institution established by treaty. This draft was acceptable to the
Economic Committee and the majority of the Social Committee, but
the dissident minority then arranged to have the whole matter referred
to the Political Committee for further study. This resulted in the preparation of a third draft which was discussed by the Assembly in the
following October. This tried to strike a balance between the two earlier projects; its institutional provisions were more complicated,
however, because it proposed the appointment of a "European Social
Chamber" rather than one on the lines of the original Economic and
Social Council. Opinions, however, were still sharply divided, partly on
the extent of rights which Governments could be expected to guarantee
to their citizens in an international instrument; partly on the question of
policy whether various social rights should be determined by Governments in their legislation or left to negotiation between the two sides
of industry; and also—and this was perhaps the most hotly disputed
point—whether it was necessary to set up some new international
machinery to supervise the implementation of the Charter. Faced with
irreconcilable differences of opinion on these (and other) points, the
Assembly refrained from endorsing the latest draft that had been submitted to it, but recommended that the Committee of Ministers should
"establish a European Convention on Social and Economic rights,
taking into consideration the present draft and the observations and
suggestions during the debate in public session..." The ball was now
clearly in the Ministers' court and there it remained for two years while
the governmental social committee worked away...'

19. The slowly-ripening fruit of these two years of expert work behind
closed doors was a draft submitted by the *experts* to the *Ministers* and
published in December 1958. Acting on this, the *Ministers then invited the
International Labour Organisation in Geneva to convene a Tripartite Conference to be held in Strasbourg, with spokesmen present for workers, employers
and Governments.*

20. 1 to 12 December, 1958. The Tripartite Conference met and elected the President of the Consultative Assembly, M. Dehousse, as its own President. Before the Conference lay the *text submitted by the experts*, and its conclusions took the form of proposing amendments to the experts' text. We should notice at once that by workers is here meant the entire trade union movement in Western Europe, with the significant exception of the Communists. Of these amendments, some commanded sectional support within the Conference, some the votes of all three groups— Governments, employers, unions. All this went back to the Council of Europe's Committee of Ministers, who passed it for a further opinion to the *Assembly*. The Assembly passed the text with all its suggested amendments to its *Social* Committee, who passed it on to its own *special task force* or Sub-Committee on the Social Charter.

21. The Sub-Committee decided to act on the principle of adopting automatically all Amendments suggested unanimously by the Tripartite Conference. We have to remember that by now difficulties and documents were so inextricably entangled that the *Sub-Committee* thus found itself trying to manage *amendments* which had been agreed by the *Tripartite Conference* in the light of the draft submitted by the *inter-governmental experts*, working under instructions from the *Ministers*—and not at all on the draft worked out by the Assembly itself.

22. Nevertheless, all these difficulties notwithstanding, a final draft European Social Charter, as approved by the *full Social Committee of the Assembly*, did emerge into public view on 19 January 1960—when it was debated by the full Consultative Assembly.

This account has so far given only the dry bones of the facts. Let us now consider the nerve and flesh of human feeling and action surrounding these bones, by listening to parts at least of this all-European parliamentary debate on a document which previous centuries never succeeded in drafting, keeping in mind this question put by Professor Henri Brugmans:

'*Is there such a thing as Europe?* Can we define or describe a community so heterogeneous in time and space? Is there anything which characterises Scandinavians as well as Sicilians, Portuguese as well as Poles, mediaeval knights, Renaissance artists, philosophers of the Enlightenment, as well as contemporary trade-unionists? Is there anything which makes them belong to one and the same group, united though diversified? I think there is because all European nations and nationalities are bound together by a fundamental four-fold heritage—barbarian, Roman, Greek, Judaeo-Christian—and because their common

past is a long series of experiences they have shared and lived
through...'

The Assembly came to order in the Hemicycle of the Council of Europe
in Strasbourg at 10.25 a.m. on Tuesday 19 January, 1960. The debate
opened with the first formal and public presentation of the draft European
Social Charter by the President of the Social Committee, M. René
Radius. He was followed by the President of the special task force set up
to write the draft Charter, M. Schuijt, and then by its *rapporteur*, M.
Molter. As we have already seen from the difficulties involved in drafting
the Charter, these three men now faced an unusual problem of persuasion
and advocacy. Even though they aimed at gaining a unanimous vote of
approval by the whole Assembly, and thereby a moral ascendancy over
the Committee of Ministers who would decide the final text of the
Charter, unusual methods run unusual risks—and since the position of
these three men was risky enough already their tactics were therefore
defensive: their method was to concede quickly as much as they could,
not only to their critics in the Assembly, but also to the unseen critics
waiting in the Committee of Ministers and all the national Governments.

Their argument was simple: even after all these years of work, their
draft Social Charter was not perfect, not even very good—but the
Assembly had far better endorse it exactly as it was. Behind this argument
was the clear threat that tampering with the Charter, even over detail,
might lead to its total rejection by the Committee of Ministers. These
three men therefore so co-ordinated their speeches that between them they
all said the same thing—constantly balancing the imperfections of the
Charter against fear of the Ministers.

M. Radius (*France*):
    'Mr President, it is forty years almost to the day since Mr Albert
Thomas inaugurated the International Labour Office in Geneva. On
that occasion he suggested as the motto a slightly altered version of
the old Latin tag: *si vis pacem, cole justitiam*'—if you want peace, sow
the seeds of justice...

    'That is true in private life; it is also true in social life; and it is still
true in international life...Justice within nations is no less important
than justice between nations. Social injustice arouses hatred between
citizens of the same country and causes war between countries.

    'This was one of the guiding principles of the Consultative Assem-
bly which led it, as early as 1949, to advocate the formulation of rules
of justice and social security for every sector of European economic
society.

'Ten years have passed since then. That is a long time in the life of a man, but the life of a human society cannot be counted in decades and, in spite of the increasing pace of events today, ten years for a human society is quite a short space of time. This is true especially in this case, for the difficulties we had to overcome were immense.

'When we started our work the cold war was going on apace and the West had to counter the aggressive policy of Stalin. To ward off this threat, the West had to devote a great part of its newly emergent strength to increasing its armaments. Such conditions were hardly favourable to raising the standard of living of the working masses, and it may even be asked whether one of Stalin's objectives in forcing the West to rearm to the uttermost was not precisely that of bringing about a lowering of living standards and thus causing social unrest. Was not, in fact, the ultimate aim of this blackmail with the threat of war to achieve on a grand scale what had happened to Czechoslovakia on 25 February 1948?

'Providence and American aid, Mr President, prevented things from reaching this point, and our Assembly can be proud of having realised, even in the midst of the cold war, the importance of raising social standards. It devoted itself to this vitally important task right from the outset. Among the aims it set itself, with praiseworthy clearsightedness, was that of spreading law and justice throughout the world...'

By the end of his speech M. Radius had quietly seized the initiative by merely indicating a level of debate. He concluded:

'The European Social Charter...falls short of the ideal we had set ourselves, but it would be surprising were it otherwise. *It would seem scarcely possible that countries with such different social systems, such diverse economic structures, and such varying degrees of development oculd, straight away, set up uniform standards for European workers.* But the text submitted to the Assembly blazes the trail we can and must follow. It is the seed from which must spring the sturdy tree whose fruit will be social progress in all our member countries...Freedom means constant development; progress knows no halt. This first milestone which we shall, I hope, be setting up during the present Session will mark one stage on the road of progress and by that progress, the unification of Europe, and thus not only harmony between the social classes within the States but also peace between the States.

'I shall end...expressing the hope that the draft Charter submitted to our Assembly today may contribute, in no small measure, towards establishing the reign of social justice and, in consequence, the great blessing of peace.'

It was a dignified opening to a difficult debate and set the stage well for M. Schuijt of the Netherlands who spoke next. Both his and the third opening speech by M. Molter will be quoted here at length. Firstly, because it is seldom we have the opportunity of carefully studying the character of debates in the Council of Europe except in isolated sentences—the context and tone of voice of debate is usually omitted: here we will include it. Secondly, because these speeches illustrate characteristics for any speech designed to express the interests of an audience extending from Iceland to Sicily, Norway to the Pyrenees, Greece to Denmark. And thirdly because these particular speeches are forced by their subject matter to combine immediate effectiveness in a parliamentary vote with historical effectiveness for the future. It is fair to judge these speeches against the only standard: do they speak for all Europe—as far as was possible in practice at the time, and as far as was possible in principle for the future? This is for the reader to judge and each reader will indeed have questions and judgements entirely of his or her own character.

Thus, while these speeches are certainly concerned with what we can, if we are critical, call a limited matter, they are also prototypes from the past of speeches we shall indeed hear increasingly in the future as the European Idea makes progress. Parliamentary utterances at the all-European level will before long be a daily element in the political awareness of millions across Europe—they are already a matter of importance to all citizens of Europe, and will be more so tomorrow. So let us now listen to M. Schuijt as he guides the Consultative Assembly of the Council of Europe into an understanding of the pressures and parliamentary dilemmas which the provisional draft of the European Social Charter is here encountering:

M. Schuijt (*Netherlands*):
  'Mr President, the draft before us is already familiar to the members of this Assembly...The appearance of the draft prepared by the governmental experts, however, immediately provoked certain reactions in better-informed circles.
  '...the Sub-Committee...found itself confronted not only by the draft drawn up by the governmental experts but also by the results of the Tripartite Conference, by various criticisms expressed by members of the Assembly and, finally, by the encumbrance of three earlier drafts prepared by the Assembly, with all the views put forward in the Assembly and its committees since 1953.

'What was the Sub-Committee to do? Was it to re-examine every suggestion put forward during the past ten years, or confine itself to submitting recommendations to the Ministers on no more than three or four essential points? That was our first problem, and we chose what, to my mind, was the simplest course. We decided to examine the draft Charter prepared by the governmental experts, in the light of the various proposals already adopted by the Social Committee, and to study the criticisms voiced during the debate at the Tripartite Conference. As M. Radius has already pointed out, the more important material before the Sub-Committee, in fact, consisted of the results reached by that Conference, in spite of its having been a technical, rather than a political one.

'This method certainly obliged the Sub-Committee to abandon, often with the greatest reluctance, a number of principles and suggestions dear to this Assembly, but this was inevitable if there was to be any real hope of its decisions being taken into consideration by the Ministers.

'From the very beginning, therefore, we tried to put aside all illusions and take a realist view, accepting the facts of the situations as they had already existed for some considerable time. Accordingly we rejected from the start any idea of making radical alterations to the experts' draft...*the draft before you, though it falls short of what we in fact want, represents the most that we have any real hope of obtaining from the Committee of Ministers.*

'...It is now my task to deal with the various *criticisms of the experts' draft* that were considered by the Sub-Committee and its proposals for meeting them.

'...In the first place, the draft was criticised for being based on a somewhat out-moded or nineteenth-century conception of social conditions and many members of the Sub-Committee felt that it did not look ahead. They felt that it had left on one side a number of serious problems connected with *automation*, the role of the *trade unions*, the growing importance of *social service*, the use of *leisure* and the *housing question*.

'This is very likely a valid criticism, but the explanation is to be found in the composition of the Committee of Experts responsible for the draft.

'I do not mean, by saying this, to detract from the value of their work or of the draft Charter itself, I merely wish to indicate that, while we recognise the importance of this attempt at a common European code and welcome it as another step towards a united Europe, we would have liked something better.'

This is clearly an attempt to establish the existence of a scapegoat—tactically, it was perhaps not merely truthful but wise, as we shall now see. Today, when power is accruing more and more to expertocracies, M. Schuijt's development of his argument is even more pertinent than when he was speaking.

'The experts' draft, in fact, lags behind the instructions given by the Ministers...the Ministers called for a European Social Charter "which would define the social objectives aimed at by Members and guide the policy of the Council in the Social field, in which it would be complementary to the European Convention on Human Rights and Fundamental Freedoms".

'The second criticism also concerns the interpretation given by the experts to this bold Resolution of the Ministers. The latter had instructed them "to consider measures for the implementation of the Social Charter such as would enable employers' and trade union organisations to assist in supervising its implementation."

'Both these guiding principles, which were satisfactory to the Assembly, were whittled away to the vanishing point by the experts.

'It is, in fact, impossible to say that the draft Charter of the governmental experts is complementary to the Human Rights Convention in the social field. For example, *we look in vain for any supervisory body even remotely comparable to the Human Rights Commission or the Court.* As for participation by employers' and trade union organisations in watching over the implementation of the Charter, the experts' draft assigns to such bodies no more than a vague advisory role...

'The third criticism concerns Part Two of the experts' draft. On examination, the standards it lays down can be seen to differ very little from those of various of the International Labour Organisation's Conventions and even, in some respects, to fall short of them. The fact that the experts' draft contains little that is new while the standards it lays down constitute no more than a basic minimum for the member States of the Council of Europe can scarcely be called encouraging.

'The fourth criticism is directed against Article 19, according to which the signatories do not subscribe to all the Articles in Part Two but can only consider themselves bound by not less than ten Articles out of the eighteen or forty-five paragraphs out of sixty-two, the choice being left to their discretion.

'This provision...robs the Charter of almost all its substance.

'The Sub-Committee's proposal for dealing with this problem is that each Contracting Party should be obliged at the moment when it ratifies the Charter to give an undertaking to abide by certain selected Articles or paragraphs. In this way, all the signatories would be bound by the same clauses which would thus *constitute a nucleus of mandatory standards and provide a common denominator for the social policies of the member States of the Council of Europe.*'

We shall, in this debate, meet this principle of a mandatory nucleus of obligations more than once—for while it expresses an aim not here at first fully achieved, it is nevertheless of great significance for the future and on other matters as well as European social policy. M. Schuijt, however, continued with his eye firmly on his scapegoat and the intensity of his criticism increasing:

'The last point arousing criticism concerned the implementation of the Charter and here I should like to say a few words about the arrangements for supervision suggested by the experts. In their draft... the employers and trade union organisations have, practically, no say in the matter, nor has the Consultative Assembly. In other words, the *Governments will be both accuser and accused, judge and defendant.*

'The Committee felt obliged to propose some changes to get rid of this legal monstrosity and ensure more effective supervision.'

These changes, however, are left for M. Molter to outline in the next speech—and M. Schuijt concludes as follows with his strategic appeal:

'I would ask you to be guided by the Committee and think twice before tabling any amendments. I should be the first to admit that there is a great deal that could be altered and a great deal that could be improved, but it is often better to leave well alone. It will take more than a few years to build Europe, and more than a few hours to establish a perfect Social Charter.

'The document before you contains everything that I think is *politically possible* to achieve at the present stage. It may be only a minimum, but at least it constitutes a beginning and may well serve as a spring-board for further progress in the future.

'Let us try to realise what the present Charter, however imperfect, can mean for the working classes. At the very least, it shows that we, the representatives of the people, have their interests at heart. It shows public opinion...we have given our very best attention to a Charter which may bring a little more happiness and well-being into the lives of millions of men and women...we have come to grips with social realities in Europe, and we have assumed a heavy responsibility...

I am thinking less of the workers in the free Europe of the West than
of the workers in *Eastern Europe* for whom our Charter will be a
manifestation of the social progress achieved jointly by so-called
capitalist countries.

'...The whole free world is now competing against the Communist world. We are apt to hear rather too much about economic
competition and too little about competition in social matters.

'There I will leave the political and technical arguments and
conclude by quoting a remark made to me about the Charter by a
young trade unionist. "It contains nothing revolutionary," he said,
"but it is a weapon we can put to good use."

'Our Assembly has been considering this venture for seven years.
If today we can bring it to a successful issue we shall have served the
cause of Europe.'

The speech by M. Molter followed at once—the third and final opening
speech defending the Charter against anticipated attack. Its strategy is
tightly integrated with the two preceding speeches—but it is more
practical and more detailed, as is appropriate for a speech by the President
of the special task-force set-up by the Assembly explicitly to deal with
the Charter alone.

M. Molter (*Belgium*):

'Mr President, Ladies and Gentlemen, after the speeches you have just
heard my task will be an easy one. At all events, it is now of more
modest dimensions because you are now all familiar with the subject-
matter, and together we shall see whether the high principles of which
we have heard from previous speakers have been embodied in the
text you have before you.

'...M. Schuijt mentioned a certain number of important criticisms
...*The principles underlying these criticisms are accepted by the majority
of the Committee*, whose constant preoccupation it has been to evolve
solutions complying with these principles likely to satisfy the members
of the Assembly *and* prove acceptable to the Ministers.

'...it was said that the fundamental concept of the Charter derives
from the nineteenth rather than the twentieth century—that it
regards man solely from the aspect of the part he plays in industrial
society, meriting the special attention which would promote his
general development. But to start again from this conception would
mean calling everything in question, and this would be neither wise
nor feasible.

'Rather than try to make any entirely new departures, the

Sub-Committee confined itself to certain future prospects—at any rate three.

'The first of these deals with the rule concerning *full employment*, recognised in Article 1, paragraph 1, as one of the chief aims of social policy in the signatory countries. This rule has already won the unanimous agreement of the Tripartite Conference, government representatives included. We may therefore hope that it will be accepted by the Ministers.

'The second consists in *the right to strike*, provided for in Article 6, paragraph 4. On this point also the agreement of the Tripartite Conference was unanimous. If it is adopted by the Ministers, *this will be the first time that the right of workers and their organisations to defend their economic and social interests is recognised by an international organisation.*'

We should interrupt M. Molter here for a moment to emphasise that while on the surface he is only saying this is the first time an international organisation has recognised the right to strike, the real and hidden importance of his words is that the Social Charter, like all Conventions of the Council of Europe, is designed to fit eventually into the structure of a politically unified Europe. Thus we have to read his last sentence as a foreshadowing of dilemmas and conflicts that could some day happen— as foreshadowing positions that may have to be adopted if, for example, there should some day be a real conflict between strike-action by trans-European unions, and the decisions of an all-European legislative process. This is looking very far ahead, but this is part of the vocation of the Council of Europe and it is precisely this kind of long-term thinking which we are watching here in this debate, at its very origins. If some day the principles of social justice under the Charter should be invoked, this is where it started.

'The third concerns the *social services*, which...the Contracting Parties must undertake to promote or establish...this corresponds to a new requirement of social life, because these services are growing in importance and constitute an effective safeguard for the welfare of workers...

'Thus the Assembly's Social Committee has been concerned with the *special situation of certain categories of workers*, particularly *agricultural* workers...The *family* enjoys greater protection...The same may be said of *women and children in employment*...and also *handicapped persons*...the Committee asserts the right of *disabled ex-service personnel and war victims* to certain advantages already granted to them by national legislation. The Tripartite Conference also reached an agreement on the extension to all *Civil Servants* of the right to organise. The Assembly's Special Committee adopted this decision... The extent to which the armed forces and police may take advantage of this right will be determined by national law or regulations.

'As for the scope of these social rights, may I draw your attention, Mr President, to Article 2, which was the object of four important amendments made by the Social Committee.

'In the four paragraphs in question, the Contracting Parties (i.e. Governments) undertake, first, to fix reasonable daily and weekly working hours, the working week to be gradually reduced to a maximum of 40 hours; next, to guarantee a minimum of three weeks' paid annual holiday; then to allow workers at least thirty-six hours off per week, taken consecutively; lastly, to promote as far as possible an arrangement of working hours which will enable workers to attend to their religious observances...The rights of migrant workers, as specified in Articles 18 and 19, have also been reinforced, and the protection to these workers is guaranteed more fully than hitherto.

'...Before dealing with the measures contained in other parts of the Charter, I must first say something about three problems which have been discussed at length by the Sub-Committee and on which the opinions of the latter were divided, namely the right to retire on *pension*, the problem of *leisure*, and the extension to *refugees* of the provisions of Article 18.

'None of these three questions took concrete form in an amendment or in a new paragraph of the text of the Charter. We were told that the right to retire on *pension* will be included in the European Social Security Code. But when, Mr President, are we ever going to see this Code?'

This exasperation did not go unheard: the European Social Security Code was signed four years later—in 1964. M. Molter continued:

'The Social Committee is going to make a separate study of the use of leisure, as its importance fully justifies...As for the possibility of extending to refugees the measures specified in Article 18, I ask the Ministers, on behalf of the Assembly's Social Committee, to bear in mind this suggestion in drawing up the final text of the Charter.

'Mr President, I come now to the last two parts of the Charter, which have met with so much criticism. They deal with undertakings and implementation.

'The first of these problems is better known as the '*nucleus of binding clauses.'* M. Schuijt has already referred to it...In the governmental draft, the signatory States undertake to accept as binding, not all the provisions of Part Two of the Charter, but ten Articles only out of eighteen, or forty-five paragraphs out of sixty-two, the choice of these Articles or paragraphs being left to the discretion of the signatories.

'The Tripartite Conference had unanimously agreed that a certain number of Articles or paragraphs *were essential and would have to be ratified by every State.* The Social Committee has selected these Articles and listed them in Article 20 of its draft. The nucleus of binding clauses proposed to the Ministers consists of Articles 1, 2, 5, 6, 12 and 19, in addition to which the signatory countries will be bound by at least four other Articles or nineteen paragraphs of their own choice.

'I should also like to draw your attention, Mr President, to two new paragraphs of this same Article 20, both of which are of particular importance. Paragraph 4 provides that "within a period of not more than five years from the time when the Charter comes into force in its own country, each Contracting Part shall be obliged to accept all the provisions contained in Part Two of the Charter".

'The fixing of a five-year term, which has already been debated by the Tripartite Conference, without any agreement being reached, was also discussed at great length by the Social Committee, but the latter's decision was, in the end, unanimous. It allows for the fact that it will have to be examined by the experts, that it will have to be signed by the Ministers and lastly, that it will have to be ratified by at least five national parliaments before becoming operative. Only then will the five-year period begin to run. Thus, in practice, it will be considerably prolonged, which should enable member countries to accept this paragraph...without undue difficulty.'

This is certainly long-term thinking: at one level subject to complete uncertainty on how the political condition of Europe will develop—and at another level to the need to come to an immediate vote on these permanently intricate questions. M. Molter's next point is equally intricate: that of the implementation of the Charter—not at once, but again at some unforeseeable point in the future. Even today, with the entry into effect of the Charter in 1965 after the necessary fifth ratification (by the Federal Republic of Germany), this is a future only now beginning to unfold.

'Paragraph 5 of this same Article provides that "each Contracting Party shall, by means of an appropriate system of supervision and inspection, ensure the observance of the Articles contained in Part

Two regarding conditions of work and the protection of workers that it has already accepted".

'This is the formulation, in legal terms, of a desire expressed by the Tripartite Conference. It seemed evident to the Social Committee that a system of inspection of working conditions is an indispensable guarantee for the satisfactory observance of the provisions of the Charter in the countries which ratify it.

'With regard to the implementation of the Charter, in the draft which we submit, without venturing on any bold legal innovations, *we have made two important modifications to the governmental text. The aim of these two modifications is to enable trade union and employers' organisations on the one hand, and the Consultative Assembly on the other, to watch over the implementation of the Charter...*

'Thus, in accordance with the desire expressed by the trade unions at the Tripartite Conference, paragraph 2 of Article 27 provides that the representatives of international employers' and trade union organisations possessing consultative status with the Council of Europe shall become full members of the Sub-Committee set up within the governmental Social Committee to watch over the implementation of the Charter. According to the terms of the governmental draft, these same representatives have only an advisory capacity...'

What we are here watching is not only the drafting of a Social Charter for that quite unknown number of countries who will eventually ratify it, but the struggle on how in principle it will be implemented in each country—on precisely who, at what level, in which forum, and according to which procedures and priorities, shall in future decisively influence that implementation. For if this matter should ever come to a social crisis, it will then be of sudden importance that Governments and Parliaments, trade unions and labour, industry and agriculture, shall by then have *already* established in preceding years those working relationships and mechanisms necessary if the crisis is to be overcome. All this is contained in the one word 'implementation'. M. Molter concluded:

'Lastly, Mr President, I would draw your attention to the Addendum to the draft Charter, Parts Four and Five of which were debated at some length.

'Part Four concerns the question, repeatedly raised, even by the trade union members at the Tripartite Conference, of the *composition of the Committee of Ministers which could, in special cases, meet not at the level of Foreign Ministers, but at that of Ministers from the Department concerned* (in this case, the Minister of Labour) in accordance with Article 14 of the Statute of the Council of Europe.

'Part Five of the Addendum asks that all decisions concerning the Charter be taken only by the Ministers of those countries which have ratified it and not by the Committee as a whole, to prevent States which have not even ratified the Charter from opposing decisions taken by the States directly concerned. This result could be achieved by having recourse to the procedure on Partial Agreements provided for in the Statutory Resolution adopted by the Ministers in 1951.

'Such, Mr President, were the chief problems that the Social Committee had to deal with; and such are the solutions it proposes.

'May I remind you that *today offers the last opportunity for the Consultative Assembly to express its opinion on the European Social Charter before the Ministers establish the definitive text.* Whatever the Assembly has to say on the subject *must* be said today.

'I know only too well that the text is long and complex, and the problems on which it touches are innumerable. The Social Committee cannot hope that everyone will be agreed on all its proposals...

'May I recall the old proverb: "When the cooks fall out, the pot boils over". This Charter has been simmering for so long that it would really be a pity to risk burning it at the last moment. (*Laughter*)

'That, Mr President, Ladies and Gentlemen, brings the Social Committee and its *rapporteur* to the end of the task entrusted to the Assembly by the Committee of Ministers.

'Have we faithfully discharged our mission? That will be for the workers of Europe to say, later on. For the moment, it is your verdict that we await.'

Thus the three official opening speeches. This debate is a model in more ways than one, and we have to try to imagine how similar debate of this kind will evolve—not merely as today in the eighteen nation Council of Europe or in the six-nation Assembly of the European Community, but in a future Assembly that is itself part of a true European *Political* Community, with legislative powers, and *directly elected*. In these present days of Gaullist influence and—let us say it frankly, political bullying—it is not fashionable to refer to anything so vulgar as direct elections. Some of our foremost political leaders when faced with this question directly are afraid to answer it directly, for they fear the effect of the truth. However, the Gaullist day will pass and so we will here deliberately include the question of direct European elections, and this not for the sake of the minority today who already feel themselves concerned, but for the sake

of the majority who will be concerned tomorrow—the majority consisting of those many millions in Europe, from workers in Ulster to
schoolteachers in the Tyrol, who have so far been denied their inevitably
approaching right: a European Franchise—the right to vote secretly for
those who will represent them publicly at the European level on European
issues. For it is already a question: are we consciously shaping Europe or
is Europe blindly shaping us? The answer lies in our own hands, and the
initiative will pass, and rightly pass, to those who can seize it. Therefore
it may be suggestive and helpful if we here insert into this debate an
excerpt from the text adopted on direct elections by the Assembly of the
Six on 17 May 1960, a text virtually simultaneous with the debate we are
here watching in the wider Assembly of the Council of Europe:

ARTICLE 1.
The representatives of the people to the European Parliament are
elected by direct universal suffrage.
ARTICLE 2.
The number of representatives elected in each member state is fixed
as follows:

Belgium	42
France	108
Germany (Fed. Rep.)	108
Italy	108
Luxembourg	18
Netherlands	42

ARTICLE 3.
During a transition period a third of these representatives are elected by
the parliaments from among their own membership, according to a
procedure which ensures the equitable representation of the political
groups.
ARTICLE 5.
1. The representatives are elected for five years. However, the mandate
of the representatives elected by the parliaments shall end with loss of
mandate in a national parliament or at the end of the period for which
the representatives have been elected by their national parliaments. Any
representative whose mandate ends in this way retains his office until
his successor has been accepted as a member of the European Parliament.
2. The five-year legislative period starts with the opening of the first
session held after each election.

ARTICLE 6.
The representatives shall vote individually and personally. They may receive neither instructions nor an imperative mandate.

ARTICLE 7.
During the transition period membership of the Parliament is compatible with membership of a national parliament.

ARTICLE 10.
The electorate shall consist, within each member state, subject to the provisions of Article 11, of those men and women who meet the qualifications within each member state for participating in elections by direct universal suffrage for the national parliament.

ARTICLE 11.
The age qualification for voting may not be less than twenty-one years. Nationals of a member state living in another member state shall have the right to exercise their vote in their countries of origin, which shall take the necessary steps for this end.

In the case of the state where they are residing also allowing these persons the right to vote, they may only vote once...

ARTICLE 12.
In each member state every man or woman, who is over twenty-five years old and a citizen of one of the member states may stand for election, subject to any traditional ineligibility imposed by national law...

ARTICLE 13.
The constitutional provisions which cover the admission of political parties to elections in each member state shall apply to the election of the European Parliament.

This draft remained only a Recommendation—yet it is indicative of the future. With this scale of future events in mind, let us now look again at the European Social Charter—first, by taking an immediate preview of the Charter itself *as it was finally approved by the Governments of the Member States of the Council of Europe.*

Thus the Social Charter we have today, signed at Turin on 18 October 1961, included the following:

Preamble
The Governments signatory hereto, being Members of the Council of Europe...considering that in the European Convention for the Protection of Human Rights...the Member States of the Council of

Europe agreed to secure to their populations the civil and political rights and freedoms therein specified;

Considering that the enjoyment of social rights should be secured without discrimination on grounds of race, colour, sex, religion, political opinion, national extraction or social origin;

Being resolved to make every effort in common to improve the standard of living and to promote the social well-being of both their urban and rural populations by means of appropriate institutions and action; have agreed as follows:

Part One:

The Contracting Parties accept as the aim of their policy, to be pursued by all appropriate means, both national and international in character, the attainment of conditions in which the following rights and principles may be effectively realised:

1. Everyone shall have the opportunity to earn his living in an occupation freely entered upon.
2. All workers have the right to just conditions of work.
3. All workers have the right to safe and healthy working conditions.
4. All workers have the right to a fair remuneration sufficient for a decent standard of living for themselves and their families.
5. All workers and employers have the right to freedom of association in national or international organisations for the protection of their economic and social interests.
6. All workers and employers have the right to bargain collectively.
7. Children and young persons have the right to a special protection against the physical and moral hazards to which they are exposed.
8. Employed women, in case of maternity, and other employed women as appropriate, have the right to a special protection in their work.
9. Everyone has the right to appropriate facilities for vocational guidance with a view to helping him choose an occupation suited to his personal aptitude and interests.
10. Everyone has the right to appropriate facilities for vocational training.
11. Everyone has the right to benefit from any measures enabling him to enjoy the highest possible standard of health attainable.
12. All workers and their dependents have the right to social security.
13. Anyone without adequate resources has the right to social and medical assistance.
14. Everyone has the right to benefit from social welfare services.

15. Disabled persons have the right to vocational training, rehabilitation and resettlement, whatever the origin and nature of their disability.

16. The family as a fundamental unit of society has the right to appropriate social, legal and economic protection to ensure its full development.

17. Mothers and children, irrespective of marital status and family relations, have the right to appropriate social and economic protection.

18. The nationals of any one of the Contracting Parties have the right to engage in any gainful occupation in the territory of any one of the others on a footing of equality with the nationals of the latter, subject to restrictions based on cogent economic or social reasons.

19. Migrant workers who are nationals of a Contracting Party and their families have the right to protection and assistance in the territory of any other Contracting Party.

These were the fundamental principles and commanded general support—though in the Assembly's draft they were carefully qualified as 'initial' aims of policy only. This word disappeared: as usual the Assembly text was the more advanced, the Ministerial text more acceptable.

In *Part Two* of the Charter, each of these rights and principles is expanded into a series of paragraphs, and it was over each of these paragraphs that the years-long battles were fought.

These paragraphs include today the following:

1. *The Right to Work.* The Contracting Parties undertake...to accept as one of their primary aims and responsibilities the achievement and maintenance of as high and stable a level of employment as possible, with a view to the attainment of full employment...

2. *The Right to Just Conditions of Work.* The Contracting Parties undertake to provide for reasonable daily and effective working hours, the working week to be progressively reduced to the extent that the increase of productivity and other relevant factors permit; to provide for public holidays with pay; to provide for a minimum of two weeks' annual holiday with pay; to provide for additional paid holidays or reduced working hours for workers engaged in dangerous or unhealthy occupations as prescribed; to ensure a weekly rest period which shall, as far as possible, coincide with the day recognised by tradition or custom in the country or region concerned as a day of rest.

4. *The Right to a Fair Remuneration.* The Contracting Parties undertake to recognise the right of men and women workers to equal pay for work of equal value.

6. *The Right to Bargain Collectively*. The Contracting Parties undertake to promote joint consultation between workers and employers... machinery for voluntary negotiations...machinery for conciliation and voluntary arbitration...and recognise the right of workers and employers to collective action in cases of conflicts of interest, including the right to strike, subject to obligations that might arise out of collective agreements previously entered into.

8. *The Right of Employed Women to Protection*. The Contracting Parties undertake to provide either by paid leave, by adequate social security benefits or by benefits from public funds for women to take leave before and after childbirth up to a total of at least twelve weeks... to regulate the employment of women workers on night work in industrial employment; to prohibit the employment of women workers in underground mining, and, as appropriate, on all other work which is unsuitable for them by reason of its dangerous, unhealthy, or arduous nature.

12. *The Right to Social Security*. The Contracting Parties undertake to establish or maintain a system of social security...to endeavour to raise progressively the system of social security to a higher level...to ensure...equal treatment with their own nationals of the nationals of other Contracting Parties in respect of social security rights...whatever movements the persons protected may undertake between the territories of the Contracting Parties...

13. *The Right to Social and Medical Assistance*. The Contracting Parties undertake...to ensure that persons receiving such assistance shall not, for that reason, suffer from a diminution of their political or social rights...to provide that everyone may receive by appropriate public or private services such advice and personal help as may be required to prevent, to remove, or to alleviate personal or family want...to apply the provisions...of this Article on an equal footing with their nationals to nationals of other Contracting Parties...in accordance with the European Convention on Social and Medical Assistance, signed at Paris on 11 December 1953...

18. *The Right to Engage in a Gainful Occupation in the Territory of Other Contracting Parties*. The Contracting Parties undertake...to liberalise, individually or collectively, regulations governing the employment of foreign workers...and recognise the right of their nationals to leave the country to engage in a gainful occupation in the territories of the other Contracting Parties.

19. *The Right of Migrant Workers and Their Families to Protection and Assistance*. The Contracting Parties undertake...to maintain...adequate

and free services to assist such workers, particularly in obtaining accurate information, and to take all appropriate steps, so far as national laws and regulations permit, against misleading propaganda relating to emigration and immigration...to promote co-operation...between social services, public and private, in emigration and immigration countries...to secure for such workers...treatment not less favourable than that of their own nationals, in respect of...remuneration... membership of trade unions...employment...taxes...to facilitate as far as possible the reunion of the family of a foreign workers...to permit, within legal limits, the transfer of...earnings and savings of such workers...

These are but some of the hundred paragraphs to which this second part of the Charter runs. And *Part Three* goes straight into the problem we heard mentioned earlier in the debate—the 'nucleus of mandatory obligations':

'Each of the Contracting Parties undertakes...to consider itself bound by at least five of the following Articles...1, 5, 6, 12, 13, 16 and 19... in addition by such Articles or numbered paragraphs...as it may select provided that the total number of Articles or numbered paragraphs by which it is bound is not less than 10 Articles or 45 numbered paragraphs.'

Thus we see that the mandatory list demanded by the Assembly proved too mandatory, while the suggested list of Articles from which Governments must choose five, proved acceptable. 'If you ratify, choose five or more among the following...'—this is, in fact, such a subtly effective solution of a problem enormous in its complexity, that the evolution of this method through all the various mechanisms of the Council of Europe must rank among the Council's finest achievements.

Part Four of the Charter concerns the eventual application of *all* its provisions by signatory Governments—that is to say, both those Articles accepted under the 'choose five' system and, equally and unexpectedly, those Articles *not* accepted. If we look at all this with a certain Machiavellian coldness, we can see subtleties again at work. The mathematical permutations that can arise out of Governments having to choose five out of seven required Articles are very interesting when we remember that five ratifications were needed before the Charter became operative anywhere, and that therefore when it became operative the chances were mathematically against any single one of the required Articles being totally rejected by all signatory countries—and mathematically in favour of certain Articles acquiring considerable momentum through adoption not by one but by several Governments. As it turned out, those countries among the first five to ratify (Germany, Norway, Ireland, Sweden, the United Kingdom) did in fact accept on average more than the required five Articles—while Article 12 (The Right to Social Security) even though it was the least popular Article nevertheless was accepted at once by Germany and Norway.

Furthermore, we should remember that under the Charter each ratifying country *does* accept the total list of overall rights as *aims* at least—though not being bound to apply them all immediately. The concealed force of this is very great—a right once accepted to this extent is almost impossible to delete. There may not be major political forces demanding its acceptance—but once a move is made to delete a right once expressed, it can be quite astonishing how major political forces can arise out of nowhere in militant and vociferous defence. And since we shall in Chapter Five look at the interaction of *all* the Conventions of the Council of Europe this is therefore the point at which to insist again on the deeply thoughtful work that has gone into each Convention *separately*—as we see here from our single example, the European Social Charter.

Thus, under Part Four, ratifying countries must not merely send the Secretary General of the Council of Europe a report every two years on what they are doing about the Articles they have accepted under the 'choose five' system, but also a report 'at appropriate intervals as requested' on what they are doing about Articles 'which they did not accept at the time of their ratification or approval or in a subsequent notification'. What this amounts to is that when all these reports are considered and compared around the same single table, each ratifying country does in fact acquire the right to comment on the progress towards agreed European levels of social justice in each of the other ratifying countries. This is the first time in the history of Europe that the power to look over one's neighbour's fence has been established in precisely this way—and the first time that the right to comment on the implementation of social principles in other countries has achieved at least the beginnings of an effective political *mechanism*.

These reports, besides going in each country to 'such of its national organisations as are members of the international organisations of employers and trade unions...represented in the Sub-Committee of the Governmental Social Committee', also go to a Council of Europe Committee of Experts consisting of 'not more than seven members appointed by the Committee of Ministers from a list of independent experts of the highest integrity and of recognised competence in international social questions, nominated' by the signatory countries.

And as for the Sub-Committee of the Governmental Social Committee, it shall consist of 'one representative of each of the Contracting Parties. It shall invite no more than two international organisations of employers and no more than two international trade union organisations as it may designate to be represented in a consultative capacity at its meetings...It may consult no more than two representatives of international non-governmental organisations having consultative status with the Council of Europe...'

The reports of the Sub-Committee and of the Committee of Experts then go to the Committee of Ministers. As for the role of the Consultative Assembly—the Charter says explicitly the conclusions of the Committee of Experts shall be sent to the Assembly, that the Assembly shall then tell the Ministers its opinion on those conclusions, and in the end *by a majority of two-thirds of the members entitled to sit on the Committee, the Committee of Ministers may, on the basis of the report of the Sub-Committee, and after Consultation with the Consultative Assembly, make to each Contracting Party any necessary recommendations'*.

This is a cumbersome and makeshift system. It cannot compare with the mechanism of the Court of Human Rights, but nevertheless it exists today and included at the tail of the Convention is a quietly stinging sentence: 'It is understood that the Charter contains *legal obligations of an international character*, the application of which is submitted solely to the supervision provided for in Part Four thereof.'

When all this is put together, and related against possible future events, what it means is that if a crisis should come, there is to some extent a safety-mechanism waiting to deal with it. We have to imagine, for example, the possibility of socially retrogressive legislation in a signatory country, for example—or a trans-European strike involving, shall we say, all ports—or trans-European social unrest following indisputable large-scale discrimination against immigrants, because of their colour. The extent to which this safety-mechanism would be adequate cannot be foreseen—it depends on the size of the crisis, and issues involved, and the political weather across all Europe. It is equally impossible to predict that no crisis will ever come, or that this emergency safety-mechanism may not some day be quite unexpectedly and suddenly invoked in any one of these Member countries of the Council of Europe where it is operative. We are dealing with deep tides running below the surface of events, and with human forces not so different from those which drove Dostoevsky to demand nearly a century ago—*'Wherewith will you unite men?'* This comes from Dostoevsky's reply to Gradovsky after the Pushkin speech—delivered by Dostoevsky in Moscow in 1880. He continues:

'I will go further: I intend to surprise you. Know, learned professor [Gradovsky], that social and civic ideals, as such, in so far as they are not organically connected with moral ideas, but exist by themselves like a separate half cut off from the whole by your learned knife; in so far, finally, as they may be taken from the outside and successfully transplanted to any other place, in so far as they are a separate 'institution'— such ideals, I say, neither have nor have had nor ever could have existence at all. For what is a social ideal and how shall we understand the word? Surely its essence lies in men's aspiration to find a formula of political organisation for themselves, a possible organisation which shall be faultless and satisfactory to all—is it not so? But people do not know the formula. Though they have been searching for it through six thousand years of history, they cannot find it. The ant knows the formula of the ant-hill, the bee of the hive—though they do not know it after the manner of human knowledge, they know it in their own way and desire nothing beyond—but man does not know his own formula. If this be so, whence could the ideal of civic organisation appear in human society? Examine the question historically and you immediately see whence it comes. You will see that it is nothing else than the product of the moral self-perfection of the individual units. Thence it takes its rise, and it has been so from time immemorial and it will be so for ever and ever. In the origin of any people or any nation, the moral idea has always preceded the birth of the nation, because it was the moral idea which created the nation. This moral idea always issued from mythical ideas, from the conviction that man is eternal, that he is more than an earth-bound animal, that he is united to other worlds and to eternity. These convictions have always and everywhere been formulated into a religion, into a confession of a new idea, and always so soon as a new religion began, a new nationality was also created immediately. Consider the Jews and the Moslems. The Jewish nationality was formed only after the laws of Moses, though it began with the law of Abraham, and the Moslem nationalities appeared only after the Koran. In order to preserve the spiritual treasures they had received men instantly began to draw towards each other, and only then, jealously and avidly, working 'beside one another, for one another, and with one another', as you so eloquently express it, only then did men begin to seek how they should organise themselves so as to preserve without loss the

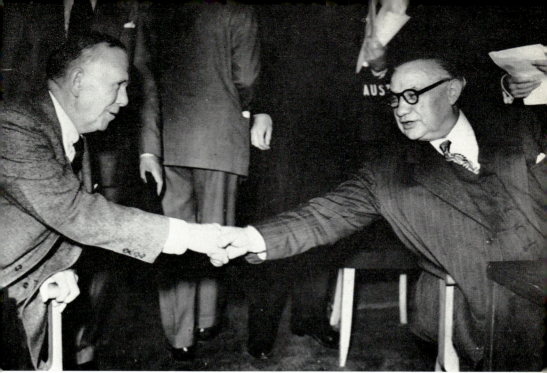

Hands across the Atlantic: General Marshall congratulates Ernest Bevin on a speech.

Ernest Bevin signs the Marshall aid agreement: on his right is Stafford Cripps, behind whom stands the young Harold Wilson

20

In witness whereof the undersigned, being duly authorised thereto, have signed the present Statute.

Done at London, this 5th day of May, 1949, in English and French, both texts being equally authentic, in a single copy which shall remain deposited in the archives of the Government of the United Kingdom which shall transmit certified copies to the other signatory Governments.

En foi de quoi, les soussignés, dûment autorisés à cet effet, ont signé le présent Statut.

Fait à Londres, le 5 mai 1949, en français et en anglais, les deux textes faisant également foi, en un seul exemplaire, qui sera déposé dans les archives du Gouvernement du Royaume Uni, lequel en remettra des copies certifiées, conformes aux autres Gouvernements signataires.

For the Government of the Kingdom of Belgium :

Pour le Gouvernement du Royaume de Belgique :

For the Government of the Kingdom of Denmark :

Pour le Gouvernement du Royaume de Danemark :

21

For the Government of the French Republic :

Pour le Gouvernement de la République française :

For the Government of the Irish Republic :

Pour le Gouvernement de la République irlandaise :

For the Government of the Italian Republic :

Pour le Gouvernement de la République italienne :

For the Government of the Grand Duchy of Luxembourg :

Pour le Gouvernement du Grand-Duché de Luxembourg :

For the Government of the Kingdom of the Netherlands :

Pour le Gouvernement du Royaume des Pays-Bas :

For the Government of the Kingdom of Norway :

Pour le Gouvernement du Royaume de Norvège :

For the Government of the Kingdom of Sweden :

Pour le Gouvernement du Royaume de Suède :

For the Government of the United Kingdom of Great Britain and Northern Ireland :

Pour le Gouvernement du Royaume Uni de Grande-Bretagne et d'Irlande du Nord :

A historic page: signatures to the Statute of the Council of Europe.

treasures they had received, how they should find a civic formula of
common life that would really help them to exhibit in its full glory
to the whole world the moral treasure which they had received...'

What then of the European Idea in our own twentieth century? What of
the Council of Europe as we have seen it in this chapter? 'Wherewith will
you unite men?' The answer is given: 'a primary great moral idea.' But
what idea? Can we find it reflected in the Council of Europe? We
have been looking at Human Rights and the European Social Charter
as they appear to us today in Western Europe—while Dostoevsky was
speaking to a Russia torn with dissension and self-distrust, and into the
teeth of men whom Dostoevsky saw as representative of the rotten
decadence of the Western Europe of his own time—men flabbily and suave-
ly pseudodemocratic in word but not in act; men dressed in European
clothes yet acclaiming the worst in Europe; men whose liberal ideas were
so rarefied that they had no gristle or muscle of meaning for men and
women who laboured all their lives long for a daily crust.

With this contrast in mind, can we now say that, even measured against
the thunderous scorn and lightning faith of Dostoesvky, nevertheless
there runs through these transactions in the Council of Europe an informal
spirit that will not be denied? Can we say that these transactions reveal a
deliberately high level of responsibility both to the present and to the
future, and a relentless though politely spoken determination to bridge
the abyss that haunted Dostoevsky? Can we say that these transactions in
their modern idiom also suggest that the questions implicit in a European
Social Charter, and behind it in a European Convention on Human
Rights, are not small things to be 'dragged about the street' by those who
cannot do better—that they are vital to the moral and physical future of
Europe? Can we say that while men and women admittedly spoke in
Strasbourg in 1960 for the record, nevertheless the record today does them
honour?

Even if all this is granted, however, when we consider all the matters at
which we have looked during this chapter, can we now take the final
step—*can we equate the primary great moral idea which should underlie what we
know today in this eighth decade of the twentieth century as the European Idea,
with the Christian principle and ideal?*

This is a question already working in people's minds—it is more powerful and widespread than public pronouncements may seem to indicate.
Yet sometimes it is unequivocally voiced—we have an example in this
same debate on the Social Charter of 1960, when M. Jannuzzi of
Italy said '...The coinage of the Venetian Doges bore the inscription

E

OPUS JUSTITIAE PAX. We have now embarked upon that work of social justice, a genuine enterprise of human justice and peace, a facet of that higher divine justice which sees all men as formed in the image of Him who created them all.' On the way this question comes to be answered through political action and social attitudes, and, on a larger and permanent scale, must eventually pivot the entire moral evolution of the European Idea. This is surely undeniable, whether we are ourselves Christian or not.

'Wherewith will you unite men?' This is for us today in Europe the question of questions. Dostoevsky was launching it with his last strength shortly before his death, and all the more powerfully because of the plausibility of the arguments of Gradovsky, who said—and not without reason, we may think, though perhaps without heart—that what Russia needed was the science of Europe, her technology, her sense and systems of inculcating social ideals into the life of society through mechanically constructed, philosophically justified, and pragmatically tested political and social institutions. 'The social perfection of a people,' said Gradovsky, 'very greatly depends upon the degree of perfection of their political institutions, which educate in man the civic, if not the Christian virtues...'

Not so, said Dostoevsky: 'The matter is important...so long as I can hold a pen in my fingers I will speak. It gave me pain to see the idea which I serve dragged about the street...Moral ideas are all of one kind; all of them are based upon the idea of absolute self-perfection in the future, in the ideal, since self-perfection bears in it all things, all aspirations, all yearnings, and from it therefore spring all our civic ideals also...' Dostoevsky's ideal was the Christian ideal and he said so—the argument of his Pushkin speech can be expressed in four words: 'God and the People'. And at the end he appealed for an eventual synthesis between his ideas and those of Gradovsky—a synthesis that Russian history has not yet permitted, but which perhaps Pasternak at least was seeking between the lines of his Doctor Zhivago.

Yet it must be said that it seems today unlikely that the Constitution of any future European Union will include the word 'God'. Where then is our primary great moral idea—and how far shall we go in publicly expressing private conviction on matters which concern us all? As far as this book is concerned, the answer is suggested at the beginning of this chapter, for when we look at Europe today, and even more when we consider how we must shape Europe tomorrow and for many generations to come, the only starting-point for action in which we can have any confidence, and the only central idea from which European public opinion can now and always derive exact solutions, must be that of the expression of Human Rights—first in principle, then in all its diverse applications: and this, not in the limited sense of demanding them for ourselves but in the positive and universal sense of recognising we must insist on them for others. This is not a question to view merely passively and subjectively, but objectively and actively and on the longest, largest scale. We do not wish to be swallowed by Hobbes' Leviathan: better surely to prefer the words of Locke—'Freedom of men under government is to have a standing rule to live by...'

This standing rule must be based on recognition of Human Rights— for Human Rights are our ladders of liberty, our rope-ladders across the abyss of tyranny, ladders very easily broken and whose knots need to be ceaselessly repaired, strengthened and renewed so that they are *at all times unbreakable because we have made them so.* The matter is not small: we shall not be safer for avoiding the question, for we have a European ship of state yet to build, and a ship that is not seaworthy cannot sail through storms.

CHAPTER FOUR

'Something More Than Common'

'... there must have been something more than common that these men struggled for ...'   ABRAHAM LINCOLN*

THE EUROPEAN IDEA depends on hidden resources in the human spirit. Sometimes these are hidden so deeply within us that we see them only when we recognise them by analogy in the outer world. Sometimes there is sense in symbol and intellect in image and yet at first we see only the image, only the symbol—and not at all the analogy it conceals. Thus while in the last chapter we considered merely two of the Conventions of the Council of Europe, we are in this chapter approaching *all* the Conventions of the Council—and as the matter is complex we can begin with an analogy chosen for its simplicity.

We can find one in London, for anyone today who walks from Queen's Gate across Kensington Gardens towards Queensway will find their shortest path leads uphill along a broad avenue between lawns. At first the ground rises, so that the avenue itself reaches up to a horizon only three hundred yards ahead. When that horizon is reached, both the city ahead and the city behind can be seen, and also on both sides of the avenue a double line of young trees. As one walked up the avenue each of these trees has probably passed separately, one at a time, and therefore unnoticed. Only now, with the whole avenue in view, can it suddenly

---

* Commenting on the implications of the battle at Trenton, New Jersey, under George Washington, 21 February 1861.

be seen each tree has been planted with purpose. Framed by the green body of the park, flanked by other trees beyond the Round Pond where both children and adults sail ships hopefully beneath a wind-swept sky, each tree of the avenue now has meaning when seen in relation to every other tree. Chateaubriand said of Kensington Gardens: 'These gardens at least have not changed; the trees alone have grown taller; here, in this still solitary place, the birds build their nests in peace.' Today, though the gardens are often still solitary, there are new trees. The Conventions of the Council of Europe are themselves like trees, and when we look at a Convention singly as we did in the last chapter, it is as if we were watching the careful planting of a tree. When we look at the Conventions all together it is as if we are looking along a whole avenue of trees—some planted twenty years ago, some yesterday, some today, and with many more yet to be planted along lines now becoming visible ahead. The Conventions of the Council of Europe are certainly but part of the politics of unifying Europe, but they have their special nature and their special place, and in years to come they can do only what trees do—grow steadily taller until either they are uprooted (perhaps by the gardeners, perhaps by storms), or until they achieve their maturity and seed their successors. When they have grown taller, it will then be pleasant to walk along their avenue and remember how they were planted.

Trees grow slowly—yet the globe spins fast. These Conventions needed, most of all in the early years, that same toughness of will, that same determination to influence the world of tomorrow by ignoring today, which is well illustrated in the story attributed to many people— among them that great European, Marshal Lyautey—about the landowner who wanted to plant some trees and was obstructed by the laziness of his gardener. When his gardener pointed out that the trees could not achieve their grandeur till after both the landowner and gardener were dead, the landowner replied: 'Good, then they must be planted this afternoon.' This realisation that future generations in their turn are quite as real as preceding generations, does demand what appears to be a certain contempt for the present.

A complete list of the Conventions is given as an Appendix, and before we look at them there are certain points to establish:

1. *A Convention amounts to a Treaty between States: it is an international document.* An exceptional aspect of Council of Europe Conventions is that they are made through the Council first, and only thereafter signed, ratified and applied within their own countries by Governments. The Governments have their part to play at all stages, but the Conventions are

the creation of the Council of Europe. They have, however, been described privately as 'the bare bones of inter-governmental haggling' and while this has the acidity of truth it is not the whole truth: for the basic text over which the Governments haggle in order to make it conform as much as possible to their own existing legislation has always been originally drafted within the Council. The 'European interest' is thus strongly represented from the first, and often most dramatically of all in the Assembly. As we saw in the last chapter, members of the Assembly take their role as guardians of the European conscience very seriously.

2. *The Conventions are not mere agreements or expressions of goodwill—they are legally binding documents on those member countries who ratify them.* A large number of Conventions create controlling organs which means that even though the powers of control often do not go nearly far enough, and in some Conventions amount only to a *droit de regard*, nevertheless the application of these Conventions within each country is supervised at European level. The Council of Europe has the status of what international lawyers call a 'legal personality' and Americans 'a corporation sole'. Just as the International Labour Organisation was able to conclude Agreements with Switzerland, and the United Nations with the United States, so it has always been accepted since the first Special Agreement between the Council of Europe and France on the seat of Council being in Strasbourg that the Council does indeed possess legal personality, both under national and international law.

3. *There is a direct link between the Conventions of the Council and another aspect of the Council's work: the harmonisation of policy between Member States.* However, harmonisation is often a pragmatic and day-to-day alignment of what is going to happen, whereas the Conventions are long-term. It is an argument of this book that there can be no lasting action at the all-European level unless based on principle—but it is a question what those principles should be. Certainly the Conventions of the Council of Europe are concerned with both the immediate present and long-term future of several hundred million people, both in the Western Europe of today and also the Eastern Europe of tomorrow. There are growing reasons why they are worthy of the respect and attention of all men and women of good will in Europe today. Yet while the Conventions are linked with the harmonisation of policy, they are not to be confused with it. Harmonisation of policy (like the roads across the park) is of immediate practical value and given immediate returns in advantage, while the Conventions (like the trees) are planted to last.

4. *The Conventions are based on a fundamental unity of principle, but this*

is hard to see because of their diversity of form. It is all the harder to see because in the earlier years their underlying unity of principle was nowhere made explicit, and this for the very good reason it was still largely a subjective and only semi-conscious unity of attitude in the minds of those individually very different people from whom the idea for each Convention first originated. It is also hard to see because each Convention has to overcome the difficulty of putting an idea into an agreed form of words able to stand up to scrutiny both in practical terms in Western Europe now, and in principle for all Europe in the future. They are therefore clothed in a mysterious politico-legalistic jargon which is both necessary and deceptive, and at first glance scarcely even hints at any unity between the Conventions as an *ensemble.*

5. *The Conventions of the Council of Europe can exist only at the European level, and yet have to gain acceptance at the harsh and gritty level of national politics in many countries: their characteristics are therefore indicative of certain aspects of the evolution of the entire European Idea.* In other words, we have as much to learn from the weaknesses of the Conventions as from their strengths—for each Convention is a simple and clear effect produced by the accumulating interaction of many complex and obscure causes—causes derived from the political condition of Europe year by year.

Since the Conventions are Treaties between Governments constructed through the Council of Europe, legally binding, linked to the harmonisation of policy, united in principle and yet diverse in form, able to exist only at the European level yet designed also to have effect at many other levels—each one of them is therefore an example of how to draft a text that aims at being both politically acceptable and humanly effective for the whole population of the Member States of the Council of Europe. The difficulties are immense yet the standard must remain high: as those who drafted the Conventions and fought them through to acceptance well know, few things are harder.

It may be asked why it should be so hard to draft a text acceptable at the European level. What could be easier than to draft a text that aims to contribute to the ideal of European unification by outlining a precisely limited course of agreed action?

It may perhaps be easiest to illustrate the difficulty in reverse by quoting an example of failure—and this not in drafting a text valid for all Europe, but merely a text on no more than European unification in general, within the limited context of one single country only, and this not even for all sectors of party-political opinion, but for only one grouping within the parties—and all this not even in a long text, but a mere few words.

Our story is taken from *Paris Match* of 25 December 1965, and describes
an incident in the French national presidential elections. The problem was
simple: in the first ballot President de Gaulle had failed to gain the necessary 50 per cent of votes for immediate victory. The second and final
ballot was to be between two candidates only: de Gaulle, and the candidate
of the left, Francois Mitterand. It had become clear already in the first
ballot that the Gaullist attitude to European integration was an issue
already affecting the votes of millions of Frenchmen.

Between the two ballots it therefore became essential that the anti-
Gaullist opposition should agree on at least a form of words stressing for
the electorate the importance of European integration. The key man in
the moves towards drafting the text was Jean Lecanuet—a candidate
already eliminated in the first ballot, yet with wide and loyal support now
awaiting his guidance on the second ballot. Here is how *Paris Match*
sardonically described what happened:

> 'What was Lecanuet doing during this time? With the future in mind,
> he founded a party called the Democratic Centre. And furthermore on
> the same day that Monsieur Mitterand, also with an eye no less on the
> future, assumed the presidency of the Democratic and Socialist Federa-
> tion. General de Gaulle was as good as elected but his successor would
> have to be found—no matter what the President of the Republic might
> have to say about it—from among the Parties. And if not, then what?—
> as Francois Mitterand very pertinently asked.
>
> 'What, therefore, did Monsieur Lecanuet do? He gathered, as he tells
> us, 40,000 supporters from his office in the Boulevard St Germain, he
> gave interviews for foreign television, he went with his daughters to
> see the play by Marguerite Duras, *Des journées entières dans les arbres*. And
> the women workers recognised him, saying "Good morning, Monsieur
> Lecanuet." And at home, the colume of Proust awaited him, whose
> reading he had never interrupted. Happiness, in one word. Happiness,
> at least, if it had not been for those four million votes he did not know
> what to do with. How was he to rid himself of this embarrassment?
>
> 'The two other candidates would have liked them very much. But
> Monsieur Lecanuet knew he was not master of those votes. To give them
> to de Gaulle was against his own ideas, his own past, and above all
> his own future. If he was to give them to Mitterand, he must first
> prove able to do so. The MRP did not wish this, Monsieur Pflimlin
> was purple with anger at the thought, and Monsieur Lecanuet knew
> that his votes would not follow him anyway...it was a "*situation
> cornelienne*', as they say in Rouen.

'Gaston Deferre—who reads Stendhal—had tried hard to offer his good services. Together with Lecanuet, Maurice Faure, Jacques Duhamel, Abelin, and Cornut-Gentille, he had drafted a European text which said—in code—that it was necessary to vote for Mitterand. The text was as follows:

"It is the problem of Europe that lies behind the vote of 5th December in which the policy of General de Gaulle was placed in the minority. The creation of a united Europe remains the key to the future of France. Every delay runs the risk of becoming irrevocable. Europe should therefore stand by the vote of 19th December, and this for the future remains the determining element in the choice of Frenchmen."

'This text was not made public. There was too much incompatibility between Mitterand, Deferre, Lecanuet and the Communists for them to be able to agree even on these few lines. I pass over the convulsions which led to this abortion, and which led from a dinner at Monsieur Izard's, at which Monsieur Mitterand and Monsieur Deferre were present, to the meeting in the National Assembly between the candidate of the left, and the Mayor of Marseilles, and Monsieur Guy Mollet. Monsieur Lecanuet therefore chose the only solution—which was to let his voters loose to do whatever they liked...'

This single glimpse into the difficulty of agreeing on a text even within a single country, even at a moment of critical importance, even among interests united at least by a common enemy, illustrates some of the difficulties any application of the European Idea must overcome. For any development whatsoever of trans-European levels of cause and effect into action manifesting at other levels of cause and effect can result in the most surprising and tangled complications. And yet this is precisely what we are today having to learn to achieve successfully more and more often. This swift interchange of reference-up and reference-down, reference-in and reference-out is a political phenomenon already commonplace within today's six Common Market countries, and in certain other Council of Europe countries also. It is potentially to be expected in all of them, and all the time. And it is a phenomenon seen at work in every one of the Council's of Europe's Conventions.

But how did these Conventions come to be made in the first place, and who first gave the Council of Europe its treaty-making power?

Article Fifteen of the founding Statute of the Council says:

(a) On the recommendation of the Consultative Assembly or on its own initiative, the Committee of Ministers shall consider the action required to further the aim of the Council of Europe, including the

E*

conclusion of conventions or agreements and the adoption by governments of a common policy with regard to particular matters. Its conclusions shall be communicated to members by the Secretary-General.

(b) In appropriate cases, the conclusions of the Committee (of Ministers) may take the form of recommendations to the Governments of Members, and the Committee may request the Governments of Members to inform it of the action taken by them with regard to such recommendations.

Thus the power was given by the Governments to the Council of Europe, in the seven words: '*...including the conclusion of conventions or agreements...*' And we have the left hand of long-term action complemented by the right hand of immediate action in the succeeding fourteen words: '*...and the adoption by Governments of a common policy with regard to particular matters...*'—or briefly, harmonisation of policy.

Given this power, what was done with it? How much has grown from these first seven words?

The short answer is usually to list at once in chronological order all the Conventions of the Council of Europe, on all subjects great and small, ignoring that they then appear casual, unconnected, unco-ordinated, lacking sense as a series and as a programme lacking power. We shall do this with the first twenty—just to see what they look like:

1. Statute of the Council of Europe (including amendments and additions), 1949–1963.
2. General Agreement on Privileges and Immunities of the Council of Europe (including the Supplementary Agreement and the four Protocols), 1949–1961.
3. Special Agreement relating to the Seat of the Council of Europe, 1949.
4. Supplementary Agreement to the General Agreement on Privileges and Immunities of the Council of Europe, 1950.
5. Convention for the Protection of Human Rights and Fundamental Freedoms (including the First Protocol), 1950–1952.

   5a. Declaration regarding Article 25 of the Convention for the Protection of Human Rights and Fundamental Freedoms (Right of Individual Petition).

   5b. Declaration regarding Article 46 of the Convention for the Protection of Human Rights and Fundamental Freedoms (Jurisdiction of the Court).
6. Amendments to the Statute, May 1951.
7. Amendment to the Statute, December 1951.

8. Statute of the Council of Europe incorporating Amendments and Texts of a Statutory Character adopted in May and August 1951.

9. Protocol to the Convention for the Protection of Human Rights and Fundamental Freedoms, 1952.

10. Protocol to the General Agreement on Privileges and Immunities for the Council of Europe, 1952.

11. Amendment to the Statute of the Council of Europe, 1953.

12. European Interim Agreement on Social Security other than Schemes for Old Age, Invalidity and Survivors, and Protocol thereto, 1953.

13. European Interim Agreement on Social Security Schemes relating to Old Age, Invalidity and Survivors, and Protocol thereto, 1953.

14. European Convention on Social and Medical Assistance, and Protocol thereto, 1953.

15. European Convention on the Equivalence of Diplomas leading to Admission to Universities, 1953.

16. European Convention on the International Classification of Patents for Invention (including Annex as amended), 1954-1961.

18. European Cultural Convention, 1954.

19. European Convention on Establishment, 1955.

20. Agreement on the Exchange of War Cripples between Member Countries of the Council of Europe with a view to Medical Treatment, 1955.

A study of the complete list of Conventions, given as an Appendix, can, however, lead the observant reader to conclude that the Conventions are of varying values—that some are of tertiary, some of secondary, and some of primary importance. This classification is arbitrary and open to argument, revision, and improvement. It depends on personal preference and judgement, which in turn depends on what scale of values we choose when looking not merely at these Conventions but at any other category of actions taking place today within the process of European unification. It is not too much to say that by forcing ourselves to classify even any *one* of these Conventions, we are also revealing by implication a great deal of both our conscious and unconscious thinking about the whole European Idea—and this means the kind of Europe we wish to see in the future.

Every Convention must begin as an idea in someone's mind, and with each Convention we are facing a problem central to all politics—given an idea to start with, how do we transmute it into action. '*The idea is the seed*' said Zola in one of his Notebooks '*the method is the earth.*' The method of the Council of Europe in making its Conventions consists of a series of well-established and tried processes, each designed not only to keep the seed of the original idea alive and growing, but each time to transplant it successfully to yet better earth. As we have seen in Chapter Three with the European Social Charter, there are many of these stages. It is sometimes hard to see where one ends and the next begins. Nevertheless, there are certain decisive transplantings of the original idea which we can identify—and the ones here mentioned are singled out because they are among those common to all the Conventions of the Council of Europe.

1. *The first recorded move.* If for instance it should some day be thought helpful to create a European Convention on Fishing Rights (a matter of perpetual difficulty for the maritime countries, and in particular between the Icelandic, Irish, British, French, Belgian, Danish, Swedish and Norwegian fishing fleets) then it is necessary that someone somewhere says so precisely in so many words. With the early Conventions of the Council this first recorded appearance of the idea is usually to be found within the Council itself—and when it happens in the speech of an individual in the Assembly, it is easy to pin-point. But there is no monopoly in ideas: credit goes where the world awards it—and the world usually awards the credit to that person most firmly and clearly first on record. And the credit is seldom justly given, for the world can apportion credit only according to the public record, and nine times out of ten the public record does not reflect the true moment of original initiative. This is certainly often true of the Council of Europe. A Convention can be inspired by a chance remark within the Committee of Ministers, or by a conversation between members of the Secretariat and members of an Expert Committee—and it would then first appear in Committee Minutes, or perhaps in private letters. Thus we often do not know—and those most concerned are often not permitted to let us know—just when, how, where, through whom and why an idea first came to consciousness and then expression. The Committee of Ministers, the Committees of the Assembly, the Committees of Experts and the entire Secretariat of the Council of Europe all work behind closed doors—and while their work is largely though not entirely on the record, it is *not* the public record.

This distinction is important—for it is now a matter of legal significance just how much of the record shall become public. Legal interpretation of a Convention can be changed decisively by the evidence being either restricted to the official public record—or expanded to include the submission in Court of the Committee proceedings which led to the shaping of the Convention. These *travaux préparatoires* were kept secret in the early years of the Council, and could not be used as evidence to clarify the original intentions of those who framed the Conventions. This, however, is no longer so—a Recommendation of the Assembly in 1965 urged that they should be made public, and to some extent the Committee of Ministers is now moving towards giving the Assembly satisfaction. And since the Conventions amount to international laws on the European level, this could become unexpectedly important.

Thus the question of individual credit for the origination of a Convention, and the evolutions of thought that first went into its making, are difficult to establish and can become controversial. Even more important, perhaps, is the larger political question of where the real areas of *first initiative* are. In the Assembly, certainly—and today increasingly in certain Departments of national Governments also. Yet the history of each Convention can be very individual: the Human Rights Convention, for instance, was already on the record as an aim as early as the Hague Congress of 1948, and thereafter derived considerable initiative from within the Committee of Ministers. Not many other Conventions have followed this particular pattern, and we can today look for the first recorded appearance of an idea for a Convention in a much wider circle—not only within the Council itself, but increasingly as the result of action by an interest-group or lobby in any Member country. Convention-making powers of the Council of Europe do offer a special opportunity—for there are many times when Governments are under pressure from particular circles to adopt very desirable legislation but fear to do so because the proposed legislation may also have vociferous enemies. When this is so, it can seem attractive to gain the desired end, not by national legislation, but by inspiring an international law which does in some mysterious way appear above party, and whose real origin can of course be kept equally mysterious. And while it is thus true that the Convention-making process offers Governments a subtle way of going round unwelcome controversy, it is equally true that the same process offers an opportunity for interest-groups within a country to circumvent opposition from their own Governments. They can go straight to Strasbourg with their idea—and this is now happening more and more often.

It is today much easier to communicate an idea direct to the Council of Europe than it was earlier. The recent establishment of an annual Work-Programme giving coherent form to all the many activities of the Council of Europe has resulted in considerable powers of initiative being given to the Secretary General. If today the Secretary General becomes convinced that any particular idea has potential value, he has power to include the idea in the draft Work Programme. Power of *decision* lies with the Ministers, but the power of first *initiative* can thus be used by the Secretary

General to sponsor ideas from other international organisations, from non-governmental bodies, from professional, regional or entirely local interests—and from individuals. This power is new, not yet widely known, and is also increasing rapidly in importance each year.

While the field within which we can expect to find the first recorded appearance of an idea is expanding, and while the chances of an idea for a European Convention achieving approval are increasing, it nevertheless remains true that the first recorded origin may not be the real origin. There is a universal fascination in beginnings and endings, and yet already the true first conception of most of the early Conventions of the Council of Europe is nearly lost to us. Big things often start so small we do not even realise they are starting—we notice nothing, so later cannot remember just when and where and how and why the tiny seed was planted. 'The avenging Gods,' said the Greeks, 'enter on feet shod with wool'—and this can be true of smiling Gods as well as stern. Even in politics we can entertain angels unawares not only in our actions but also in our thoughts —and in such a way that only inveterate diarists would pause to scribble the date. Thus even today, when attention is focussing more sharply on the Conventions of the Council of Europe, their first recorded appearance as *ideas* is often so small, so difficult to see, that to catch them adequately requires the day-to-day diligence of a Samuel Pepys.

2. *The first formal proposal for action.* This can sometimes be the same as the first recorded appearance of the Idea—but not usually. Power lies with the Committee of Ministers, and it is therefore usually in the form of a directive from the Ministers—perhaps direct to the Secretary General. Thus the Ministers in 1949 instructed the Secretary General 'to collect all useful material on the question of the creation of a *European Patent Office* and to report to the Committee on the best method to be employed for handling it'. More often it is a direct instruction entrusting the work to a committee of governmental experts to be convened for the purpose. Whatever the technical form of the instruction, as long as it is a formal proposal for action then at least a first decision has been made, and therefore a choice has been made between alternatives. The mechanisms of the entire Council must begin to move, even if at first imperceptibly. From that moment a number of possible future courses of action are automatically excluded, while others become immediately relevant. From now on it is no longer primarily a question of where, when, how or through whom to start—but of keeping things moving.

Thus with the *Extradition Convention*, the idea was first put forward by the Assembly in 1951 for a Convention 'with a view to the punishment of those committing crimes on the territory of one of the Members of the Council of Europe, and taking refuge on the territory of another Member'. It was 'to improve the existing system of granting and refusing extradition'. The first action of the Committee of Ministers was, as is usual, to obtain privately the opinion of all member Governments—an immensely complex process. The first formal proposal for *action* did not come until May 1953 and took the form of creating a Committee of Experts. This choice of action resulted in broad agreement at the beginning on general principles among the experts—but thereafter led to disagreement on whether to attempt incorporating all these principles in a single multilateral convention for all Member States, or in a model bilateral agreement to be adopted separately between pairs of States. And this was, by comparison, a fairly straightforward and predictable beginning to a Convention.

More complex were the events determining the first official decision to act on the *Convention on the Peaceful Settlement of Disputes*. In December 1950 the Assembly accepted the opinion of its own Committee on Legal and Administrative Questions, and recommended to the Committee of Ministers that there should be a Convention providing that disputes between Member States should be settled by the International Court of Justice in the Hague. This was sent to the Governments for their opinion— and while the Governments were still making up their minds, the Assembly decided in December 1951 it would be better to seek the creation of a European Court of Justice. This was followed within a few months by a compromise text calling for both a European Court, and a European Act for the Peaceful Settlement of Disputes—this to be based on the precedent of the General Act of Geneva of 1928 as revised by the General Assembly of the United Nations on 28 April 1949. It was not until thinking had evolved to this complexity that any official decision was taken by the Committee of Ministers—it was only after this considerably detailed and far-spread process of consultation and debate had at least outlined possible alternative solutions, that the idea was first officially handed over to an Expert Committee.

There is thus a paradox—an unfair contrast—between the drama of events leading up to the first official decision to act, and the sometimes imperceptible action entirely behind the scenes that then follows, and can indeed endure for years while nothing appears to be happening at all. Of course this is not so. The first official decision for action has mobilised new minds into the project, it has created a new combination of human energies that did not exist before, but which now exists as an official and additional part of the Council of Europe. It is true there is a well-founded

feeling that the mere phrase 'Committee of Experts' is itself ominous—
that these committees somehow tend to achieve the extraordinary position
of being both indispensable and useless. Yet this depends on the instructions to the Committee and the calibre of its members—and membership
of the Council of Europe inter-governmental expert committees is usually
of a standard hard to surpass, recruited as they are from the highest and
most select talent available throughout all the Member States, and acting
under instructions to find ways of enabling every Member State to act
simultaneously with every other Member on a project precisely defined.
It is of course necessary that each Committee should be both placed under
political pressure and given political leadership—and while in the earlier
years of the Council of Europe this was not always so, action is today
intensifying to make sure it shall be so. The immense delays which seem
to characterise the work of Council of Europe Expert Committees are
usually the result of the complexity of what they are asked to do—and it
should be remembered they are being asked to solve new problems in
unprecedented ways. Thus our public patience and understanding of the
value of what they are doing is not always what it should be. A little
thought about these committees should be enough to make us think
twice before we criticise too swiftly—for these committees all work
in camera, they have no right of reply to criticism, and our criticism
should perhaps be focussed, when necessary, more on the political context
within which these committees must work. This is often decisively determined by the exact nature of the first official decision to act, the first
terms of reference for which the members of the Committee are recruited
and under which they must work. There must have been many times
when members of expert and highly select committees in Strasbourg must
have wished they had power to strike back at both the uninformed public
and the impatient politicians after the immortal manner of Congressman
John Steven McGroarty of California, who in 1934 wrote to one of this
constituents: 'One of the countless drawbacks of being in Congress is that
I am compelled to receive impertinent letters from a jackass like you in
which you say I have promised to have the Sierra Madre mountains
reforested and I have been in Congress two months and haven't done it.
Will you please take two running jumps and go to hell.'

3. *The polarisation of individual initiative*. After the first official decision has
been taken to act, there usually occurs a polarisation of initiative between
two extremes—and usually this happens through individuals. By polarisation is here meant a concentration of personal energies around two contrasting centres of opinion. The contrast may be no more than that between

inertia and slow progress. Or it may be more: between radicals and traditionalists, the bold and the careful, those who have much to gain and those who have much to lose—or, we may even think, between the wise and the stupid. And it can be deceptive, as we saw with the European Convention on Extradition, where polarisation occurred between those on the one hand who wanted a multilateral Convention, and those wanting a model bilateral agreement drawn up as no more than a suggestive blueprint to be copied by those Governments who liked the look of it. It was deceptive, because here the division in opinion appeared to be no more on the surface than a superficial argument on method—whereas in fact it reflected fundamental and profoundly opposing *political* attitudes on European integration itself.

This polarisation of individual initiative can occur only within the context established by the first official decision to act, and is therefore limited. Often it takes place entirely behind the scenes, not appearing at all in the official record. However, sometimes it does become visible: a good example is again to be found in the evolution of the *Convention on the Peaceful Settlement of Disputes*.

Initiative here polarised around Mr Osten Unden, Swedish Minister for Foreign Affairs, who had been an active leader in drafting the General Act of Geneva in 1928. He put his view very strongly to the Legal and Administrative Committee of the Assembly of the Council of Europe—whose Chairman, Professor Rolin, had also helped to draft the General Act. Mr Unden's view was that it would be most unwise to ask Governments to commit themselves in advance to accept compulsory arbitration of legal disputes. In the previous thirty years compulsory arbitration had not once succeeded. Legal obligations were one thing: political possibilities were another—when the two did not coincide, what was to be done? He quoted the Saar as an example—and a good example it proved to be, the Saar eventually being lost to France and gained by Western Germany not as the result of arbitration at all, but of a popular referendum. Mr Unden felt very strongly that compulsory arbitration would succeed only if the *political* possibility of its success had been previously agreed—and he proposed that this should be decided by a two-thirds majority of the Council of Europe's Committee of Ministers.

Mr Unden nearly succeeded. The Assembly Committee went so far as to recommend that those States which wished to take advantage of the procedure he advocated should be able to do so. This was the compromise they suggested, and even this was only under his persistent pressure, for already there were a growing number of Member States who had already said they would indeed accept compulsory arbitration. The Committee of

Ministers decided in favour of the original and stronger text, with, however, a safety-clause inserted enabling Member States to declare at the time of ratification they would not be bound by its provision on arbitration, or even conciliation. To this extent Mr Unden succeeded. The Convention was signed in 1957, and within three years had been ratified by six Member States. Italy opted out of the provisions on both arbitration and conciliation, the Netherlands and Sweden out of arbitration only, Austria, Denmark and Norway accepted the Convention in full. West Germany, Luxembourg, Malta and Switzerland have ratified it since.

A second visible example of the polarisation of individual initiative is to be found in relation to the Convention on Human Rights—and indirectly concerns all the other Conventions also. In October 1957, Professor Wahl of Heidelberg—a member both of the Bundestag in Bonn and the Consultative Assembly in Strasbourg—proposed that there should be a *European Supreme Court empowered to interpret the application of all Conventions of the Council, and this at the request of individuals*. When the European Court of Human Rights was created for interpretation of the Convention of Human Rights, Professor Wahl proposed that this Court should in fact become the Supreme Court he wanted, with power to interpret all the Conventions of the Council, and perhaps other treaties also. His aim was to secure uniform interpretation of all the Conventions of the Council of Europe in all its Member States, and by insisting on this to secure the yet greater thing—that European Supreme Court which must eventually come into being if European unification is indeed to be based on the rule of law uniformly applied.

The more complex political problems become at the European level, and the more they seem to expand beyond the capacity of individuals to grasp, and the more these problems seem to demand the resources of great organisations before anything at all can be done—then there is all the more need for the powerfully convinced individual, not less. It may seem a paradox that when matters become too complex for any individual to know fully, they come to depend all the more for their solution precisely on the individual. But as the pressure increases, so the need. Even within the strictly limited context of each Convention of the Council of Europe, this is becoming more and more apparent. Just as we live today in a time of complexity increasing, speeds accelerating, of historical transition and flux and change and always the daily possibility of the completely unexpected, so each of the Conventions of the Council of Europe is an example of some of these problems overcome—problems all the time inherent in the process of European unification itself.

4. *The polarisation of conflict.* It is perhaps a good working rule that if a
Convention of the Council has not been achieved without conflict, that
Convention is probably not of primary importance. As we saw in Chapter
Three, the twelve-year Odyssey of the European Social Charter was
tortuous, its conflicts many. Nevertheless, the Convention now exists.
To say that a Convention achieved without conflict is unlikely to be a
primary Convention is not to say that conflict is a good thing but that
conflict *overcome* is a good thing. Nevertheless, the price paid has often
been heavy, and to some extent the polarisation of conflict has also always
been a result of deliberate choice. Thus in the eyes of those resolved on
conflict it may appear that a proposed draft Convention is too big, too
unmanageable—like a shapeless granite boulder that is too heavy to move
and must therefore be chipped with little hammers—or split with sledge-
hammers—before the pieces can fit where they are wanted. In the eyes
of those opposed to conflict it can appear that to split the boulder is to
ruin it. And as stone-breakers, masons and sculptors know, it does take
an experienced eye and a steady hand to know whether a stone can be
usefully split at all, and if so where, and how, and along what line, what
angle, and with precisely how much strength.

As a first example, the original idea for a *European Patents Office*, which
was proposed at the opening Session of the Assembly in 1949 by its
Committee on Economic Questions under the Chairmanship of M. Paul
Reynaud, with Mr David Eccles as *rapporteur*, ended by being split down
into several small separate splinters: into Conventions standardising formalities required when applying for patents; and creating a uniform
system for classifying patents—first in more than a hundred main classes,
and then hundreds of sub-classes. The splinters were finely shaped no
doubt—but they lacked the weight of the original idea, which has still to
be achieved on the wider European scale.

As a second example, we saw in Chapter Three how conflict within
the Assembly on the *Social Charter* centred between the two opposing
poles of the Economic and Social Committees of the Assembly. Nor was
the conflict merely between economic viewpoints and social aims, but
over methods of applying the Social Charter, and it was thus a conflict
on the entire shape, weight and momentum of the Charter as a whole.
And as we saw, it is no small matter to devise a design for applying uniform social standards from highly evolved industrial societies like Sweden
or Britain where the problems and solutions are already very well known,
to societies like those of the highlands and lowlands of Turkey, the
sparsely peopled slopes of Sicily, or the island of Cyprus. Even when they
are known, there can be the sharpest differences on method again: thus,

for example, some countries have opted for a contributory pension scheme, others for a non-contributory. The differences can prove fundamental and the conflicts therefore serious and well-founded on both sides. And as we saw, on the all-inclusive question of the method of application of the whole Charter, conflict polarised very strikingly between those who wanted ratifying Governments all clearly bound in advance to apply common standards within a common time-limit, and those who thought it foolish to insist too loudly, and wiser rather to be thankful that Governments ratified at all.

A third example of polarisation of conflict at several levels simultaneously is to be found in the early stages of the evolution of the *Convention of Human Rights*. 'A serious difference of opinion', says Dr A. H. Robertson, '...arose on the fundamental question whether a European Court of Human Rights should be created at all. The representatives of a number of countries were definitely opposed to the creation of a Court, on the ground that the needs of the Conventions would be covered by the institution of the Commission (on Human Rights) and the reference of its reports to the Committee of Ministers: others felt, however, that only the creation of an impartial tribunal would ensure the efficient protection of human rights...Another contentious issue during the course of the negotiations was the question whether the Convention should apply to the overseas and colonial territories of the High Contracting Parties. One view held that it should be so drafted as to apply automatically to such territories unless they were specifically excluded; the other view was that it should only apply in the first place to the metropolitan territories, but be capable of extension to overseas territories by express declaration... The right to education trod on equally delicate ground. In modern society, where the education of children is primarily—at least in most countries—the function of the state, the right of parents to choose the education to be given to their children involves as a corollary the duty of the State to furnish education in accordance with the individual convictions of its nationals. How far is this duty to be carried? Must schools of all denominations be provided in every village? If not, where is the line to be drawn? These questions immediately evoked in many Continental countries the long and bitter dispute between Church and State over education and the support of Church schools. They also raised a newer and even more controversial question. If parents have the right to choose the education to be given to their children, have Communist parents in a non-Communist State the right to have their children educated in the doctrines of Marx and Lenin?'

Here is conflict enough—the problem with the polarisation of conflict, in its early stages at least, is that the more it is important, the less it is usually allowed to be public. Thus neither in the Committees of the Assembly on the Social Charter, nor in the Committee of Ministers on the Convention on Human Rights, does the public record include any indication of which parties or Governments argued or voted which way. Throughout the evolution of almost every Convention, real conflict has tended to polarise at deeply subtle levels—sometimes involving Governments directly, and sometimes completely different levels of political organisation.

5. *Emergence of effective compromise.* European unification is today a process that cannot *endure* if not based on principle, yet cannot *continue* if not based on compromise. Thus compromise on the European level dare not mortgage future principle for the sake of present profit—it must rather insist not only on gaining the maximum present profit possible that does not damage future principle, but also on investing that profit to further and guarantee future principle. The tensions here are enormous, for the stakes are enormous—the board across which the game is played is already the whole of Western Europe—and the character of the compromises that emerge depend on the character of their makers; whether individuals, or an organisation such as the Council of Europe.

As suggested earlier, the Conventions are both united in principle and diverse in form. Their very diversity of form indicates the astonishing complexity of compromise that has been necessary to maintain principle. In the making of nearly every Convention polarisation of conflict has preceded a time of stress—and as we know from the laws of magnetism, a condition of stress does not manifest at or around either magnetic pole, but in that intervening space between them where their magnetic forces are most nearly equal. It is precisely here, in this intervening space, that the resources of the Council of Europe as a whole have been most consistently, effectively and subtly used. The consistency has been in the maintenance of principle, the subtlety and effectiveness in the shaping of compromise.

In the early Conventions at least, there are certain principles which can be observed at work in their making:

Each Convention must be acceptable to all the Member States of the Council of Europe—and of course, also to any other States that may later qualify and wish to join the Council of Europe. At present countries like Portugal, Spain, Yugoslavia or Roumania are disqualified *a priori* under the terms of the Statute from membership—nevertheless, this can change, and the fact was probably not absent from the minds of the makers of the Convention.

Each Convention must be so written that it can command respect as a document embodying the ideal of the Council of Europe—and not only now, but at any time and place in the future.

The Convention should not provoke insuperable opposition, not challenge powerful interests directly, not attempt immediate revolutionary change —in other words, it should not come in direct conflict with existing social and political circumstances.

This necessity to achieve legal texts for all Europe that are constructive, acceptable, worthy of respect and non-controversial has usually meant lengthy and nerve-wracking to-and-fro manoeuvring by mediators until the condition of stress is replaced by an agreement on all sides which does somehow satisfy these three conditions. These mediators have been found sometimes in the Committee of Ministers, always in the Secretariat of the Council. To some extent this is symbolic of the entire European Idea on the widest scale: it is not too much to say that the future character, might and majesty of a united Europe does depend—right now and today—on the emergence of tough, skilled and imaginative mediators.

In the Council of Europe the difficulties surrounding the first pioneer mediators were formidable, have evolved with passing years, and are today even more formidable. Let us take as an example a Convention not yet mentioned, and survey the difficulties that surrounded its making.

The *Convention on Establishment* is concerned with the rights to be accorded to citizens of one Member State when they are on the territory of another. The word 'establishment' means the status of the citizen, and closely linked to this is the right of free movement by any citizen from one Member State to another. The difficulty of achieving any agreement on this is shown by the fact it had never been successfully done before— and this not for want of trying, for in 1928 and 1929 the League of Nations had tried and failed.

It was generally agreed in Strasbourg as early as 1950 that a Convention on establishment would be welcome—the idea was first put forward by the Italian Government. It was agreed that its basic principle should be that citizens of Member States should, when on each other's territory, be placed in a more favoured position than citizens from other countries. A number of bilateral Conventions already existed between separate pairs of Member States: the problem was to find common ground for a multilateral Convention agreeable to all Member States. When asked for its opinion by the Committee of Ministers, the Assembly urged that the Convention should cover the whole field, including 'admission and right of sojourn; private and civil rights; the exercise of professions and trades; legal protection; the status of commercial companies; taxation; benefits from public services; and civic rights'. This is not only a formidable list in itself, it becomes more formidable when we realise the repercussions of such a Convention in terms of adjustments to the separate legal frameworks within all the Council's Member States.

Understandably, this complexity of difficulties caused delay and prolonged consultations—between the Committee of Ministers, all the national Governments, an Expert Committee set up by the Ministers, and a Special Committee set up by the Assembly. And compromise was reached—not by a struggle over principle, not by wrangling over detail—but by a severe pruning of the list of problems to be touched at all.

To some extent this was painless—other Conventions had already partially extended their area of agreement over that properly described as 'establishment'. The Convention on Human Rights, the interim agreements on Social Security, Social and Medical Assistance, and the Convention on the Equivalence of Diplomas had all included decisions with direct effect on establishment. And the list of what the Convention did include remained formidable—the right of entry and freedom of movement; prolonged and permanent residence; the conditions under which expulsion is permissible; personal rights and rights of property; legal protection and the right of access to the courts; the exercise of gainful occupations and professions; the activities of commercial travellers; admission to educational institutions; taxation; expropriation.

The price of compromise was the exclusion from the Convention of any action covering *minority rights, military service,* or *companies* incorporated in one Member State and working in another—and more besides, but these are enough to spotlight as acutely controversial. All three were questions where even the most suicidally inclined politician might well have hesitated to raise even a finger for fear of consequences. The question of companies was considered so difficult it was eventually dealt with separately in a Convention that even then did not achieve signature until 1966; the establishment aspect of military service has not yet been dealt with at all; while the fact that the Convention on Establishment came into existence by avoiding all mention of the fate of minorities is perhaps the vulnerable point where justifiable criticism should begin.

However, we are here considering the advantages of compromise—and we can see from this Convention some of the lines along which compromise was achieved. Politically explosive subjects were excluded; politically complex problems were either approached with some courage or postponed in the hope of a better solution later; politically innocuous problems were at once included. This critical struggle to achieve creative compromise is to be found in the evolution of every Convention—and has to be successfully overcome, for without compromise not one Convention of the Council of Europe would ever achieve the stage of effective application—and with it, its aim of influencing positively the lives and circumstances of the individual European citizen.

This perpetual need for creative compromise is outstanding in the struggle to unite Europe—for our European situation is exceptional and will be so for years to come. We do not yet have a stable framework of union within which to work. Our need to achieve working agreements which contribute in both large and small ways to building this framework is thus far greater than in national politics—while our obligation to achieve them while simultaneously refusing to abandon one inch on principle is also far greater. The principles that will later be indispensable if Europe is to survive as a healthy and developing social organism are today not yet incorporated in Europe's social structure. Thus the stakes on either side are so great that although the choices for action seem wide the margins of safety are in fact small. They are not only small—like channels in an unknown seaway, they are today scarcely charted.

To continue our example, even after the Convention on Establishment had been successfully drafted, within a few years a new necessity for compromise became clear. The Convention was signed in 1955—and in March 1957 the Rome Treaty was signed, creating the European Economic Community of the Six—all also members of the Council of Europe. And Article 52 of the Rome Treaty dealt explicitly with establishment: 'Within the framework of the restrictions set out below, restrictions on the freedom of establishment of nationals of a Member State in the territory of another Member State shall be progressively abolished in the course of the transitional period. Such progressive abolition shall also extend to restrictions on the setting up of agencies, branches, or subsidiaries by nationals of any Member State. Freedom of establishment shall include the right to engage in and carry on non-wage-earning activities, and also to set up and manage enterprises and, in particular, companies within the meaning of Article 58, second paragraph, under the conditions laid down by the law of the country of establishment for its own nationals, subject to the provisions of the Chapter relating to capital...'

And with the success of the EEC the necessity increased, leading to negotiations between the Council of Europe in Strasbourg and the Community in Brussels—negotiations today still in progress, and themselves again symbolic of both the importance and difficulty of this question of compromise: for it does not diminish as the European Idea continues—it increases with it, extending up and down through all levels of action—and outwards to a steadily increasing number of countries.

Thus 'compromise' in Europe is becoming a loaded word—and tends, most oddly, to provoke most uncompromising and even violent emotions. It is often the most valuable compromise that invites the most vicious criticism, the most immediate impugning of motive. 'Compromise', said Reginald Wright in *The Way of Peace*, 'is never anything but an ignoble truce between the duty of a man and the terror of a coward.' Edmund Burke, in his speech on conciliation with America, said: 'The concessions of the weak are the concessions of fear.' Emerson, writing in his *Miscellanies* on *The Fortune of the Republic*, said: 'Everything yields. The very glaciers are viscous, or relegate into conformity, and the stiffest patriots falter and compromise.' Yet even the violence of these emotions is not always consistent. Even the sternest men find themselves suddenly faltering, compromising in spite of themselves—as we see again from Burke, who was able to say in the same speech: 'All government—indeed every human benefit and enjoyment, every virtue and every prudent act— is founded on compromise and barter.' George Herbert, in his *Jacula Prudentum*, said 'A lean compromise is better than a fat lawsuit.' Sidney Smith, in his *Essay on the Catholic Question*, said: 'All great alterations in human affairs are produced by compromise.' In a letter to Boswell in 1766, Dr Johnson said: 'Life cannot subsist in society but by reciprocal concessions.' And in George Canning's *The New Morality* we find the compromise view on compromise:

> '...and finds, with keen discriminating sight
> Black's not so black—nor white so *very* white.'

So—compromise is not a word to approach carelessly. It appears to depend very much whether a compromise is designed to defend, or to influence, or to change events—and our judgement of each of these three kinds of compromise may be differently coloured. When we consider the European Idea, it is perhaps possible to suggest that when compromise is designed to *change* events constructively, it is probably right. And when compromise is designed not to change but merely to *influence*, that there will always be genuinely respectable differences of opinion on all sides. And third, that when compromise is designed only to *defend* an already existing state of affairs, nine times out of ten it is wrong.

As the Conventions of the Council of Europe show, Europe today is in exceptional need of successful compromise. The actions quoted in

Chapter Three can be read entirely as examples of varied attitudes to this question of compromise—and while it is true that the ideal compromise must combine adherence to principle with an awareness of the facts of practical possibility, it is probably also true that the more a compromise achieves this ideal in Europe, the more it is likely itself to have three effects. It is likely to be condemned by disappointed and fanatical supporters. It is likely to be condemned by outraged and fanatical opponents. And it is likely to gain the quiet, practical and often silent approbation of those men and women of a realistic temper who wish to see not merely something done regardless of consequences, but something done that will succeed.

When we look at the Conventions of the Council of Europe, or at the European idea itself, perhaps what it all comes to is that compromise is always the opening of a door, and must be judged solely by who and what comes through that door.

6. *The first irrevocable approval.* Sole and final power for the approval of a Convention lies with the Committee of Ministers of the Council of Europe. It is customary to consult the Assembly and we have seen the part the Assembly plays, but nevertheless much proposed by the Assembly has been rejected by the Ministers and there have been Conventions where the Assembly was not consulted. And the approval of the Ministers must be unanimous in the negative sense that while not every Government need sign, every Government still has power to block the signature of a Convention. To this extent each Convention does express a common denominator between all the Member countries of the Council of Europe —or, to be exact, the political parties forming their Governments.

Every Convention must pass through this stage. It is not the final stage, but it is irrevocable in the sense that the *text* of the Convention is now *fixed*, once it has been initialled by the Ministers. These texts do sometimes specifically provide for their own amendment and improvement, and they are sometimes extended or completed by Protocols—thus there are no less than five Protocols to the Human Rights Convention, two of which do actually modify Articles of the Convention, while the Standing Committee established under Article 24 of the Establishment Convention has the task of 'formulating proposals designed to improve the practical implementation of the Convention and if necessary to amend or supplement its provisions'. Nevertheless once the text has been initialled, and thereafter formally signed, it has been approved to the extent it can no longer be stopped or changed, and as a text is now irrevocable.

The decision of the Ministers is taken in secret, but the formal signing of the Convention is usually public—and very public it can be. The vellum and parchment, the superb calligraphy of the lettering, the streamers of silk ribbon to take the imprint of state seals in burningly hot and coloured globules of wax—even the astonishingly squiggly-wiggly signatures of the men of state who sign—all these are properly symbolic, done now as they have always been done through the centuries, and attracting our instinctive respect. There are few of us who do not feel a certain awe, a certain mystery in how power can be compressed into a scribble of ink. 'Great is the hand that hath dominion over man by a written name', wrote Dylan Thomas.

The names signed on the Conventions are usually as numerous as the Member States of the Council of Europe at the time. Places of signature have been not only Strasbourg, but very often Paris, for its geographical convenience to Ministers, and other cities as well: the Statute of the Council itself was signed in London, the Convention on Human Rights in Rome, the Social Charter in Turin.

It may be thought that a Council of Europe Convention should always be signed in Strasbourg because there is the seat of the Council. Yet any extreme centralism in European unification is a sensitive matter, and just as Committees of the Assembly often deliberately choose to meet not in Strasbourg at all but in other cities like Berlin or Dublin for the excellent reason that the work of the Council of Europe belongs equally to every city and region in Europe—so the Conventions can be signed wherever the Committee of Ministers chooses. It could follow from this that the places of signature of future Conventions may continue to be deliberately widespread and varied. Indeed the choice of place and time can be invested with deep meaning, as was done with the Social Charter—which was signed not merely in Turin, but during the International Labour Exhibition held there as part of the celebrations to commemorate the hundredth anniversary of the proclamation of Italian Unity. Mazzini would have been pleased to see the inscription on the plaque in Turin marking the signing of the Social Charter—'Here the peoples of Europe gathered...and hope shone...*Effulsit spes...*'

And after the wax of the seals has dried, and the photographers have flashed their pictures and departed, and the Ministers have been swept away in their glossy limousines with national flags fluttering, what remains? For the Convention now is seen to exist, the thing is presumably done. The first visible recorded origins are already sliding into history, the first official proposals for action have led to action, the emergence and polarisation of initiative, conflict and compromise have shaped that action

into an irrevocable text, stamped now with seals of state, and to be preserved in the archives of the Council of Europe in Strasbourg and brought
before the public gaze again only under circumstances of solemnity. The
thing is done—or is it? The Convention exists—but does it? Every Convention of the Council goes through these stages and up to this point, but
what in fact has happened? The truth is that the Convention has been
born, no more; all its life has yet to grow.

For Article 15 of the Statute as enlarged by the Committee of Ministers
in a Resolution of May 1951, reads:

'The Conclusions of the Committee may, where appropriate, take the
form of a convention or agreement. In that event the following provisions shall be applied:

    1. The Convention or agreement shall be submitted by the Secretary
General to all Members for ratification;

    2. Each Member undertakes that within one year of such submission,
or, where this is impossible owing to exceptional circumstances, within
eighteen months, the question of ratification of the Convention or
agreement shall be brought before the competent authority or authorities in its country:

    3. The instruments of ratification shall be deposited with the Secre-
tary General.

    4. The Convention or agreement shall be binding only on such
Members as have ratified it.'

Ratification is not the initialling of the Convention by Governments, but
approval by a national parliament of what its Government has initialled.
Nor is ratification the same as the entry into force of the Convention, for
that depends on conditions laid down within the Convention itself—
which usually means not until after the second, or third, or fifth ratification—depending on the already agreed text of the Convention.

Thus once the Convention is at last a finished text in Strasbourg, its
progress thereafter at once separates in as many divergent directions as
there are Member countries of the Council of Europe. Furthermore, in
each of these countries, progress towards the ratification of the Convention again goes through all six stages all over again—for again the first
recorded appearance of a move towards ratification can be separately
seen within each country, again we can pinpoint eighteen first official
proposals for action, eighteen separate processes of initiative, conflict
and compromise; each either leading or not leading to a full parliamentary
ratification in that country—whether Italy or Denmark, Britain or
Iceland, Norway or France, Malta or Sweden, Turkey or Ireland. And

in each country the result will be one of three clear signals: yes, no, or wait. This means that if we consider merely ten Conventions awaiting ratification at any one time, we have *one hundred and eighty separate parliamentary operations to think about.* This is a complex matter of some significance for the future of the Council of Europe: the lay observer would assume there is constant and effective pressure from Strasbourg designed to increase the speed of ratifications. This is not so at all—there exists at present no organism for generating sufficient pressure to ensure the ratification at national level of Conventions already agreed at European level.

Let us go through our six stages again quickly to see what in fact happens at the national level—remembering we are here concerned with the continuing success of a Council of Europe initiative in eighteen very different frameworks of national parliamentary politics.

1. *The first recorded move.* Looking at it from Strasbourg, this is clear. On a precise day a letter goes from the Secretary General to each of the Governments. Looking at it from each of the capital cities it is not clear —for the letter arrives, is passed to the relevant Ministry or Ministries, and at once eighteen very different processes start. What then happens in each city depends on the policy of each Government towards European unity, its policy towards the Conventions of the Council of Europe, its attitude to the subject matter of this particular Convention, its awareness of the attitudes of other Governments on this Convention—it depends on the political philosophy of that Government, its strength in its parliament, and its entire mood and feeling in both internal and external politics. It depends, above all, on whether or not there exists a will to act towards ratification in the minds of those men and women carrying the responsibility: whether in Reykjavik, London, Rome or Ankara. And it depends on the procedure required for ratification—this can be very different from country to country. For if, as in the United Kingdom, ratification does not in practice demand parliamentary time, then the real problem becomes that of whether the Convention requires the amendment of existing legislation or the introduction of new. Or if, as in perhaps half the Member countries of the Council, the provisions of an international Convention automatically take precedence over domestic legislation, then the problem becomes more one of lengthy and very serious parliamentary scrutiny.

2. *The first formal proposal for action.* The form this takes can be subtly different in each country—for it depends on official opinion and advice crystallising behind the scenes to the point where the Convention is put

forward—usually to a particular Minister—as worthy of ratification as part of that Government's policy. The power here of Civil Servants is not merely influential, but often decisive.

Yet while the first official proposal for action is usually made within Government Departments, it need not be limited to these circles. It is open to parliamentarians of all parties, to leaders in all forms of public life, to professional and trades union and indeed any concerned interest-groups to take the initiative and themselves make the first official proposal for action. Just as in Strasbourg not everyone has waited for the Committee of Ministers, so in each Member country it is not always necessary to wait for the Government.

3, 4 and 5. *The polarisations of inidividual initiative and conflict, and the emergence of creative compromise.* The key is the seizure of initiative. It is here that the danger-point comes—but a negative danger, that of doing nothing. It is dangerous because each Convention needs a minimum number of national ratifications to bring it into force—thus a failure to seize the initiative in one country can be the cause of the Convention failing to come into force even in those other countries which have previously ratified. A failure, for example, of Civil Servants, parliamentarians, Ministers, trade union leaders, journalists or professional spokesmen in Norway, Britain or Germany to seize a good opportunity can thus result in desired action being indefinitely delayed in Cyprus, Switzerland, France or Holland and vice versa.

Furthermore, even on the largest matters this initiative can be seized by the smallest number of people. It is their attitude of mind that matters: one person is enough to start a move to ratify, two people are better, and three are already an effective working team. This determination to seize and keep the initiative is well illustrated by the British ratification of the Convention on Human Rights—when a team of two kept the matter always moving: Lord Layton and Sir David Maxwell-Fyfe (later Lord Kilmuir). And most of the Conventions do leave room for compromise in their acceptance—as here with Human Rights, for British acceptance of the Right of Individual Petition was not insisted on at first, and came only recently under a new Labour Government.

6. *The first irrevocable approval.* This comes with the approval by a national parliament of a Convention, and when the instrument of ratification has been deposited with the Secretary General of the Council of Europe. Only then is the full circle complete, and it is a circle that must be completed separately in *each* country on *each* Convention.

Whose then is the responsibility for keeping up the pressure so that these ratifications are achieved, thereby complementing the Convention-making process in Strasbourg? It is officially no one's responsibility. The obligation to maintain initiative does not centre anywhere. The Council of Europe in its full capacity can officially do no more than inform Governments the Convention exists. Governments are officially bound to do no more than submit the Convention within a year or eighteen months to 'the appropriate authority or authorities in its country'. The proof that initiative and pressure towards ratification has no effective centre of action, and is not being effectively maintained in motion, is that this undertaking by Governments is frequently ignored. This casualness of attitude is a symptom with many causes, and is itself not to be ignored. And it is also true that even if a Government does submit a Convention to its Parliament, nothing at all will happen unless the Government itself has already decided it shall happen. We have here the first weak link in the chain—and we should remember that in the strict and technical sense even members of parliamentary national delegations to the Consultative Assembly of the Council of Europe have no official responsibility—they go as individual representatives, not official delegates. It is an interesting phenomenon indeed—and symbolically characteristic of the entire progress of the European Idea in our time—that *so much hard work at one level should be vitiated by a failure to establish communicative action linking it to other levels.* Responsibility for ensuring continuous action towards ratification of the Conventions of the Council of Europe throughout all the Member States of the Council today still remains, as it has for many years, a European Portfolio without Minister.

This has been repeatedly and publicly recognised in debates of the Consultative Assembly. When responsibility for seizing and maintaining an initiative can find no official context or structure within which to act, it is then especially for individuals to raise their voices and many Members of the Assembly have done so. And while it is easy to say that the links here missing between initiative at the European level and complementary initiative at national level should of course be created, the fact they have not yet been created is also proof that the difficulties are fundamental—difficulties of information and communication, of man-power, money, precedent, method and motive. Yet even in the early years of the Council attempts were made to overcome them, and they originated nearly always in the Assembly.

The means open to grasping the initiative in national Parliaments were limited to the time and talent available from members of the Assembly themselves. They, as always, were over-worked and therefore sometimes under-informed, able to give Europe usually far less than a tenth of their time. And each year the answer was found to be exactly what it was in the beginning—that whenever progress was made it was nearly always by individuals sufficiently determined to seize any exceptional chance that came—and sufficiently devoted to the aims of the Council of Europe to do so unprompted.

Even when the question quickly arose of trying to mobilise the collective energies of not merely individual members of the Assembly, but national delegations—whether all together, or by parties—even then the answer was still usually the same. When effective action came it was still nearly always the result of leadership by one, two, or three determined individuals within a delegation. And whereas in Strasbourg, pressures tended to encourage national delegations to work together, at home in their national parliaments the pressures worked the other way, and were often most quickly eased by throwing off the European harness. A great burden was carried, most of all in the early years, by Members of national Parliaments who did not look upon their European conscience and their Strasbourg experience like a passport—indispensable abroad, useless at home. Of all those who went to Strasbourg—which amounts to some hundreds of Members of Parliament from the eighteen countries—only some fully assumed their dual function: that of representing and working for their country in Europe, and for Europe in their country. It was true then, and it is still true today, that a Parliamentarian who takes the trouble to write an effective personal letter at exactly the right moment to his Party Whip or his parliamentary leader or even to colleagues not of his own party—merely drawing attention to something in Strasbourg perhaps—or putting down a formal Question for debate—or beginning a drive to focus attention on ratification of a particular Convention—or seeking Parliamentary time for full debate on an aspect of the Council of Europe's work—that such a Member, who not merely writes the letter but takes the further trouble of actually walking along the corridors and delivering it personally to the right place at the right time, perhaps on a dull slow-moving day when his colleagues are taking a holiday from politics—such a Member has probably done more for the real future of Europe than he or she could have done by ten times the work on a public speech.

Initiatives of this kind have often made the difference to the ratification of a Convention. Nevertheless, there is also a limit to what an individual can do, and on the organisational side the picture is not entirely black. The Assembly's Working Party on Relations with National Parliaments has been persevering steadily, year after year, seeking always to erode

those difficulties blocking its way. Much of its work is behind the scenes—
but it is worth noting that roughly every six months it publishes a list
of every public intervention made by a Member of the Consultative
Assembly at home in his or her Parliament. That is to say, an intervention
in Bonn or Oslo or London or Paris is very quickly on the public record
for the attention of parliamentarians in all the other capitals of Europe.
And since all the Members of the Consultative Assembly—and other
people also—do tend to keep a weather eye open to every nuance of their
colleagues' orientation on Europe, we have here a form of political
communication with direct effect on reputation. For the question:
'*Is he a brother?*' is today a question increasingly urgent in many people's
minds, in many contexts and permutations—its nuances are not becoming
simpler, they are becoming increasingly complex and sophisticated as the
European Idea progresses.

There is also an increasing number of Parliaments who have followed
an example first set by Bonn, and have taken care to create facilities
strengthening links between what their Members do at home and in
Strasbourg. The Bonn example first took the form of appointing a
permanent official, paid by the Bundestag, with secretarial assistance,
and responsible for assisting members of all parties in their official work
with all European organisations. It was a small beginning, but along the
right lines. There are Parliaments in Europe today who have not yet
even got this far. There are other Parliaments who have evolved even
better methods—and this is important, for Parliamentarians have no more
than twenty-four hours a day like every one else, and any method that
can save time, ensure that work is concentrated and not wasted or duplic-
ated, and that information is both centralised sensibly and also widely
distributed, does make action easier for everyone. These methods have
resulted in the initiative being seized when otherwise it would not have
been possible. Though seizure of the initiative often appears to be solely
the dazzling product of sudden inspiration, when problems are complex
—as they are here—it is indeed far more often the result of a
methodical mastery of immediate detail, in the context of a long-term
plan.

And while the problem of gaining the initiative towards ratification of
a Convention is fundamentally similar in each country, the polarisation
thereafter of conflict on a Convention is exactly the opposite, varying
sharply from country to country, and from Convention to Convention.
The conflict is determined by the results which ratification is thought
likely to have in the politics and life of the country. Let us look at an
example from the London *Evening Standard* of 7 June 1967:

F

'Another loophole for the pirate radio stations is to be sealed off. Amsterdam, usually considered a safe refuge for the pirates, will be barred to them if the Dutch Government goes ahead with plans to ratify the Strasbourg Convention and pass a law outlawing illegal broadcasting.

Holland's own pirate radio, Radio Veronica, which broadcasts on 192 metres from a ship off the Dutch coast outside territorial waters, is making plans to operate independent of the shore. Already most of the programme preparation is done on board the ship. The three brothers Verwey who own this oldest of all the pirate stations are confident that they could operate should further legislation be passed against them. Meanwhile they are quite happy to see the other pirates join them in Holland, and are not the least worried by Radio Caroline's plans for a separate Dutch programme.'

The new Dutch Government has not yet firmly stated its policy on pirate radio. It is having enough trouble with the legal radio, which is controlled by five separate companies, four of them concessionally based. The Dutch are very fond of Veronica, which puts out a basic diet of pop music with a couple of hours of light classics in the evenings twice a week, and programmes for Indonesian workers from Southern Europe on other evenings.

At the moment any pirate radio can establish an office with impunity in Holland, but they had better keep a weather eye on the political scene.'

This brief summary of *some* of the factors shaping up to conflict in *one* country on *one* of the smaller Conventions of the Council of Europe, gives an idea of the complexity involved. And if we now take the first *sixty* Conventions of the Council, and multiply them by the *eighteen* Member countries, we find that if the Conventions are eventually to achieve what they are designed to achieve, we are now dealing with the necessity of first achieving no less than *one thousand and eighty* separate parliamentary ratifications.

If we take the negative of this, and consider in a darkly clairvoyant mood all the reasons for ratifications that have *not* been achieved, and if we concentrate solely on the black side as we plot them Convention by Convention, and country by country, we would emerge with a horrifying picture—it would limn for us a Europe of nationally inbred small-mindedness, internecine departmental wars alternating with departmental sloth, of provincial small-mindedness, sectional stubbornness, and political myopia—a Europe showing the symptoms of prejudice rampant, courage dead and conscience dying. We deceive ourselves if we say the dark side is not there. Yet when it comes to conflict over ratifying a Convention, we should perhaps also note that opposition which is more than merely negative, and according to its lights indeed reasonable, tends to be identifiable at one of the following levels in each of the capital cities of the Member States:

1. A feeling that while the Convention is probably a good thing simply because it does come from the Council of Europe, it is in fact *ahead of its time*, not immediately urgent, and need not be ratified just yet. This is the argument to delay perhaps just a few months.

2. A feeling that the Convention may not be a good thing for its consequences *will not be acceptable until things have changed*—until, for instance, after the next election on the national level, or until after the next phase at the European level.

3. A feeling that the Convention may be all very well for others, but is *unlikely to be acceptable in this particular country for a long time*—that it should, in fact, be shelved indefinitely.

4. A feeling that, while the Government may have felt it wiser to avoid blocking the Convention in Strasbourg, it is at home thoroughly understood to be *completely unacceptable* in practice.

Whether the feeling is this year, next year, sometime or never, the result is to move the Convention downwards in the always overburdened list of governmental priorities. The object of supporters and friends of the Convention is, of course, to move it upwards—and unless the Convention is labelled outright as unacceptable, conflict will revolve round this single question of priorities. For the Convention cannot now be immediately modified, the possible alternatives for compromise in its complete or partial implementation have already been written into the Convention, and the facts are clear. If ratification cannot be immediate, it is important to know why not. If ratification is desired, it is important to know when it may be possible. For while no ratification means very simply no action, successful ratification can lead to action whose consequences can extend far. Article 63 of the Convention on Human Rights, for example, which permits signatories to extend the Convention to people overseas, has resulted in the Convention now being operative in countries as far apart as Greenland, Surinam and the Netherlands Antilles, and an immense list of British colonies and dependencies and states now independent that ranges from British Guiana to Malaysia, from the Channel Islands to the island of Napoleon's exile, St Helena, from Gibraltar to the Falkland Islands and even the faraway Kingdom of Tonga in the Pacific.

If persistent pressure is therefore to be methodically exercised on Governments to persuade them to ratify waiting Conventions, it is necessary for those exerting the pressure to be able to know at a glance at any time the existing condition of ratifications, and the relevant circumstances in each country. This is true for parliamentarians, Press, Civil Servants, all interest-groups or lobbies who are concerned. And just as there is at present no organisation for fully co-ordinating and exerting this pressure, so there is at present—and this is astonishing—not even any single method whereby those most concerned (and often they are also those with the least time) may learn swiftly what they must know if they are to act.

The problem with most official charts published by the Council of Europe itself is that they are intelligible only to those already informed— even then, they do no more than say which Conventions are being applied, which are ratified, and which are awaiting ratification. Futhermore, it is not possible to get even privately a thorough unified briefing on the exact up-to-date circumstances relevant to each Convention in each country. As we have seen, in Strasbourg itself at the Ministerial level, work towards effective ratification of Conventions is a Portfolio without Minister: while at the Assembly level it is limited to the Working Party on Relations with National Parliaments, who are doing the best they can. No single person, no single office, can at this present time put their fingers instantly on *all* the essential facts. The facts, of course, are known—but they are not all known consciously and simultaneously in relation to each other. Different people know different aspects of the facts: the essential sequences of information which should be immediately available to anyone who could use them well do not exist—and to track them down at all on the part, shall we say, of an individual member of the Assembly, requires a kind of mathematical skullduggery in forcing a number of very busy officials to answer a number of very difficult questions, until all the answers do arrange themselves at last into that intelligible sequence which should be always available automatically. Thus while it should be possible at any time to take any Convention in any country and ask: what are the facts, problems, and possibilities, and who are the people sufficiently informed in that country to be able and willing to contribute to exerting that pressure towards ratification which all agree is necessary, this is not merely not possible, but it is at present not even anticipated that it should be made possible. And it should be pointed out—unbelievable though it is—that in all the years of its existence the Council of Europe has never yet published, propagandised and developed into the powerful weapon it could be, one very simple thing—a handbook, written for those whom it might concern, and explaining clearly in detail what every Convention does. Those who take it for granted that such a publication exists will find they are mistaken —for while the texts of the Conventions are available, an explanation of each separately is not. The sooner such a handbook is made available the better—it would be a valuable contribution to the aims of the Council of Europe. Much could turn on even so simple a thing: the aim being constant, that of enabling complex and effective pressure to be brought to bear on Governments in such a way that the rate of ratifications steadily increases.

It is worth remembering here that Governments have an Achilles heel—for there is one thing Governments are powerless to prevent and unable to avoid hearing: a steady, dignified, factual, and repeated public listing of what each Government has *not* yet done. The French Government, as we saw in the last chapter, has not ratified the Convention on Human Rights—the fact needs to be implacably and repeatedly publicised: it should not be lost in silence. And while there is to some extent communication from the Committee of Ministers to the Assembly giving explanation on particular points, this is not quite the same thing. For the Achilles heel is there and we should keep our eyes upon it—for what the Governments can scarcely change is that the Assembly is master of its own agenda, and with the exception of military matters may discuss publicly whatever it thinks useful.

If this is accepted as a starting point, it suggests several possible lines of action, some of which could possibly be combined to great effect. If we express them negatively, we find the Assembly itself has no Standing Committee on Ratifications. The Assembly lists no inclusive debate on ratifications as a whole. There is no method yet whereby even a progress report is submitted to the Assembly giving in a codified form the information available on what is happening to each Convention and why. There is no single Member of the Assembly charged with keeping a watching brief on what is happening to all the Conventions seen as a whole. All this is of course also true at the level of the Committee of Ministers, and of the Secretariat, but we are here keeping our eye on the Achilles heel of Governments. Thus if at each Session of the Assembly merely no more was done than to include in the Agenda the single item, '*Report on the progress, ratification and application of all the Conventions of the Council of Europe*', it is possible that from this first action more would follow. And this would perhaps be welcome to those who have already contributed so much to the evolution of the Conventions, and would

perhaps be of benefit to those whose interests the Conventions are designed
to serve—the general public.

'*There must have been something more than common that these men struggled
for...*'—that is the motto at the head of this chapter. We have looked at
some of the stages in the making of the Conventions, and though—as we
have seen—when it comes to the critical stage just before ratification we
find a tangle of insufficiencies, and though—as here suggested—it might be
useful to keep in mind that the Conventions are not mere seeds to be
planted and forgotten, but are growing trees, and that it would be good
to hear each year how they are growing—there is perhaps something
more to see. For when we look at the stubbornly obstinate effectiveness
revealed in the making of the Conventions, does this not appear inexplicable unless we acknowledge something 'more than common' in
the minds of their makers? What can this thing have been if not the
European Idea at work—not merely in its already accepted sense of knowing both that Europe must be united and why, but in the deeper and
often necessarily subtler sense of seeing how action may contribute to
that, and when, and through whom, and how? What can this thing have
been—this something more than common—if not a particular aspect of
the European Idea working through particular European minds in a
particular historical context? What can this thing have been if not a
dogged insistence on combining both a search for the immediately
possible, however small, with an equally dogged insistence on always
seeing also the wider and larger view, no matter how far away it may
appear. It may have been no more than this: it cannot have been less.

It was suggested at the beginning of this chapter that the Conventions
are, nevertheless, no more than part of the politics of unifying Europe.
That is very true. It was suggested also that the way we talk and act about
the Conventions reveals a great deal about how we really feel about the
European Idea, and that is perhaps also true. They are a very subtle test
of attitudes, and will be so for years to come. For their very creation,
evolution and character suggest that the easy way may not always be the
safe way, and the fast way may not always be the best way. It is an
attitude worth bearing in mind when we remember that, when all is
said and done, it is in our own highest and best interest to create and maintain a truly united Europe—that we have today a European ship of state
to build, and that though whichever way we choose may be hard,
nevertheless it must be done and done well. A ship that is not seaworthy
cannot sail through storms.

CHAPTER FIVE

'Citizen Of Novara'

'And thou Milan, thou seekest to supplant Cremona, to overthrow Pavia, to destroy
Novara. Thy hands are raised against all, and the hands of all against thee . . . Oh,
when shall the day dawn in which the inhabitants of Pavia shall say to the Milanese:
"Thy people are my people", and the citizen of Novara to the Cremonese: "Thy
city is my city".'*

THE EUROPEAN IDEA will be justified only when it makes daily sense to
every individual European citizen. If the citizen of Novara introduced
above could be reborn today and stroll along the lobby beside the
Representatives' Lounge in the Council of Europe, and could pause to
glance there at the texts of the Conventions displayed as they sometimes
are in glass showcases, he would doubtless doff his feathered cap, hitch
up his jewelled sword, swing his fur-edged cloak, and bend forward
to gaze closely, questioning what these documents of state can be. If a poor
citizen of Novara, to whom communal rivalries are but a grim and daily
harassment and hazard, he would doubtless shuffle in his shabby shoes,
and wonder—as we would say today—if there was anything in it for him.

In the previous chapter on the individual making of the Conventions
of the Council of Europe it was suggested that the full list of the Conventions appeared casual and unco-ordinated, lacking sense as a series
and as a programme lacking power. In this chapter we shall look at all
the Conventions as an *ensemble* and through the eyes of our latterday
citizen of Novara—and as we do, we shall find this criticism an understatement. The truth, on the surface, is worse.

* 'An obscure priest of Milan', probably fourteenth century, quoted by Frederick
L. Schuman in *International Politics* and by D. J. Hill in *History of Diplomacy*.

Do they appear casual? Surely yes. A glance at the full list in the Appendix gives an impression of a curiously casual choice of subjects— blood-banks, patents, exchange of television films, cultural activities, criminology, the peaceful settlement of disputes between Member States, extradition, motor vehicle insurance, the liability of hotel-keepers, human rights, academic recognition of university qualifications, a European pharmacopoeia, and many more—up to a total of over sixty subjects. It is casual in the sense big things are succeeded by small and superficial things by fundamental things; some fields appear to be touched several times yet not completely, and other fields merely once and never again. Its general impression is that if one made a list of five hundred useful actions in support of the European Idea, and then idly closed one's eyes and jabbed with a pin seventy times the result would be a list every whit as orderly as the Conventions now displayed in the Lobby before our puzzled citizen of Novara.

Do they appear unco-ordinated? Surely yes, on the surface. Though this list could understandably have begun casually, it is seldom that human affairs which continue for any number of years do not in the course of time attract to themselves a certain co-ordination. The list covers fully twenty years of intricate work, and in politics twenty years is quite a long time. And even if we divide the list into five year periods, and seek an underlying evolution, a sense of co-ordination does not immediately strike us.

Do they appear to lack all sense as a series? What happens if we do no more than seek some one common denominator of purpose? We have seen in Chapters Three and Four the immense work that goes into the making of each Convention—work extending through all the Member States of the Council. Can it be that the result of all this is no more than a zig-zag list of incoherent items?

As a programme, do the Conventions of the Council of Europe appear to lack power? Whatever power it may have does not appear unified or consistent. We cannot look at it and say clearly: this list of European Treaties exercises today the following form of power in the practical affairs of Europe, and in the following defined way, for the following expressed purpose...

If complicated politics are serving a realistic aim, if they are justifying the time, trouble and energy people are putting into them, then one way of proving it is if their value can be made plain to anyone who asks. What then are we to say to our citizen of Novara?

Suppose he first asks: 'Who is to *enforce* all this?' We have to tell him this is the wrong question—that although he can ask it about each treaty separately, there is at present no way of asking this question in relation to this list of Conventions as a whole. It is true that a number of Conventions require Governments to report and justify their actions to the European body created for the purpose by the Convention (as for example, with the Social Charter or the Establishment Convention). Governments can be brought under pressure in Strasbourg by the Assembly as a whole, or by interested groups and individuals at home. Certainly there is a special situation in those countries where every Convention acquires immediate force of law on ratification. Yet each Convention must still be viewed separately, and when it comes to enforcing all the Conventions as a whole it does remain largely a question of the good will and integrity of each Government.

Let us suppose our citizen asks: 'What is the *purpose* of these Conventions seen as a whole?' We are forced to tell him that the only official answer so far approved by Governments is that every Convention contributes separately to the 'greater unity' of Europe, but that if he persists in asking us precisely *how*, there is no detailed official answer.

And if we face the fact that our citizen of Novara may well finally ask, in twentieth-century paraphrase of the fourteenth-century question— 'When shall the day dawn in which the inhabitants of Brindisi shall say to the inhabitants of Barcelona or Brest, of Birmingham or Bergen, "Thy people are my people and thy city is my city",' we shall very likely be at an ashamed and stumbling loss for words. He wants an honest answer, but the more we know the less likely we shall find the words to tell him. For we face here a special problem with which our citizen of Novara may already be familiar—that of translating the abstruse into the actual. An example of this problem as it appeared centuries back merely in the field of law is quoted by F. W. Maitland in his *Year Books of Edward II*, where he gives as an example of the difficulty of communicating law to laymen the following hypnotising description: 'an heir in tail rebutted from his formedon by a lineal warranty with descended assets'.

Yet far from condemning this he defends it by saying: 'It is forgotten that during the later middle ages English lawyers enjoyed the inestimable advantage of being able to make a technical language. And a highly technical language they made...Precise ideas are here expressed in precise terms, every one of which is French: the geometer or the chemist could hardly wish for terms that are more exact or less liable to have their edges worn away by the layman.'

Yet the layman whose life is governed by the law can scarcely like this. Though in law he might grudgingly accept it, he would be unwise to accept it in politics—or to insist on anything less than the clearest possible

F*

explanations. Throughout all the processes of European unification today, our citizen of Novara still stands before us, asking his questions, expecting honest answers. If we give him an answer we know he cannot understand that is already deception. Worse is an answer denied.

Yet when we look at this list of Council of Europe Conventions, how are we to answer him? We wander here through a labyrinth, but are we wrong even to seek an Ariadne's thread? Or does this list of creative European achievement with all its talk of high ideals reflect no more than what T. S. Eliot in *The Waste Land* described as a 'heap of broken images'? Does our Europe of today sicken still from the malaise of the thirties? Is our mental image of Europe itself still fragmentary, itself nothing more than an unco-ordinated list of things to be done? Cadmus, brother of Europa, sought her everywhere and was told by the oracle at Delphi: 'You will not find her.' Is there perhaps an indication in the dictum of Denis de Rougemont, who, telling of Cadmus, concludes: '*To seek Europe is to make her. She exists in her own quest. She cannot be anything but a never-ending search...*' Perhaps we should then ask our citizen of Novara if he does not feel in his bones that it is better to travel hopefully than to arrive—and that it is simplest to see the Conventions of the Council of Europe as themselves a search?

If a search, then for what? In the beginning, in the grand years, when the first Conventions looked as if they would form into a constellation round the first shining stars of the Convention on Human Rights and the European Social Charter, they were certainly *part* of a search for unifying action—but a search to be undertaken by the Council of Europe as a whole. The early Conventions were unhesitatingly shaped to accord with the spirit of such a search. They were to express the highest ideal of the European Idea, and help towards making that ideal a daily reality for people. But they were also to be only part of the larger search, and it is ironical that at the very time when the Conventions appeared to play a lesser role in the activity of the Council of Europe as a whole, the Conventions made were major ones. As we have seen in Chapters One and Two, the structural imperfections of the Council prevented it from pursuing any single all-inclusive search with all its faculties. The separate parts of the Council began instead to pursue individual but not always co-ordinated searches of their own—and after the emergence of the Coal and Steel Community the evolution of the European Idea enabled effective things to be done elsewhere than in Strasbourg. The context—the matrix as it were—of European unification became one more likely to give birth to twins or even triplets than a single sturdy child, as had been the original hope in Strasbourg.

If we consider the effects of this on the minds of the makers of the early Conventions, when those with a wider vision found themselves forced to don blinkers and live with the fact that the horizon of possible action had narrowed, we can understand their problem. These were days when a full European Political Community had been at least on the drawing board. We cannot say that the Convention of Human Rights had been explicitly designed as a moral yardstick for an awaited European Constitution—yet we also cannot say that this possibility was absent from the minds of its makers—and it is true that when the Treaty for the European Political Community was being written, its authors found the Convention on Human Rights most conveniently at hand. The European Social Charter was intended as a complement to Human Rights. The Mackay protocol had hoped to secure recognition for the Council of Europe as the sole mechanism for creating European laws. Yet this entire sequence of events was now destroyed—what therefore was to be done?

It was perhaps easier to see the one thing not to be done, and that was to give up. Those men in the Council of Europe whose position, temperament and European consciousness enabled them not to abandon the idea of continuing to construct European Conventions, did refuse to give up and did continue to think positively—and this with an admirable obstinacy, at a time when the chains of hope, logic and expectation had all broken. If they had been asked exactly what they hoped to achieve they would have been hard put to it to say: the political calculus of European possibilities would scarcely then have justified their action, and we must look outside it for their real motive.

Or to be more precise, we must look deeper. A great deal has been said and written about what is called the need for a 'European consciousness', and this is the first chapter where we have been driven to face the phrase. Yet it has never been defined. Many people have a feeling of what it could be, but this feeling can seldom be expressed consciously. As soon as it is expressed consciously it appears inadequate. We are driven to subterfuges: we are forced to say there have been moments in European history when a European consciousness was reflected: as in the letter by Metternich to an English friend when he suddenly confessed he felt the whole of Europe to be his country. Or we are forced to say there are works of art like Goethe's *Faust* or Shakespeare's *Hamlet* which we agree at once reflect a European consciousness—yet do not contain in themselves a definition of that consciousness, for they are themselves part of it.

Europe is always unhappy unless she feels a sense of creative movement, and this always involves struggle. If we look again at the evolution of the Conventions of the Council of Europe, at this puzzling list of European treaties that has never ceased to grow, we can perhaps say they did express a double impulse within the minds of their makers—whether in the Assembly, the Committee of Ministers, or the Secretariat: first, a need to continue creative movement towards they knew not what; secondly, an acceptance that this would involve struggles they could not yet fully justify. This combination of uncertainties would deter most people: it did not deter the makers of the Conventions, and we shall ourselves be unable to understand the real meaning of this list of Treaties unless we try to find out why.

The root of the trouble is that while the phrase 'European consciousness' is convenient, it is incomplete. The awareness of a society moves at many levels. A European consciousness cannot exist without both a European *sub*-consciousness, and also a European *supra*-consciousness. Sub-conscious awareness is derived from the raw material of past memory. Supra-conscious awareness is derived from a sensitivity to the ideal in all things, and a creative attention to the future. It is seldom these three levels are perfectly co-ordinated. It is certain that all the time they interact with each other. When we are considering the evolution of what in our time we call the European Idea, and the related phrase 'European consciousness'—and this in terms of millions of people both of the older and of the younger generation—the complexity of the politics of European unification cannot be explained unless we are aware of the far greater complexity from which it grows.

Our twentieth century is the first century to possess disciplines of thought devoted to handling questions of this size and subtlety. Three quotations may here be illuminating—and all the more so if we take as a hypothesis the argument that the laws we find at work in the individual are also very similar to laws at work in society as a whole. We are here considering the psychology of the European Idea, and asking ourselves what lies behind a 'European consciousness'—let us first look at a quotation from Coleridge's notebooks, picked out by Aniela Jaffe as the motto for her edition of Jung's Autobiography (*Memoirs, Dreams, Reflections*): 'He looked at his own Soul with a telescope. What seemed all irregular, he saw and showed to be beautiful Constellations: and he added to the Consciousness hidden worlds within worlds.'

If we transpose this attitude to a larger scale, it is not inappropriate as a guide to the hidden unity behind the European Idea today—for at times it does need a telescopic view to be seen in perspective at all.

Now let us look at a second quotation, taken from the glossary to the same book, and quoted directly from Jung himself: 'When one reflects upon what consciousness really is, one is profoundly impressed by the extreme wonder of the fact that an event which takes place outside in the cosmos simultaneously produces an internal image, that it takes place, so to speak, inside as well, which is to say: becomes conscious.'

If we read this in terms of a 'European consciousness', and remind ourselves that at present the dynamic is working the other way—that today the image of a united Europe is still an image created by the imagination of many individuals, seeking to create its own objective counterpart through the medium of external and very practical politics— then it is certainly suggestive.

What is also striking about the Conventions of the Council of Europe in the years when immediate political justification was difficult is that they do display a remarkable consistency of character. In their practice they are puzzling, not in the principles from which each in turn was derived. This must lead us to suppose that in the minds of their makers there was a coherent combination of impulses at work. But it was not so conscious that it was repeatedly expressed. While any one of those concerned in the making of a Convention at this time could have given in private a thoroughly intelligent account of why the provisions of a Convention would have a good effect, few could have explained why the making of the Convention merely *as a Convention* would have any larger effect. This is understandable, for it could not then be proved that the Conventions of the Council of Europe would acquire any cumulative force as an *ensemble*—or how exactly the existence of any one Convention would eventually both contribute to the value of the others, and also itself gain from them.

We see this failure of conscious justification well illustrated in the speeches in the Assembly already quoted in Chapter Three. There it is the criticisms of the draft European Social Charter that are conscious, rational, objective, and well-argued. They stem from intellect, their strength is rooted in intellect. In revealing contrast is the defence of the Charter, which is based far more on the feelings shared by its supporters—a feeling hard to express, and which in M Schuijt's speech took the form of quoting François Mauriac: '*Our work is worth what it cost us in labour*'. There could hardly be a more eloquent example of a conscious conviction. Similarly, if we notice how the Social Charter was criticised for not coming up to the standard set by the Convention on Human Rights, we can read that as implying there was already a feeling becoming conscious that *all* the Conventions of the Council must somehow evolve into a visibly coherent whole. Yet never once in the debate was this positively said—which is understandable, for the difficulties of European unification at that time made it impossible to say *how* this could happen, and thus no conscious and objectively argued declaration of what this coherent whole should be was ever made. That would have been the next logical and decisive step—and as we shall see by the end of this chapter, the Council of Europe today faces this identical question again, but now in a more urgent and even more complex form.

Thus we find that the makers of the Conventions continued to create these European Treaties without the benefit of any official and conscious justification or explanation, at a time when the intrinsic value of each Convention was not susceptible to ordinary calculation, when the individual future of each Convention was uncertain, when the collective evolution of the series as a whole was unpredictable. Yet their makers nevertheless insisted on making headway without delay: they did not wait for the turn of events throughout Europe to make everything easier. It is as well they did not: for events have not made things easier. To some extent their problem was the grindstone problem, for a grindstone shapes things and makes the sparks fly—and once it is turning and has momentum it needs much less energy to keep it turning than it does to start it again after it has stopped. The grindstone mechanism of the Council of Europe's Convention-making has never ceased to turn—let us now look at some of the tactics that evolved out of this constant effort to ensure it kept turning.

They were tactics of survival: limited and subtle. They are best described in terms of working attitudes which still hold good today, and are themselves still evolving.

1. *The aims of each Convention must be irreproachable in the negative sense, yet valuable in the positive sense.* This was true from the beginning, but as the difficulties increased so also did a certain caution in choosing subjects for a Convention, particularly when unanimous approval was required from the Committee of Ministers, and the use of the 'Partial Procedure' method had not yet come to be adopted as widely as it could have been. The aim of a Convention thus had to be one which would not arouse persistent or vehement opposition from any Government, and which therefore did not touch any vital interest, privilege or principle.

A dramatic example of an irreproachable yet positive Convention was that establishing a *European Blood Bank*. Caused by the Dutch Flood Disaster of February 1953, when local supplies of plasma were exhausted, further supplies were rushed in, and survivors of the flood then died after transfusions of the wrong types of blood, the Convention laid down agreed standards of pharmaceutical preparation, medical handling, and administration. This sounds a small and obvious matter to arrange. Yet people had died because it had not been done, and as every medical administrator will realise, it was in fact extremely complicated—involving the co-ordination of standards in use by all the separate medical services of all the Member Countries.

2. *The Conventions sought to fill vacuums of power.* They exploited to the full the advantages of choosing those lines of advance which were least spectacular, those mere loopholes in events where nothing yet was being done. An excellent example is the *Convention on the Liabilities of Hotel-Keepers*—another the *Compulsory Insurance of Motor Vehicles*—another the *European Cultural Convention.* At the national level these were all areas of difficulty: at the European level, of opportunity. The first two are fields of precisely limited cause and effect—the third, of course, a field as expansive as the human spirit. All three Conventions filled a vacuum of power, whether small or large, in the sense that each Convention initiated action at the European level where previously there had been none.

3. *The Conventions sought to bring about what we can call the minimum necessary effective change.* It was politically necessary it should be the minimum, but morally necessary it should be effective. With every Convention this balance had to be estimated throughout *all* Member States, and the tactical skills required within the Council of Europe to gauge this to a hair's-breadth became through the years a fine political art. Delicate examples of this are the Convention on the *Equivalence of Periods of University Study* and the Convention on the *Equivalence of Diplomas leading to Admission to Universities.* Each of these is but a small part of European cultural and educational harmonisation, and yet each Convention did achieve the minimum necessary effective change. If they had aimed at less they would have been ineffective: if they had aimed at more they would have been unattainable.

4. *Each Convention must nevertheless have a long-term potential.* In the early years there were exceptions to this, when Conventions were created to salve some of the wounds of war—for example, the Agreement on the *Exchange of War Cripples* between Member Countries of the Council of Europe with a view to medical treatment. And there have been Conventions to meet a sudden special need—as with the *Convention on Pirate Radio Ships.* But nevertheless, even so there is always a long-term potential somewhere there behind the scenes, often in the form of legal precedent—and the more carefully we look at the Conventions the more

we see with what subtlety this long-term potential has been so implanted that as time passes so it must increase. It is a characteristic of human nature not to notice what will not have immediate effect, and this has been used in the Conventions to great advantage. What is not noticed can scarcely be opposed.

5. *Each Convention should be politically non-controversial*. This is meant in the sense it should not provoke intense debate on the fundamental *principles* of European unification. To some extent the makers of the Conventions have been much helped by the fact that those who might have opposed them on fundamental principle often did not realise that the very existence of the Conventions as a growing *ensemble* could in time lead to such a debate. Even quite recently it has been known for those advising Governments on the Conventions of the Council of Europe to admit in private conversation that they could see no fundamental principles involved in the Conventions, and preferred to advise their Governments according merely to the immediately pragmatic and visible pros and cons of each Convention separately. Here the extraordinary technical complexity of the Conventions has certainly had a smokescreen effect—it is a fact that some of those officially responsible for advising Governments have been kept so busy rubbing the technical smoke out of their eyes that they have not thought to advise their Governments on whether there was perhaps behind the smokescreen a political fire burning.

Where Conventions have proved controversial it has usually either been in circles *below* Governmental level, or when at Governmental level, then long *after* the first creation of the Convention. Thus the Convention on *Pirate Radio Stations* is certainly controversial—but not with Governments themselves. The Convention on Human Rights, which is certainly controversial at the highest Governmental level, has not in fact become so until a number of years *after* its creation. The following letter in the *Daily Telegraph* of 17 July 1967, written by the London representative of the Council of Europe, illustrates this process at work in at least one Member State of the Council:

Sir,

In December, 1965, the United Kingdom Government recognised the optional clause in the European Convention on Human Rights permitting the right of individual appeal.

Since then certain individuals have appealed to the European Commission on Human Rights and it is open to justifiable conjecture whether the Convention itself has not been violated many times over by the law of the land.

Since the signatories of the 1950 Convention, of whom Britain was one, undertook to bring their national laws into line with the Convention, the time would appear over-ripe for some consolidated action in this direction by the United Kingdom.

It is no use trying to be European, which is the policy of both H.M. Government and Opposition, if one blandly ignores first principles—in this context the *legal paramountcy* of the European Convention on Human Rights.

As a first effective step the Lord Chancellor might appropriately appoint a Commission to report to him on the changes necessary to bring all the law into harmony with the rights listed in the Convention. The task should be revealing.

Yours faithfully,

Cosmo Russell.

And so far, the Conventions of the Council have usually succeeded in avoiding fundamental controversy at Governmental level at least during those critical first years when each Convention must accumulate a reasonable number of Ratifications. They are, in fact, so designed that they tend to be left in peace until they have grown sufficiently tall and strong to stand, first, against contrary breezes, and second, against winds that could in time become strong enough to shake them even at the roots.

This list of five tactical attitudes is not at all complete. It does no more than emphasise some characteristics of the Conventions, and includes no statement of strategic aim. Yet if we consider the implications of an accumulating series of actions, all of which are fulfilling a need, are politically non-controversial at their beginnings at least, tend to seek out and fill vacuums of power, and do all have long-term potential effects at many different levels of European life—if we look at this through the eyes of our citizen of Novara, remembering that he is well accustomed to an age of labyrinthine power-politics where the longest way round is often the shortest way home and the road to a citadel is often a side-street, where a tangle of complex actions, many apparently quite unrelated, and yet all sharing certain recognisable characteristics, do usually indicate that very simple thing—a disguised aim—if we look through his eyes, the eyes of the era that led up to Machiavelli's *Prince*, we would perhaps not be very surprised if out of the complexity he suddenly asked one sharp shrewd question—*was there a plot?*

The answer is no, not at first. Yet by 1962, the question could no longer be evaded: the European Ministers of Justice meeting in Rome went so far as to say 'a veritable European community of law' had been formed among the Member States of the Council of Europe. And on Europe Day, 5 May 1965, Dr Hans Furler went so far as to make the following public assessment of the Council of Europe:

> '...The Council of Europe is not only the first European institution, but also the widest inclusive grouping of free European peoples...Its importance lies in its successful work towards the creation of a *European consciousness;* in the creation of a *form of European Law;* and in the debates of the Consultative Assembly where parliamentarians from seventeen (today eighteen) countries gather regularly as a great forum of European public opinion. More than fifty (today over sixty) Conventions—among them ones as important as the European Convention on Human Rights and the European Social Charter—are laying the foundations of a *common structure of law* in which not only member-states are taking part, but beyond them other European nations in addition...'

And a fifty-page brochure published by the Directorate of Information of the Council of Europe in 1967 felt able to put the words 'A Community of Law' as a major heading, and continued as follows:

> '...the Council of Europe's legal programme has been considerably expanded, and over fifty European Conventions and Agreements have now been opened for signature.
>
> '...mention should...be made of: the European Convention on *Establishment:* the European Convention for the *Peaceful Settlement of Dispute:* the Convention on the reduction of cases of *Multiple Nationality* and on *Military Obligations in cases of Multiple Nationality:* the European Convention on *Extradition:* the European Convention on *Mutual Assistance in Criminal Matters:* the European Convention providing a uniform law on *Arbitration:* the European Convention on the *Formalities required for Patent Applications,* the international Classification and the unification of certain points of substantive law on *Patents for Invention:* the European Agreement concerning *Programme Exchange by means of Television Films.*
>
> 'In 1963, the Committee of Ministers decided to set up a *European Committee on Legal Co-operation* to prepare a legal programme for the Council of Europe and co-ordinate work already being done.
>
> 'The European Committee on Legal Co-operation is composed of a delegation from each of the Council of Europe's Member States. The Consultative Assembly is entitled to three seats on the Committee and Spain and Finland send observers.

'In particular, the Committee implements the legal programme of the Council of Europe and co-ordinates and supervises work arising from it. It supplements, or modifies, the expanded legal programme, particularly in the light of Assembly recommendations and proposals by Governments or international organisations.

'The Committee also examines drafts or conclusions resulting from the proceedings of specialised committees of experts before submitting them to the Committee of Ministers, and follows developments in other organisations or bodies in order to achieve effective co-ordination of work and promote co-operation with them on matters of common interest.

'The Council of Europe also provides the Secretariat for the periodic Conference of the European Ministers of Justice, who send their resolutions to the European Committee on Legal Co-operation.

'The Consultative Assembly holds an annual debate on reports submitted by its Legal Committee and has made proposals leading to the conclusion of several European Conventions. At present the Legal Committee is studying such subjects as: *press legislation:* the *nationality of married women:* the right to *conscientious objection:* European *immigration laws: industrial espionage;* and a *European Highway Code.*

'...Most of the items now under study by Committees of Experts in the legal programme are concerned with the drafting of European Conventions or Agreements. A Convention on *State Immunity* will establish to what extent a State shall continue to enjoy immunity from jurisdiction when it engages in economic or commercial activity on the territory of another Contracting State. A Convention on *Consular Functions* will supplement the 1963 United Nations Convention on Consular Privileges and Immunities by defining the powers of consular officers, and, in particular, their functions in respect of estates and shipping. Another Convention, on the *Abolition of the Legalisation of Documents* drawn up by diplomatic or consular officials, will remove the need for any formality to prove the authenticity of signatures on such documents.

'Several Conventions will seek to: standardise certain basic legal concepts such as 'time-limit', 'domicile' and 'residence'; provide for effective ways of circulating information on foreign law for the benefit of domestic courts when they are called upon to decide matters relating to a foreign law; standardise, as far as possible, national legislation on investment trusts, private companies and hire-purchase.

'Draft Conventions are also planned to introduce into municipal law certain rules governing the place of payment and the procedure for discharging foreign money liabilities and to bring in measures to prevent bearer securities, which have been lost or stolen in one country, from being sold in another.

'Other work in progress is designed to make the law of the various European countries more widely known and to encourage better contact among jurists. In this context, mention should be made of: the publication of digests of State practice in public international law; the translation into the languages of the Member States of the principal codes or other legislative instruments in force in those States; the organisation of meetings between practising lawyers from all Member States: the study of the best ways of promoting teaching and research on European comparative law and the development of co-operation between European law libraries...'

Yet even this does not tell us *how* a 'community of law' is to be achieved or what its achievement will mean. If we are to take the claim seriously that the Conventions of the Council of Europe are designed to create a European Community of Law, then we find ourselves contemplating a difficult matter—for if we achieve a genuine community of law across at least Western Europe, are we not well on the way to achieving all? A genuine community of law must postulate a genuine enforcing authority. Does this not mean a *democractically elected Government* of a unified Europe? Can it mean anything else? If we imagine, an enforcing authority that is tyrannical in either principle or practice, is not this or any other alternative something we must not merely reject but actively oppose? If we accept that the rule of law must become the paramount principle in the unification of Europe, then we must accept that the phrase 'community of law' does postulate a European government—for just as a structure of government is at all times best measured by the character of the law it upholds for its individual citizens, so a common structure of law cannot survive without a common structure of government.

To accept such a proposition all at once in what Churchill called one single 'spasm of resolve' is usually too much for most of us, and in history happens only occasionally, and then only under enormous pressures. Thus to say that acceptance of a 'community of law' means we ought now to work towards a European Government often provokes the impulse to seek some easy way out. And in the realm of law, and in the context of the European Idea in our time, this can lead to the Gaullist fallacy of seeking to overcome the weaknesses of our present national state system by seeking all the more to buttress that system.

As we have seen, the processes of European unification are themselves characteristically untidy owing to the very nature of our times, and this is certainly true of the present evolution of the Conventions of the Council of Europe. The Conventions depend for their effect on ratification and implementation by separate and very individual Member Governments, and thus each Convention accumulates round it an individual combination of supporting countries. For each Convention we could take a map of Europe, and colour in those countries where the Convention is operative, and by the time we have done this with what will soon be a hundred Conventions we will have as many maps of political effect as there are Conventions, and many of them will be strikingly different.

Our map of the Social Charter, for example, would show that its social ideals and methods are closest to implementation in a very particular Europe—the north-western Anglo-Scandinavian-Teutonic Europe. As further ratifications accumulate we could predict from this map that the influence of the Social Charter will come to be accepted in a general easterly and southerly direction, thus extending into the Latin and Mediterranean area, and ultimately, we must hope, also to what used to be called Asia Minor, as well as eventually upwards again through the Slav and Baltic peoples.

Yet only one Convention of the Council of Europe has yet achieved ratification by all Member countries. With even most innocuous, genuinely minor and utterly irreproachable Conventions, some Government somewhere has either itself succeeded in finding fault with the Convention, or has not been put under the necessary minimum of persuasive pressure to ratify and apply. In the previous Chapter we looked at the mechanics of this. When we look at the ratifications of the Conventions it has to be realised that the avoidance of ratifications through the adoption of a 'this year, next year, sometime, never' attitude is happening all the time. What this means is that however much we accept the expressed aim of a 'Community of Law', and however much we seek to discover the real plot behind the Convention-making of the Council of Europe, we are perpetually baffled and hindered by the fact we are seeking answers at a time when not a single one of the Conventions has yet achieved its full potential.

We are thus dealing with a complicated and interrelating series of still only *partial* influences. To give them coherent force, both will and skill are needed; either without the other will fail. And the skill is almost a lumberjack skill—an ability to look at enormous political log-jams, and see how to move the one log that will allow all the others also to move with the current—and then, while all the time keeping our balance upon all these logs on the move, nevertheless to wait patiently for the next log-jam to occur all over again, as it certainly will. When we look at the European Idea we shall not help ourselves by wasting breath on cursing its difficulty, but rather by giving thanks that the river does run strong, and the logs are not too few but happily too many. Very often in politics a wealth of difficulty can also indicate a wealth of hidden opportunity.

Let us therefore now look at some of the varied ways by which the Conventions are already contributing to a common structure of law.

1. *Influence through internal legal modification.* By agreeing to ratify and apply a Convention, Governments do often thereby accept certain changes within their own national law—changes which when effected will bring their own law into harmony with that of all other countries which have also signed the Convention. This method of inducing Governments to introduce parallel changes in legislation is not of course limited to the Conventions, for a method similar in character has been in proved use for a long time by, for example, the Nordic Council of Iceland, Norway, Sweden, Finland and Denmark. There unification in law is done by each country introducing within its own parliament legislation already harmonised in advance with the parallel internal legislation of its partners. The method is good—and similarly, ratification of the Conventions of the Council of Europe does often lead to parallel legislative action within countries hitherto ostensibly linked in few other ways.

2. *Influence by precedent.* The previous existence of a Convention or group of Conventions—for example, the medical or criminological groups—can tend to influence subsequent related legislation in Member States, legislation not necessarily directly connected, but perhaps in some field where the same sort of problem or need can well be met by the same sort of solution. In the same way, the existence of Council of Europe Conventions can influence similar legal work by other people also but at the European level—whether the influence is by way of legal precedent, or political precedent. We saw this happening, for example, with the Establishment Convention, which led to work on establishment within the European Economic Community.

3. *Influence arising from the application of the Convention.* An increasing number of the Conventions have precise legal and political methods of application and control written into them—for example, the *Establishment Convention* and the *European Social Security Code.* Thus the progress each year of these Conventions does steadily strengthen patterns of action that did not earlier exist, and which do now exist but *only* at the European level. The more this European level of common agreed action is intensified,

the more national levels of action are forced to take its existence increasingly into daily account, and do what is necessary to keep everything moving forward in harmony.

4. *Influence arising out of interpretation of conflict.* Whenever the application of a Convention in any country or group of countries raises questions of legal conflict and therefore interpretation, for which no legal or political machinery already exists, then the resolution of the point at conflict will in itself tend to bring such a machinery into being. This of course can happen entirely within the orbit of the Council of Europe, as with the Human Rights Convention—or in conjunction with other organisations, as for example the Hague Court or the Court of Justice created by the European Community to adjudicate questions arising out of the Community's foundation Treaties. Either way, in the long run the very creation of a structure—however small and embryonic—to interpret a Convention of the Council can prove to be of more enduring influence than the Convention itself, for it is only by fruitful interpretation of law that a structure of law can healthily grow. And although the fact is not widely publicised it is already true that intensive work within the Council of Europe designed to open up the way for a mechanism enabling uniform interpretation of *all* European Treaties is making serious progress. And indeed it has to, for the sheer numerical complexity of the Conventions is now beginning to achieve such an interactive network of effects that uniform interpretation will soon be indispensable.

These are only four among some of the more obvious ways by which the Conventions do justify the aim now publicly attributed to them of seeking a 'community of law'. It is a beginning only, and yet when we consider that this concerns eighteen *national* structures of law, as well as the unifying levels of *European* legal action, we are forced to muse a little on what may be coming towards us in the future, and the different ways in which it may come. If we also consider that, very broadly speaking, any legal interpretation of an agreement confirms the original validity of that agreement—and secondly that any subsequent reference back to that agreement does confirm the validity also of interpretations that have taken place in the meantime but are not yet directly in question—and if we apply this across all Western Europe—then we have a visible phenomenon at work which is of interest not only to lawyers, not only to politicians, but also to our citizen of Novara.

We have, however, already seen that the Conventions as an ensemble are only partially in operation—for they depend on a network of ratifications only partially completed. Furthermore, adherence to them by

Governments is entirely voluntary up to the point at which a Government does or does not decide to ratify and thereafter apply. Above all, this decision is voluntary in the sense that Governments are not being bound to a structure of principles by any foundation treaty comparable to that binding the six countries of the European Community—though we may wish they were. Thus the Conventions of the Council not only lack the strength such a Treaty would give, but also its disadvantages. As agreements, the Conventions are ill-defined, complex, elusive in character, entirely voluntary for Governments, and steadily increasing in number. This flexibility has been aided by what has already been referred to as the 'Partial Agreement' method—a method of very great interest indeed, and now worth looking at closely. The Resolution of the Committee of Ministers adopted in August 1951 says:

'...having regard to Article 20 (a) of the Statute, which provides that recommendations by the Committee of Ministers to Member Governments require the *unanimous vote of the representatives casting a vote and of a majority of the representatives entitled to sit on the Committee:*
'Having regard to Recommendation 3 adopted by the Consultative Assembly in August 1950;
'Desirous, whenever possible, of reaching agreement by unanimous decision, but recognising, nevertheless, that in certain circumstances individual Members may wish to abstain from participation in a course of action advocated by other Members;
'Considering that it is desirable for this purpose that the procedure of abstention already recognised under Article 20 (a) of the Statute should be so defined that the individual representatives on the Committee of Ministers should be able, by abstaining from voting for a proposal, to *avoid committing their Governments* to the decision taken by their colleagues;
'Resolves:
1. If the Committee, by the unanimous vote of the representatives casting a vote and of a majority of the representatives entitled to sit on the Committee, decides that abstention from participation in any proposal before it *shall* be permitted, that proposal shall be put to the Committee; it shall be considered as adopted *only* by the representatives who then vote in favour of it, and its application shall be limited accordingly.
2. Any additional expenditure incurred by the Council in connection with a proposal adopted under the above procedure shall be borne exclusively by the Members whose representatives have voted in favour of it.'

Which is to say, first, that whenever this procedure is adopted then those Governments wishing to opt out may do so—and second and far more important, that those Governments nevertheless resolved to go ahead may do so. There is, of course, great strength in a method like this as soon as a sufficient number of Governments begin to realise its potential value for them each individually. This method has evolved directly out of the difficulties experienced by the Council of Europe, and though it is at present unique to the Council, there is little reason why this should continue to be so in the future, and good reason why the method may in time come to be very widely adopted. This is of importance to the European Idea as a whole, for it is undeniable that a sufficiently wide-spread adoption of partial agreements can in time contribute directly and effectively towards the creation of unified and eventually complete frameworks of action.

Nevertheless, it also remains true that a genuine and enduring community of *law* in Europe cannot exist until it is the product of a democratically elected European Parliament with real legislative power. This may not happen for years—and in the meantime, the Conventions of the Council of Europe can do only one of three things—continue with exactly the same character and effect as they have today, which is unlikely—or fall into decay, which is unlikely—or evolve in character and increase in effect. They are in fact suggestive models for future patterns and modes of European legislative action. And when the day at last comes for them to be cheerfully superseded by something better—by, for example, real and enduring European legislative action genuinely endorsed by direct individual franchise—then these Conventions will themselves be a fundamental part of the basis for such legislation.

However, our citizen of Novara—whose attributes may include a surprisingly shrewd and even sceptical curiosity—may ask us at once whether these three alternative futures for the Conventions of the Council of Europe are the only ones, and whether we can really be so sure of our judgement. His questions should not be blinked: during the rest of this chapter we shall anticipate his attack by looking even more carefully at some detailed characteristics of the Conventions—and asking some questions about them which are not usually asked:

1. *What is the reparative factor in the Convention?* To what extent will it heal a wound in European life, supply a counter-balance to some black evil still coming at us out of the past, contribute to the satisfaction of some long-neglected need or necessity? Our heritage in Europe is both black and white, and it is a pernicious negligence of mind that blandly assures

us that because the sun in shining there are no shadows. More to be preferred is a reparative vigilance that unceasingly seeks out opportunities
to repair those mistakes we have undoubtedly made—and which, if we
are honest, we must admit we are likely to continue to make. As the road
goes forward, so pot-holes constantly appear behind the road-makers—
if the road is to go continuously forward, the pot-holes must be continually repaired.

2. *What is the simplifying factor in the Convention?* To what extent will
it not merely tie up loose ends or introduce order where there was disorder—but *replace compound problems by simpler problems*, thus making
them easier to understand and therefore to solve? The Convention creating
a *European Pharmacopoeia* is an excellent example—for it does not in itself
solve the problems of pharmaceutical work, yet by introducing an agreed
common language of terms, standards and methods it does at least make it
easier to understand and express what those problems are.

3. *What is the stabilising factor in the Convention?* In our present era of
flux and change we must all the time be concerned, whether we like it or
not, with considerations of the elements of balance, continuity and the
fundamental and long-term strengthening of principle. Yet this factor is
also the opposite of the dramatic, for it is often oddly invisible. A mere
stolid accentuation of the enduringly valuable—that can seem very dull.
It is a quality which in public affairs we often do not notice even when it is
right before our eyes because of course it does not move. The paradox
of the stabilising factor in any political action is that—like the great beams
within a house or ship—the less it seems to do the more it is proving its
worth.

4. *What is the pace-making factor in the Convention?* To what extent does
the Convention show us a first example of *what* can be done where it was
not done before, and of *how* it can be done? To what extent does it exem-
plify a method which previously was not prominent—or even had no
part—in the politics of Europe? The function of a pace-maker in a race
is not just to stay out in front to show that speed or power are possible,
but to do so with such skill that the will of others to follow is increased,
and those labouring one step behind can then come forward later at the
perfect tactical moment and win. The pace-making factor in a political
action can often afterwards be best measured by the speed with which
that action enabled itself to be superseded by something related but better
—which explains why it is so often the fate of the pacemaker to be
forgotten.

5. *What is the obsolescence factor in the Convention?* What elements within
the Convention indicate the possibility of it exhausting its own potential,

or falling behind because of its own inherent weakness, its own inability to keep up with other events? We are accustomed in this radio-active age to talking about the half-life of active elements—there are sometimes phenomena in politics we can think about in the same way. We can sometimes learn to estimate when they will no longer be active, and thus even in their time of strength to measure their rate of extinction.

6. *What is the traditional factor in the Convention?* The instinct to preserve is so profound in Europe that for all its apparent variety, it can have a unifying function—for it enables us to maintain in our consciousness a true sense of the past. Our European mind is in some ways constructed like our churches—which even in their architectural maintenance, expansion and modernity often keep their Norman crypt or Gothic arches. When we insist on preserving that which can hand a meaning forward to us from the past, we are also taking care to construct a common denominator for the present which is all the stronger. Our monuments and memories, our curiosities and customs, our communal heirlooms and happily inconsistent inheritances, all have value. And the same in politics: the *Cultural* and *Educational* Conventions of the Council of Europe do in fact reflect the old traditions of an earlier Europe when barriers had not yet been devised, and when freedom of communication within an expansive and rapidly growing European culture was taken for granted. The very new is often merely the very old come into its own again: our respect for the traditional is often a shrewd defence against seeking to impose solutions that are too facile on situations which under the surface are deeply complex, and this in ways we may not realise, and for reasons of the past. There are such immense gulfs and contrasts hidden deep within our European consciousness that we must be perpetually careful, perpetually sensitive over what we do—and a respect for tradition encourages this care, sharpens this sensitivity. Our city-dweller thinks he is the pinnacle of his time, our country-dweller feels he is the foundation of his time: both are merely part of their time, each sees and knows things the other does not and preservation of things past, of methods long known, of attitudes whose roots within us run deep and subtle—this very preservation can create a permanent bridge of common meaning between all of us.

7. *What is the catalytic factor in the Convention?* The art of catalysis lies in studying thoroughly all the existing elements in a mixture and then adding just that little extra something which supplies what the existing elements need in order to change into a new form. So often in politics we are tempted to seek to solve big problems with big answers, and thus do not see the tiny catalyst lying right before our eyes. It is so small we think it must be insignificant. Thus we have here to look at each Convention and for a

moment close our minds completely to its apparent size. We must ask simply whether it might or might not release change quite out of proportion to its own size as soon as it begins to work within the fermenting yeast mixture of what we see as the contemporary process of European unification. The Convention may be tiny—but match it with the immense political and human permutations of our time, and we may suddenly perceive it has a catalytic factor within it. As soon as we realise this, our own estimate of the value of that Convention must itself change.

A striking example of a catalytic effect is given us in a different connection by Professor Arnold J. Zurcher in his book *The Struggle to unite Europe*. Here the catalyst is merely the founding of a school. But to Professor Zurcher its effect is sufficiently impressive for him to make it the concluding page of his entire book. He says:

'What the future holds for the European Movement has never been expressed more appropriately than in the inscription that appears on the cornerstone of the building in Luxembourg that houses a European secondary school. This school was established for the children of officials of the Schuman Community…the Latin inscription of the cornerstone inscription reads as follows: "*The young pupils educated in contact with each other, freed from their earliest years from the prejudices which divide one nation from another, and introduced to the value and beauty of different cultures, will have a growing sense of their common solidarity. Retaining their pride in, and love for, their own countries, they will become Europeans in spirit, ready to complete and consolidate the work that their fathers have undertaken for the advance of a united and prosperous Europe*".'

8. *What is the inter-reactive factor in the Convention?* All the Conventions are, of course, meticulously designed to interact constructively with each other, and also with situations already existing elsewhere within the context of the European Idea. We are here dealing with what we can call the dovetailing problem—and in particular with the dovetailing between the Conventions themselves. Thus every Convention at the moment of its creation must dovetail with all existing Conventions—this at least in the negative sense that it does not run counter to them. As soon as it is created, its existence then automatically poses the same problem for all subsequent Conventions. And it is one thing to write a Convention when there are only three or four others with which it must be co-ordinated—another when there are already more than sixty, and their number increasing every year.

As we have seen, a great strength of each Convention is that it exists in an exact written legal form. It is thus possible to consider exactly—and to the last dot and comma and nuance of translation—what legal ground the Convention covers, and what its possible effects may be. The full inter-reactive effects of a Convention can become very complex—as we saw with the Establishment Convention and the European Economic Community, but the aspect not often emphasised is that some Conventions are designed to have an inter-reactive effect with events that have *not yet taken place*—but may take place, and which the existence of one or more Conventions may indeed help to bring about. As the legal influences of the Conventions extend, so their inter-reactive effects must become increasingly complex—and it is at the legal level we can see this most quickly and clearly.

A quite unpredicted inter-reactive effect between two Conventions occurred with pirate radio stations. Under the terms of the Convention on common national legislation against these stations, the British Government passed the necessary law against them—whereupon the *Guardian* of 17 August 1967, reported the following:

'Radio Caroline International is to take its case against the British Government to the European Commission for Human Rights and possibly to the United Nations,' said Mr Ronan O'Rahilly, founder of the station...'The poet and writer, Ronald Duncan, is writing a poem to be broadcast over Caroline...the poem will deal with individual freedoms and Duncan is signing a contract for sixpence allowing Caroline to broadcast the poem. After the first prosecution by the Government under the new act an appeal will be made to the Human Rights Commission.'

Thus the consequences of British application of one Convention did provoke the threat of immediate reference back to Strasbourg under the terms of another Convention, also ratified by Britain. This bizarre example, is of course, one that caught the public attention—but there are in fact inter-reactive effects quietly arising out of all the Conventions all the time, and their cumulative effect should not be under-estimated.

9. *What is the evolutionary factor in the Convention?* The word 'evolution' summons up associations with Darwin and the survival of the fittest—and is in politics very necessary to enunciate clearly lest it be confused with that other word—revolution.

The European Idea, when fully achieved and perpetuated, will itself be the accomplishment of a revolutionary idea but by evolutionary processes. By evolution we mean here the continuing development of the inherent dynamic of the European Idea, and its gradual unfolding into action. In this sense every Convention of the Council is part of this evolution—but some Conventions demonstrate its unfolding more harmoniously than others, and some have greater effect than others in furthering its future unfolding. If revolution is the correction of past failure, evolution is the avoidance of future failure.

When we consider the lessons of Darwinian evolution, it is of course irresistible to consider also the lesson of the dinosaurs—some of whom were the most heavily armoured and terrifying creatures ever to shake the earth with their tread, and yet died because when the climate changed they could not change with the climate. Our European dinosaurs of today are those who adhere to nationally limited concepts of responsibility—and the climate is changing. Thus today the idea that existing frameworks of sovereignty are adequate for future survival is not only wrong, but morally irresponsible—for this idea weakens our power to survive as peoples, regions, countries, *and* as Europe.

10. *What is the revolutionary factor in the Convention?* While the dramatic quality of revolution is in what we see destroyed (streets burn, houses tumble, chains of office are torn link from link, and sometimes men limb from limb) the essential quality of revolution is in what it enables to begin, and that takes a long time to see. The dynamic of a revolution springs from the simple fact that it is not usually possible to create without destroying, or when destruction is successfully avoided, without change. The sweetest revolutions are invisible.

Nevertheless, there can be hidden lessons even in the more rawly melodramatic, as we can hear from the *Memoirs* of Cardinal de Retz, written around 1660:

'The Swiss seemed as it were crushed under the weight of their chains, when three of their powerful cantons revolted and formed themselves into a league. The Dutch thought of nothing but an entire subjection to the tyrant Duke of Alva, when the Prince of Orange, by the peculiar destiny of great geniuses, who see further into the future than all the world besides, conceived a plan and restored their liberty. The reason of all this is plain: that which causes a supineness in suffering States is the duration of the evil, which inclines the sufferers to believe it will never have an end: as soon as they have hopes of getting out of it, which never fails when the evil has arrived at a certain pitch, they are so surprised, so glad, and so transported, that they run all of a sudden into the other extreme, and are so far from thinking revolutions impossible that they suppose them easy, and such a disposition alone is sometimes able to bring them about; witness that late revolution in France. Who could have imagined three months before the critical period of our disorders that such a revolution could have happened in a kingdom where all the branches of the Royal Family were strictly united, where the Court was a slave to the Prime Minister, where the capital city and all the provinces were in subjection to him, where the armies were victorious, and where the corporations and societies seemed to have no power?—whoever, I say, had said this would have been thought a madman, not only in the judgement of the vulgar, but in the opinion of a D'Estrees or a Senneterre.'

And on this same passage, Saint-Beuve in his *Causeries de lundi* two centuries later had this to say:

'The vague humours of public discontent are very quick, in hours of crises, to be caught by emulation, letting the example of a neighbour decide them, and taking the particular form of malady that reigns and circulates. Retz understands and makes us understand all that admirably. Do not suppose that he understands seditions and riots only; he comprehends and divines revolutions. He describes as an observer gifted with an exquisite sensitiveness of tact, their period of oncoming, so brusque sometimes, so unforeseen, and yet so long in preparation. I know no finer page of history than that in which he paints the sudden passage from the discouragement and supineness of minds, making them believe that present evils can never end, to the contrary extreme where, far from considering revolutions impossible, they then think them, in a moment, simple and easy.'

We should, however, also look at the less dramatic side of revolution, when new harvests rise where earlier nothing was ever planted or when the unfruitful ceases by a quiet withering, for all genuine novelty, all true innovation is revolution. When we consider the revolutionary factor in the Conventions it is *this* for which we are looking—those aspects of the Conventions that are revolutionary in the sense that they originate processes which are not completions along old lines, but beginnings along new.

11. *What is the disaster factor in the Convention?* The disaster most to be feared would be anything that undermined fundamental principle in such a way as to sap the future, and so contribute to an eventual cave-in. Even if principle is preserved, is there anything in the Conventions that could, in any imaginable future circumstances, shock, disrupt, or dismay? Where in the Convention are the necessary safety-mechanisms, the necessary safety-valves that will lessen pressure before it can explode?

What, for example, could happen if a trans-European strike by transport or shipping or aviation workers invokes the provisions of the European Social Charter—not just in theory, but on a massive scale and as a deliberate test-case of principle?

What could happen if a judgement of the European Court of Human Rights is in diametrical conflict with the policy a Government must pursue if it is to survive, and if nearly equal political forces thus find themselves ranged on opposite sides of the question whether the ruling of the Court shall be respected?

What, for example, could happen if the need of the Council of Europe —indeed the duty—to extend co-operation, and communication to the countries of Eastern Europe—or to Portugal or Spain—leads to results that in time prove so successful they appear to justify equivocation on the principles of conscience enshrined in the first Convention of all—the Council's own founding Statute? Is there not therefore a disaster factor in the Statute itself, in that by defining ideological standards clearly it invites them to be challenged directly, and that the consequences of their being challenged successfully could be disastrous?

The greater the radius of action, the greater the circumference of risk, and the swiftest invitation to disaster is a refusal to admit it is possible, and the safest insurance against disaster is to foresee it.

12. *What is the integration factor in the Convention?* To what extent does the Convention counter-balance the sad fragmentation of our times? The answer to this question will in fact summarise our answers to all the preceding questions—and also to as many other questions as we may like to ask, for this list of twelve questions is in no way complete, and is merely suggestive. And if we ask the character, nature and real strength—both obvious and hidden—of the integration-factor, we shall find the real answer will extend beyond the realm of politics, or of so-called public affairs, or indeed any objective and limited field, discipline or activity. *The New Frontier in Europe is not in politics at all, it is deep within ourselves as individuals.*

The whole process of European unification serves no lasting purpose if it does not unify our subjective attitudes as much as our objective. In easy times emotions may be ignored, in difficult times not. 'It is pleasant to observe' said Thomas Paine in his *Common Sense* of 1776, 'by what regular gradations we surmount the force of local prejudices, as we enlarge our acquaintance with the world. A man born in any town in England divided into parishes, will naturally associate most with his fellow parishioners (because their interests in many cases will be common) and distinguish him by the name of *neighbour;* if he meet him but a few miles from home, he drops the narrow idea of a street, and salutes him by the name of *towns-man;* if he travel out of the county and meet him in any other, he forgets the minor divisions of street and town, and calls him *countryman*,...but if in their foreign excursions they should associate in France, or any other part of Europe, their local remembrance would be enlarged into that of *Englishman.* And by a just parity of reasoning, all Europeans meeting in America, or any other quarter of the globe, are *countrymen;* for England, Holland, Germany, or Sweden, when compared with the whole, stand in the same places on the larger scale, which the divisions of street, town, and county do on the smaller one.'

Our citizen of Novara, with his own inborn sense of the city as micro-cosm might well be the first to feel this to be very true, and understand it. As always, the real question is that of relative attitudes—and most of all those attitudes least often expressed. The integration-factor in any Convention must therefore be measured—and this quite deliberately—as much by subjective as by objective values, and not by either alone—for that way lies danger—but by both equally, and in *balance.*

To sum up, the purpose of these twelve questions is merely to suggest some possible lines of thinking whenever we try to estimate the real value of any Convention of the Council of Europe. There are Conventions to which some of the questions are not relevant. There are Conventions to which they are all relevant—so relevant, indeed, that we then face the necessity of reconciling the possibly contradictory or complex answers that these questions may provoke. If a Convention has, for example, a marked catalytic-factor, but also a marked disaster-factor, then it is a matter for individual judgement how in fact we decide to value that Convention. And the commentary here given under each question is designed not to provide ready-made judgements on the Conventions at all, but to clarify the question itself.

These questions can equally be applied to all the Conventions seen as an ensemble, to every separate aspect of the European Idea, and to the entire European Idea itself.

Nevertheless, it is also true that the weakness of these questions is that the more they are applied, the more they can result in our thinking becoming ever more and more complex. Something more is needed, something arising out of these questions, but intended to simplify rather than complicate. Let us merely ask: is the importance and value of each Convention to be judged as Primary, Secondary, or Tertiary?

This question implies a judgement of relative dynamic value—of movement in *relation* to other events on the move. If we ask this question

G

we find we are forced to a bold step, for we are forced to place the Conventions in an order of value. This has never yet been done—least of all officially—but it should be attempted, and a suggested order of value, arising out of consideration of the twelve questions already given, could be added to the list of Conventions in the Appendix. This division of the Conventions into three groups—Primary, Secondary and Tertiary- is entirely personal, arbitrary, and open to criticism. It could be expanded —to five groups, or seven—the method here described is again no more than suggestive. It does, however, grow directly out of the questions we have been asking, for it is certain that regardless of difficulty there must be some method, and some form of systematic and also *final* questioning, and some determination to arrive at a system of values and say so—we scarcely do justice to the Conventions or indeed any other aspect of the European Idea if we attempt anything less.

In explanation of this system of grouping, one point should be made. The Conventions do not and cannot exist in isolation. It will thus be more helpful if we adopt the attitude that even in politics all things are interdependent, inter-connected—that the utterly big does connect with the utterly small and the utterly small with the utterly big. The Conventions are intricately connected with the web of European life—because they are themselves strands of that web they are in turn directly linked to other strands. It is thus not possible to test the tautness or strength or resilience or elasticity of any one strand without thereby becoming aware of very many other strands also. And though the connecting strands may be spun so thin we notice them only when sunlight glances on them—or perhaps even only if they should suddenly snap asunder—nevertheless they are there, all around us and working through us and all the time, and when any one strand is touched, other strands must vibrate. Though the vibration may be so big we feel the shaking, it can also be so small we deny it is there. Sometimes it can take time for the effect to travel to us, and we can fall asleep even though already it is on its way. And just as the value of any strand in the web must change because of the changing value of others, so the dynamic rating of any Convention of the Council of Europe must also change—however imperceptibly—because of all else that is simultaneously changing not only in Europe, but also around the globe. And just as a web is usually made of both radiating and concentric strands, so we may find it helpful to remember that while the Council of Europe forms an outer circle in the web—ringing together as it does eighteen countries already, so also is the European Community a circle in the web, though smaller, closer to the centre, thicker and tougher, and at present tightly limited to its six countries.

Our *Tertiary Conventions* must therefore be those we consider to be the least energetic, the slowest and least forceful. This sounds as if every Convention here considered Tertiary is thereby damned. Not so at all. For these groupings are relative, and a Convention already exerting effect that must command our respect can nevertheless be Tertiary in relation to other Conventions. And nearly every Convention is at some time on the move upwards or downwards from one rating to another, and just as there can be Primary Conventions slowing down to Secondary, so there are Tertiary Conventions which are today only in the waiting stage and may tomorrow accelerate swiftly straight up to Primary. Yet there is a cruelty in politics by which action not seen to be immediately and dramatically successful is immediately dismissed as failure, and we must guard against this in looking at the Tertiary Conventions. Most of them would be classed as Tertiary because while their action is effective, their function may still be strictly limited, or because they are still held back from moving up to Secondary or Primary because of delay in Ratification or application; or because though they have been ratified and applied their action has nevertheless to some extent been impeded—or indeed, simply because their time has not yet come.

An intriguing example of a Convention that must still be classed as Tertiary, is the *Convention on European Companies* which arose out of the difficulties in creating the *Convention on Establishment*, was in turn itself extremely difficult to create, was finally opened for signature in January 1966, yet has been ratified by remarkably few countries. It is not yet on the move, therefore it is Tertiary—but if the right things begin to happen both in Strasbourg and elsewhere, it will in time certainly move up to Secondary, and possibly—again depending on the entire evolution of European politics, industry, technology and commerce—right up to Primary, and this overnight.

Our *Secondary Conventions* are those with sufficient Ratifications to be in application, and whose effects are sufficiently advanced to have acquired momentum, to be already visibly on the move. Because of this we usually find that we are now dealing with larger, more formidable frames of action. They may be Secondary because already they clearly affect principle and are already clearly contributing directly towards a 'community of law' or, and this is equally important, because in their application they are beginning to affect directly an increasing number of people in an increasing number of countries. Yet they must be distinguished from the Primary Conventions by the extent to which they are nevertheless still clearly limited in their effect—or because even when not so limited, they have not acquired sufficient momentum to make their full potential active.

An example of a Convention that *used* to be Secondary is the *European Social Charter*. From the moment it was open for signature it could scarcely have been classed as less than Secondary and yet nearly five years passed before the necessary five Ratifications were achieved to enable it to come into operation. During all that time it was exerting real, but secondary, effect by the mere fact that it was widely known to exist—yet it was not until the fifth Ratification by the Federal Republic of Germany that it did—and overnight—come into its own as Primary.

Our *Primary Conventions* are rare—far fewer in number than the Secondary. They would be classed as Primary in the sense that they are in themselves prime movers—which is to say, that as a moving force they contain within themselves the source of sufficient continuous further energy not merely to keep themselves moving, but also to exercise continuous effect outwards on people and events.

The founding Statute of the Council of Europe is in this sense Primary. This may come as a shock to the critics of the Statute, who tend to see its imperfections so clearly they are sometimes reluctant to admit its real potential. This quickness to condemn arises from a fundamental difference in attitude to the dynamics not merely of politics, but of the European Idea itself. It is not entirely just to deny the worth of a prime mover merely because of the undisputed fact it is not a *perfect* prime mover. Even if we accept at once every sound criticism that has ever been made of the Statute—and that includes the criticisms in earlier chapters of this book—nevertheless it is possible to say that the Council of Europe has been a moving force in the politics of European unification for fully two decades, that during all this time it has supplied its energy from within itself, and that it has all the time continuously exercised influence outwards. Every action of the Council of Europe derives its motor energy from the permissive and regulatory and self-perpetuating characteristics of the Statute—and it is, therefore, whichever way we look at it, Primary.

A second example is the *Social Charter*, but *after* its entry into force. Its function is potentially very wide, its momentum since its first entry into force is now real—but its undeniable claim to a Primary rating is that it includes within itself the provision that each signatory country may exercise a right of supervision and enquiry into the social policy and standards of other signatory countries. This alone—influential as it may become through its extension as a principle into many other processes of European unification as well—is sufficient to make the Social Charter rank, despite its many admitted inadequacies, as Primary.

A third example, is of course, the *Convention on Human Rights and Fundamental Freedoms*. No one who walks past the Council of Europe in

Strasbourg to its recently completed building of the *Palais des Droits de l'Homme* can deny that a document which can result in this first building of its kind in the world, is a prime mover. The Convention on Human Rights has already drawn to itself its own Secretariat, administration, bibliography, appointed Judges and practising Court. Most important of all, it exercises definite and continuously increasing influence on men's minds throughout Europe on the highest question of all, the great and central issue coming steadily closer to us year by year—that of the moral imperatives that must eventually achieve lasting and indestructible expression through the writing of a Constitution for a United Europe: which, if so expressed, will become not merely the pride of Europe—but an example to the world. A Convention which can do this is not merely Primary, but irresistibly Primary.

A fourth example—and this may come as a surprise—is the *Convention on the Punishment of Road Traffic Offences*. Its subject matter is at a superficial glance almost unimportant—and yet its method is the tiny tip of a wedge very big, now strategically tapped into the jamb of a door also very big. For the Convention establishes the principle that it is possible for any one signatory Government to require another signatory Government to prosecute and sentence one of the latter's citizens for a road traffic offence committed on the territory of the former. The extension of this principle to other crimes also, and therefore to other fields of law, is being pressed forward within the Council of Europe's Committee on Crime Problems— the wedge is thus being hammered a little further home each year. This Convention thus not merely serves the individual directly, but also the entire cause of European unification and a Convention thus already exercising influence in this way at *both* ends of the spectrum of society, must be admitted to be already Primary.

To ask no more than whether each Convention is Primary, Secondary or Tertiary is itself no more than suggestive. The method is no more than a deliberate over-simplification, for many other questions are always involved. But just as no prime mover in politics is ever perfect, so also no decision in politics ever achieves real success except by way of over-simplification at the very end of the argument—for the human mind is so organised that we can transmute the inexplicably and overwhelmingly complex conjunctions of all our levels of consciousness into action *only* by working from thoughts that are recognised to be over-simplifications. Our worlds within worlds are so complex that we must always be amazed by the fact that we do always *act* from thoughts that are so simple. Sometimes the paradox seems alarming—yet simultaneously we know it must always be so.

Thus our citizen of Novara, as he looks at the Conventions of the Council of Europe displayed in their glass show-cases in Strasbourg—or as reported in the daily newspapers—may on the one hand understand exactly how in our present time we tend to regard them, and yet on the other hand remain puzzled in many ways—and still wondering when he is going to get an honest answer to the simple question of whether or not there is behind them a plot. He may well be able to classify and categorise with the best of us: he may well understand what we mean when we say that the Conventions as an *ensemble* are already directly touching issues that can one day become living issues; that the Convention on Human Rights touches the issue of human dignity, rights, responsibilities and duties versus human tyranny; that the Establishment Convention touches the issue of individual status within the social organism; that the Convention on the Peaceful Settlement of Disputes attempts to cure a cancer of our times before it can anywhere become malignant; that the Convention on Patents touches the issue of what is to happen to those future prime movers—new ideas—which will determine the evolution of our technology; that the Social Charter touches the issue of our attitudes to the trans-European existence, application and defence of working standards. He may agree at once that every one of these Conventions is an example of what we can call Ideals-In-Action, that every one of them demonstrably springs from a plain awareness of duty—and a dual duty, to the present and equally to the future. He might even approve the words of Churchill, who said: 'The destiny of mankind is not decided by material computation. When great causes are on the move in the world, stirring all men's souls, drawing them from their firesides, casting aside comfort, wealth and the pursuit of happiness in response to impulses at once awe-striking and irresistible, we learn that we are spirits, not animals, and that something is going on in space and time, and beyond space and time, which, whether we like it or not, spells Duty.'

Let us merely add what must already be apparent to our citizen—that part at least of the plot behind the Conventions of the Council of Europe is that by encouraging a multiplicity of actions all tending towards legal harmonisation in a very large number of nation-states, it is thereby forcing into both public and official awareness the increasing necessity of a *paramount legal structure*—if for no other reason than to re-introduce order into a situation being deliberately made ever more complex by the Conventions themselves. Every one of the Conventions increases the solemn obligations of Governments to act according to an agreed, unified, yet still evolving structure of legal thinking—the more the complexity of these obligations increases the more the necessity of their logical consequences and remedy becomes both apparent and acceptable, and in the end, by one way or another, that community of law which must in time grow to become the backbone of a truly unified Europe will in fact come into being. The plot is subtle, its scale epic—and its aim what we must admit to be the primary necessity of our time. The Conventions of the Council of Europe are as an ensemble now sufficiently numerous, and have acquired sufficient momentum, for them to withstand the attack of even the most able opponents of a European Community of Law. In this and other ways they do contain already a deeper wisdom than it is yet fashionable to realise, and of which we would do well to be aware if we do not wish to encounter the future blindly.

Yet even with this much said, it does remain true that the thinking and strategy behind the Convention is a process still to evolve in many ways. Let us therefore conclude this chapter by emphasising two possible aspects of its future evolution.

Firstly, it has been true of every Convention up to the present time that it has been required to command the assent of every member-country of the Council of Europe before it could be even opened for signature to those countries already interested. It is possible that the European Idea would be more effectively and swiftly served if it became possible for the Council of Europe to make Conventions in the greater freedom that would result if this insistence on the right of one country to veto seventeen others could be lifted. As we saw earlier in this chapter, it is still necessary to gain unanimous Governmental approval within the Council of Europe's Committee of Ministers before even the Partial Agreement Procedure can be used at all. In other words, a veto can still be used on the question whether the power of veto shall be lifted on any particular Convention, and there is considerable opinion today advocating that this work could be accelerated and improved if the process of Convention-making could be amicably reformed to permit the existence of Conventions—as a matter of course—commanding at the first no more than a majority assent among Governments. This is to say that action should be taken to apply some more flexible method (doubtless modelled along the lines of the present Partial Procedure method) to the making of every Convention —automatically, and as of right.

Secondly, it is possible that both public and official attitudes to the Conventions would be at once clarified and strengthened throughout Western Europe—from Iceland to Italy, from France to Norway—if the doctrine implicit in them were repeatedly and officially made available in an agreed Declaration, approved by Governments, and originating from the Council of Europe itself. An expanded, helpful, official statement of the philosophy

188 Done this day

guiding the Conventions, the principles they seek to further, the aims they seek to realise, and the methods they are now evolving, would not only be an immense achievement, but also by its mere creation become a new prime mover in the process of European unification.

This combination of greater flexibility in how the Conventions are made, with a sharper and more authoritative definition of what is being done, will doubtless be very difficult to achieve—but often in politics it is the mood in men's minds that gives meaning to the matter, and perhaps here the swing and ring of Schiller's *Song of the Bell* is not inappropriate to what we may hope to see in the Conventions of the Council of Europe and their moulding. Here is Longfellow's translation:

> Fastened deep in firmest earth
>   Stands the mould of well burnt clay.
> Now we'll give the bell its birth;
>   Quick, my friends, no more delay...
> To the work we now prepare
>   A serious thought is surely due;
> And cheerfully the toil we'll share,
>   If cheerful words be mingled too,
> Then let us still with care observe
>   What from our strength, yet weakness, springs;
> For he respect can ne'er deserve
>   Who hands alone to labour brings...

The European Idea is today a great bell ringing but it is *not* yet 'stirring all men's souls'. It could in time become a ship's bell: the image is irresistible and we need this reminder as a call to duty—for it is necessary it should be made to swing and ring ever louder until a most stubborn obstinacy will be needed for anyone to turn a deaf ear and deny that it rings. 'To the work we now prepare a serious thought is surely due'— and most of all when we have a European ship of state yet to build. A ship that is not seaworthy cannot sail through storms.

CHAPTER SIX

'Look At The Map'

'If you want to know the future of Europe, look at the map.'

GIUSEPPE MAZZINI

THE EUROPEAN IDEA contains two fundamentally different quantities—for geography is a constant, people always a variable. In the last chapter we looked at some of the constant and variable quantities in all the Conventions of the Council of Europe—here we shall look at their frame, the unchanging map of Europe herself. And as we look at it, we may well ask: why, when so much today is changing all around us so fast, should something that is in essentials unchanging be able to tell us of our future?

If we look at the map from a long way away, all we see is an island-fringed promontory to the north-west of the Afro-Asian land-mass. If we look more closely, we see a complex but fundamentally unchanging system of mountain-chains, river-networks, farming-land and forest-land and city-land—a system of plateaux and plains, semi-tropical sea-coast and Alpine heights, estuaries, harbours, inlets, fjords, hamlets, villages, little towns, big towns and smoking areas of giant metropolis. We are looking at a region of the world where more than three hundred million of its most creative, intelligent and experienced people live, a region which when united has the possibility to make itself one great power, a region therefore of gigantic opportunity and potential, and yet also a region inescapably influenced by its geography, climate and resources.

This is the map of Europe as it really is, the Europe we experience or see if we travel through it or fly overhead. We are not looking at the

G*

outmoded stereotype map we inherit from the nineteenth century—
where Europe is a cardboard outline, cross-hatched with crazy-paving
lines in black, each enclosing a proudly separate nation-state. That sort of
map makes little sense today. Yet we are used to it because as children we
were brought up to be used to it, and today we still tend to hold up the
same style of map to our own children—which is a visitation of the sins of
the fathers for which succeeding generations will scarcely bless us.

Here is a story from our own time, around 1960. It comes from the
wheatlands of the Danube, not far from the steel-yards of Linz, not far
from where the Alps loom silently above the southern horizon, their peaks
even in summer capped with snow and flashing under the sun as if they
were the polished helmets of sentinels. It comes from near the same Andau
made famous by James A. Michener in his book *The Bridge at Andau*,
written at that earlier time when Andau was a crossing-point for thousands
of dispirited refugees, fleeing for their lives from a Hungary in flames to an
Austria offering at least blankets, safety and food. Yet this story, though
it comes from a region quivering with memory of war, is of peace. For if
around 1960 anyone had walked along a certain rutted cart-track road
that leads towards the barbed wire and minefields of the Austro-Hungarian
frontier, and had paused at a certain obscure village—just a line of rough
houses clinging to the road in the midst of an enormous flat plain of grain
rippling to the horizon—scarcely even houses, in fact, just tumble-down
farmers' cottages strung along that raggle-taggle road—if they had gone
into one of those cottages set aside as a school-house, paused in the door,
looked down at the tiny desks and benches and up and out through the
windows at the wheatfields beyond, they would have seen something at
exactly eye-level, and nailed firmly to the wall between the two windows
—a large piece of white paper, and on it two signs roughly drawn by hand,
yet carefully. One would have been the *twelve golden stars in a circle on a
blue ground of the Council of Europe*, the second would have been the *large
white capital letter E on a green ground of the European Movement*. It is quite
possible they are still nailed there today. It is possible they were nailed up
then because the school teacher had no money for even an ordinary
map of Europe. What is certain is that today a schoolful of young Austro-
Hungarians are growing up and into the world aware from their most
vividly impressionable youth that there exists a Council of Europe, and
a European Movement—and therefore a European Idea. Somewhere is a
teacher who can be truly proud. The story is so simple, its meaning is
so clear.

The map published with this book is merely one example of the way
cartography is responding to the needs of the European Idea. It was

drawn specially by the Secretary General of the *Conférence des Régions de l'Europe de Nord-Ouest*, Dr I. B. F. Kormoss of the College of Europe in Bruges, himself also a Hungarian refugee and today a notable pioneer in new and revolutionary cartographic methods.

If we use this map as an immediate example for testing Mazzini's dictum, we can see already various ways of looking at the map. We can break our accustomed stereotypes by tilting the map, or even by deliberately looking at it upside down—not just briefly but until our eye is accustomed to this new view, and so begins to see new meanings. For whichever way we turn our map its geography cannot change, while our vision can. Whichever way we look at this map of the European Idea, we may find it more suggestive than maps drawn to older fashions. This particular map derives its character from two heart-shaped circles— the inner circle representing the European Community, and the outer circle representing not merely the Council of Europe area, but something more important. For it is drawn in a bold and freehand way, and it uses the blue and gold of the Council of Europe flag to indicate that this is the general area of *influence* of the unified Greater Europe we seek to build. The outer and more vivid circle thus relates to the future more than the present: it represents the *aim* that guides the European Idea, it is the form our ideal must some day assume if it is to become a real and moving magnetic force in the world.

When we look at these two heart-shaped circles together, they also suggest that progress towards the unification of Europe during this decade depends on consolidating and extending the inner circle, while also combining it with the outer circle—which is in fact only a little in advance of what is already the present area of interest of the Council of Europe. This would bring us to a Europe both geographically and humanly harmonious in construction, and potentially capable of enduring for centuries. And if we take this process yet further forward, and en- visage all Eastern Europe as part of this greater circle, we find ourselves beginning to see the future form of a yet larger circle of magnetic in- fluence—an influence extending not only deep into Russia but also rimming the entire Mediterranean coast and extending into the Middle East, from Gibraltar to Suez and the Dardanelles. Areas not even on this map will then become of increasing and immediate importance to all Europeans—as, for example, that area centred on the Atlas mountains: Morocco, Tunisia, Algeria and the Sahara. Perhaps the day will even come when we can ring with a single peaceful circle what is today no more than a struggling hope—the entire 'fertile crescent' which the geography of Israel, Jordan, Lebanon and Iraq suggests is possible—that area where today oil flows either abundantly or not at all, where blood flows often, and water still too often in a trickle lost in sand.

It is here worth remembering that both the Mahgreb countries and Israel have been careful to conclude agreements with the European Community, and that Israel in addition attaches considerable importance to her connection with the Council of Europe. This connection has been nursed most astutely for a number of years. Israel is thus at present still the only country always to send a delegation of observers to the Sessions of the Consultative Assembly—has adhered to several of the Council of Europe's Conventions, and participated in several of the Council's inter-governmental expert committees. It is no secret at all that, considering herself an essentially European state, Israel would consider it logical if ways were found not only to allow her to adhere to Conventions, but to become a full Member State of the Council of Europe, thereby not merely enjoying the privileges and advantages this would bring, but also accepting the duties and obligations. It is equally no secret that when the Lebanon attempted to emulate Israel and send a delegation to the Assembly under the same conditions as those already enjoyed by Israel, a decision was politely evaded.

If we take our map, and project it against the whole world, and if we draw all Europe as one strong circle, and North America as another, then we find we have two circles balanced in counterpoise. These two circles— whether seen as two wheels in tandem, or as some Americans prefer, the two ends of a dumb-bell which can be lifted by a harmoniously agreed political will—are going to be a dominant factor; and while the future of what today we call the Atlantic Alliance and the free western world may now be preserved from year to year by America, it can tomorrow be certain of a continuing and sure existence *only if also permanently guaranteed by a United Europe.* Those Europeans among us who are tempted to rely first on America, and to place America always first in their thinking, can never reach any sound basis for action. Yet the key to the preservation of the Western world is right here in our own house.

At the same time, as Mazzini suggested, the one fact we cannot deny is the geography of Europe. Let us admit our present limitations: we may be able now to tunnel under the English Channel or Mont Blanc, but we cannot yet drain the Baltic, inundate or even irrigate the Sahara, raise or lower the level of the Mediterranean. We are still circumscribed by the facts of geography—and though this in time will change, and with it our thinking, this is unlikely for decades, and even the year 2,000 may see us only beginning. Yet all modern maps show us already a different face of Europe, and what they give is a visual knowledge of the networks of cause and effect that exist now. This knowledge is fundamental to the question of political communication and understanding in Europe today.

We can, for example, take a map emphasising clearly all the railways and waterways of Europe. Or a map of all major industrial regions coloured to show distribution of man-power by activities. How many of us—above all, how many of our younger people whom this will come to concern most of all—have ever studied such a map and considered its implications? Or a map showing simply the distribution of people throughout Europe—where in fact we all live. This comes as a surprise when visually plotted in colour—for the belt of densest population is very definite, and runs in a broad curve, starting in the British Midlands, following the Rhine, and reaching to the north Italian plain. If we are concerned most with where most people live, this is our Europe. Or we may study climate and farming and seek the granaries of Europe— which are around the Wash in Britain, across the Pas-de-Calais in France, and include even the rice crops of the north-west Adriatic in Italy. All are equally real, and can represent our Europe. Rice or railways? Wheat or waterways? All these are Europe.

Or perhaps we are more conscious of cities. If we take the widest possible view, then our cities in terms of people, and starting with the largest, are London, Moscow, Paris, Leningrad, Greater Berlin, Madrid, Rome, Budapest, Hamburg, Athens, Vienna, Milan, Barcelona, Lisbon, Bucharest, Kiev, Istanbul, Munich, Warsaw, Naples, Birmingham, Brussels, Turin, Glasgow and Prague. These are cities with a population of over a million—though Copenhagen and Amsterdam come close, and we should perhaps also include the Manchester agglomeration, which equals Rome with over two million.

If we care not about cities, but rather about technology and science, then we can look at the map of electrical grids, and superimpose on it all nuclear power-stations, both built and planned, and with them centres for mining uranium deposits, refining ore and creating fuel elements, centres dealing with heavy water, treatment of irradiated fuel and above all, nuclear research itself. This is the Europe of Calder Hall and Dungeness, Delft and Karlsruhe, La Rochelle and Garigliano.

Or we may prefer a map coloured simply to show who speaks which language where, or a map showing regions and local communities. This is more directly political—for now we see a Europe where the Rhine, for example, runs through North Brabant, Zelderland, North Rhine, Westphalia, Baden-Wurtemburg, Alsace...Or perhaps we prefer another

Europe—that of Liège, Luxembourg, Pas-de-Calais, Lorraine, Saar, Niedersachsen, Ruhr, Milan, Newcastle...our Europe of coal-fields and heavy industry, capable already of surpassing both Russia and the United States.

Even if we restrict our view merely to our accustomed map of nation-states, there are new ways of looking at that. Let us tilt it so that east is at the top and look with fresh eyes at Europe. What we see is a solid double cube formed by France and Germany, balanced on one side by Britain and Ireland, and on the other by Italy—with Scandinavia in a new visual relationship to the whole, and right under our eyes, in the foreground of our vision—Portugal and Spain. We have so many possible views of Europe. They can all be drawn on maps. And if we want to know the future of Europe...

Let us now look at the innermost of our two heart-shaped circles— the European Community or Common Market. And let us do so at a very carefully chosen level of reality—that of the Commission of the Community expressing itself to the public, and not only its own public but that of the greater Europe as well, and indeed the world. We shall take the apparently routine handbook published officially by the Commission in 1964, and distributed to the public from all its Information Offices—and see precisely what the Commission has to say, and how much of this continues to be true today in spite of our contemporary turmoil, uncertainty and political convulsions. As we do so, we should, however, keep two points in mind:

1. As we look at this handbook, let us remember that this economic stage in European integration is no more than a stage and will be super-seded by others which may be very different. In Chapter Two we looked at the origins of the Coal and Steel Community, and at the motives and methods of Jean Monnet—and we must here again stress what it is fashionable to forget—that the Coal and Steel Community was the first and decisive proving ground of what could be done in this way, and how. The Common Market is no more than the child of the Coal and Steel Community—and if the European Defence and Political Communities had not miscarried, things would today be very different. Those feder-alists of the school of Altiero Spinelli, who hoped so hard for popular rather than institutional federalism, were not completely wrong to describe the Common Market as 'an accident'. They were even right in the sense that a slight change of circumstances could have created a situation in which we would now be primarily concerned with Europe's

Community command of nuclear strike-capacity and the place of con-
scription in European life—or with the evolution and manoeuvring of
newly-born trans-European party-political groupings—instead of, as
we now are, with the political consequences of economics.

2. We can make little sense of this handbook if we do not face the
truth of what this is all about, which it never says in so many words.
If we wish to face the naked realities of power then it can only help to
have the central question clearly stated, and that by an unquestioned
authority—for one of the most relentlessly truthful statements of our
European predicament on the public record comes, typically, from
John F. Kennedy, to whom Theodore Sorenson attributes this:

> 'There is no "Europe". I understand their objection to my speaking
> for them on nuclear matters, but who's to be my opposite number?
> I can't share this decision with a whole lot of differently motivated and
> differently responsible people. What one man is it to be shared
> with—De Gaulle, Adenauer, Macmillan? None of them can speak
> for Europe.'

True of defence earlier, this is true of other matters also today—and is
fundamental to any critical view of the European Idea as today evolving.
For it is merely another proof that no one will listen to Europe—and
indeed no one *should* listen to Europe—until Europe decides to speak
with a single voice.

This handbook of 1964 appears deliberate and skilled propaganda for a
purpose, and invites judgement on the spirit and ethos it expresses. Its
first words are: 'The Common Market is now a reality. It has made its
impact on everyone who lives in it...' That, we can probably agree at
once, is in a certain sense nearly true—we have only to read the newspapers in Rome, Brussels, the Hague, Luxembourg, Paris or Bonn to
see the reality of the impact. It is here listed as having effect on:

> '...the man-in-the-street and the housewife; when they buy a refrigera-
> tor or a washing machine, they can choose from a large number of
> models from all the Community countries; on the manufacturer, who
> must plan his production in terms of a market of 175 million con-
> sumers; on the statesman, who on a growing number of subjects can
> only take political decisions in agreement with his opposite numbers
> in the other Community countries.
> 'The Common Market already has a history. Through its economic,
> psychological and political effects it has, in a short space of time,

appreciably altered not only the material world in which Europeans
live, but also their ways of thought.

'A glance at this history makes it easier to understand the sense of
adventure which has gripped the old countries of Europe—and also
to see just *how much has still to be done* before Europe is finally united...'

The glance at this history follows—a Commission glance. The war
ends—Europe, 'cradle of modern civilisation', is divided and in ruins—
one part 'liberated', the other 'enslaved'. The two world wars have been
caused by 'aggressive, extremist nationalism' and there are two questions:
economic ('how can the material destruction of the war be repaired, and
the wheels of industry made to hum busily again?') and political ('how
can Europe be given new political strength and stability, and the self-
respect and confidence which will prevent the re-emergence of aggressive
nationalism? How can old hatreds be eliminated and the long conflict
between France and Germany ended?')

With 1946 the word 'idea' appears—'Winston Churchill undertakes
his United Europe campaign in Western Europe. In a celebrated speech
at Zurich, he declares: "We must build a kind of United States of
Europe." The idea is launched. These words will soon become the
slogan of a new, peaceful revolution.'

In 1947 the word 'sovereignty' appears, in an account of the Marshall
Plan, the Organisation for European Economic Co-operation, and the
European Payments Union. 'These bodies', says the handbook, 'cannot
do more than their objectives permit; and their objectives are strictly
limited to economic recovery. The member countries retain full sovereignty and any one of them can veto new proposals. Nothing has so far
been done to meet the second, political desire—the desire for stability
and self-respect.'

On the next page of the handbook is a photograph—Churchill in a
bow-tie and spectacles, speaking in Brussels in 1949, appearing somehow
puzzled, ponderous, and pertinaciously seeking the final word all at the
same time, and with both those curiously sensitive hands spread out low
over his papers, which we cannot see. On his left is Paul-Henri Spaak,
on his right Guy Mollet—and in the background those impassive im-
personal masks of faces to be seen in every political photograph, and
here enlivened only by a lady wearing that great rarity—a hat that is
both political and feminine. It is a powerful photograph, combining
purposes and personalities into good visual propaganda.

The text below the photograph slips back to the previous year of 1948
and the Congress of the Hague, where we are told 'Europe's political

leaders advocate the establishment of a European Parliament. They hope that this body will be able to bring about the political unification of Europe.'

So far all appears happy, and there is an impression of inevitability that can comfort us if it continues over the pages covering the next few years. It does not. The next paragraph tells us of 1949:

'The Council of Europe is set up at Strasbourg. Although it serves as a forum of opinion for Western Europe's parliamentarians, the Council does not live up to its founders' hopes—it cannot bring about political unity in Europe. The reason for this is simple; the governments have given it wide terms of reference, but no real powers. In practice, almost all the efforts which the Council's Consultative Assembly makes in the cause of European integration founder on the procedural rules of its Ministerial Committee. This body can only take decisions unanimously—i.e. it is subject to the veto—and its meetings degenerate rapidly into brief, infrequent and inconclusive diplomatic conferences.'

It should be remembered that this was the Commission view in 1964— but while we must deplore this sad factionalism between those really on the same side of the barricades, we also have to note there is no other mention of the Council of Europe throughout the rest of this handbook— or of the European Movement—or of the European Free Trade Association. Brevity means omissions, certainly. Intensity of concentration can even be measured by the always equal intensity of its refusal to look outside its circle of concentration—yet we are here concerned as much with *failures* of communication within the European Idea as with successes and we should note that while the handbook continues to communicate firmly, it does so only on its own wavelength.

'Drawing the lesson from this failure', it continues, 'a few far-sighted European politicians launch a revolutionary scheme based on a principle which is entirely new to international agreements: the transfer to a *common organisation of real powers over a limited field.*'

This wording is very close to that quoted in Chapter Two—the federalist formula first evolved in the Pension Eliza in Strasbourg by M de Felice, so perhaps the sad factionalism just mentioned is only on the surface. Or perhaps not. For next in the Commission handbook comes the description of Robert Schuman's Declaration of 9 May, 1950— printed under the heading 'Point of Departure', and facing a pomp-and-circumstance photograph of the Declaration being made in the Salon de l'Horloge of the Quai d'Orsay. The pomp is provided by the Salon—

Schuman stands speaking with Monnet sitting on his right hand, in front
of an immense marble and chandeliered background, complete with
sporting cupids and a semi-gowned and triumphant female figure, and
this all in the grand, the balanced harmony of the Second Empire. The
circumstance is provided by the Declaration—and the two together, as
action within the frame of history, are Europe indeed.

'The Declaration's aims are two-fold', says the Commission handbook
(after swiftly hailing Walter Lippman's words that they are 'the most
audacious and constructive since the end of the war'—and a 'blueprint
for the future integration of Europe'). These aims are, first, to reconcile
France and Germany, and second 'the setting up of a European federation
—a United States of Europe'. Here we have it at last, in official black and
white, and not in an esoteric text for the initiated only, but in a clear
statement to the entire European public—from this moment on no one
can doubt that the Commission's real and avowed aim is exactly what it
says it is—a European *federation*.

Now let us see how the Community describes its method, which is:

'1. To begin by creating *de facto* solidarity between Europeans through
concrete achievements, rather than by attempting to unite Europe in
one move; 2. To lay the foundations of economic unification in Europe
by pooling basic products—coal and steel; 3. To set up for this purpose
a High Authority which would be independent of Governments, but
whose decisions would be binding on them. The Schuman Declaration
represents a realistic approach to the problems of uniting Europe,
and it remains today the charter of European integration. It is the first
real signpost to the contributions an organised living Europe can
make to civilisation; to the abolition of hunger and poverty, to the
fostering of economic strength in the under-developed parts of the
world, and to peace…'

What says the handbook of the British response to these possibilities?
Without mentioning at all that the hardness and vision of the Commission's determination is the direct result of British weakness of determination and lack of vision, it merely records the British Government
of the time in its own damning words as being '…reluctantly…unable
to accept…a commitment to pool resources and set up an authority with
certain sovereign powers as a prior condition to joining talks…'—and
says no more.

On the next page of the Community handbook, under the heading
'The first steps: a Coal-Steel Community', appears immediately and
uncompromisingly the key word—'*federal*':

'The Six...solemnly declare themselves "resolved to substitute for historic rivalries a fusion of their essential interests; to establish, by creating an economic community, the foundation of a wider and deeper community among peoples long divided by bloody conflicts; and to lay the bases of institutions capable of giving direction to their future common destiny." By ratifying this Treaty, the Parliaments of the six countries set up the first European organisation with federal characteristics. Previous international organisations were composed of member countries' representatives, and their decisions were the results of fragile compromises between national interests. For the first time, the Coal and Steel Community sets up a common European Authority, to which member Governments transfer part of their sovereign powers, and whose members carry out their tasks, in full independence, for the general good of the Community as a whole. This Authority, the "High Authority", is subject to democratic control, through an Assembly composed of representatives from the six national Parliaments, and to the rule of law, through the judicial control of a Court of Justice.'

After then relating the success of the Monnet Community, the hopes that a Defence Community would also lead to a Political Community and the smashing of these hopes—the handbook then accounts for the creation of the European Economic Community as follows:

'...Following this spectacular failure of the second stage in European integration, it seems to many as if the grand design underlying the Schuman Plan is buried for ever. But the Coal-Steel Community continues its successful course, and the rejection of EDC merely alters the direction of the drive towards European unity. Its new direction is the natural outcome of the successful experiment in economic integration—in a limited but crucial sector—represented by the Coal-Steel Community. The European Idea is re-launched. The field of European integration widens. Two sets of reasons lie behind the new moves: Europeans are becoming more and more aware of changing world conditions, and are discovering the real significance of their struggle towards unity. The weakness of the old powers, as their colonial empires gradually dissolve, contrasts glaringly with the growth of two continental giants whose agreement or lack of agreement largely determines the fate of the world. Western Europe is still dependent on American support for her defence, as she was earlier for economic stability. It is becoming clearer than ever that a nation's influence is based on its economic strength, on its rate of technical

progress, and on the stimulus of a large home market. The Six Governments, meeting at Messina on 1 June, reflect this increasing awareness
when they decide to continue the development of a united Europe
"in order to maintain Europe's place in the world, to restore her
influence and prestige, and to ensure a continuous rise in the living
standards of her people." ECSC has rapidly achieved three of its main
aims: full Franco-German reconciliation, a smooth-running institutional
structure and *de facto* solidarity through the merging of basic interests.
The inherent logic of the venture begun in 1950 requires the extension
to the whole economy of methods similar to those tried and tested in
the ECSC. At Messina the Ministers of the Six instruct a committee
of experts, under the chairmanship of Belgian Foreign Minister Paul-
Henri Spaak, to examine the possibilities of general economic union,
and joint development of the peaceful uses of atomic energy. The
Six are poised for another step towards unification.

'1956. When the Foreign Ministers of the Six meet again in Venice
at the end of May, they decide to go ahead with negotiations on the
basis of the Spaak Committee's report. They aim at drafting two treaties
which will set up:

1. *A European Economic Community* (Common Market) to bring into
being a vast single market for all goods, with a wide measure of
common economic policies, which would constitute a powerful production unit and generate steady expansion, greater stability, and a
more rapid rise in living standards.

2. *A European Atomic Energy Community* (Euratom) to further the use of
nuclear energy in Europe for peaceful purposes and to ensure that
Europe does not lag behind in the coming atomic revolution...on
25 March, 1957, in Rome, the Ministers of the Six sign the Treaties
setting up the Common Market and Euratom. Both Treaties are
ratified before the year's end by the Parliaments of all the six member
countries, with even greater majorities than the Treaty which set up
the ECSC.

'The six countries then decide to apply to the whole of their economies the principles which have been proved in ECSC. They agree to
the gradual merging of their six separate markets into a single area of
common economic policy with the same characteristics as an individual
national market, throughout which men, goods and capital will be
able to move freely.

'While the sceptics continue to voice their disbelief, Europe thus takes
a giant step towards the unity which will provide a powerful stimulus
to her economy and help restore her national stability and influence...'

So far, so good. But remembering that this is selective propaganda, let us see whether this propaganda does or does not avoid the heart of the matter. It is worth noticing that this handbook has so far not only been written in the present tense to convey immediacy, but now accelerates into the future tense:

'How will the Common Market be established? By a double process which reflects the two essential aspects of the European Community of today.

'A customs union will be set up to remove the obstacles hindering the free movement not only of goods, but also of people, firms, services and capital. The customs union will also harmonise the conditions under which imports from the rest of the world enter the new unit—in other words, it will institute a common tariff at the Community's external frontier.

'This merging of separate national markets into a large, single market cannot be achieved in one move without economic strain. The authors of the Treaty propose therefore that it should be done gradually over a transition period, tentatively scheduled to end in 1970.

'A common economic policy must be applied in all six countries. As every Government in our age exercises considerable control over its country's economy, the Six recognise that the Common Market would have little chance of success if each of them remained free to apply divergent economic policies. The Treaty therefore specifies that the Common Market must harmonise national economic policies and apply common policies for the whole of the Community, particularly in the spheres of agriculture, competition, transport, and trade with the rest of the world.

'To achieve these aims, *the authors of the Treaty use an institutional structure which is basically federal in pattern.* They take over, with slight differences, the ECSC system; an Executive which will be independent of Governments and private interests and which, by stimulating and initiating common action, will be the Community's main driving force; a Council of Ministers, composed of representatives of the Governments, which will decide proposals put forward by the Commission—increasingly, as time passes, by majority rather than unanimous votes; a European Parliament exercising democratic control over the Executive; and a Court of Justice to ensure the rule of law.

'1958: The institutions of the new Communities begin their work. They are located, provisionally, in Brussels...'

We must recognise that the propaganda quoted here from the Brussels

Commission handbook does approach the heart of the matter, and is truthful. 'The institutional structure' of the Community is described as 'basically federal in character'—certainly that is propaganda, and equally certainly it is the plain truth.

What Edgar Allan Poe said of literature is also true of politics, that its makers '...would positively shudder at letting the public take a peep behind the scenes, at the elaborate and vacillating crudities of thought—at the true purposes seized only at the last moment—at the innumerable glimpses of ideas that arrived not at the maturity of full view—at the fully matured fancies discarded in despair as unmanageable—at the cautious selections and rejections—at the painful erasures and inter-polations—in a word, at the wheels and pinions—the tackle for scene-shifting—the step-ladders and demon-traps—the cock's feathers, the red paint, and the black patches...'

The handbook can scarcely take us behind all the scenes, but some at least it does indicate. Flanking the pages already quoted are deliberately chosen photographs of its New Style Europe—of men 'who were instrumental in making European unity a corner-stone of their countries' policies...former German Chancellor Konrad Adenauer...the late Alcide de Gasperi, Italian Prime Minister almost continuously from late 1945 until August 1953.' We see Jean Monnet pulling the lever to cast 'the first European pig-iron' at the Belval works in the Grand Duchy of Luxem-bourg—followed by another photograph of Paul-Henri Spaak—and then of 'the representatives of the Six at Messina'—Johan W. Beyen, Gaetano Martino, Joseph Bech, Antoine Pinay, Walter Hallstein—and yet again, Paul-Henri Spaak. Their nationality is no longer felt to be their *primary* characteristic and is ostentatiously not included—which is, after all, now no more than European good manners. And there follows another photograph, this time of Hallstein alone, as 'Common Market Commission President'.

Next we see the signing of the Common Market and Euratom Treaties at Rome on 25 March 1957—an immense long straight table, with the signatories sitting very upright for the photographers—microphones in front of them, and behind them a triple row of aides, and behind their aides a tall wall covered with gigantic pictures. Edgar Allan Poe would perhaps have appreciated the fact that we cannot make out what the pictures are—they might be oil-paintings, they might be tapestries—we cannot quite tell, and it does not matter, for they represent those scenes of yesterday always present behind our scenes of today.

On the next page of the handbook come photographs of Robert Marjolin and Sicco Mansholt, Common Market Vice-Presidents, and we might suppose by now the essential points have all been made. Not at all. For next comes the central double page of the handbook, opening out wide before our eyes in colours both vivid and careful. It is the master illustration of the handbook: it is, of course, a single carefully chosen map.

The Europe here chosen to convey the Commission's interpretation of Community feeling is the Europe of Regions. It is already a map of more than the present Community, a map of the wider Europe of our not-too-distant future—indeed, nearly the same Europe as that of the Council of Europe. If we start in Wales, we can cross this map through the Midlands, London and Southeast England, over the Channel to the Pas-de-Calais, Champagne and Lorraine, over the Rhine in Alsace, to Baden-Wurtemburg, the Alps and Bayern and Tirol, to Slovenija, Hrvatska, Bosnia, Hercegovina. Every name is now scrupulously printed in its own mother-tongue. Or, if we like, we can start in Aragon, cross the Pyrenees to the Midi, Auvergne, the Rhone Alps, Franche Comté, Alsace, Baden-Wurtemburg, Hessen, Erfurt, Halle, Berlin. Every region is accorded as much respect as every other: seen together as an *ensemble* they suggest an irresistibly greater whole.

Inset are two smaller maps. One shows a Europe coloured with broad curving currents of pink, green, yellow, orange-brown—the Europe of climate and crops. Vineyards, Olives, Potatoes, says the legend, Oceanic climate, Semi-Continental, Mediterranean, Steppe, Alpine—and carefully drawn across them are the July Isotherm of + 20 degrees and the January Isotherm of + 10 degrees. The second shows the yet greater Europe. The Community of today is coloured white: everywhere else a neutral distinguishing yellow, reaching out from Ireland to Turkey, from Atlantic to Black Sea, from Norway to North Africa, and suggesting a Europe now over three thousand kilometres from south to north, three thousand kilometres from west to east.

With this firmly in our mind's eye, the text and photographs thereafter become immediately contemporary. On the next page is a photograph of a lorrydriver, and a benevolent policeman in front of a lifted barrier-pole opening the way across a frontier. 'The customs union is well under way,' says the handbook, 'and the removal of trade barriers is proving far easier than originally expected...' Next comes a conference-room photograph, with long straight tables set now in a complete square, many flags grouped on standards behind the chairs, and the caption: *Partnership with Africa.* One of the meetings in Brussels between representatives of the six Community countries and 18 independent African countries which led up to the signature of the new Association Convention in July, 1963. And on the next page—against text headed '*The balance-sheet to date*', a picture of a lady, her high heels poised squarely on a chess-board pattern of tiles, her skirt-line just below the knee in the fashion of the early 1960's, on her elbow a super-market basket, and behind her a man in white collar and striped tie directing her eye upwards to the topmost shelf. We cannot see what is on that shelf; the photograph might be of anywhere in Europe. The lady and the man both have individual personality—but the super-market is standardised, and in its quiet way the illustration is a commentary on the fact that no sooner does real standardisation become possible than it must—if Europe is to become really Europe—be deliberately counter-balanced by individual diversity; whether of regions, as already suggested in the map, or by people, as in the photograph.

The next photograph is of coalminers' flats built with Community money at Heemskirk in Dutch Limburg—five-storey apartment blocks, with a church tower just beyond, and in the foreground a Volkswagen and other cars, shining, highly polished. Next is a photograph of Dino Del Bo—President of what is still somehow the Coal and Steel Community 'High' Authority. Over the page is a large photograph of a white-coated scientist juggling what appears to be a rubber-tubed retort at the Euratom Joint Research Centre's Laboratory in Ispra, Italy. Underneath, much smaller, is a photograph of 'Euratom Commission President Pierre Chatenet.' And next comes a half-page diagram: 'The Community Institutions up to the end of 1964'.

This shows the three Communities of Coal and Steel, Atomic Energy, and Economic, as they were before their recent fusion into one Com-munity. The diagram combines three elements—at the top, circles representing the Commissions of the organisations, with round them individually drawn figures of their members, each individually sworn to act in the interests of the Community as a whole, and not—explicitly *not*—under governmental instructions or influence. Below them comes a single square conference table with six figures round it, representing the six Governments. And below these Ministers comes a double and exactly balanced drawing, showing on the one hand the Hemicycle of the European Parliament of the Six (which holds its Sessions in the Hemicycle of the Council of Europe in Strasbourg) with the legend 'DEMOCRATIC CONTROL'—and on the other hand, the legend 'JUDICIAL CON-TROL' and a drawing of eight judges in hats. Each judge is holding up a hand, and above them are exactly balanced scales of justice. The female figure of justice is not blindfold, and it is hard to know whether the central upright of the scales is or is not intended to represent the unsheathed sword of justice. This is carefully ambiguous, surely with intent, and is no more than exact as a representation of the evolution of the European Idea in our time, as seen through the eyes of the Commission in Brussels.

Meanwhile, the text of the handbook has been marching, with a steady left-right, left-right of facts, facts, facts:

'1959, January, sees the beginning of the irreversible process which is to lead to complete abolition of trade barriers between the Six…the the first cuts—of 10 per cent in internal customs duties…the Common Market Commission also prepares a whole series of steps to align the rules of competition…and drafts its first proposals for common economic policies, particularly in the realm of agriculture…1960: the Community economy moves into top gear…industrial expansion expands by a record 13 per cent; the Community's balance-of-payments position rapidly improves; trade between Community countries has increased by nearly 50 per cent in two years. In France…the spectacular financial recovery is consolidated. The Six decide to speed up the development of the Common Market…internal customs duties on industrial products will be reduced by 60 per cent by 1963 instead of by 40 per cent…The first stage towards bringing national tariffs on imports from non-member countries into line with the common external tariff is taken one year ahead of the timetable laid down in the Rome Treaty.

'1961…the Community moves into a more difficult phase, in which its main task is to work out common policies and put them into force. The first detailed anti-trust regulations come into force…External affairs loom larger in the Community's activity…an Association Agreement with Greece…*Great Britain decides to apply for membership…Denmark, Ireland and Norway also apply…Austria, Sweden and Switzerland apply for association.*

'1962: The Common Market enters Stage Two…Community affairs take on an increasingly political character as common policies start to take shape. January sees the painful but triumphant birth of the common agricultural policy…the Community's relations with the United States move increasingly into the forefront. In September Congress gives the US Administration sweeping new powers to expand trade…President Kennedy proposes that his Trade Expansion Program should be the start of an Atlantic "partnership of equals" between the US and the growing union emerging in Western Europe.

'1963: Foreign affairs and the Community's political future again dominate the scene. *The negotiations with Great Britain are abruptly suspended in January following a veto by France. The crisis which this provokes among the Six eases only gradually under the pressure of the work still to be done*, and in particular, the need to respond to the important US initiatives of 1962...Turkey becomes associated with the Community...The Community signs its first trade agreement—with Iran—and negotiates with Israel. It re-establishes contact with Britain through Western European Union (WEU) and has talks with Denmark, Ireland, Nigeria and East African Commonwealth countries. The common agricultural policy takes a giant stride towards completion, bringing 86 per cent of total Community farm output within its jursidiction...Partnership with Africa is brought on to a completely different plane. In July the six Community countries and 18 independent African states sign a new association convention on a basis of complete equality and freedom.

'1964: The Common Market has passed the half-way mark in its transition period; it is beyond the point of no return. In April, the Ministers of the Six take a series of steps which form the first act of Community economic policy; they agree on a Community policy to halt inflation; they adopt measures to co-ordinate "medium-term economic policy"; they decide to strengthen the structure of their monetary and financial co-operation; and they at last make a move towards a common energy policy. The Six have entered the stage of economic union...a broad decision is taken to merge first the three Community Executives...and the three Communities themselves... *Direct election of the European Parliament and extension of its powers continue under discussion...*'

This is the voice of the Commission speaking directly to the public. Its method is a clear repetition of aim, plus a relentless accumulation of facts. Criticise as we may, the facts presented are indisputably facts, and the aim is clear—'a system of government'.

Where, however, do these words stand in print in this handbook? They have not yet been quoted, for they appear on the very last page, in a statement of aim headed '*A federation in the making*', and concluding significantly with the word 'confidence'. Let us look very carefully at this page, *ex cathedra* as it is:

'The success of the Common Market, the deepening community of interests between its member countries, the spirit of cooperation proved by many sacrifices, and the need to ensure that Europe becomes capable of playing the role of a strong partner to the United States in

President Kennedy's vision of an Atlantic partnership—all these are pushing the Six beyond the stage of economic integration towards union in other fields, notably diplomacy, defence and cultural affairs,

'The Six took a first tentative step in this direction on 1 July, 1961. when they solemnly reaffirmed in Bonn their determination to set up a political union and to give it a statutory form.

'In practice, however, European political unification has already begun. In the first place, the real point of impact of Community action is...the economic policies and legislation of the six countries. The Community is therefore already a political union, limited to the fields of economic and social policy. Secondly, the Community is a political entity through its institutions, which are not only already taking political decisions, but which are also organised in such a way as to form the basis for a *system of government*. This constitutional mechanism is still imperfect and incomplete, but it is *federal in form;* the joint Community interest is effectively represented, alongside the interests of each member country, by the three Community Executives, and it will be strengthened when the three Communities become one, administered by a single Executive. The Member States are represented in the Council of Ministers; the Community Court of Justice represents the rule of law; and the European Parliament represents democratic control, which will be reinforced if current proposals for direct election of the members and extension of its powers are adopted.

'*The European Community is a federation in the making;* if the move towards European unification has shown remarkable resilience, it is because it is in line not only with the main trends of historical development, but also with the needs and aspirations of the European today and tomorrow.

'The people of Europe are now taking part in a historical process whose aims and main lines of development were defined fourteen years ago. The achievements of their past, their present vigour and adaptability, and the inescapable needs of the future all point towards the full democratic union, in free and equal partnership with America and the rest of the world, which alone can bring them security and confidence.'

And there it stands in black and white—in words mentioned once only in this official Commission message to the public—'*A system of government*'. And it is the *real* issue, courageously and plainly stated, the deep, powerful and irreversible issue that will continue to live and reverberate throughout our time and after.

This issue of 'a system of government' is nevertheless even today not always acknowledged. Its supporters still avoid its bald statement, while its opponents rightly attack their avoidance. Relevant to the consequences either way is a story being told—perhaps apocryphal—of a French Minister in the Cabinet of President de Gaulle talking to Professor Hallstein, then President of the Common Market Commission. 'You fool', said de Gaulle's Minister to Hallstein, 'do you not realise that for years we have succeeded at great cost in keeping hidden from him the real meaning of what you are doing in Brussels, your methods, your aims? His eyes were on other things, we kept them there, and he did not believe that what you are creating in Brussels is real. Then you began to speak out. You began to explain, defend, attack. De Gaulle heard you. We could no longer prevent him looking behind the scenes. When he discovered that what you are doing is real, and what you say you do also mean, he realised he had no time to lose if he was still to stop this thing—or at least slow it down, deprive it of initiative. So now we have had the Community crisis, and this increasing confrontation between Gaullist principles and Community principles. If only you had said nothing the old man would have done nothing—you fool!'

This Community crisis was not mentioned in the handbook we have quoted, for it happened after 1964—when President de Gaulle, confronted as he was by the timetable of the Community, attempted to paralyse the Community before it moved on to the stage of decision-making by majority vote. He did this by withdrawing the support of France—the 'empty chair' method—and this absence of French representation at all decisive levels of its institutions certainly succeeded in paralysing the Community. Yet he proved unable to destroy it, unable to mould it to his purposes. His minimum aim was achieved—but not his maximum, which was to impose his will on the Community, and on the other five member-Governments. The Community was already too strong, de Gaulle already too late. Nevertheless, the struggle was intense—in essentials it is the same struggle that continues today with an even fiercer intensity. At its beginning it was most easily understood as a conflict between the views of these two men: de Gaulle representing the Gaullist view of a Europe building upon the nation-state, and Professor Hallstein the view of Europe growing as a newly designed Community. The struggle was bitter and dramatic—it culminated in 1966 in both the vindication of Hallstein's view of the Community (as shown, among other events, by the British application to join) and then in 1967 by de Gaulle's revenge in successfully forcing Professor Hallstein's exclusion from the Presidency of the new unified Brussels Commission (which today, under the Presidency of Mr Jean Rey, combines the Common Market, Euratom, and the Coal and Steel Community). Yet in this first crucial struggle—when Europe of the past confronted Europe of the future across Europe of the present—not even the angry trampling of the strongest of our old men was able to destroy what must be seen today as our finest and increasing hope: the genuine purpose of the European Idea. And though Professor Hallstein has disappeared from the Community, his ideas have not.

Could the potential causes of this conflict be deduced from the handbook of the Community as here quoted? Scarcely—for one of its characteristics is its careful avoidance of any power-currents *not* of the Community. The aim of the handbook is to communicate the Community's aim and the facts in support of that aim; it is not an explanation of either tactics or strategy.

This, however, we do have from Professor Hallstein—and we owe it to that very outspokenness of his which caused both his permanent triumph and his temporary fall. Professor Hallstein spoke on 4 December, 1964 at the Royal Institute of International Affairs (Chatham House) in London, giving the Fourteenth Sir Daniel Stevenson Memorial Lecture. His problem is the same as that of the handbook—political communication—but whereas the handbook seeks only to define and inform, Hallstein's method is to seek out and destroy the opposition. He is speaking privately to a selected audience, and yet he is speaking publicly, for his speech—exactly like the handbook—has been widely distributed as a foundation text. It is witty, urbane, penetrating. It is a powerful statement of a powerful case by an utterly committed man and today reads more powerfully than ever.

The very title of his speech is aggressive—'Some of our *faux problèmes.*' And his method is aggressive: Hallstein takes the questions one by one, and deals with them—he is, of course, more often than not directly attacking the Gaullist thesis. He begins by explaining what he means by 'false problems':

'...They are problems in a subjective sense: the questions are asked, and people argue about the answers. But they are "false" in an objective sense: the options offered to us do not really exist, since we do not have to make a choice at all—either because the choice has already been made and is binding, or because the various solutions proposed are in no way exclusive. It is all the more necessary to recognise this now that we no longer have any overt opponents of European unity. There are still opponents, but today they too sail under the

European flag, and they make use of counterfeit problems as one
would use counterfeit money—which is only coined to deceive
people.

'Moreover we have an ample supply of real problems and cannot
afford to misapply our political acumen and political imagination...'

The first false question which Professor Hallstein says that people tend to
ask runs as follows: *is there a hegemony within the Community, or does it
rest upon a balance of power?*

'False', says Professor Hallstein, false, because it springs from nation-
state thinking, from the 'pre-Community stage of European politics.'
Instead of hegemony by one state, or precarious counter-balancing
between many states, there is 'an institutional order which is the expression of a unity designed to last.' The Community cannot be expressed in terms of the old for it is itself new. Its growth takes place by
'the amalgamation of economic and social policies'. It is a system with
'the features of a *federal* constitution; a structure that depends on co-
operation between the higher entity and the constituent states...to put it
briefly; within the Community a problem of foreign policy has given
way to a constitutional problem...'

*Second false question: does the choosing of integration mean relinquishing
'sovereignty'?* This is dismissed by Hallstein as a myth, one of 'those
extinct stars which we see shining long after they have burned out.'
The key definition of the Community view is that it 'respects the sovereignty of the member states. Although the political dynamics of integration may extend further and further into public life, the ultimate aim is
not a unitary state. The constituent states of a European Federation would
be legally sovereign, since a federal system has the advantage of allowing a
division of responsibilities which leaves each member its ultimate sovereign power.'

This, however, is still only the legal aspect—the real argument is that
the sovereignties of still separated European states are all simultaneously
wasting away by reason of their separation. With each year the states
themselves become further devalued—and 'in isolation they are too
weak. None of them can deny that the countries of the free world are
spiritually, economically and militarily interdependent.' The 'pseudo-
sovereignty' of the state is a wasting asset. What is missing, what must
be created, is its opposite—that greater sovereignty that would accrue
to a united Europe by reason of its unification. 'Only by joining in the
unification of Europe will the states again be able to speak with a "sovereign" voice in world politics.'

Third false question: does European integration mean giving up the 'national'
for the 'supra-national'? False, because based on the plausible but erroneous
logic of the French Revolution that *'il n'y a que l'individu et l'etat'*—when
in fact 'most of the states of this world are federal states in which the
citizens are subject to two different states'. Europe must build precisely
upon its own nations and its own people, upon 'France and her Frenchmen...Italy and her Italians'. Hallstein rejects a 'streamlined Europe'—
on the contrary what is needed is to 'keep alive the fruitful diversity of
Europe, which is a source of constant emulation. Respect for the individuality of Europe's peoples is a source of strength and not of weakness
for the Community, *provided that its power to act is preserved.* No one is
asked to disown his country. But this does not exclude the awakening of
a *new European patriotism.* A double allegiance is required of our citizens,
so that the new Europe may be built with the nations for its foundation.
It will not be governed by an international Areopagus, a coterie of men
owing no national allegiance...Let those who consider that the bond
between the Community and the nations is too weak bind it faster;
there are many ways in which the Community can be made more democratic and its Parliament strengthened. Let those who complain of the
Community's lack of authority give it authority in those matters where
the individual states are too weak. Perhaps it is true that only states can
act politically. Then let us create the European state—or is Europe finally
to abdicate?...I should like to recall what Rousseau said about the Abbé
de St Pierre's plan for perpetual peace: "There is considerable difference
between being subject to a neighbour or only to a body of which one
is a member and of which each member in turn becomes head. In the
latter case, the pledges that one gives ensure one's freedom. Entrusted to
an overlord, these pledges would be lost; but in the hands of fellow
members they become stronger".'

Fourth false question: can we not, must we not, make our choice between the
systems of 'federation' and 'confederation'? False, because 'when we look at
the reality of European integration, we see at once that it cannot be
"grasped" in terms of either of these concepts'. And this for the excellent
reason that 'integration' has much in common with the traditional view
both of federation and confederation. It is a process in itself, drawing from
both these two sources. And here we must look very closely at the exact
words chosen by Hallstein, for every nuance has increased meaning today.

'One federal aspect is that member states finally hand over some of
their responsibilities to the Community. In practice this applies...
to the whole of economic policy and to social policy.

'This combination of tasks is accompanied by a corresponding pooling of sovereign powers. From this there is emerging a new economic and social order which has its origins in the Treaty establishing the Community and in the Community's own legislation. This body of law is hardly less extensive than that of the member states in the field affected. Its administrative and jurisdictional implementation is vested partly in the Community institutions but mainly in the organs of the member states. In this the Community's constitution follows the German Federal pattern and not the American (according to which Federal laws can in principle be implemented only by the Federal organs). *Only such a federal conception can reconcile the unity and diversity of the states and nations of Europe, for it alone ensures an adequate concentration of political powers while at the same time respecting—in contrast to the centralised unitary state—the proud and vigorous individuality of the member states.*

'...Integration...is a dynamic concept, that is to say its very implementation constantly creates new reasons for widening the field of integration...The common orientation of the economic and social process also means that the sinews of war must be made a Community matter, and furnishes an important argument in favour of the integration of defence policy. A common commercial policy... suggests a common foreign policy on non-economic matters also... Integration is thus a process and not a static thing, and this process is one that tends towards *complete federation, that is, to the federal state.*

'Of course, a European state does not exist until the final position has been attained—and this is in conformity with our concept of a confederation.

'...there is no hard and fast distinction between federation and confederation that would require us to choose between the two. Perhaps the Swiss were not far wrong when they called their constitution *La Constitution fédérale de la Confédération Helvétique.*'

Fifth false question: must we choose between self-interest or Community interest? False, because 'it is perhaps naïve and unrealistic to imagine that in the decision-making organ of the Community, the Council of Ministers, only the "Community interest" is heeded and particularist interests play no part'. What Hallstein prefers to suggest is that 'European unity is intended to take a federal form, and the interests of the member states are therefore perfectly legitimate. Do not the United States Senate and the German *Bundesrat* often give forceful expression to particularist interests?...If federation is unity in diversity, the Commission represents

the unity and the Council (of Ministers) the diversity. The balancing of
individual interests and Community interests is accomplished by discussion between these institutions, culminating in the meetings of the
Council of Ministers...The Community is all the stronger for serving
particular interests...what the common agricultural policy is to one
country, the common commercial policy is to another. We welcome
the energetic pursuit of such interests where they further the progress
of the Community. The ideal situation is, of course, when all member
states have an interest of their own that coincides with the Community
interest. The most recent example of this is the campaign against inflation.'

*Sixth false question: must we choose between 'economic' and 'political'
unification?* It was, of course, Hallstein himself who had caused uproar
several years earlier by calmly saying of the Community, 'We are not in
business, we are in politics'. Now, with that behind him but another
uproar already around him caused by the Gaullist confrontation with the
Community, he takes the matter further:

'I have no need to repeat what has now become common knowledge:
that what is called economic fusion is in fact a political process, since
the motives for economic integration, the field to which it applies,
the instruments it uses and its repercussions are all essentially political.
Everybody knows that the Community's institutions are not "in
business", that they are neither producers nor dealers, bankers nor
forwarding agents, consumer co-operatives nor trade unions. The
European Economic Community is already an economic and social
union, democratically based and constitutionally secured...The
expression "political union" has, however, a second implication:
the improvement and completion of the Community's federal constitution; and with this is bound up another specious "either...or".
Either, it is said, political union must be implemented at once, and we
must break through to a European federal state, or there can from
now on be no further progress in "economic" integration.

'This contention is the miracle weapon of the opponents of
European integration. It is the easiest thing in the world to claim
that the examples of economic and monetary policy have shown
that economic integration has now developed a so highly political
character that no further progress is possible, even in the economic
field, without completing European federation. And nothing is
easier than to assume an air of special enthusiasm for Europe by
demanding maximum European unification at once. This is an ideal

H

device for justifying an *immobilisme* which, once applied, would destroy not only the unification work accomplished so far, but also all hope of a comprehensive political union...this "all-or-nothing" argument is also specious...The argument "either political unification or no advance in economic integration" is wrong, since it turns political logic upside down. "Politicial" integration is not a condition of economic integration but its consequence.'

We are here listening to what we can term the Community philosophy of *irreversible gradualism*. These two words go far to account for the emotional opposition which the Community method does provoke. Just as the tone of Hallstein's speech reflects that suavity which arouses dissidents to fury, so we can understand how these dissidents feel as they watch the tide of events slowly creeping higher, lapping indeed round the feet of some of the giants of our time. Economic integration within the Community is today already nearly complete, and no matter how fiercely enemies of the Community may rush to construct dykes, at the end of their day one fact will still remain quite unchanged—the consequence of economic integration *is* political integration.

Professor Hallstein now comes to the second part of his speech. He is building up to his conclusion—the *moral* value behind his understanding of the European Idea.

Another false question: should we not look at the problem of European integration as a choice between 'greater' and 'little' Europe?

'...The two Europes are complementary and indeed depend on one another. It was only the success of the Common Market that led to the foundation of the European Free Trade Association of our European neighbours, and finally in the pending General Agreement on Tariffs and Trade negotiations, to new opportunities for the European Economic Community and its European partners to move closer together in economic matters...it would have been a mistake to desist from the highly intensive integration policy of the Six because not all European states were parties to it from the beginning.'

This defence of the Community's limited but hard policy was at the time very necessary. For there was then widespread criticism, motivated by pique in countries outside the Community at the Community's own determination. It was the pique of runners on the starting line of a race who had lacked nerve to start, and deeply resent being shamed by the success of those who did.

'Where then is this larger unit which was supposedly broken up by the integration policy of the Six? If only it existed. The OEEC (and OECD) and the Council of Europe can hardly be what is meant. No: the European Community is the work of the countries which were the first resolutely to turn their backs on a tradition of discord and to place what is common above what divides.'

We can agree that neither the Council of Europe nor the Organisation for Economic Cooperation and Development are as tightly institutionalised structures as the European Community. What is interesting is that, after this mention of the Council of Europe comes immediately the following paragraph, which expresses the voice of the European Idea as seen both from Brussels and Strasbourg, and this in its highest and widest sense.

Hallstein quotes from a resolution of the Europa-Union, (the West German branch of the European Movement) adopted in Frankfurt in 1964: '*Six European states are not the whole of free Europe. Wherever human rights and freedom reach in Europe—up to the Iron Curtain and, once it has been overcome, even beyond it—there unification will be our task, our mandate. At the end of the road stands the whole of Europe united in freedom. The smaller Community is an advance battalion, whose ranks must be open wide to welcome any European state willing to recognise the law of the Community.*' And he then turns to the global scene. *Third force or alliance with America?*—a false question, for it is not a case of 'either-or':

'Europe has no choice, Europe belongs entirely to the free world. Its dialogue with America is of vital significance to the free world. Our objective is therefore to work in partnership with the United States—as President Kennedy was the first to put it—on the basis of complete equality in all tasks for the strengthening and defence of the free nations—partnership means the opposite of a monolithic Atlantic Community in which the European states would play the part of a bridgehead towards the East, as were the Hellenic settlements in Asia Minor...Free Europe must develop its own personality in order to become a partner for America and to serve as magnet for the countries of Eastern Europe.

'Atlantic partnership is no alternative to the unification of Europe, but assumes that such unification has occurred.

'Atlantic partnership is a long-term aim...because of this—we must begin forthwith to approach it step by step. The point, then, is not to lose sight of the basis of partnership, no matter whether we are making commercial policy decisions in the Kennedy Round or

discussing how responsibility for the defence of the free world can be
better distributed.'

This is, oddly enough, closer to the Gaullist view than it seems. Unlike
President de Gaulle, Professor Hallstein was of course under the necessity
of holding American political opinion to its blessing and support of the
Community—an American bi-partisan policy at this time not yet under
severe strain, and to some extent already growing traditional roots in
American politics. Yet there is, even here in Hallstein's careful understatement, a hardness which can only be invigorating for Europe—and
for Americans, just possibly, already a little disconcerting.

And then comes his final statement—in reply to the final false question,
as expressed in that one word which in Europe we know only too well—
Realpolitik:

'To conclude, let me turn to an age-old problem that is always with
us and that I suspect of being also a specious problem. I am referring
to one of the many aspects of the equivocal concept of *Realpolitik*,
which some people take to mean an "amoral" policy. It is no accident
that the question is a favourite one when our relations with totalitarian powers are being discussed. The question leads us into philosophical waters, and I will therefore do no more than state my belief
and make a few suggestions.

'*I do not believe that any policy can be divorced from moral values.*

'Admittedly, men do not agree on what is good and what is evil,
on what is—from this point of view—a right policy and what a
wrong. But that is quite another matter; that is a real problem.

'*Realpolitik* belies its own strongest point—its reference to reality—
if it does not acknowledge at least the subjective reality of the morality
that motivates men's actions. The rightness of the moral judgement is
not at issue here; just as the existence of a lie proves the authority of
the truth (which those guilty of the lie are in fact trying surrep-
titiously to usurp), belief in Good, or even the abuse of this belief,
bears witness to the supremacy of morality.

'Furthermore, I contest whether the politician can even find a firm
footing if he evades the real alternative—good or evil. Where is he
to find the criteria that determine his aims and means of attaining
them? How is he to distinguish between friends and foe? Words like
"task" and "responsibility",...lose all significance if politics is merely
a matter of power. And if it is, then we can abandon all hope of peace;
the most we could count on would be an armistice.

'I believe not only that Europe's cause is strong, but also that it is right.'

Here as an immediate and satirical postscript to this speech is an item from the London *Daily Telegraph* of 30 August 1967, published while Professor Hallstein was still at the head of the Commission of the Economic Community, and which while pointing its humour at de Gaulle, simultaneously underlines the argument running through this entire account of his speech:

Striped Pants for Rome
Murmurs arose among Ministers at the Common Market 'summit' meeting in Rome yesterday when leading members of the Commission trooped from their hotel in full morning dress and decorations.

Last year General de Gaulle sought to enforce the 'striped pants' clause in a list of rules he wished the Commission to follow. This banned ceremonial wear when visitors from foreign Governments arrived at its headquarters.

His idea was to discourage the Commission from behaving as if it were a European Federal Government. But yesterday even the General could not complain. The Commissioners were being received in audience by the Pope.

In America over a century ago the same problems of canals, railways, roads, shipping—of commerce, banking, currency, industry and agriculture—and above all, of the interrelation of geography and people and the evolving patterns of new politics these two together dictate—were all fiercely alive. Then the problem was to maintain a union already achieved and defend it from disintegration. Today in Europe our problem is to achieve a union in such a form that it can thereafter be maintained. The raw materials and issues of politics in the America of the 1860's and in our Europe of today are in many fundamental characteristics closely related, and not least in the scope, nature and difficulty of their problems. We can see this dramatically from a speech in Congress remarkably close to what we are hearing today in our Europe of the Economic Community, of the European Conference of Ministers of Transport, of the lowering of tariff barriers so that refrigerators and nylons may sell more cheaply and further afield—to say no more. It is a rather unfamiliar Abraham Lincoln, speaking in 1848:

'Nothing is so local as not to be of some general benefit. Take, for instance, the Illinois and Michigan canal. Considered apart from its effects, it is perfectly local. Every inch of it is within the state of

Illinois. That canal was first opened for business last April. In a few
days we were all gratified to learn, among other things, that sugar
had been carried from New Orleans through this canal to Buffalo,
in New York...Supposing benefit of the reduction in the cost of
carriage to be shared between seller and buyer, the result is that the
New Orleans merchant sold his sugar a little dearer, and the people
of Buffalo sweetened their coffee a little cheaper than before—a
benefit resulting from the canal, not to Illinois, where the canal is,
but to Louisiana and New York, where it is not.'

And just as Professor Hallstein, discussing the European Economic
Community, found himself logically led to consider the 'sinews of war'
and the 'defence of the free world', so in 1862, discussing exactly the same
canal, Lincoln said:

'...this suggests...the favourable action of Congress upon the projects
now pending...for enlarging the capacities of the great canals in New
York and Illinois, as being of vital and rapidly increasing importance
to the whole nation, and especially to the vast interior region...The
military and commercial importance of enlarging the Illinois and
Michigan canal and improving the Illinois river...I respectfully ask
attention to.'

As for political communication today at the *legal* level, what we hear is
surprising. In Chapter Five our citizen of Novara had his wits and perception exercised merely by regarding the Conventions of the Council of
Europe—here they would be even more exercised, yet in different ways.
For the legal effects of Community law can be easily summarised—
perhaps too easily, for this appearance of order is deceptive. Very briefly,
they include the following:

1. Influence is exercised through international private law—in the sense
it is now becoming increasingly necessary for judges in any one country
of the Community to examine the law of another member country before
giving judgement.

2. Influence is exercised by the increase in the number of cases which
involve nationals of the Member countries of the Six, and which arise
out of the implementation of the Treaty of Rome. Examples are cases
concerning nationality, international contracts affecting employment and
trade, and legal questions arising from differences in law in different
countries concerning companies.

3. Not only will the number of cases increase, but the increasingly
numerous cross references between Community law and national law

must combine to force consideration of the very principles of law in the Member countries of the European Community. Just as with the Conventions of the Council of Europe, so within the Community this ever-increasing network of causes and effects is proliferating to the point where it is not merely a source of potential political crisis, but is by its very complexity and inconsistency forcing attention to that harmonisation of supreme legal principles which alone can restore harmony—and a new harmony, at a new level.

This is the problem. M. Michel Gaudet, then of the Legal Service of the European Executives and Maître des requêtes au Conseil d'Etat de France, spoke recently to the Union Internationale des Magistrats on the theme 'Le Marché Commun devant les Juges'.

> '…The Common Market therefore leads to a call upon comparative law, which in the European Community will become an essential instrument in the search for a coherent legal system. The remedies will be found in the gradual unification of law, which in itself has two classic aspects. One is the harmonisation of legislation…The other is the narrowing of divergences in jurisprudence within the limits that the written law leaves to the discretion of the courts. There is no doubt that judges can exercise a direct or indirect influence on these two processes by which law is unified. In conformity with a long tradition, this influence will make itself felt in favour of clarity and coherence. Nevertheless, the slowness and complications of the traditional methods of unifying law are scarcely compatible with the economic impulse behind the Common Market and the requirements of the time-table fixed for its introduction. The founder states of the European Communities have therefore had the foresight to couple with the measures of economic integration so far adopted a certain degree of legal integration.'

M. Gaudet then defines 'the emergence of Community law' as 'the introduction of common rules which are directly applicable to all Member States on the model of domestic laws, and the institution of a common jurisprudence to watch over their interpretation and application. This ensures both the strict unification of written law, by the application throughout the Community of a single text, and unity of jurisprudence in the application of this text.'

He goes on to point out that Community law is at present manifest in five forms: *Recommendations* and *Opinions*, which are not obligatory—*Regulations*, which must be applied throughout all Member States—*Directives*, which are binding on the Member States as to their aim, but

leave it open to the States to choose their own means of reaching the aim
—and *Decisions*—which may be addressed either direct to Member States
or to individuals. These all derive from the Treaty of Rome (under today's
unified Community, from all three Founding Treaties), and from the
mechanisms set up for their implementation.

The juridical supervision of all is through the Court of Justice of the
European Communities, whose authority is derived from, and limited by,
the Founding Treaties. Legally this is clear, and if Community law were
the only law, it would be indisputably clear at all times. But this is not
so—as M. Gaudet is not alone in pointing out, what matters is that with
every year we have an ever-growing complexity of interaction between
Community law, national domestic law, and all the various evolving
cross-relationships at all levels of law within the Community. This, of
course, includes also the Conventions of the Council of Europe.

M. Gaudet's emphasis is not quite what we might expect: he points not
at the level of law interpreted by the Community judges, but that interpreted by domestic and national judges—for it is here the law is most
uncertain, here that it is most susceptible to interpretation. We are thus
already well into a time in which it is the domestic judges themselves who
need to be the most fully informed on the daily evolution of this new legal
map of Europe—and it is the Community judges themselves who must
watch all the more attentively how this evolution is being shaped not only
by themselves but especially by the domestic and national judges.

If we study very carefully this legal map of Europe of the Six as it is
now shaping before our eyes today, we find we are watching an entirely
new context of legal, political and social communication. Already visible
are two areas where crisis is predictable—but not yet its scale. The first
is the area of legal interaction within the Community of national and
Community *law*. The second is at that mysterious level where law is partly
politics, and politics also partly law—for Community *law* derives from
the Treaties, and the Treaties have *political* intent. As M. Gaudet puts it:

'...by its very object this law is profoundly novel. Community law
serves a venture in economic integration which has no precedent in its
scope and method; it is linked with an institutional structure tran-
scending the traditional categories, transposes into a new framework
concepts borrowed from all branches of law, and presents simultaneously the features of an international convention, an institutional
charter, and a code. It therefore calls for a collective effort of research
and interpretation on the part of every jurist in the Member States,
and more particularly, of the judges.

'As the jurisdiction of the Court of Justice already shows, the final aim of the Treaties establishing the Communities constitutes one of the essential criteria of interpretation in this new field of study and action. This final aim alone will make it possible, in many cases, to guard against hasty and misleading analogies with state-dominated structures or with the rules of domestic systems of economic law designed for other ends.

'The emergence of Community law thus opens a new creative period of law in which the function of the magistrate takes on its highest significance. It is not indeed a question of filling in the lacunae of an incompletely sketched written law, but of contributing to the working out of the *legal rules which a new stage of European civilisation postulates...*'

Are we here in politics or law? It is not easy to say. This was no more than a third routine Community handout for information and publicity to the general public—exactly as were the Community handbook and the speech by Professor Hallstein. Of the three, it is in some ways the furthest reaching—between the lines it is unceasingly concerned with the construction of a rule of law throughout a unified Europe. The challenge is so tremendous that we might suppose that this legal guide to what is being planned in the Community was the product of a giant legal administration in Brussels, calling on the services of national, specialist, and international lawyers—lawyers of every imaginable and necessary speciality and competence. Not at all. This legal map is no more than one single man's determined attempt to communicate directly and regardless of difficulties. As Balzac said, 'difficulties were made to be trampled on'—and M. Gaudet himself makes no bones about it:

'Allow me to conclude on a more personal note, which is intended both as an expression of thanks and as an appeal. The few dozen jurists from all the Member States who make up the Joint Legal Services of the three European Executives are endeavouring to blaze the trail in the still too little explored field of Community law. They know the joys of pioneers, but also their anxieties.

'They welcome with gratitude and a lively feeling of encouragement gestures which...are proof of interest and a promise of aid on the part of the judiciary...in the interests of new dimensions in which we are all engaged...'

Thus when we consider this legal map of the Europe of the Six, and remember the 'few dozen jurists' at present contributing to this map, we

see another of the giant problems increasingly involved in the process of
European unification—that of co-ordinating talent not easily available with
difficulties not easily solved.

This is true of every level of political communication here quoted—and
the quotations given in this chapter have been carefully chosen from
earlier years because this does enable us to see them in better perspective.
The overlapping between the Community and the Council of Europe
has perhaps become clearer—and the federalist impetus of the Community
aims has perhaps now been sufficiently documented to make it indisputable. Nevertheless, these are official quotations—here, as a deliberate
contrast, is an extract from a forthright article by Anthony Hartley in
the London *Daily Telegraph* of 5 May 1967. To what extent does it
confirm the underlying suggestions of this chapter?

'...It is useful to ask what kind of Europe now exists, and how it is likely
to evolve in future...At the end of this year the Six will achieve a total
Customs Union with a common external tariff. By July 1968, their
most important decisions on agricultural policy should have been taken.
The Commission in Brussels is proposing that freedom of movement
of labour should be introduced by the same date...The Six have survived
the 1965 crisis over agriculture and even managed to present a common
front in the Kennedy Round...Now, however, the problem facing
Europeans has begun to change its shape. In future, they will have
to consider, not so much the completion of a programme of economic
integration, as the extension of co-operation to new fields of common
activity; financial and foreign policy, defence and technology. Here the
obstacle will not be France, where President de Gaulle's successors,
intent on enlarging their majority in the National Assembly, will
probably abandon his dislike of European integration...Those Europeans who once worked for the development of the Six into a tightly-
knit political community are faced with the fact that, if Europe wishes
to compete with the two global Powers, it must enlarge its basis...Only
a wider Europe can exert significant political influence. If this lesson is
learned...then it is certain that E.E.C. will be enlarged by the addition
of other countries in the next decade. And it is hard to think that a
successful leap forward of this kind would not bring in its train political,
as well as economic, institutions. Sooner or later peoples accustomed to
Parliamentary Government are bound to demand a direct political
voice to express their approval or criticism of the way in which
European institutions are being run. From the moment that Community
decisions are taken by a majority vote, direct democratic control would

appear essential and inevitable. And it is not easy to see how this could be exercised except through some form of federalism...it should be possible for a wider Europe...to learn from the experience of its Member States...to look for the most efficient type of Civil Service, the most discriminating form of social policy, the most human approach to education and to scientific research. These are quests in which past dogmas will have little part to play. Europe may keep its ideals, but it should not make the mistake of confusing ends with means. The free exchange of national experience, a willingness to learn from others and a heightened tolerance for new ideas are not the least of the benefits that a European federation will confer on its members. Such a federation would also have to decide its policy towards the rest of the world.'

This line of thinking is entirely in harmony with the previous quotations in this chapter, and they in turn are all in harmony with Mazzini—'*If you want to know the future of Europe, look at the map*'. With this as our starting-point, it becomes all the more curious to notice how easily we tend to ignore two very simple, powerful, obvious facts. The first is that all our discussion of the European Idea in terms of the European Community is at this time determined—yet will not always be so determined—by the fact that the Community today still consists of six countries, six very special countries, and six only. This is so obvious it is seldom presented as a phenomenon that must change, and therefore scarcely justifies its present hypnotising power over all our attitudes. For it must be kept relentlessly in mind that our thinking on this entire matter *must change both quantitatively and qualitatively as soon as one or more additional countries enter the Community and accept its obligations of membership.*

President de Gaulle was thus dressing a naked half-truth in over-rich robes when he said in 1963:

'It must be agreed that the entry of first Great Britain then of those other states will entirely change the complexion of adjustments, industrial understandings, checks and balances and rules that have come into operation between the Six, because all these states, like Britain, have very important individual peculiarities. But then, it is a different Common Market which undoubtedly would have to be envisaged. A Common Market on a basis of eleven, then thirteen, then maybe eighteen would unquestionably bear no resemblance to one erected on a basis of six. What is more, a Community committed to expansion in this way would come up against all the problems of its economic relationship with a whole series of other states, and first of all, the United States. It must be presumed that the coherence of all the numerous and very different members of such a construction would not long stand up to the strain, and that in the long run it would take on the semblance of a colossal Atlantic Community, under American direction, and dependent on America, which would make short work of absorbing the European Community.'

It is true we shall have a Community different in the balance and composition of its membership: it should not be—or to be exact, will not be if our political determination can prevent it—a Community different in principle, purpose, or method. It must never be a Community diminished in essentials—it may well be, and this must be our great hope—a Community in essentials always improving.

The second fact to notice is that our thinking today is about a Community where national sovereignties are still being merged only in certain tightly defined sectors, where decision-making is still not yet done by the democratic method of the majority vote, where Parliamentary control still does not exist at the European level, and where legal adjudication and the rule of law is still limited to interpretation of the foundation Treaties.

Thus the Community must inevitably change, and whether it changes by outer enlargement or by inner evolution, with it must change our thinking, information and attitudes. It is a most curious aspect of the Community that while the facts of its daily operation change before our eyes every day, its essentials do not change and are not so easily seen. Thus when the Community does succeed in merging sovereignty in new sectors, or in fully accepting decisions at the top by majority vote, or when effective European Parliamentary control, expression and initiative become part not only of the mechanics of Community politics but of the awareness of the Community's people, then a great deal of our present problems will at once disappear. They will be replaced by others, but these will be new and thus in themselves a proof of evolution. A great deal of our present thinking will become obsolete and even dangerously inadequate. We shall have new questions to think about. We shall need new methods for solving them. And while this will not only be the glorious opportunity of our epoch—an opportunity practical enough to make us both rejoice and roll up our sleeves to get on with it—it will pose also immediate problems of action.

Some forerunners of these problems are already so real and pressing that those among us who do not agree either with the federalist aim, the Community method, or even the moral imperatives implicit in the European Idea, see their reality as a growing threat—and they react accordingly with the power at their disposal. Hence we have the Gaullist counter-attack—of which the various Gaullist-inspired anti-Community crises are but examples, and of which it is safe to say there will be more examples to come, some of them probably yet more dangerous. This is not a counter-attack limited to Government supporters in France, but the attack of a school of thought whose adherents are to be found in many countries, and whose basic attraction is that it appears to justify a plausible postponement of the real questions. These questions are hard: their postponement is naturally attractive.

The First Gaullist premise is that Europe must ultimately learn to stand on her own feet. We should not here be forced by our own instinctive opposition into injustice: better for us to agree at once that so she must. Long years of life-saving transfusions of the American dollar, ever since Europe was saved by the Marshall Plan, and long years of enervating reliance on the American atomic shield, have certainly weakened our habits of will. They have delayed our realisation of the necessity for Europe to gather together that combined strength essential for her to create those new habits of will that can enable her to think alone, act alone, and lead alone. The best thinkers in America have long accepted that the Atlantic Alliance—which means the leadership of the free and democratic world— can be strengthened by a Europe strong, confident and also wise enough to act alone when and if she so wills. This appears a paradox and yet it is a truth, for wisdom and power are left hand and right hand: those who fear the power of a united and independent Europe are sometimes not fearing her power but merely its possible misuse. It is one thing for Americans to welcome the idea of a united and even independent Europe—another for them to contemplate a Europe whose policy in their eyes may become increasingly opposed to American policy. Yet there is no other way. For both sides of the Atlantic it will in the end be safer for Europe to be bold. And from the American point of view there is truth in the German saying: *nichts bindet so als freilassen*—nothing binds so tight as freely releasing the bond. For we all know that the best partner of all is always a partner strong enough to go it alone if necessary, yet cooperative and also wise enough not to wish to do so—thus preferring partnership, but out of free will. Whether this can continue between exact equals is the question we have not yet had to face and is the most difficult question—it may be that when it comes it will prove to be the question on which the real future of the Atlantic Alliance will in fact turn.

The second Gaullist premise is that only national Governments in Europe have the proved power, and only the present nation-state consciousness of our peoples have the proved cohesion, on which to build safely. The

nation-state today cannot reach any wider or higher form of expression—
so runs instinctive Gaullist feeling—and only groups of Governments can
today form an enduring foundation for our future Europe. We have, in
other words, reached the apex already—we can in essentials do no better
now than we have done in the past. These arguments are richly robed
indeed but their colours are the panoply of decadence. They catch the
eye, they comfort with their richness—and yet all in fact they do is clothe
a half-truth, and that feeble, shivering, starved, and without long to live.

For the Gaullist argument would be true if we were not already changing its basis. Much of it will remain true until it has been superseded. The
Community method threatens to supersede it completely, and is already
succeeding partially. The strength of its success is already proved by the
very vigour of the Gaullist attempts to check it.

We thus have today the whole of Western Europe coloured as it were
with three intermingling colours of technical advocacy. First, the *Community* method—demonstrating a method already in progress, aiming at a
Federal Union of Europe, and in practice progressing towards this by
means of a practical compromise between traditional inter-governmental
relations and the simultaneous evolution of its own increasingly supra-
national mechanism. This is not a method aiming at federalism overnight,
or at federalism tomorrow—but it does aim at federalism the day *after*
tomorrow.

Second, we have the Gaullist method—aiming at a partial political
Union by means only, and exclusively, of inter-governmental mechanisms
and at all costs hostile to the creation of any federal structure that might
prove successful in evolving a new, higher, and more effective life of its
own.

Third, we have the *Council of Europe* method—which at first sight can
appear superficially Gaullist, for it works by means of inter-governmental
agreements, but which is itself also committed to an aim which in intent—
though never in official words—is federalist. As we shall see in the next
chapters, the Council of Europe method works by developing a diversity
of tactical methods all designed to further unity wherever possible, and
already extending not merely beyond the present countries of the Community, but in a number of increasingly subtle ways to all the countries of
Europe—and furthermore, is doing all this without prejudice to the present confrontation between Gaullism and the Community.

These three colours of technical argument run today through every
country of Western Europe—they change, merge, mingle, forming inces-
santly varying patterns, and tomorrow there may be new colours. The
fundamental question remains: are we or are we not determined to

create a Federal Government of Europe—yes or no? It should be clear by now that this book, partisan and federalist as it deliberately is, argues that we must say yes—and say yes today—and not merely say yes privately but say yes publicly—and not merely say yes publicly but act on what we say. The decisions coming so swiftly upon us during this next decade are likely to prove critical for all Europe and it would be helpful to agree and know not merely whither we are tending, but where we intend to go.

Even if the construction of Europe proceeds during these critical years by means limited to increasingly close association between independent national governments—*l'Europe des Etats*, Europe of the Fatherlands and nation-states, *Europe of the great half-measures*, even if this should succeed within its narrow limits, this very success must sooner or later bring us face to face with the identical question we already face today: do we or do we not admit the necessity of creating a Federal Government for all Europe and for all time: yes or no, and if yes, then when and how do we intend to do it? We have today, regardless of contemporary difficulties, an opportunity that could be lost until well into the next century or even permanently if we do not now grasp it, rather than fall into the error of postponing it until long after many of our leaders are all safely dead, and have thereby dodged the consequences of their present actions whether bitter or sweet, and with them that sole opportunity that makes our epoch unique. And if this opportunity *is* grasped and a Federal Europe *is* created, it will then of course become nonsense to suggest we shall thereafter make more progress by backsliding into any form of European unification that is less than federal—indeed, it will by then no longer even be possible.

Thus either way it is the federal question we shall eventually have to solve, and the entire Gaullist argument is no more than an attractive and sometimes seductive detour, enabling us to avoid the hard question at the cost of wasted years for hundreds of millions of people. Is this not a heavy price to pay merely for the questionable pleasures of remaining blindfold?

We must furthermore remember that at present all these matters are decided by a limited number of people, some tens of thousands, no more, and most of them concentrated in specialist fields of governmental and integrationist politics only. Our people as a whole have little opportunity to share in the construction of their own future—indeed, the Gaullist argument unashamedly bars this opportunity from them. And yet we are also simultaneously on the verge of moving into a new and better stage, where it will become increasingly possible for all of us to so participate— and gladly—and this perhaps sooner than we may at present think, and yet only if we make it unmistakeably plain it is our will that this *shall* happen. The extent to which this popular will is or is not made clear must affect the public and private lives of all of us.

We have here the components of a great change. These must eventually combine to cause an unprecedented evolution in all our thinking. And when they do, a flash-point of changing opinion will come, and it will come when sufficiently important principles become simultaneously alive as issues in the hearts and minds of a sufficiently important number of individual men and women. Then all may start to change—for the ship-builders will be finishing their work, and decision-making will be coming to be more and more where it ultimately must be—in our own hands, the hands of *all* our people.

The strength of this thriving truth has long been recognised by de Gaulle, though he vainly attempted to starve it into a half-truth when he said as early as 1953: 'As to institutions, I considered the simplest to be the best: a Council of Heads of Governments, a deliberative Assembly, and a referendum organised in every country so as to bring the nation into the process and to furnish as a basis for the confederation the explicit decision of an immense mass of Europeans.'

Our answer is that 'the explicit decision of an immense mass of Europeans' must be something better, and that we insist upon creating a Europe where we, the people, are regularly and unavoidably given power over all events through true, regular, and constitutionally guaranteed elections.

Nevertheless this is still in the future, and the facts today remain—that in the Community we already have an embryonic federal structure but not yet with direct European elections; that in the minds of Gaullists of all nationalities we see a stubborn attempt to avoid the creation of anything new in character—direct European elections most of all; and that in the Council of Europe we have an embryonic attempt to get on nevertheless with everything that can be done right now, and this in a style which by insisting at all times on the direct relationship between man as an *individual* and European society as a *whole* is by constant implication contributing to the eventual manifestation of a genuine European electoral will.

If we now take an opinion-map of Europe we find this all at present expressed by the fact that among many millions of people there is a level of opinion regarding the European Idea that is changing only slowly, and yet has the feeling it would like to change faster. And among some hundreds of thousands of people, perhaps already even millions, there is a perceptibly evolving layer of somewhat puzzled opinion, adjusting as best it can in the light of the information it has to new facts, necessities, problems and hopes. And among some tens of thousands of people, no more, carrying the day-to-day responsibility, there are currents of conflicting arguments, aims and actions.

This understanding of the extent of the conflict and confusion in public opinion today must force us again to face the fundamental question: are we or are we not determined to work unswervingly towards the creation of a Federal Government of Europe? If we can say yes to this, then the entire matter can be expressed in the following chain of propositions: that the European Idea posits a European Federal Government; that a European Federal Government posits an unbroken succession of individual minds carrying all-European responsibility; that these first two propositions both posit European direct democratic elections; that these first three propositions together posit unceasing and increasing support, both popular and governmental, for the maintenance, strengthening and improvement of the Community principle and method; that the Community method and principle must also always be complemented by improved, widening and coherently organised inter-governmental co-operation; that this inter-governmental co-operation must not only support the Community but also be simultaneously expanded beyond the Community circle of influence outwards to all Europe; and that our ultimate aim, to be achieved by a harmonious combination of a steadily strengthened Community with a steadily widening inter-governmental co-operation, must be a European Federal Government not merely of Western Europe only, but for all Europe, for all time, and founded on the perpetual defence and extension of Human Rights.

This may sound complicated—but it is itself a proof of how far we have come since the events described in Chapters One and Two. 'Have we a flag?' asked Churchill in 1948. Today, of course, we do have a flag: the twelve gold stars on an azure and electric blue background—the flag adopted by the Council of Europe, approved by its member-countries and representing the ideal of a unified greater Europe—and the flag that flew in alternation with the Union Jack from flagpoles facing the House of Commons on Europe Day, 5 May 1967—for the first time in British history.

We have come a long way since Churchill first asked for a flag; yet we have a yet longer way to go until this flag acquires its *real* meaning—as is shown by the very complexity of this circle of propositions. Let us now comment briefly on each proposition in turn—briefly, because they are here no more than introduced and we shall be looking at them again from a different viewpoint in Chapter Ten.

1. *That the European Idea implies a European Federal Government.* It is

noticeable that in nearly all contemporary discussion of the European Idea this question is consistently avoided. Why? Because it is thought psychologically disturbing for us to contemplate at present the ultimate logical consequences of our present actions. This at least is the conviction of most of those at present responsible for leading public opinion. Yet the time for this hesitancy is passing; it is no compliment to the people of Europe to suggest we are not yet able to contemplate the real questions involved in the construction of Europe. Are we really so unintelligent, are we really so lacking in judgement, are we really so devoid of fibre that we must be talked to as if only the men in power are adults, and the rest of us are children? Surely not. Churchill himself felt able to raise the question by implication as far back as the war years. Today, over twenty years later, enough time has passed and sufficient progress has been made for us to be able to admit this issue to its rightful dignity. We have already a younger generation growing up who are far more prepared to accept the real implications of the European Idea than their elders. Whereas those of us who remember the war will always see European unification as a radical innovation—a most disturbing novelty—not so our younger generation: they take its advent for granted, and for this we can all be thankful.

'Hearken not to the voice,' said Madison, 'which petulantly tells you that the form of government recommended for your adoption is a novelty in the political world, that it rashly attempts what is impossible to accomplish. No...shut your ears against this unhallowed language.' There are still many today who would say that the creation of a European Federal Government is impossible to accomplish: there are more who while admitting it may be possible insist on reminding us it is a novelty in the political world—thereby suggesting it will not merely be difficult, but may be dangerous, undesirable, a thing to be avoided only because it *is* new. Certainly it is a splendid novelty. For that reason it is all the more important that a steadily increasing number of people should feel themselves directly and personally concerned with this question. It is already a sign of moral equivocation to advocate a united Europe without making it unmistakeably clear whether or not a European Federal Government is also advocated—that is to say, a united Europe responsible for all her actions. For it must be admitted that only a *Government* of Europe can guarantee the continuing unity of Europe, and only a *Federal* Government of Europe can justifiably invite the continuing and indispensable support of the *people* of Europe. We thus come today full circle to the question implicitly suggested to us by Churchill so many years ago. A Federal Government of Europe can be created only by the combined ability, judgement, action, example and good-will of very many men and women—and yet at the popular level this has all yet to start: it cannot ever start unless the question is first clearly posed.

2. *That a European Federal Government implies an unbroken succession of individual minds carrying all-European responsibility.* It is a truth in human affairs that government by committee cannot long endure, and is least of all successful when successful government is most needed—in time of crisis. This is not merely the heart of the matter: it is the pace-maker within that heart. It is the thing that few will say. It is the question on which the destiny of Europe will depend. Yet the phenomenon of individual minds carrying all-European responsibility still seems new to us— and so we fear it—and yet it is a phenomenon already appearing around us. Since this phenomenon is already upon us it will scarcely help us to deny the fact. For when on the one hand we have so to construct a Government of Europe that the door to progress is always open as far as we, the people, wish and permit; and when on the other hand we have so to construct a Government of Europe that the door to tyranny is always bolted, barred, and everlastingly locked—then the problem must go further, for it is not only a question of individual responsibility, but even more a question of the structure of events within which that responsibility can manifest. The men who in the future will carry the burden of Europe in turn on their shoulders will do so within that context of events which we ourselves are already beginning to create. It is thus upon our own responsibility now that our attention should be focussed.

If we accept that the maintenance of a United Europe will depend upon an unbroken succession of individual minds carrying all-European responsibility then we can begin to approach the greater and more immediate problem of *creating* the structure of responsibility within which these individual minds will best work. Monsieur Lecanuet in France—even in the hurly-burly of French party-political elections—felt able to put to the French public the first half of the matter and was one of the first to say in public what many in informed circles have long known to be true— that *a unified Europe must eventually have an unbroken succession of European Presidents.* And at a more technical, limited, and immediate level, Lord Gladwyn in Britain, in his 'Outline Plan for the Institution of a European Political Community' has not only gone so far as to advocate the creation of a Political and Defence Commission but goes on to suggest that 'the Council of Ministers (acting by a qualified majority), should then nominate the President for a given number of years...The Commission would have its own budget and its own staff recruited by its President. Once appointed, officials would be answerable only to him...' This is certainly not the same as openly advocating a Government of Europe, but the tendency of its logic is clear.

3. *That the two preceding propositions both imply European direct democratic elections.* Here we face the fact that if European unity can be guaranteed only by a continuing European Government, then a European Government can itself survive only if endorsed by a European electorate from whom it derives its mandate. Much will therefore depend on the speed and wisdom with which we create a European franchise: that is to say, the right of all Europeans to vote regularly, directly, secretly and individually on all questions affecting all Europe.

Expert opinion is here more vocal. Mr Hugh Beesley, of the Council of Europe, whom we shall quote again later, has written:

'...to neglect the traditional forms of democracy is out of the question inasmuch as to the vast majority of ordinary men and women these forms represent the reality—and indeed afford them their sole opportunity of participating in the affairs of their State...In a "United Europe"...the Executive will recapture some of its erstwhile powers and the Parliament regain its former powers of initiative, effective criticism and meaningful control. In debates on this question at the Consultative Assembly of the Council of Europe the formula has been evolved that in the measure that control escapes national Parliaments (e.g. if Ministerial Councils operate by majority vote) it should be entrusted to international parliaments.'

If a directly-elected European Parliament is not practical politics today, then it is today that we must start working towards making it practical politics tomorrow. This means a massive adjustment in public opinion.

The full effects of these first three propositions all lie in the far distant future. The next three propositions, however, are on the contrary concerned with the facts of European unification as they are today. Let us again take them briefly one by one.

4. *That the first three propositions together imply unceasing and increasing support, both popular and governmental, for the maintenance, strengthening and improvement of the Community principle and method.* At the governmental level, we have here at present a watershed, a critical dividing of the ways in the present crisis of European unification. It is here that the Gaullist attack is sharpest, here that some national positions are weakest, here that the questions involved in the future political union of Europe and also any immediate enlargement of the Community, all come to a focus. The tactical necessities in each country and for each party here form such a labyrinth that the strategic necessity is seldom expressed—and when it

is expressed, it causes controversy of a kind which Ministers tend not to wish to encounter.

A classic example is Mr George Brown's speech at Bergen—of which Mr John Gordon wrote in the London *Sunday Express* of 22 May 1966: 'What an extraordinary fellow Mr George Brown is. He made a remarkable after-dinner speech at Bergen last Saturday. The *Sunday Express* reported him next morning as saying, "We British now feel we have a mission to create a new Europe where there are no economic divisions and no political divisions", which means, if it means anything, a full European federation in which national sovereignties would be subservient to the federal authority and even the position of the Queen might eventually be in question. Obviously what he said was politically sensational. Challenged in the Commons to disclose exactly what he did say Mr Brown told Mr Shinwell that he hoped he was not being misled by the *Sunday Express*. When Sir Alec Douglas-Home suggested it might make everything clearer if a copy of the speech was put in the Library for M.P.s to read, Mr Brown replied evasively "like so many after-dinner speeches, all texts are neither prepared nor, happily, kept". To another question he gave the explicit reply that he made no speech or statement to the effect that his view of a united Europe including Britain would be a supranational federation.'

The missing element here is the pressure of informed public opinion, sufficiently convinced to be able to sustain pro-Community Ministers and policies actively. We are in a sorry state when pro-Community Ministers dare not say what they really feel because they know that at present only anti-Community opinion will understand them. It is becoming increasingly necessary that informed opinion shall extend not only through all political parties but also through all interested pressure groups and so to the public as a whole—and that this opinion shall speak out not only for the maintenance of the Community principle and method, but even more for its deliberate strengthening and improvement with each succeeding year—and notably in the direction of popularly based democratic control, exercised through a European Franchise. The Community institutions exist only to serve the interests of the people of Europe: it is the Community itself which waits to be *allowed* to hear the popular voice.

5. *That the Community principle and method must also always be complemented by improved, widening and coherently organised inter-governmental co-operation.* For all its strength, it is a fact that the European Community as we know it today can operate only within certain precise fields, and these only within its own member countries. The fact that these fields of action *may* extend, and that the number of member countries may increase,

must not blind us to the fact that a great deal of work towards European unification is simultaneously making progress (both within the member-countries of the Community and an even larger number of countries outside it) by means of inter-governmental co-operation, agreements, and programmes—and as we have already seen, notably through the Council of Europe. Yet there is at present no organic link connecting the work of the Community with these other simultaneous patterns of work. This link can be created only by the combined action of Governments and the need is becoming acute. Since it is apparent that not for many years to come will the European Community include *all* the countries even of Western Europe only, it is clear that a formula must be found to harmonise the harmonisers, to co-ordinate the co-ordinators, unify the unifiers. To take only the most obvious example, it is already necessary to evolve a formula combining the use of the Community method through Brussels by a relatively small number of states, with the use of the inter-governmental method through Strasbourg by a larger number of states, and this in such a way that each method assists the other. It is possible this could be done by a formal Treaty of Association between the two organisations. It is possible it could be done more easily by dividing the question in two, and seeking an arrangement at the governmental level enabling the ministerial bodies of both organisations to work far more closely together—and also an arrangement at the parliamentary level doing the same for the Assemblies of the two organisations. And there is yet a third way of approaching the problem: at the Civil Service level, by means of an agreement between governments to create a unified *European Civil Service*. Yet even these three possibilities are merely aspects of the problem: the coherent organisation of inter-governmental work alone is another aspect, and even this is already so large that governments may find they prefer to deal with it first and separately. We shall look at this more closely in coming chapters —what can be said here at once is that if action is not taken then confusion must increase.

6. *That this inter-governmental co-operation must not only support the Community but also be simultaneously expanded beyond the Community circle of influence outwards to all Europe.* This does not merely mean to Finland, Turkey or Portugal but to *Eastern Europe* generally and it is not yet widely realised this is already beginning to happen. On 19 June 1966, Mr Robert Stephens, Diplomatic Correspondent of the London *Observer* was able to report as follows on a projected 'British plan for a Code of Co-operation between countries of Western and Eastern Europe which was outlined by Mr Michael Stewart, the Foreign Secretary, at the recent meeting of NATO Foreign Ministers in Brussels.'

'Mr Stewart's idea is to try to work out a statement of principles and purposes to which many of the members of NATO and countries in Eastern Europe could subscribe. Politically the statement would have to be conceived in very broad terms to secure such agreement but in cultural, social, scientific and economic matters it could be worked out in more detail. A possible development is an eventual invitation to East European countries to join or become associated with some European organisations which have no strong cold war character. Both the Council of Europe and the European Free Trade Association (EFTA), for example, have neutral as well as NATO states from West Europe. The Council of Europe would appear a promising forum for promoting all-European co-operation in social and cultural matters, and eventually perhaps a means of maintaining continuous political contacts between western and eastern Europe. Non-member states such as Portugal (and) Spain...already take part in the work of some of the Council's committees of experts...'

This was at the governmental level. At the European level Sir Geoffrey de Freitas, President of the Assembly of the Council of Europe, felt able as early as 1966 to advocate an all-European Assembly. In a letter to *The Economist* we find his own first public exploration of the idea:

'Western European integration is proceeding without the participation of the East European countries. For a long time to come they will not be able to join or become associated with European institutions. In the meantime should we not try to devise some means of enabling them to acquaint themselves with the West European organisations? It could be argued that private organisations such as the European Movement could pave the way. However, their action is always limited. Should we not therefore try to devise a half-way formula to go further than collaboration between private organisations, while falling short of an association with governmental institutions such as the Council of Europe, EFTA, or the EEC? It would have to provide for the institutionalisation of the East-West dialogue so that the resulting organisation would be an ante-room to European organisations, would be recognised and would have access to governments and European institutions. The answer to the problem might be in the setting up of an organisation having some sort of semi-official status. There are precedents for it and there is a fund of experience to draw on. It should be a forum for the confrontation of views and for improving mutual understanding. The participants should include people connected with governmental organisations, European institutions and industry, the banking trade and organised labour, and their counter-parts in Eastern Europe...'

These are but first indications of the tendency of our times—they illustrate again that what cannot be done through Brussels must be done elsewhere: that if it can be done elsewhere then ways must be evolved for it to be done coherently; and that in the creation of this coherence it is governments which have at this present time the most responsible part to play.

7. *That our ultimate aim, to be achieved by a harmonious combination of a steadily strengthened Community with a steadily widening inter-governmental co-operation, must be a European Federal Government not merely of Western Europe only, but for all Europe, for all time and founded on the perpetual defence and extension of Human Rights.*

Here we are again contemplating our far distant future, but we are also contemplating a question we shall not be able to avoid. The success of Western European unification must force this question increasingly upon our attention, and by a logical necessity—for if we turn this question into the negative, what do we find ourselves having to say? Namely, that if we do not advocate the union of all Europe then we are advocating the perpetual *division* of Europe. We might just as well face the future logical consequences of our present position now—which is that the creation of a Federal Government of Western Europe will not eliminate the question of the unity of the Greater Europe, but on the contrary will make that question loom larger on our horizon—until it may some day become the most difficult issue in our politics. It is this very difficulty that should brace us now to start facing the question early—while there is still time for our thinking to evolve slowly, unhurried as yet by crisis, and therefore the more likely to create in good time those patterns of action and thought we may later suddenly need.

To these seven propositions one further note should be added—it is that the one word relevant, whether directly or indirectly, to every proposition is the word 'federal'. This is not a word we can evade. Even though the shining virtue of its early years has in recent years been increasingly and publicly prostituted, and thereafter mocked, by men who felt the moral reproach of its inherent dignity and therefore preferred to bring it low, all the more must we restore this word to its real meaning, and guide it back, dishevelled and dusty though it is, to its proper place—which is at the centre of our political thinking and our political action. Those who say that federalism is *dépassé* thereby only prove their own thinking *dépassé*—as years to come will show. The word 'federal' is the word at the heart of the matter for all of us in Europe today, and while it is not a word for weaklings it is certainly a word for all who hope. 'Let us stand by our duty fearlessly and effectively', said Abraham Lincoln in 1860 in New York, 'let us be diverted by none of those sophistical contrivances wherewith we are so industriously plied and belaboured—contrivances such as groping for some middle ground between the right and the wrong; vain as the search for a man who should be neither a living man nor a dead man...such as Union appeals to true Union men to yield to disunionists, reversing the divine rule, and calling, not the sinner, but the righteous to repentance.'

These seven propositions, and this one word that unites them, form a picture of our time as some at least of us today now see it. Nevertheless, perspective cannot be seen unless we stand outside the frame of the picture, well back from the object of our vision, and a real vision of Europe in depth comes to different men in very different ways. Balzac saw Europe as a pantheon of artists. Dostoevsky tells us he first saw Europe through a single painting in Dresden Museum by Claude Lorraine, while Jung first saw Europe by talking to an American Indian, a chief of the Taos Pueblos, named Mountain Lake. As Jung tells us:

'In talk with a European, one is constantly running up on the sand bars of things long known but never understood; with this Indian, the vessel floated freely on deep, alien seas...
    "I asked him why he thought the whites were all mad.
    "They say that they think with their heads," he replied.
    "Why, of course, what do you think with?" I asked him in surprise.
    "We think here," he said, indicating his heart.
'I fell into a long meditation. For the first time in my life, so it seemed to me, someone had drawn for me a picture of the real white man. It was as though until now I had seen nothing but sentimental, prettified colour prints. This Indian had struck our vulnerable spot, unveiled a truth to which we are blind. I felt rising within me like a shapeless mist something unknown and yet deeply familiar. And out of this mist, image upon image detached itself; first, Roman legions smashing into the cities of Gaul, and the keenly incised features of Julius Caesar, Scipio Africanus, and Pompey. I saw the Roman eagle on the North Sea and on the banks of the White Nile. Then I saw St Augustine transmitting the Christian creed to the Britons on the tips of Roman lances, and Charlemagne's most glorious forced conversions of the heathen; then the pillaging and murdering bands of the Crusading armies. With

a secret stab I realised the hollowness of that old romanticism about the Crusades. Then followed Columbus, Cortez, and the other conquistadors who with fire, sword, torture, and Christianity came down upon even these remote Pueblos dreaming peacefully in the Sun, their Father. I saw, too, the people of the Pacific Islands decimated by firewater, syphilis, and scarlet fever carried in the clothes the missionaries forced on them.

'It was enough. What we from our point of view call colonisation, missions to the heathen, spread of civilisation, etc., has another face—the face of a bird of prey seeking with cruel intentness for distant quarry—a face worthy of a race of pirates and highwaymen. All the eagles and other predatory creatures that adorn our coats of arms seem to me apt psychological representatives of our true nature.

The warning is a stern one: we would do well to keep it in view—for the real character of a unified Europe has yet to mature; it will be many years before it is even partly unveiled to us, and even then it will become visible only through our actions. The new character of our new Europe is in fact forming now, but still in secret—we shall not even be able to see it until it begins to manifest itself in a federal context. The warning is all the more important when what we have to do is still so hard—for we have a European ship of state yet to build, and a ship that is not seaworthy cannot sail through storms.

CHAPTER SEVEN

'Consider More The How'

'Consider the What, consider more the How.'

GOETHE: *Faust* (trans. Louis MacNeice)

THE EUROPEAN IDEA is predictable in principle, not predictable in practice. During the last five years the Council of Europe entered a critical point in its evolution, and when we consider the present uncertainty facing the European Community in Brussels, and that since May 1969 we have a new Secretary General of the Council of Europe (Dr Lujo Toncic-Serinj of Austria) and a new President of the Assembly of the Council of Europe (Professor Olivier Reverdin of Switzerland), it seems likely that the next five years may be equally crucial. Yet they will find the evolution of the Council of Europe (and of the European Idea as a whole) at a stage unthought of five years ago. In the next three Chapters we shall examine some of the reasons for this.

It is a curious fact that most accounts of the Council have been able to describe much of its work without ever naming individuals. This was not true of the very early years: as we have seen in Chapters One and Two the individual influence and example of men like Winston Churchill, Paul-Henri Spaak, and R. W. G. Mackay was central to the story—but it was true of the middle years and has been true until very recently. Today it is no longer true. It is now no longer possible to make sense of the Council of Europe without describing its life as interpreted, represented, and influenced by certain individuals. This change is fundamental, and is most clearly to be seen in the office of Secretary General.

Least of all have accounts of the Council during both its early and its middle years felt it necessary to focus on the successive Secretaries General. This is understandable, for we have reason to feel that in most organisations the title 'Secretary General' means no more than a general sort of secretary. Formerly this was often so, but today the patterns of European politics are forcing it to be different—and of global politics also, for there is a parallel in the Secretary Generalship of the United Nations. The problems of the internal structure of an organisation, its external relationships, and the power it exercises whether officially or unofficially must all be kept in view—and in the European context they must be kept especially in mind because they are all constantly changing.

In the early and middle years of the Council of Europe the office of Secretary General was strictly confined both by the nature of the organisation as it then was, and by the conditions imposed upon it from without by the context of political events. It was not an office of political leadership. It was not an office where primary decisions could take place. It was an office where no real responsibility—and therefore neither credit nor blame—could be said to centre. Yet even by the end of the 1950's there were signs of a possible change. This change was visible also in other institutions. It was the change whereby the increasing interdependence of all political administration on the European level had jumped far ahead of the existing mechanisms for political decision. Political decision-making itself thus tended increasingly to find an unconscious, unofficial, unrecorded home in the offices of the great administrators—at first perhaps imperceptibly, with just a word murmured or a nod seen. Yet the change was coming, and took public form in a question: should great administrative, technical and organisational offices at the European level be entrusted to individual men who were themselves primarily men of political decision? And the same question was being asked at other levels: the evolution in the United Nations from Trygve Lie to Dag Hammarskjold, and in NATO the appointment as Secretary General of Paul-Henri Spaak are both intriguing examples—for Dag Hammarskjold led too well, while Spaak was prevented from leading enough—an example, perhaps, of the right man heading the wrong organisation. And it is of interest to note that while Spaak himself believed at first that his very dedication to Europe meant he must accept the NATO post, some of his own good friends went so far as to say his acceptance was a betrayal of Europe's real interests.

In the Council of Europe the first attempt to answer this question came with the election by the Assembly of Mr Lodovico Benvenuti as Secretary

General in 1957. A Christian Democrat, member of the Italian Resistance during the war, leader of the Italian delegation at the Common Market Inter-governmental Conference, well versed in European unification at both Ministerial and Parliamentary levels, he was the first practising politician to be appointed Secretary General. His election was an experiment, his tenure was watched with sharp eyes, and though his period of office was at first judged disappointing, it was not so disastrous that a continued political occupancy of the Secretary General's chair became unthinkable. Quite the contrary; the question by 1964 had already become subtly altered—to what extent should the office of Secretary General provide political leadership, what form was that leadership to take, and *how* was it to be done? And as so often happens, the word HOW? re-arranges itself to ask WHO?

The Secretary General of the Council of Europe is directly elected by a secret vote in the Assembly, but the names of candidates are presented by the Committee of Ministers, and therefore with the approval of Governments. Before a name can formally emerge, all the following things must happen.

1. Action must begin not less than six months before the end of the term of the incumbent Secretary General. It is open to him to present himself for a renewal of his term, and if he does then the details of that term must be agreed between the Committee of Ministers and the Assembly through their Joint Committee. A term renewed can thus be of variable length. For all other candidates, nominations can be submitted by one or more Member Governments only. Candidates for the office of Secretary General can be sponsored either by a Member Government or by the Secretary General himself—provided they are already permanent or temporary members of the Secretariat. Members of the Secretariat are also eligible for nomination as Secretary General. Some years earlier when the then Deputy Secretary General, Mr Dunstan Curtis, was widely tipped for the position. It should also be noted that the following guiding principle in regard to nominations is officially included in the Rules of Procedure of the Assembly, which advocate the '...desirability of ensuring an equitable *geographical* allocation of appointments among nationals of the Member States subject to the overriding interests of efficiency. No appointment to the Secretariat shall be considered to be the prerogative of any particular Member State.'

In the early years of the Council this rule was not always applied. The two top positions in the Secretariat were in fact a Franco-British tandem. The first two Secretaries General were French (Jacques-Camille Paris, 1949-1953; Leon Marchall, 1953-1956) while the first three Deputy

Secretaries General were British (Aubrey Halford, 1949-1952; Anthony Lincoln, 1952–1955; Dunstan Curtis, 1955–1962). Pressure, however, from within the Assembly and from other Member Governments led to this arrangement being discarded—(not only did Mr Lodovico Benvenuti become the first Italian Secretary General in 1957, but in 1962 Mr Polys Modinos became the first Greek Deputy Secretary General)—and since then this rule has become increasingly accepted.

Yet as a principle it is applicable to far more than the election of the Secretary General: it is today to be found in operation within nearly all workings of the European Idea. There must be no monopoly of any one position by any one country, and at any one time there will be an equitable distribution of offices between countries making it impossible for any focus of power to become even the unofficial prerogative of any one nationality. At the top levels this is also coming to be taken for granted, not only as a matter of political bargaining but of sheer necessity, for there is no other way to maintain the necessary equilibrium. Thus wherever we find the European Idea working creatively we shall also expect always to find a stable but alternating equipoise, between Celt and Latin, Scandinavian and Turk, Anglo-Saxon and Swiss—and also between nominees of parties in power and parties in opposition. Not always, as we shall see—but the principle stands nevertheless, can be disregarded only for exceptional and agreed reasons, and in its insistence on mere geographical factors, is an indication for the future—for it will be a long time before the unity of Europe becomes so well established that this principle can safely be discarded. And with nominations for Secretary General of the Council of Europe this in practice means that nominees must have not only the support of a Member Government (usually their own, though this is not obligatory) but must also be of a nationality different from that of the outgoing Secretary General, and if possible not of the same political party, or even the same Church.

2. Not less than thirty days before the Assembly votes, the Committee of Ministers is required to consult the Assembly through their Joint Committee for final approval of the candidates. On one occasion the Ministers put forward one name only: the outcry that followed from the Assembly was so effective that the Ministers agreed thereafter there must always be a choice. Thus the Ministers are today required to send two or more names, but have the right to indicate their own order of preference. And once the candidates have been agreed through the Joint Committee, the Ministers themselves have—officially—nothing further to say. What this in fact means is that every candidate has to survive this first preliminary period of inter-governmental bargaining and discussion. It means that any

Government can veto any candidate—and therefore every candidate must be acceptable to all Governments.

3. With the candidates agreed, initiative passes to the Assembly. The same pattern is now repeated. The Bureau of the Assembly (its Committee of elected officers) have like the Ministers the right to interview candidates, and the right to submit their names to the Assembly in their own order of preference—while repeating formally the preference previously indicated by the Ministers.

4. With the names agreed, and the orders of preference indicated—the final stage is the election of the Secretary General by secret ballot in the Assembly. An absolute majority at the first ballot is decisive—failing that, a relative majority at the second ballot. Once elected, the successful candidate will hold office in the first instance for five years.

It should be stressed that this process has certain characteristics. First, that a candidate cannot succeed in face of government opposition. Second, that Governments cannot impose a candidate on the Assembly. Third, that the Ministers and the Officers of the Assembly have the right to interview each candidate. Fourth, that final power rests in the hands of individual Representatives in the Assembly, but that individual Representatives have no official right to satisfy themselves on the intentions of each candidate.

It may also be noted that while the evolution of this electoral process over the years has shown an increasingly democratic tendency—to the extent where today the individual Representatives in the Assembly amount to a genuinely unfettered and all-powerful electorate—nevertheless they may not yet amount to an *informed* electorate. It is today entirely possible that Members of the Assembly may find themselves voting for a Secretary General on merely private, governmental, or party-political recommendation, or on the more direct word of men they respect within the Assembly, or perhaps on their own personal experience of the candidate in European or other circles—all of which are admirable reasons, but are not reasons of policy. In other words, it is entirely possible for the Assembly to elect a pig-in-a-poke, for the very good reason that individual Representatives have not been able to satisfy themselves—or have not even been informed—of the policy of the candidates. In the earlier years this did not matter—but today it does. As we shall see in coming chapters, the office of Secretary General is today a policy-making office, and therefore when each individual Representative in the Assembly casts his vote the real issue at stake is in fact the desired orientation, policy and vocation of the entire Council of Europe for at least five years to come, and maybe more.

When we consider all the inter-reactions of all the various levels of the European Idea today, the vote of each individual Representative thus becomes individually important—and while this is not to say that the future of the Council of Europe is now entirely determined by the Secretary General, the influence of the office of Secretary General has already acquired some quite remarkable characteristics. And while the attitude of each individual Representative to each of these characteristics is itself determined by a multitude of other factors, it is of interest to note that within the Secretariat of the Council of Europe itself there is at present a very strong feeling that a Secretary General cannot succeed unless he is—all other considerations apart—a man of political courage.

This is the situation today—and it is so very largely as a direct result of the vote by Representatives in the Assembly which took place in 1964. For the Secretary General then elected has in the years since wrought a change in the Council of Europe—and a fundamental change—which was at the time of his election not anticipated.

Let us now see what happened at this election. The three candidates, in alphabetical order, were:

FERNAND DEHOUSSE

POLYS MODINOS

PETER SMITHERS

The official biographies of the three candidates, submitted presumably with their approval, were published for the information of Members of the Assembly by the Committee of Ministers. Each biography is indicative of currents then running deep in the practical evolution of European unification. We have in each a view in cross-section of part at least of what was going on in Europe at this time—and this seen each time from a different angle. It is to men of this calibre and character that the unification of Europe is today very largely entrusted, and we sometimes forget how few they are, or how heavy the burdens they carry.

M. Fernand Dehousse, according to his official biography, was born at Liege in Belgium on 3 July 1906.

Education: Doctor of Law, degree in Special Science, *Agrégé* of Higher Education.

Professional life: in 1935 Lecturer and in 1940 Professor at the Faculty of Law of the State University of Liège. President of the Institute of European Legal Studies at Liège University. Author of four books and numerous studies on problems of public international law, comparative constitutional law, the history of diplomacy and foreign policy.

ÖSTERREICH

BELGIQUE-BELGIË

KYPROS-KIBRIS

DANMARK   FRANCE

B REP DEUTSCHLAND

HELLAS   ÍSLAND   ÉIRE   ITALIA

LUXEMBOURG   MALTA   NEDERLAND

NORGE   SVERIGE

SUISSE-SCHWEIZ-SVIZZERA

TÜRKIYE

UNITED KINGDOM

How it works: ABOVE *the member states,* BELOW *a diagram showing the organisation of the Council of Europe.*

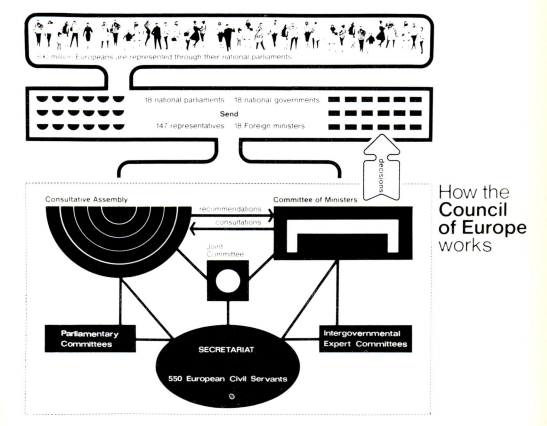

How the **Council of Europe** works

The House of Europe, Strasbourg

A new generation of Europeans visits its Consultative Assembly

Political life: Co-opted as Senator by the Belgian Socialist Party in 1930 and subsequently Member and frequently *rapporteur* of the Belgian Foreign Affairs Committee, the Committee on Foreign Trade and the Senate Committee for Constitutional Amendment. Chairman of the Senate Cultural Affairs Committee, and Belgian representative at many conferences and international meetings.

International political life: United Nations—Delegate to the San Francisco Conference of 1945; Delegate or substitute at the General Assembly in 1946, 47, 48, 50 and 51; Representative on the Economic and Social Council 1946, 49, 50; Member of the Commission on Human Rights 1946, 47, 48. In addition: Delegate to the Peace Conference in Paris of 1946.

Record in the Council of Europe: took part in the negotiations in 1948 on the creation of the Council, as Delegate to the Committee for the study of European unity, and in 1949 at the London Conference and the Preparatory Commission. From 1954 to 1961: Representative to the Consultative Assembly, and *rapporteur* in the Assembly for several projects. Chairman from 1959 to 1960 of the Assembly Committee on Local Authorities.

Political life at the European level other than in the Council of Europe: Chairman of the European Commission for the Saar Referendum and of the Western European Union Saar Commission in 1955–56; Member of the Assembly of the European Coal and Steel Community for its duration from 1952 to 1958; Member of the *ad hoc* Assembly and *Rapporteur* for the then proposed European Political Community in 1952, 53; Member of the European Parliament of the Common Market countries since 1958, Chairman of its Working Party on European Elections from 1959 to 1960, and Vice-Chairman of its Parliamentary Socialist Group.

And in addition to all this: Member of the Permanent Court of Arbitration in the Hague since 1957, Joint President of the Franco-German Arbitration Tribunal for the Saar since 1957, and President, then Honorary President, of the Association for the Study of European Problems in Paris—as well as holder of numerous decorations, not only from Belgium, but West Germany, Italy, Luxembourg, France and Turkey—where he was a Freeman of the City of Istanbul.

Senator Dehousse was thus a thoroughly experienced leader in national, European and world politics. His candidature alone is enough to demonstrate dramatically the evolution that had taken place in the Council of Europe since another Belgian, Paul-Henri Spaak, had thought it best to resign from what was then a far more important post, that of President of the Assembly itself. Senator Dehousse was thus the dynamic candidate. His biography did not mention that he had been President of the very

I

Assembly whose votes he was now soliciting—it did not mention the fact that the Secretariat of the Council regarded him with mixed feelings—or that he was equally well known as a Federalist of proved intelligence, conviction and practical determination.

In curious contrast was the second candidate, M. Polys Modinos—a contrast of unexpected colour, dignified understatement, and discreet revelation of activity behind the scenes. He was born on 11 October 1899 at Alexandria in Egypt, was a student at the Faculty of Law at Paris University, and in 1921 a Member of the Bar at the Mixed Tribunals in Egypt. This must have appeared to both Ministers and Assembly a career with a note very much of its own. His early years in Egypt led to an appointment by the Egyptian Government in 1937, and after that to the Montreux Conference as Judge on the Mixed Tribunals—leading in 1944 to election by his colleagues as President of the Chamber. These were the war years—during which M. Modinos, acting as Secretary General of the Greek National Committee in Egypt on the request of the Greek Government-in-exile, organised aid for the families of members of the Greek armed forces and was decorated—doubtless for this but perhaps for more besides. And in 1949, after the dissolution of the Mixed Tribunals, he was given several official missions, including that of drafting the establishment treaty between Greece and Egypt.

In September 1951 came what must have appeared a turning-point in his life—M. Modinos joined the Secretariat of the Council of Europe. He held in turn the posts of Counsellor in the Political Directorate, Director of Human Rights, and Registrar of the European Court of Human Rights. In 1961 the Committee of Ministers conferred on him the rank of Deputy Secretary General in his personal capacity: an appointment to which he was formally elected by the Assembly in 1962. The final paragraph of his biography reads: 'M. Modinos is the author of numerous works and studies in Greek and French. He is an associate member or honorary member of several institutes and learned societies and is the holder of high honours.' The honours are not listed.

All in all, a most puzzling candidature—and yet also the safest, for what could be safer than to elect as Secretary General the previous Deputy Secretary General? The quotations from M. Modinos in Chapter Three are illustration enough of his quality—yet it was not a candidature including any record of elective office or public leadership, but rather one based on varied experience, a mastery of the inner workings of the Council of Europe itself and the proved confidence of those working behind the scenes within the Council.

The third candidate was Mr Peter Smithers. Born in 1913, educated at Harrow and Magdalen College, Oxford—a First in History and a Doctorate of Philosophy for a thesis on the life of Joseph Addison—recently re-issued in a revised form.

And after Addison? In 1936 Mr Smithers was called to the Bar, in 1939 he was commissioned in the Royal Naval Volunteer Reserve, and after a short period of active service went to the Admiralty—Naval Intelligence Division. Then to Washington as Assistant Naval Attaché; then to Mexico, the Central American Republics, and Panama as Acting Naval Attaché. At the end of the war he went straight into politics, but unexpected politics—the politics of local government. In 1950 he entered Parliament as Conservative Member for Winchester. It is a smoothly upward progress, and yet with individualist excursions, not entirely predictable. The Addisonian analyst of prose, the Naval Attaché in Panama, the modest devotee of the politics of the parish pump—they do not at first sight fit together.

The Parliamentary career that follows is on clearer lines. 1952 to 1956, Parliamentary Private Secretary to the Minister of State for the Colonies; from 1956 to 1959 PPS to the Secretary of State; 1962 Under-Secretary of State in the Foreign Office. At the same time, from 1956 to 1959, Mr Smithers was Chairman of the Conservative Party Overseas Bureau, and from 1958 to 1962, Vice-Chairman of the Conservative Parliamentary Foreign Affairs Committee. From 1960 to 1962, he was a Delegate to the United Nations Assembly.

The record, in fact, is thus far so impeccable that we consult it in vain to discover why Mr Smithers should be standing as candidate for Secretary General of the Council of Europe. Where is the key? Married with two daughters; Chevalier of the Legion of Honour—these are not entirely an adequate explanation of how this candidate hopes to command a majority vote against both a former President of the Assembly and the incumbent Deputy Secretary General. Mr Smithers' entire claim to head the Council of Europe Secretariat in succession to M. Benvenuti is expressed in three laconic sentences. 'Mr Smithers was an active member of the European Movement from its first beginnings. He was one of the two joint secretaries of the Brussels Conference in February 1949. In the Council of Europe, he was a delegate to the Consultative Assembly from 1952 to 1956, and again in 1960. From 1959 to 1962, he was Vice-President of the European Assembly of Local Authorities.'

Thus the three candidates—Senator Dehousse, the pugnacious federalist; M. Modinos, the judge and administrator; and Mr Smithers, the Conservative

ex-Minister—each in his way representing a different evolutionary
strain of European political man. But whereas in Darwin's theory, it is
those most fit in themselves who survive, in politics it is sometimes those
most necessary to others who survive—which is not at all the same thing.
And when the election was held in the Assembly on 15 January 1964, with
128 Representatives voting in the first ballot (and the required absolute
majority thus 65), the results were:

PETER SMITHERS	60
POLYS MODINOS	35
FERNAND DEHOUSSE	33

Mr Smithers was thus already within five votes of election, and when
M. Dehousse withdrew his candidature, the results in the second ballot,
with 132 Representatives voting, three spoiled votes, and two inexplicable
votes for M. Dehousse, were:

PETER SMITHERS	75
POLYS MODINOS	52

From this it would appear that the supporters of M. Dehousse divided
roughly fifty-fifty between the two other candidates. With a secret vote,
however, we cannot of course be sure—it is easier to point out the mathematical fact that if even merely twelve of those who in the second ballot
voted for Mr Smithers had at the last moment jibbed, and gone for M.
Modinos, the result might have been reversed. Twelve votes, no more—
but it did not happen, and when M. Pierre Pflimlin, Mayor of Strasbourg
and then President of the Assembly, declared Mr Smithers elected, a
decision had been taken which was to affect the evolution of the Council
of Europe in ways which at the time of the election not only few Representatives voting in the Assembly anticipated—but not even the Committee of Ministers, and Member Governments.

Why, however, was Mr Smithers elected? It can be said there was a
strong feeling in the Assembly that a British influence would in itself be
welcome, and this in direct reaction to President de Gaulle's earlier veto
of British entry to the European Community. When Britain had been so
damagingly rebuffed and when the repercussions were having such
lamentable consequences on the whole progress of the European Idea, it
seemed not merely appropriate but also shrewd to favour the election of
a British Secretary General of the Council of Europe for five full years to
come. This at least is known to have been a powerful motive, but it is
doubtful if the detailed political motivation of those voting for Mr
Smithers went much further than this. How, indeed, could it go further?

Neither the pattern of events in the next few years, nor Mr Smithers'
own intentions could be guessed—all that was clear was that for the
second time the Council of Europe had chosen as Secretary General a
practising politician of Ministerial experience.

Let us now consider the circumstances in which Mr Smithers began his
term of office. Europe at this time was in a period of crisis, exasperation
and deadlock. While the Gaullist refusal to permit an enlargement of the
Community had not broken the Community will to proceed, it had
induced a *malaise* extending far beyond the Community, and very evident
in Strasbourg. The Council was then in some ways very different from
what it is today, and if we look at descriptions published at that time the
impression we get is puzzling. It is not at all like the impression we had
in the previous chapter when we considered the European Community:
the contrast is striking. Yet if we look, for example, at the most
notable account of the Council of Europe, that published in a revised
edition by Dr A. H. Robertson in 1961, we do find symptoms of *malaise*
already unmistakably charted:

'By 1960, it seemed that the following conclusions could be drawn from
the experience of eleven years—
1. That the Council of Europe had a good record as an instrument of
European co-operation in the social, cultural and legal fields, but that
this was insufficient to achieve the aim of 'greater unity between its
Members' which was conferred on it by the Statute;
2. That the Assembly had done valuable work on political and economic
subjects, but for one reason or another the Committee of Ministers had
not been able to seize the opportunities thus afforded to it;
3. That the main driving force towards European integration had now
shifted to the three Six-Power Communities for coal and steel, atomic
energy and the common market;
4. That the Council of Europe could still perform a most valuable role
as the framework in which to bring together, and harmonise the
development of, the Six and the other countries of free Europe. If this
were to happen, however, a greater degree of political determination
would be necessary...

'Did the political will exist or could it be created? That was the big
conundrum...It was above all in the political field, that action was
necessary to give the Council new life. The Assembly was doing its best
and could be relied on to continue doing so, but it could not play an
effective political role without more support from the governments; in
this domain, the inter-governmental machinery was inadequate...a study

of this problem was certainly necessary if the Council of Europe was
to discharge the essentially political task which both the Committee of
Ministers and the Assembly had agreed was its principal function.'

Yet in charting the symptoms, Dr Robertson was also quietly sketching
the outline of a possible cure. 'Did the political will exist?...more support
from the governments...the inter-governmental machinery was inadequate...a study was certainly necessary...essentially political task...' And
he was also careful to note that the Council was in no more than the
'early days of a process of evolution'.

Mr Smithers thus took office at a time of compound difficulty and
psychological crisis. What followed has proved remarkable. There are
lessons in it of very wide application indeed. In this and the coming chapters we shall therefore focus very closely on what can happen when a
determined man in a difficult position succeeds in applying the right idea
with a new method—and as we do so we shall find we are watching not
merely Mr Smithers, not merely the Council of Europe—but certain
aspects of the struggle to unite Europe in the middle 1960's which are not
merely history, but in their characteristics and dimensions are a preview
of the struggle yet to come in future decades—decades when the difficulties will be yet more complex, the scale of events yet larger, and the
necessity of achieving success all the more imperative.

Let us begin by following the key passages in a speech which Mr
Smithers made to the Assembly a little over a year after his election, in
May 1965. Let us listen as if we knew nothing of what was later to come;
let us imagine we are sitting in the public galleries and hearing him
through our earphones perhaps in direct English or in the simultaneous
French, Dutch, German or Italian translations—considering all the time
what is the effect of this speech upon us, what is being said, what is *not*
being said, and why? Mr Smithers begins:

'There are three questions to which an answer seems to be required:
   How should we proceed to greater unity between our Member States?
   What should be our relationship to European non-Member States?
   *What is the place of our organisation in the emerging structure of
   world-politics?'*

Mr Smithers here takes his stand on the single Statutory aim of the Council
of Europe—'greater unity'. He has in fact no other choice for a firm
foundation. We have looked at the Statute in Chapters One and Two—
here we have again to keep it in view, for its presence is behind the whole
philosophy and handling of this speech. By the end of it the word

'greater' has undergone a subtle transmutation—it refers no longer merely to an abstract 'unity' but to a Greater *Europe*.

Next comes a paragraph of flash-back, leading up to the situation as it appeared in May 1965:

> 'First of all it must, I think, be said that greater unity between our member States presents today a problem of a quite different kind from that which existed in 1949. Then we were an unorganised group of nations and the problem was how better to organise ourselves for the common benefit. Since then much progress has been made in organising the economic affairs of Europe and, as a result, the problem of greater unity amongst our members is essentially that of the relationship of the rest of Europe, including EFTA, to the European communities.'

In the last chapter we looked at what today we call the Community, and through this speech we are now hearing exactly the same problems, but now from outside—not as they appear from Brussels, but as they now appear from Strasbourg. And already we have unfolding before us one of the master-themes of our time; the intricate and changing relationship between European *organisations* and European *states*. As early as 1939 Clarence Streit was insisting that our European states are not really sovereign, for not one of them is totally independent: today the same is already true of European *organisations*. In this speech we are reminded that the structure of the Common Market was based from the beginning on the opportunities, conditions, and necessities of Europe's *economic* health—not political, not military, not social, but economic. Regardless of the aims, the means were economic—for this reason the simultaneous existence of the Common Market as an inner and of EFTA as an outer economic circle is here mentioned not merely as a fact, but as a fact creating a problem. Mr Smithers goes on: 'While on the one hand the European Commission evidently finds it difficult to envisage a substantial extension of its activities to us...'

What we have here is a problem that can be solved only by two levers operating against each other with the common aim of cracking the problem between them. One lever here is the Brussels Commission, the other the Secretariat of the Council of Europe. The nut to be cracked is the power-relationship between the two organisations. And nutcrackers, of course, can be used in two ways. Either each lever applies equal and simultaneous pressure, or one lever alone applies pressure, while the other is so placed that it does not move and so provides passive strength. Clearly, from what Mr Smithers has just said, the Community half of the nutcrackers, for all its strength, is somehow condemned to be passive—the very word 'difficult' reveals it—and already an implication is suggested that initiative must come from the Council of Europe.

During Mr Smithers' first year of office, initiative did come from Strasbourg. The story is interesting as a commentary on the importance of personality and temperament in European questions, for the first direct talks between Mr Smithers and Professor Hallstein on the possibility of a division of work between Brussels and Strasbourg evoked no response from Brussels. Yet a second initiative, this time in talks between M. Modinos (who had resumed in good heart his work as Deputy Secretary General under Mr Smithers) and M. Rey of the Brussels Commission (subsequently to become President of the Commission), succeeded where their two superiors had failed. The beginning at least of a working relationship was evolved—and while this at first amounted to no more than clear suggestions from Brussels that on some questions no more was expected of Strasbourg than to keep off the grass, on other questions a more practical and positive attitude did emerge. Yet even now much still depended on personal contact at different levels and on quite separate questions between representatives of both sides. And here again progress was often determined quite simply by the personality and temperament of the pairs of men meeting—and while the Commission as an official body still continued to be not entirely co-operative, the effect of this was tempered more than once by the actions of men like, for example, M Emile Noel—who could be relied on to make a special effort when often only a special effort could succeed.

On the Brussels side this was perhaps understandable, for this was a time when the Community was having trouble enough defending its existence, principles and progress against President de Gaulle. Yet Mr Smithers in his speech does not say 'the Community'. In spite of the difficulties he refers explicitly to the 'European Commission'. He thereby excludes the Council of Ministers of the Community, and its Member Governments— and thereby also the peoples of the Community, for this was still a time when to exclude national Governments also meant to exclude the populations of their countries. And his emphasis on the nine sworn men of the Brussels Commission is indicative of a determination to strike only at what really mattered, an understanding that it was only from these nine men and the mechanisms at their disposal that real co-operation and initiative could effectively begin.

Mr Smithers continued: '…it (the Commission) has suggested to me that the Council of Europe should proceed by way of action analagous with that of the Communities in which a limited number of its members would take part...'

Here we have it at last, the first formal and public expression on the nature of the relationship now evolving between the two organisations. We are watching something here very important—the first visible and recorded origin, and very small it is, of something later to become very large. And Mr Smithers was able to do even this only because he had at last gained a private but official expression of the Community's view *in writing*. He was thus quite certain of what he here paraphrases for the public—and yet, as we have seen, even this first cautious agreement on a formula of words had already taken over a year of negotiation to achieve, and even now he can go no further than say the Commission 'has suggested'.

Wherein lies the 'limitation'? Is Mr Smithers here thinking of countries like Finland or Spain? Surely not yet, they were not even members of the Council of Europe. Is he thinking of countries like Britain or Austria outside the Community, or of countries inside the Community like Germany or Italy? Probably both, but it is not at all clear. And what is meant by 'analogous'? We are driven to adopt the definition of analogy as used in natural history—there it becomes the 'resemblance of form or function between organs essentially different'. To the extent the Community and the Council of Europe both seek to forward the European Idea, their function is similar—and yet their organs are indeed 'essentially different'. We are thus here being asked to think about resemblances of function in practical instances of action: precisely what this speech is already suggesting must be created. If this is the 'What' we have yet to hear about the 'How'.

> 'This is an extremely important suggestion which offers possibilities for development, with or without reciprocity according to the subject matter, in some cases by way of *partial agreements* limited to those members desiring to take part in them and drawn up in the light of what is being done by the Communities...'

There is here a marked contrast with the style and method used by Professor Hallstein and quoted in Chapter Six. This is a speech of suggestion, of anticipation—challenging earlier assumptions. The first of these assumptions is that the Community and the Council of Europe did not need any formal understanding or relationship—that harmonisation of their work was not necessary.

In earlier chapters we have seen the thinking behind the partial agreement procedure—we saw it becoming central to the Council of Europe's

I*

method of creating Conventions. It is noticeable how this first signpost to
what is going to happen, and *how*, is most carefully concealed in the middle
of its containing sentence. No one can say it was not said—but it is not at
first being said so loud that we are compelled to listen. Yet having made
his point that perhaps there is something valuable in the partial agreement
procedure, Mr Smithers brings it up again, bigger, and now with an
anticipatory barrage of counter-arguments already around it. The paragraph is revealing: what is the attack he feels he must forestall?

> 'Such a procedure of inter-governmental co-operation in the Com-
> mittee of Ministers would involve no new institutions or machinery.
> There is, for example, already a well-established partial agreement
> procedure with a respectable history of achievement to its credit.
> Furthermore, consultations between the Services of the Commission
> and the Secretariat of the Council have already shown the value of
> discussion of our activities in relation to one another.'

In suggestions concerning the European Idea it is often helpful to see
whether a precise level of action is indicated. Here it could scarcely be
clearer. Action is to be inter-governmental by way of the Council of
Europe's Committee of Ministers and not by way of any new institution
or machinery. To those in Mr Smithers' audience already uncomfortably
aware of too many European organisations doing not yet enough in far
too many different ways, this must have come as a relief. For instead of a
new machinery, what is now being proposed is progress by means of an
acceptably dull precedent, in harmony with Brussels, doubtless, but with
the actual work being done in Strasbourg. Immediately there follows a
key sentence: '*The problem is not one of principle but of programming: that is
to say, choice of the subject matter.*' And who, we must immediately ask, is
to be entrusted with that gigantic weapon—power of choice? We are not
told; at least not yet. Instead we hear again a massive and defensive
build-up of facts and argument:

> 'The Council of Europe is a complex organisation which, on the inter-
> governmental side, operates through a series of just under sixty
> inter-governmental expert committees. As we are an organisation for
> inter-governmental co-operation, no important project will succeed
> unless it is likely to command unanimous support or at least an
> absence of objection.
> 'Yet no determined or systematic effort has been made to ascertain
> and define the areas where agreement is possible; on the contrary,
> attention—at least public and political attention—has been focussed

almost exclusively upon those important European matters in which
there is disagreement, and often sharp disagreement. On such matters,
this Assembly has held many valuable debates which have had substantial results in public and parliamentary opinion...'

Apart from the suggestion that in fact the debates of the Assembly,
however 'valuable' they may have been, and however 'substantial' their
results, were forced by events to focus far too often on the negative, there
is here a quite astonishing affirmation of past failure. We have seen in
Chapter Three at least one debate which did not become a mere gnawing
on bones of contention, yet as we saw in earlier chapters, the history of
the Council of Europe had always revolved in a spiral around the twin
poles of the conflicting purposes and powers of the Committee of
Ministers and of the Assembly. And the larger criticism here—a criticism
to be applied elsewhere in Europe also—concerns not the Assembly but the
Ministers—that same Committee of Ministers perpetually blamed for the
weaknesses of the Council of Europe. Mr Smithers does not approach
them in the usual way:

'On the other hand, the Committee of Ministers, which is not ideally
suited to deal with such contentious matters, is ideally suited to reach
agreement upon all those matters of detail where such agreement
should be possible...'

This was probably the first time in the history of the Council of Europe
that someone had said this. Yet the facts have not changed, only the handling of the facts. By that alone the facts themselves now at last appear on
the edge of transmutation. And Mr Smithers not only repeats his point,
but extends it to the whole Council, and this against not merely the Six-
Power Europe of the Community, but the larger Europe. '...So far as I
know, it is in fact the only organisation in Europe capable of undertaking
this neglected task.' The neglected task is quickly defined:

'In the vast field of human activity in technical, social, public health,
legal, educational, cultural and other matters, there must be literally
hundreds of activities in which agreement on common practices
between our Member States would be of benefit to them. While each
individual matter may now itself be of small consequence, the sum
total of agreement upon them, reached over a period of years, would
become a political factor of the first order.'

Now follows what we have already seen cannot be avoided, the open,
courteous, and yet now repeated affirmation of past failure: *'No systematic
and comprehensive attempt has been made up to now to use the Council of Europe*

for such an organised effort to identify the grounds where agreement is possible,
and to build upon them. This attempt, in my submission, should certainly be made.'

If we here keep in mind the earlier key sentence: 'The problem is not
one of principle but of programming: that is to say, choice of subject
matter...', we can perhaps be forgiven if already curiosity is swinging our
thoughts to computers and magnetic tapes punched full of dotted codes.
It is always fascinating when we hear someone dare to propound a
'programme'; we hope to sit back without further effort and see the future
unrolling before us. Do we not all enjoy previews?

Yet the preview does not immediately appear. We never hear what the
'programming' will be, nor any more about the 'choice'. In a way this is
a Salome-speech and Salome-speeches in politics usually imply hard
purpose. Veil after veil is most carefully dropped but we somehow never
see the naked truth. Not yet, that is. One explanation is the date of this
speech, for we are listening only to what could be safely said in May 1965.
It should be clear from what has been suggested in earlier chapters why
this caution was indispensable, and it is partly because of the date of this
speech that we have not yet heard the word 'policy'—yet there can be no
doubt it is a policy-speech as well as a Salome-speech. Even more surprisingly, the next paragraph again repeats the affirmation of past failure,
but this time relates it to individual and group motives:

'When one comes to contemplate such a Programme, a second surprising fact comes to light; *no adequate machinery for drawing up a coherent*
programme of work has been evolved in the Secretariat. There has never been
a proper mechanism which would enable a new proposal to be envisaged in
relation to the activities of the Council as a whole or which would enable the
activities as a whole to be examined systematically, in order to obtain an idea
as to where its deficiencies lay and where advances could possibly be made.
Indeed, it has been difficult for any member of this Assembly, as I was
once myself, or for a representative of a Government, or indeed for the
Secretary General himself, to get a clear idea of what the Council is
really doing in a particular field without a prolonged series of inquiries
in different parts of the House in each particular case.'

As a revelation this is not only alarming in itself, but is in fact often true
not only of the Council of Europe but of other levels of European
unification as well.

'No international organisation such as ours could hope to achieve a
sense of purpose and direction without such a machinery. I have therefore established a modest *Programme Unit* within the Secretariat...'

At these words, all cynics will swoop on that most vulnerable word—
'modest'. It has notoriety as a word able to conceal most plausibly purposes that may politically not be at all modest. Yet, in an unexpected
sense, this word is here exact, for the 'modest Programme Unit' was at the
time of Mr Smithers' speech able to command as its entire directing,
executive, research and advisory staff no more than two heavily overburdened and yet—as events have shown—extraordinarily effective members of the Council of Europe Secretariat. And we can pause at the thought
that it is in fact becoming usual in Europe today for problems to prove so
complex that in the end they can often most effectively be solved only by
a personal and prolonged focussing of thought and action in no more
than three, two, or even only one individual mind. This paradox is
entirely appropriate to our time: the paradox that the more matters
extend to affect giant complexes of society, the more often they come to
be solved with the equivalent of a pencil and a piece of string.

We now wait to hear the effect of what has been already going on with
pencils and pieces of string behind the scenes.

'It is still very small in size but is already giving valuable results and
will probably become an important nerve centre of our activities in
the future. Let me make it clear that this unit has no authority of its
own. It is a piece of analytical and critical apparatus available for use
by members of this Assembly or by Governments for obtaining information on what we are actually doing and studying and evaluating
ideas submitted to it in the light of the rest of our activities...'

We do not yet know what it is, but already we know who will be entitled
to use it. Among others, certainly members of the Assembly before whom
this speech is being made. Nor is this swift appeal to motive without its
reason. To any who are half-asleep, a firm statement of action approaching
is always a crack of the whip, and is for the first second not welcome till
the result of what it announces is experienced—*movement*.

'...in the light of the rest of our activities. So far as I am concerned,
it is the mechanism on which I shall rely for the compilation of all
activities for the inter-governmental work of the Council to be proposed over a period of years to the Committee of Ministers.

'Although the Council over the years has been engaged in a number of extremely useful projects for agreement or for joint action, *the
ultimate purpose of these activities, each valuable in itself, has never, so far
as I know, been defined*. In fact, in deciding whether or not to include
an item in its programme the Council has hitherto been content

merely to ask whether it seemed useful in itself. No sense of unity of purpose can, I believe, be achieved by us unless the Assembly and the Governments are able to judge projects not merely by their intrinsic ability but by the contribution which they may make to ultimate agreed objectives common to our programme as a whole.'

We must here at once consider the phrases 'ultimate purpose' and 'ultimate agreed objectives'. Whatever is here already in mind is going to be planned for 'a period of years'—and yet, how otherwise could it be effective? It is a hard truth that few ultimate objectives concerning the unity of Europe make any sense at all if they are not planned in terms of decades. Yet since both our personal and professional lives seem so short, and since we instinctively live with such feverish haste from year to mere year, any estimate of how long it will really take to establish enduring effects always comes as a shock. We are here listening to a speech in 1965, and the next paragraph—while remarkable for its personal leadership at the all-European level—is also of interest as an illustration of how fast events change on the surface and of how slowly events underneath change in fundamentals. This is how these problems appeared in 1965—we may well ask today, how much since then has fundamentally changed?

'I have already said that, in my own view, as I think in yours, the problem of European unity is mainly that of the relation of the rest of Europe to the Communities. Their establishment has altered the nature of the problem formerly existing and has created a new one. Since all the members of the Community, nearly all those of EFTA, and some other States as well, belong to the Council, it is in the light of the work of the Community that our objectives have to be determined. *If we consider the problem of any individual State which is not a member of the Community, its interests lie in one of three directions; that of ultimately joining the Community, whether individually or as part of a larger group; that of living alongside the Community in such a manner that the interests of both sides can best be adjusted to one another; or that of deferring a decision as to which of these courses it should adopt.*'

There is again a swift change of focus—whereas previously our attention was directed to the Committee of Ministers of the Council of Europe because there is centred the power, we are now told that the co-ordinates for the use of this power must be derived from the objectives not of the Council of Europe but of the European Community. And in what follows, our attention must change focus as fast again: this time from the Community to all the Governments of all the Member countries of the

Council of Europe both now and in the future. The tone is now a calculated persuasiveness and a direct appeal to self-interest:

'A planned programme of harmonisation carried out in the Council of Europe in all matters except those of tariffs and trade and problems intimately connected with them would be helpful to all our members, *whatever their ultimate objective may be, without prejudicing the choice of an individual State as to which course it would adopt.*

'Such a programme of work will probably offer attractions to all European States. To some which are internally divided on the issue of entry into the Common Market it will offer a means of making progress and solving some problems without raising the main issue.

'To those who desire entry but cannot expect it in the near future, it provides a ready means of detailed preparation for that event. In the case of those who wish to remain outside the Community, it will provide opportunities to arrive at practical agreements to ease the position on both sides...

'Such an agreement would in addition bring in the question of and give substance to the often forgotten Article 230 of the Treaty of Rome, which states that there shall be established with the Council of Europe all the necessary forms of co-operation without dividing off from the Community any part of their activity. On the contrary, such a programme, far from subtracting from the work of the Community, would serve to supplement it.

'To EFTA such a programme of work would offer no threat since most of its members would be present, and it might well provide means for achieving agreements which would supplement its work upon tariffs and trade in a useful way.'

We now come to a turning point in a speech which was itself indicative of a turning point in the fundamental evolution of the whole Council of Europe.

'*More important, however, than any of these individual considerations would be the overall political effect of the execution by eighteen Governments of a work programme which would demonstrate the will and ability of Europe to co-operate effectively, at a time when such a demonstration is badly needed.*

'Moreover, it would provide a flexible framework for such co-operation on an inter-governmental basis over a long period of development and would thus enable those within the Communities and those outside to foresee a future of collectively and intelligently planned progress towards the ultimate objectives of their own choice within the general objective of greater European unity. In short, such a development might well mark a decisive turning point in the long-term progress of European unification, by orientating the activities of all our member-states in certain defined fields in the same direction even if they are proceeding by different methods.

'At its meeting yesterday the Committee of Ministers unanimously instructed me to draw up a programme of work in the terms which I have described, taking account of all existing programmes and, of course, subject to their approval of the programme in due time. In my view the Committee of Ministers took what could be one of the longest steps forward for many years to the realisation of a greater Europe. This then is the modern meaning of the statutory phrase "greater unity amongst our Members".

It would be naive to accept this literally as merely a beginning: it is a *fait accompli*. This is already the end of possibly the most critical and laborious stage of all in a political enterprise—that of achieving a sufficient concentration of energy, and from that a sufficient impetus and thereafter momentum for the entire process to begin its intended movement.

What is now revealed in this speech, for the first time, is that the Secretary General of the Council of Europe has succeeded in so shepherding his Committee of Ministers that they have now at last officially instructed him to do precisely what he himself had hoped and intended. The principles of a programme of work must have been shaping in his mind throughout 1964—and they were certainly helped towards crystallisation by, for example, a most constructive conversation towards the end of 1964 with Mr Kristensen of the Organisation for Economic Co-operation and Development in Paris. Now, in May 1965, they are no longer a hope, they are a *directive*. This is very fast work indeed, and while in the next chapter we shall look behind the scenes to see how this shepherding was done, here we are still listening to its first presentation in public, and there is more to come. We are not yet allowed to sit back and applaud. We must again concentrate, and most of all if we feel ourselves concerned with the lives of people in Bucharest or Belgrade, Budapest or Sofia, Warsaw or Helsinki—with the lives of people living today along the Oder and the lower Danube, among the Carpathians or on the west coast of the Black Sea—and even eastwards further still towards the very furthest rim of what is today the present accepted horizon of our European vision. For Mr Smithers' speech does not hesitate to lead our eyes eastwards, into an area of great difficulty demanding equally

great care. The words that follow appear casual but they are Mr Smithers'
statement of attitudes towards the still semi-totalitarian regimes of
Eastern Europe:

> 'I turn now briefly to the second main question which confronts the
> Council. *What should be our relationship to European non-member
> States?* After prolonged discussion of this matter between Member
> Governments and myself, and taking account of the views expressed
> by the Assembly, the Committee of Ministers considered this
> question at its meeting in Paris in December (1964), and after the
> meeting it was stated in the *communiqué* that "an exchange of views
> was held on the subject of relations with other countries. In this
> context, the development of the situation in the countries in Eastern
> Europe and its possible consequences were reviewed. The discussions
> brought out clearly that the Council of Europe does not form a
> *bloc*, and remains open towards the outside world, within the
> limits set by its Statute".'

This was, of course, being said at the beginning of the thaw in Eastern
Europe—and while the democratic ideological requirements of the
Council's Statute have here been most scrupulously included, the eventual
logical consequences of this attitude are potentially far-reaching. For if
the Council of Europe could evolve a programmed policy covering many
multiple activities, harmoniously analagous to the aims and methods of
the Community, and if over years this *combination* of magnetic forces
continued to radiate an intensifying and increasingly attractive influence
across Eastern Europe as well, then it would contribute towards the creation of what all Europe must some day become—a world power.
Interesting things would then happen to the arguments of thinkers like
M. de Riencourt, who argue that the present condition of the world
reveals an unalterable tendency towards global Caesarism, polarised
between Russia and America. We shall encounter M. de Riencourt in the
next chapter—but these issues and more have already been raised by
implication in Mr Smithers' speech. And having given us an indication of
the 'What', he now continues with great care to approach the 'How':

> 'So there is in fact a clear distinction between those States which are
> members of the Council and those which, though geographically
> eligible, are not members because they do not wish to belong to the
> Council or because they are not eligible under other provisions of
> the Statute. In the worst days of the cold war, co-operation with many
> of these States was clearly unthinkable. But under present conditions

to refuse to co-operate with non-member States in uncontroversial technical or juridical matters, if they so desire, could not, in my view, be justified. At the present time there is such co-operation in juridical or cultural matters, or both, with four non-member States, and I expect there to be a gradual further development in this important direction with a corresponding improvement in the political climate of Europe as a whole.'

We are here watching the question of what to do and how to do it being moved up to the scale of Europe as a whole—and the deeper question implied is of the utmost seriousness: to what extent should we ease up on the rigid advocacy of principle in its purest, most absolute, and most astringent form in order thereby to gain a wider, sooner—but not necessarily deeper—*partial* acceptance of that principle? It is even a question whether partial acceptance of an absolute principle in politics is itself ever acceptable, and even whether it is ever in practice possible. The principle here immediately at stake is the democratic nature of Member States of the Council of Europe, while the ultimate principle thereby implicitly at stake is the democratic nature of those States to be granted a decision-making power and responsibility within any eventual All-European Union. The political litmus-test is here always human rights—we shall see in the next chapters how important this test may soon become.

This is a dilemma of increasing importance, for it concerns not only Europe to the east, but also Europe to the south-west. What of Spain? What of Portugal? And what of unexpected and today quiescent regions where this dilemma may some day suddenly arise in dimensions of which we do not yet even dream?

Yet before we can start answering these questions, a yet larger question confronts us:

'The third and last question which confronts us is "*What is the place of our organisation in the emerging structure of world politics?*" A year ago, the Committee of Ministers encouraged me to increase our co-operation with other international organisations. Since then, much has been done, and it can be said that we enjoy the closest and friendliest of relations with those with whom we have to deal. In every case there is an increasing realisation of mutual interest, and the role of the Council of Europe is becoming increasingly clear. As a regional organisation working over a great range of technical matters, we traverse the same ground as the United Nations Agencies. But this does not mean that we need to be in conflict with them, but just the contrary.

'It is clear that an organisation such as ours, consisting mainly of highly developed and technically advanced societies, can proceed much further in the direction of international co-operation than the totality of United Nations members can yet hope to do. Many matters now of immediate concern to us will not become so to many United Nations members for some years. Provided, therefore, that we work in close harmony with the United Nations members, the same process of co-operation in technical matters which will promote greater unity in Europe can also make a valuable contribution towards the work of the world organisation. By acting as a regional advance guard in international co-operation we can thus lay down the precedents and carry out the procedures which may be of service to others in due time. This is a truly acceptable and characteristically European contribution to the emerging world structure. In numerous projects of co-operation or consultation between the Council of Europe and the United Nations agencies it is coming to be an accepted and welcome reality.'

And there is yet more to come. Just as Mr Smithers began this turning-point speech with three clear questions, so now we hear his three clear answers.

'To sum up, after some years of confusion in Europe I see no reason why we should not now enter a period of greater clarity, in which Governments and international organisations will be working towards clearly defined and recognised objectives. The three-fold aim of the Council of Europe can easily be written on the back of a picture postcard...'

These aims can be expressed as answers to the three original questions:
1. *How should the Council of Europe proceed to greater unity between its Member States?*
Answer: by promoting 'greater unity between Member States by inter-governmental co-operation in those fields of human activity where agreement between governments is possible, in consultation with other international organisations, by means of a comprehensive programme of work drawn up in the light of those of the Communities'.
2. *What should be the relationship of the Council of Europe to European non-member States?*
Answer: the promotion of 'co-operation with European non-member States in social, public health, juridical, educational, cultural and other technical matters, wherever such co-operation is mutually desired'.

3. *What is the place of the Council of Europe in the emerging structure of world politics?*

Answer: the making of 'a constructive European contribution to the work of the United Nations and its agencies and thus to the establishment of a better world order'.

And Mr Smithers concludes:

'It will not have escaped the attention of the Assembly that these three aims are all closely interconnected and that the more our work programme prospers the more useful will we be as a partner in the world scene, and the more attractive will we be as an organisation to those who might wish to co-operate with us as non-member States.

'These aims have come to be accepted in principle and in large part explicitly by Governments. I believe they also reflect much of the thinking of this Assembly. Their realisation over a period of years will depend upon the combined and planned efforts of the Assembly, of Governments and of the Secretariat which seeks to serve them.'

This speech has indicated a direction, level, and above all a *method* of action—and it can stand as a model of the kind of political judgement needed at this time. 'Judgement', as John Locke said in 1690, in a passage singled out for approval by Joseph Addison, 'lies...in separating carefully Ideas one from another, wherein can be found the least difference, thereby to avoid being misled by Similitude, and by affinity to take one thing for another...' And while Mr Smithers' speech has not hesitated to aim at the unity of the Greater Europe, or to suggest that although the unity of this Greater Europe may be many decades ahead of us, nevertheless it insists also that action towards that aim can and must start today. Yet there are things which this speech has itself quite deliberately *not* said.

A work programme is to be established, but not one word is said of who shall control it—whether Secretariat, Ministers or Assembly. A planning and programming unit is also to be established—has indeed already been established—but not one word is said of what it will try to do, the categories of thinking under which it will work, the powers it will enjoy, or its ultimate aim. The 'What' has been half sketched; the 'How' has been half outlined. Is this speech really a turning-point, and if so, why?

Less than four weeks later an authoritative commentary was added by Mr Hugh Beesley, Counsellor to the Political Directorate of the Council of Europe, in a public speech to the Council of European National Youth Committees on 1 June 1965. After filling in some of the background to

Mr Smithers' proposals, he proceeds to more direct comment on the Secretary General's speech:

'You remember that...when the Secretary General made his speech he had on the previous day obtained the unanimous agreement of the eighteen Governments on the substance of what he had to say. Now it will occur to you, of course, that among these eighteen Governments there are those of the European Communities—the Six—and that they should agree that we should base our own work here on that of or be inspired by that of the Communities is not very difficult for them. On the other hand to have got such a statement from the EFTA countries or from those countries which, unhappily for them, take part in neither of the big economic groups is, you may think, rather more amazing.

'...there is a general recognition that *the* economic and political fact in Europe at the moment is the European Communities and therefore any realistic programme of work of this body (the Council of Europe) must necessarily and at all times take the very closest account of what the Communities have done, are doing, and plan to do.

'In what fields can this be done? I think the answer must be *all* fields, with two exceptions. We are not competent for defence and military matters...We think also that we ought to stay out of the tricky, desperately tricky, business of tariffs and trade which is, of course, a direct business of the Communities, the direct business of EFTA...

'But we do feel that a comprehensive programme of work which we...are in process of drawing up, should extend to every other field of European co-operation...

'We think again that within this comprehensive programme we should set up priorities. Most of us around this table could probably agree on the sort of Europe we want to see, the sort of united Europe that we hope we will see within our lifetimes. Where perhaps agreement is a little more difficult is when you come to assess the priorities, to decide on which work you should start first. And yet it is evident that to have a realistic programme that does not merely trail all over the place with no clear indication of priorities we must reach agreement on the tasks that command immediate attention...

'...I think that what I have said will convince you that we have a fairly ambitious programme of work ahead of us. In a way *this is going to be the supreme test for a rejuvenated Council of Europe*. Will it prove equal to the task that this programme sets it? The years will show, but I think there is a reasonable hope that it will.'

Thus Mr Beesley as early as 1965—and we have saved his opening and best point for last. It was brief and astonishing:

'I think that if you had come here as late as four weeks ago I could not have told you at least in as definite terms just what the Council of Europe's *doctrine* was. But it happened that on May the 4th the Secretary General addressed the Assembly in a public statement...'

Which is where we came in earlier in this chapter. The Council of Europe, and indeed all concerned with the European Idea, owe more than we like to realise to those few men who will go so far as to express their entire understanding of the matter in a single explicit and comprehensible word—and then to go yet further, and insist on placing that word boldly before the public eye. This particular word—*doctrine*—had been missing entirely from the history and even the thinking of the Council of Europe for fifteen years—the turning-point is evident. The voices we have heard in this chapter knew where they were going, but such voices are too few. We all have to consider not merely the decades to come in Europe, but the centuries, and make the effort to say to those among us still rubbing the sleep out of their eyes—'Consider the What, consider *more* the How'.

Separately we are each little and very different, yet together we are Europe—and when we are Europe, what are we? Why, we are the oldest and also the newest; we are the weakest and yet we can be the strongest; we are the most foolish and yet we can be the wisest; we have the longest and most troubled past and yet ours can be the longest and most triumphant future—for after all, we are Europe. It is good that we should know this, for we have a European ship of state yet to build, and a ship that is not seaworthy cannot sail through storms.

CHAPTER EIGHT

'Whither We Are Tending'

'If we could first know *where* we are, and *whither* we are tending, we could better judge *what* to do, and *how* to do it.'   ABRAHAM LINCOLN, 1858

THE EUROPEAN IDEA knows where it is going, but not how it will get there. Towards a 'greater unity' says the Statute of the Council of Europe. Towards an 'ever closer union' says the Preamble to the Treaty of Rome. The 'where' is indicated though not defined—the 'how' we have to work out for ourselves. And whenever we touch the European Idea what we are actually dealing with is a quite deliberate process: the transmutation of forms of power, ill-defined though the process may be. It has to be accepted that a united Europe will eventually evolve its own characteristic and recognisably European modes of handling political power, and when, as in the previous chapter, we watched a particular aspect of the European Idea in progress, we were watching not only how the introduction of a coherent Work Programme was first presented to the Assembly in a public speech by the Secretary General of the Council of Europe but also an aspect of how modes of power at the European level are today being transmuted into new forms before our eyes.

In this chapter we shall see a further stage of the same process but in a different dimension. Instead of watching public events, we shall instead follow the process by which this same Work Programme was *privately* expounded to all the Member Governments of the Council of Europe— and we shall again be able to catch glimpses of yet larger questions. Above all, we shall see before us at least one documented aspect of 'where we are' in our present experience of the European Idea.

Yet, in Europe at least, when we consider where we *are* it is as well to recall where we come *from:* the Europe of stuttering machine-guns, poison-gas, Paschendaele and barbed-wire—the Europe of the dive-bomber and the diplomatic smile—the Europe where a Franco must climb out of the rubble and a Mussolini must march on Rome—the Europe where the handshakes of statesmen were measured in millions of dead, and the signatures of statesmen in more millions of dead, uncounted millions—from the Europe of Theresienstadt and Auschwitz, the Europe where murder, blackmail, betrayal, torture were daily playthings, the Europe where good men stood still until it was too late, the Europe where truth was used more diabolically than lies, the Europe where the highest prayer for millions of men, women, and children became every day a prayer merely to survive.

Less than thirty years ago our Europe was again a killing-ground for mankind, a charnel-house. Those who were alive in the war and survived need no reminder, but those who were then not even children certainly do. It is as well our charnel-house was photographed in all its folly so that we may view again our past as an everlasting warning. No one should discuss the unity of Europe who has not, for example, at least sat though some of the films—notably Paul Rotha's dispassionate documentary *Mein Kampf*—and not just once but several times until the images and sounds are printed deep. Ours is, after all, the continent that produced both the artist that was Goya and the cruelty he depicted—Goya, who began by designing tapestries and ended etching torture. These films show a Europe to surpass any nightmare of Goya's—a cruelty apocalyptic in extent, intensity and duration, and yet a Europe where unthinkable horror became entirely commonplace. These images of people live, talk, walk, run, shout, kill, scream, cower and burn before our eyes—and this as often as we have courage to regard them. Perhaps they died merely so that their suffering might be shown to us: these were real people, this is what we come from. Let those who discuss the unity of Europe study carefully these images upon the screen—the rag-wrapped feet of a five-year-old boy shuffling in a starvation-dance for alms to save his life some few days longer in the Warsaw Ghetto, or the demented mother howling aimlessly up and down the pavement—trudging sightlessly up and down between corpses sprawled out upon that pavement—her child in her arms. Nor can we turn aside like Pharisees blaming all on Hitler. As the film carefully says: 'He was one of us and we permitted this.'

Let those who discuss the unity of Europe therefore study carefully the expression on the faces of those about to die, dying, and having died; the expression on the faces of those about to kill, killing, and having killed. Let them study the faces of partisans about to hang and the faces of men about to do the hanging. If this repetition sickens them, let them bear with their nausea: this is the truth of where we come from. Let those who discuss the unity of Europe therefore consider the under-tones of the public speeches, the over-tones of the public misery. Let them study carefully the beginning, the middle, the end—the price of a cracked, black loaf of bread in the German inflation; the sight of modern armies in this age of oil and rubber and steel reduced to horse-transport, and the horses soon to be eaten. Let them study the sight of victims become captors, and captors become victims. And let them not ignore as trivial the sight of a long line of tiny identical twins, toddling hand-in-hand and two-by-two out of their concentration camp, spared from the incinerators merely because they were ear-marked for merciless scientific experiment.

Are we so blind as not to remember where we come from, so careless as not to care whither we are tending? If this is the truth of the Europe we come from, what then of the Europe towards which we *wish* to tend? If we are formed by the past, to what extent dare we allow the past to fetter us? To what extent is it true that evil always comes at us out of the past and that—to adapt the modern French song—'Les *souvenirs* en sont la cause, les *souvenirs* sont assassins...'? How shall we find the balance between the pain of remembering and the balm of oblivion, the balance between forgiving (which we *must*) and forgetting (which we must *not*)? Above all, how shall we learn to choose what the past must teach us— and having chosen, what does that tell us of our future?

One thing is certain—we have nowhere to go now in Europe except up, and Europe has no chance of doing so unless this time we go upward all together. Yet equally it is folly to deny that this very progress upwards, for the very reason that this time we are trying to do it by working all together, must in time bring us face to face with problems of unprecedented magnitude, complexity and certainly, at some time we cannot yet anticipate, of soul-rending difficulty—and this both for individuals and for peoples.

It is an argument of this book that we are tending towards a Government of Europe. We can see something of the progress we have made towards this if we consider some possible implications for the European Idea of what the Secretary General of the Council of Europe had in mind when he announced his establishment of a 'modest Programme Unit' inside his Secretariat. He was introducing to a public session of the Assembly his project of a coherent Work Programme for the Council of Europe, as already approved in May 1965 by the eighteen Member

Governments. It is easy to say today that the creation of a Programme Unit to co-ordinate the work of the Council was a self-evident necessity —but we can now safely say this only because we also now know it has proved possible. Previously it was not realised that it was possible —and if we merely compare the idea of creating a Programme of Work with the events described in Chapter Three, we shall see the extraordinary change taking place within the Council of Europe. In Chapter Three we followed the progress over many years of a single and immensely complicated social initiative which finally achieved birth at the all-European level in the form of a Convention of the Council—the European Social Charter. In this Chapter we are again dealing with an unprecedented initiative, but now at the scale of an entire European organisation proposing to spell out in detail *all* its present and future inter-governmental activities, complete with defined aims and agreed time-tables. And we find that central to this project is to be a Programme Unit consisting at first of no more than two or three people.

Even if we knew no more about the Programme Unit than has already been mentioned, we could work out something about its future characteristics and evolution from first principles. As we know from cybernetics, a flow of information which starts from a centre of policy and diversifies outwards into action can be fully efficient only if the results of that policy not only happen but are known to happen and are transmitted back as new corrective information to the policy-making centre—not haphazardly but exactly, swiftly, in detail and with discrimination. Effective action depends on information travelling this full circle. This simple theory of feedback is today so well known, and now it is familiar to us is theoretically so obvious, that what is astonishing is how seldom we give the necessary time and attention to making certain it is happening in daily practice. Yet is it so simple—in Norbert Wiener's own words: 'Feedback is a method of *controlling a system by re-inserting into it the results of its past performance*. If these results are merely used as numerical data for the criticism of the system and its regulation, we have the simple feedback of the control engineers. If, however, the information which proceeds backward from the performance is able to change the general *method* and *pattern* of performance, we have a process which may well be called learning.'

This is especially true in politics. If we reverse the proposition, we could well say that a political system with no feedback is not a system that can effectively learn, improve, evolve—or in the end even survive. If we apply this criteria of feedback to the Council of Europe in its earlier years, we find it was confined within separate organs and functions of the Council.

In other words, a number of limited and unconnected feedback systems were active, but no overall system. Similarly, if we apply this criteria to the whole European Idea today we find the same—that feedback systems are still fragmentary, limited to separate organs, functions, and areas where the Idea operates.

Thus we could expect this modest Programme Unit to become a concentration of skilled minds inside the Council of Europe Secretariat devoted first to knowing everything that is already being done within the Council of Europe, then what may be done in the future, and thereafter extending this process to a consideration of what is also being done elsewhere than in the Council. We could expect this tiny group of people to exercise influence merely through their unceasing co-ordination of incoming and outgoing information—and that once they have achieved momentum in their method, experience and thought, they would tend to acquire *increasing* influence. If our professions of faith in the European Idea are genuine, we must of course welcome this increasing influence. We must hope that it will be emulated elsewhere than in Strasbourg. And we must hope that ultimately all these newly created political nerve-centres will themselves be harmoniously linked right across Europe.

This speculation on what we could expect from a Programme Unit may seem straightforward, yet it does itself take a great deal for granted. It is an astonishing and shocking fact that there is at present no single inclusive list, no single codified means of knowing precisely who is supposed to be doing what in Europe, where, how, or with what aims. The information exists, but it is sealed off into nearly thought-tight compartments, whether in the offices of organisations and departments, or the memories of individual people. There is no common pool of even essential information.

It is a fact, for example, that while there is a confidential system called the '*Indexage*' in the Council of Europe, this is limited to providing immediate cross-reference between all documents handled by the Council, and there is *no* single index of the right type available to all parts of the Secretariat, or to all Members of the Assembly. The information is there but split up piecemeal in different minds. Much of it is in documents, but there is no codified—least of all computerised—method of extracting swiftly a digest of the information as needed by the questioner.

Thus for example, if anyone in the Council of Europe should wish to know in a hurry the names of the twenty-five men in Europe best qualified on, shall we say, transport problems, it is necessary to ask Jacques who will ask Gustaf who will ask John who will perhaps know two names only, and that only because he happens to have met them personally. It is not

possible to check any index under TRANSPORT—(a) political, (b) industrial, (c) trade unionist..., and see at once twenty-five names. This is all
the more extraordinary when the Council itself has already mobilised
sufficient expert talent of the highest calibre to man more than sixty
expert committees. No list of these names is immediately available—and
thay have not been programmed into the basic memory of any central
indexing system for the very good reason no central index yet exists.

The same is true of course very often in America—but there the problem
is known, and when something difficult has to be done, the cybernetic
aspects are often given a first priority, and attacked with determination in
proportion to difficulty. It is commonplace in many American political
organisations to work intensively from card-indexes of this type. The
Rockefeller, Nixon, Kennedy methods have become well known (and
the ethical problems were well dramatised in the American novel *Convention*, with its questionable computer 'Oscar')—yet these are all no more
than an intensification of methods taken for granted in many areas of
American industry, law and education. In Europe we do not take it for
granted. If we consider merely our libraries, we find that all-European
bibliographies (as for example, those developed in the College of Europe
in Bruges) are today still considered pioneer ventures and surprising. If we
consider political information centres, we find that an organisation of the
calibre of the Atlantic Institute in Paris does not reflect the norm at all—
on the contrary, its increasingly streamlined procedures for handling
information appear today revolutionary. For we are often in Europe so
spoilt in our sophistication, so convinced we already automatically know
better, that we do not trouble to check whether we do know better. If we
did check, we would often be dismayed to find we do *not*.

Oddly enough, any suggestion that information-theory should be
applied on this scale to the work of unifying Europe is often met either
with the criticism that it smacks too much of naive and crude Americanisa-
tion—or, at the other extreme, of ruthlessly sophisticated totalitarian
techniques. Our European memory is such a cluttered museum of
formerly admirable models for doing almost anything, that if an idea
comes along today with no obvious European predecessors, we usually
dismiss it as either naive or unwelcome. If we need this idea today, then
we must surely have already done something like it yesterday—so runs
our instinctive thinking. Yet is it not equally naive, equally unrealistic, to
think we can get along without new ideas, of many new kinds, and most
of all in the politics of European unification? Is it in fact even *safe* to deny
we are in urgent need of new ideas—which at first sight may seem not
merely surprising but deeply disturbing?

The idea of a Work Programme for the Council of Europe, when first put forward as a firm personal commitment by the Secretary General, was certainly surprising—and his idea that it must have a Programme Unit was certainly disturbing. It would have been yet more disturbing if the Assembly had known at the time of Mr Smithers' speech in May 1965 that neither he nor his Secretariat had yet achieved any clear idea of the form the Programme should take, or what it should contain. The truth is that the hard thinking was done *after* his speech—during July and August—and that the entire Programme of Work was evolved during September, October, and November.

Yet even without knowing this, we could anticipate that an effective Programme of Work, with an increasingly experienced Programme Unit behind it, would automatically tend to attract increasing attention in the Committee of Ministers, the Assembly, and the Press—and thereafter also in all Member Governments, all Member countries of the Council of Europe, and eventually in other continents—not least Latin America and the Middle East. This we could anticipate merely by knowing its *method*. And even though this Work Programme was not yet at all a *plan for Europe* in the full sense, it was certainly already an indispensable first step towards a far larger application of the same method. In cybernetic terms the simplicity of compressing everything into one document was structurally sound, and this is the moment to point out that even this first preparatory step, this first idea of a single coherent Work Programme being published to the world as a *single lucid written document*, was initiated solely by the personal action of the Secretary General, and that his repeated personal insistence was necessary to get it done, approved, and on the move.

Thus while in May 1965 it was possible for Mr Smithers to announce an agreement in principle on the creation of a Work Programme, and while by November a draft Programme did exist within the Secretariat, nevertheless this had yet to be finally approved by the Governments. All could yet be lost. What, therefore, was to be the essential strategic aim? As will have become apparent from the previous chapter, it could only be to secure an absence of opposition within the Committee of Ministers. If one or more Governments had at the last moment drawn back from the spirit of their previous approval in principle, the Programme could nevertheless have gone ahead in some form (for there was no formal requirement that the Ministers must be unanimous on every item)—but this would have been damaging. What was needed was a Ministerial atmosphere of wholehearted approval—and on particular disputed items a cheerful decision by majority vote: this for the very good reason that every time a Government expressed approval on any single item, that much at least was gained for the future. And while the draft Programme already contained over two hundred proposed activities, its real aim was to *transform the character of the Council of Europe into a more dynamic, precise instrument for the European Idea, and to introduce a fundamentally new structural element into the European picture.* The strategic long-term aim can be symbolised by the map at the end of this book, which we have already examined in Chapter Six—the unchanging aim of a truly united Greater Europe. Yet this could scarcely be stressed at the time: the very size of the strategic aim required in the presentation of the Programme to Governments a deliberately *quiet* approach. Above all, there must be no sense of crisis.

If the strategic aim was simple, the tactical problems were complex. To appreciate this we have to keep in mind not only the inherent complexity of a list of over two hundred activities, but we have to imagine this list being presented to eighteen Foreign Ministers separately—one each in Dublin, Reykjavik, Oslo, Luxembourg, Bonn, Rome, Athens, Copenhagen, London, Stockholm, Brussels, the Hague, Valletta, Vienna, Berne, Nicosia, Paris, and Ankara—and in each Ministry a group of advisers gathered round their Minister, and each group in turn finally advising him on the exact extent to which he can approve the Programme as a whole, and also each activity separately. These advisers had therefore to consider the extent to which every single detail in the Programme did or did not seriously accord with the fundamental circumstances within their country, and if we pause a moment to consider what is really happening when a project involving over two hundred activities is then cross-multiplied by all that is happening in eighteen separate countries, we have to admit that it is, to say the least, complex.

It was in these circumstances that in November 1965 the Secretary General of the Council of Europe addressed himself to the Governments in a private explanatory memorandum. We shall now follow this memorandum very carefully—for it was with these arguments that the battle was fought and won where it really mattered: *inside* the Governments of the Member countries.

Its tone—as we would expect—is that of a very quiet soft sell. The Programme was so close to success that scarcely more than a whisper of suggestion could be risked. Mr Smithers' argument was thus on the surface no more than a gently rational mustering of logic and fact. And yet, though it appears as smooth as butter, if we look closely we shall see the butter has been spread with a very sharp knife, and that we are watching a masterly example of how to grasp, hold, and use the initiative. The initiative, after all (to paraphrase Napoleon's dictum on power) belongs with justice to those who know how to use it.

Mr Smithers began: 'The aim of the draft Programme of Work is to increase the usefulness of the Council of Europe to Governments and, through them, to the people of Europe.' The thrust is at the Governments —but already the word 'people' is in the collective and unified singular.

'The Programme is conceived as a continuous process developing in balance and coherence from year to year and gaining in relevance to the needs of Europe as they change and develop. The document presented here (the first draft Programme for 1966/67) thus necessarily contains only some first steps in this direction...it consists essentially of an enumeration and classification of existing inter-governmental activities, as precise as possible and giving an indication of the results proposed in each case. A few new activities are proposed, and a few suggestions made as to activities to be discontinued. These suggestions are necessarily modest since time has not permitted adequate discussion with governments of important but controversial matters. This continuation of existing work needs in principle no justification, for in every case the inter-governmental activities on which the Council of Europe is engaged have already been specifically approved by the Committee of Ministers. Their inclusion in the 1966 Programme nonetheless reflects three features which are novel.'

'Firstly, every item has been reviewed by the Secretary General against the background of certain criteria which are set out below.

'Secondly, the preparation of a complete detailed list of the Council's inter-governmental activities is in itself new. The existence of such a list, which will be published and will be revised in each annual statement of the programme, will enable Governments, the Consultative Assembly, other international organisations both inter-governmental and non-governmental, and interested public opinion to make an assessment of the work of the Council as a whole, and in the various sectors. It will thus for the first time be possible to criticise its substance and its balance upon a comprehensive basis.

'Thirdly, except in respect of "permanent" activities, approximate dates are given for the beginning and, where possible, termination of each particular project...some idea can be obtained as to the likely state of work for several years ahead, and priorities can be expressed in practical terms of a timetable.'

These are lines to which 'interested public opinion' and even more interested expert and governmental opinion will have to come back again and again as successive annual Work Programmes follow each other. Mr Smithers' words appear mild, their general impression is that nothing startling is going to happen—merely a general tidying up—and yet the messages are clear between the lines—a *continuous* process...', 'balance and coherence...', 'criteria...', 'a *complete* detailed list...', 'an *assessment* of the work of the Council as a *whole*...', 'for the first time possible to *criticise*...' When we unwrap the hard words from their packaging of soft words, the impression is different.

And these lines of Mr Smithers are also approaching a submerged reef of difficulty, to be encountered repeatedly by anyone attempting real action in the context of the European Idea—our fundamental dislike and even fear of timetables and priorities. We do not like being pinned down. We hesitate to commit ourselves more than one step in advance. We sometimes fear to give our word for fear that we shall break it. This dark reef of difficulty is not to be underestimated. Its rocks are only just below the surface of our daily conscious actions—we shall navigate safely round it only if first we know it is there. It is even possible to say that one of the surest ways of testing how genuine any alleged willingness to co-operate in European unification really is, can be found by simply seeing whether hard timetables agreed in advance, and scales of priorities so real they involve sacrifices by someone, can or can not be agreed in principle and maintained in practice. Mr Smithers approaches this difficulty quietly. We would not think there was a reef at all:

> 'These dates, which can of course be neither rigid nor binding, are put forward as a basis for discussion and decision by Governments. They should, when confirmed, serve both as target-dates which committees of experts will do their best to respect and as an indication of the priority which Governments attach to each activity. Thus the fixing of an early completion date in relation to the amount of work involved means that work has high priority. It has been found possible to suggest dates up to and including 1968, and in a small number of cases beyond.'

Thus while this first Work Programme was presented as aiming to run only within a three-year span, it must even in 1965 have already appeared inevitable that this span would tend to lengthen—that with some projects (the investigation of cancer, for example, the control of water pollution, or the European Pharmacopoeia) we can scarcely expect any results at all except under timetables running up to five, seven, nine and more years. This first private introduction of the Work Programme was of course designed to understate—to woo Government Departments rather than

Behind the Scenes: Henri Brugmans, President of the European Union of Federalists, and R. W. G. Mackay, MP for Hull, N.W., until 1950

The President of the Assembly of the Council of Europe and its senior officers: LEFT TO RIGHT: *Gerhard Schloesser (Clerk of the Assembly), Polys Modinos (Deputy Secretary General), Peter Smithers (Secretary General), Sir Geoffrey de Freitas, PC, KCMG, MP (President)*

A unique body: the European Commission of Human Rights in session.

A building with a unique purpose: the 'Palais des Droits de l' Homme' in Strasbourg.

astound them—and it is not irrelevant that Governments do tend to think and react in terms of their own electoral time-span. While the combination in any country of a powerful Civil Service with the facts of that country's own situation does tend to limit the boundaries of possible policy, it is also true that any change of Government can lead to decisive changes within those limits. And Mr Smithers is dealing not with one Government but eighteen, whose elections do not occur concurrently. Scarcely a year or even six months can pass in Europe without decisive changes of emphasis and policy occurring in one or more countries. And while this crazy-paving pattern of politics across the map of Europe makes any co-ordinated and stable timetable on even small things inordinately difficult, it also makes the necessity of holding to timetables and priorities all the more evident. Given the circumstances of this first Programme, a three-year time-span was probably the most that could be reasonably suggested to Governments—for if this could safely gain acceptance, later it could safely grow.

As for the new activities for which approval was sought, nothing more was suggested to Governments than that '...these are few in number... insufficient time has elapsed since the Ministers' decision of 3 May to permit the Secretariat to ascertain which of the many questions of undoubted European interest are also of interest to enough national governments and offer a chance of leading to practical results. In future Programmes the section "New Work to be Undertaken" may be more extensive, both because a certain amount of existing work will by then have been completed and because consultations with Governments will have revealed which problems are ripe for inter-governmental action... this year it was difficult for the Assembly and for the many organisations consulted to make suggestions for work to be undertaken since no existing programme was before them as a starting point. Next year they will have such a basis before them on which to found their consideration; in consequence it may be expected that a greater number of relevant suggestions for new work will be received. Study of some of these problems is already proceeding within the Secretariat...'

The harder the matter, the more necessary a delicacy of approach—so it here sounds. It is clearly suggested to Governments that this first Work Programme is imperfect—and why? The explanation cannot be avoided: most of its activities have been inherited. And since its form is new but its content old, since this new bottle still awaits new wine and of a new vintage, who then in fact will tread the grapes, and who will drink the wine? This question is here most carefully avoided but as we shall see in the next chapter it could not be avoided for long.

K

And a second point is indicated—true certainly of the work of the Council of Europe but with wider implications for all concerned with the European Idea—the point that there are many problems in Europe today whose solution would be of value to many people, and which are susceptible of solution now as soon as there is a will to solve them, but which—most mysteriously—Governments tend to ignore. Or perhaps it is not so mysterious: Governments, after all, demand a quick electoral dividend on all they do. On this depends their survival. The value of what a Government does is thus determined in its priorities by the electoral system which has put it in office and will choose its successor. This would suggest we can hope for effective solutions only to those problems national Governments feel to be of electoral advantage—and most of us would feel this a sad limitation if final. And yet simultaneously, there are in Europe today—and this does mean from the West of Ireland to the Upper Danube—problems of the most urgent human concern which do not yield immediate electoral advantage. On national agendas these problems thus sink to a priority so low that nothing even starts to happen. These problems thus become perpetual. Their evil accumulates. Their solutions become increasingly difficult, and as they become more difficult so their national priorities slide ever yet lower. Yet when these problems are common to many countries, when many Governments face the identical difficulty of seeing no immediate return for effort invested, and when these problems are nevertheless admittedly susceptible of solution, then we have problems of 'undoubted European interest'. Which, to put it less modestly and more truthfully, means they are problems which can be solved *only* at the European level and *at nothing less*.

It is also clearly suggested to Governments there is no question of waiting for them. If they prefer to stand aside, so be it—but within the Council Secretariat 'study of some of these problems is already proceeding.' Who now is acquiring the initiative? In the next passage, let us watch closely this question of initiative—for it is central to the evolution of the European Idea and its handling here repays study. Mr Smithers continues:

'Of the proposed new activities to be started in 1966 (or, occasionally, later) the majority have been suggested by committees of experts themselves, which provides good *prima facie* evidence of their feasibility. Others, notably in the social and public health fields, have been proposed in the light of what was in May agreed to be one of the fundamental features of the Council's Work Programme, namely that it should have regard to the activities and achievements of the European Communities...Proposals falling in neither of the above categories reflect simply my personal conviction that here are problems (whatever conclusions may have been arrived at previously in some cases) which now call for early European action and are unlikely to raise major difficulties for Governments, particularly given the possibility of recourse if necessary to a Partial Agreement. In several instances they reflect a suggestion by the Consultative Assembly.'

Do we shy at that phrase 'simply my personal conviction'? If we do, are we justified? Regardless of how we value it, this phrase has to be recognised as merely one among many signs around us of an emerging managerial revolution in both the style and method of the politics of European integration. If this were not so, would we not have even greater cause for alarm? Is not this quiet determination to get on with the job—and to accept public responsibility for that determination—an aspect of our times which we in Europe must increasingly welcome?

Mr Smithers' next point is on '*Work to be discontinued*':

'That the list of such projects is short is, again, understandable; for each of them was in its time approved by the Committee of Ministers. However, in some instances the work has not progressed as planned, while in others it has failed to lead to the results expected; in these circumstances revision of the original decision is justified. This list would have been longer if I had not felt that in several cases the studies already undertaken had reached a point where it would be more wasteful of money and work to postpone their immediate cessation than to bring them as quickly as possible to some kind of conclusion, such as the publications of a report.'

The sense of initiative continues—'If I had not felt...'—the personal decision is there, and with it acceptance of personal responsibility. That we must respect. Yet at the end of it all comes no more than 'the publication of a report'. This appears such anti-climax, such a minor point. Merely another report, to be heaped on heaps, already piled high, of papers upon papers? If some activity is not going well, would it not be better for it to be instantly axed?

This point is vital to the present handling of the European Idea, for the visible frontiers of our national states in Europe are as obstacles nothing beside the very many invisible frontiers dividing off our knowledge. The real frontiers in Europe are the frontiers within ourselves. They include all information-barriers which starve us of understanding, and wherever these barriers can be lowered the achievement is great. Again we are in the realms of cybernetics: to turn it the other way, the worst waste possible of even unsuccessful work is for there to be no record of what went wrong, and how, and why. When the unification of Europe is today as difficult as it is, do we have any right to deny knowledge of our present mistakes— as well as our efforts—to our neighbours of today—and also tomorrow? To take merely one example among thousands: a book by Mr Finn Moe (*rapporteur* of the Political Committee of the Assembly of the Council of Europe), discussing the desirability of creating a European Research Institute to examine causes of international conflict and to develop peace research studies, while on the one hand it opens up a gigantic subject, on the other hand was published merely as yet another 'report of the Assembly'. And the reports of the Secretariat or of expert Committees, to which Mr Smithers is here referring, are often each equivalent either to an entire book—or, alternatively, to just one sub-aspect of one activity in the Work Programme. We are thus today in a stage of European unification where our problem is not the *amount* of information available—for we can never have too much—but its *organisation in relation to our needs*. Energy invested in improving the mechanics of our communication processes is no longer a luxury—it is a necessity of immediate political importance. And in this context, it will by now have become clear that the principles of political organisation and communication on the European level here being quietly indicated by Mr Smithers are themselves potentially capable of far wider application than the Council of Europe itself—they are in fact a blueprint of how these things can not only be done now, but can tomorrow be done on the all-European scale. If we look at it this way, and speculate on the decades to come, we shall perhaps come to read such an apparently innocuous phrase as 'the publication of a report' in its true perspective.

Mr Smithers continued with '*Work in progress*':

'Included in the Programme…are many items on which work should also cease, in the near future, for more satisfactory reasons. These are the activities for which it is now possible to predict successful completion in 1966. Thus no idea of the balance of new work with work ceasing can be obtained unless work being completed is taken into account as well as work being stopped. The perpetual replacement of "Work in progress" by "New work to be undertaken" should indeed be the main feature of the Programme, which will gradually determine its character over a period of years.'

This attitude is in sharp contrast to those who see European unification as an end in itself instead of as an indispensable means towards something larger—Europe's list of unfinished business is not only enormous, but will always be enormous if Europe is to be truly in character with herself.

What will change is the scope and scale of what is being done—therein lies the achievement. This is a hard criterion for constructive criticism— and yet, within the terms of this document to Governments, it is shrewdly chosen. All success provokes a shock-wave. We have here an anticipation of this shock-wave, for anything which is going to determine the character of action over a period of years is likely to be sharply scrutinised during those years—and it is sometimes not unwise to point out in advance where criticism can best start.

Next comes something even harder, criteria for action:

'In general all the Council's activities will be judged, by governments and public opinion alike, by their practical consequences. If they lead to a mutually profitable *pooling of experience and resources, to raising economic, social and educational standards, to reducing the causes of discord and tension between neighbouring countries and an alignment of national laws in spheres where there is demonstrable need for uniform or similar regulations, then their value cannot be doubted and both the national and general European interest will have been served.* If the progress made along these lines can be directed particularly to the more important and urgent problems, then its significance is the greater. These must be the constant criteria when selecting the Council's work, both immediate and longer term, and thus determining priorities. Conversely activities having no definite practical aim or unlikely to give tangible results in a reasonable space of time must be given low priority or be dropped altogether.'

And there follows again a double attack on past inadequacy. Its truth cannot be denied and in the *way* it is here said privately to Governments it serves the strategic purpose by merely pointing out what was earlier not done. A hill looks highest when one points out the low ground.

'An overall examination of the Council of Europe's work reveals two major gaps, which the Programme of Work will seek to remedy over the years. The first is that certain activities of obvious importance for the realisation of the Council's statutory aims, and indeed certain entire sectors of activity, have been neglected. The second is that where a problem is so large that it transcends the divisions within which we have fallen into the habit of working (cultural, social, public health, etc.) it has been tackled piecemeal, with the result that particular aspects of the problem, though perhaps vital to its solution, have sometimes been neglected.'

The two gaps are then illustrated—the first (that in which sectors of activity have been neglected) through economics. This of course touches

282   Done this day

the work of the European Community, and a clear though subtle de-
marcation appears of what the Council of Europe definitely can not do—
and also perhaps of what it can:

'...Naturally, there are reasons why the Council has been almost completely inactive, at least at inter-governmental level, in this sphere...at
the time of the Council's creation there was already in existence a
specialised organisation [the OEEC] having virtually the same membership, a general competence in economic matters, and enough expert
staff, which the Council could legitimately regard as its economic arm.
Today this situation has changed fundamentally, for our Member
States no longer have at their disposal a European organisation with
general economic competence. The OECD [which replaced the OEEC],
with a membership extending to North America and Japan, cannot
regard the Council of Europe as its 'opposite number'...Again, the fact
that six of our Member States, together with two others associated with
them, pursue their economic integration and co-operation primarily
within the Communities, while seven others work mainly inside EFTA,
is in strong contrast to...1949.
     '...it would be an error for the Council to attempt to play...a nego-
tiating role in...tariffs and currency questions...On the other hand a
concerted attempt to reduce or eliminate non-tariff barriers to the free
movement of goods and persons is not only in the direct interest of
Member Governments but is a task which the Council of Europe is
excellently fitted to fulfil...it has been working in this field already,
though, because the task has been undertaken by committees of legal and
social experts, the fact has not always been realised. This work should
now be enlarged and made part of a planned programme. It will no
doubt continue...to be entrusted to governmental experts who are not,
or not primarily, economists...A second consequence of a new determination on the part of Member Governments to achieve faster and
more considerable economic results by such indirect means could be
additional work in the fields of transport, posts and communications,
using other competent organisations to make the necessary technical
studies, and the Council of Europe to draw up, where appropriate,
international legal instruments based thereon. For this task the Council
of Europe is particularly well suited.'

Is this a concealed take-over bid? We shall look at this in the next chapter,
and if it is, then this is where it started.
     The second gap is even more characteristic of our present stage in
European unification than the first. It is our piecemeal, fragmentary, un-

co-ordinated and often openly conflicting approach to problems. To some extent it is obliquely reminiscent of the story about the man who mounted his horse and rode off furiously in all directions—it cannot be done but we would all like to be able to do it. When we look around us today at the network of organisations, activities, and people all concerned in most genuine ways with furthering the European Idea, it does sometimes look very much like a large number of men on horseback all riding furiously hard—but in cross-directions. We immediately ask: why do they not all ride together in the same direction? Yet in thus being so quick to criticise and see the fault, we are also forgetting how hard it was in the beginning to get anyone on horseback at all, and even then to get the horse moving at anything more dramatic than a funereal amble. We are now coming to the stage where as soon as we see a considerable number of our men on horseback at last starting to ride together all in the same direction, we are quick to criticise in advance, and to say with real and justified trepidation: yes, but in what *direction* are they riding? This image is relevant to the democratic unification of Europe—for taken to its black extreme, the image of the man on horseback is also that of the dictator—it is the image of Cromwell and of Napoleon, the image we know so well in Europe, and which is so justly feared in America. It comes logically to our minds as soon as we consider the implications of any re-shaping of power on the large scale and of any political tide in history that involves very many people. In Europe today the perils implicit in massive co-ordination are as serious as are the perils already explicit in *non*-co-ordination and thus our real fear is that of failing to control the consequences of what we know we were in honour bound to begin, and must now continue.

All this is evoked merely by mention of the piecemeal approach today so characteristic of European unification. Let us follow Mr Smithers in his private note to Governments, as he documents one aspect at least of the piecemeal approach to European unification. The example he chooses is one known to us all, one of daily, callous, careless tragedy, resulting each year in Europe in a steadily higher mounting pile of hundreds of thousands of maimed and dead.

'As regards the second gap—that caused by the piecemeal approach— examples are also easy to find. Several expert committees are already working, or have proposed to the Committee of Ministers that they should work, on the subject of road accident prevention. The topic is of course of immediate concern to all Member Governments and, equally certainly, is one where the exchange of ideas and experience (e.g. as between road research laboratories), and direct collaboration

between national administrations (e.g. in the detection and punishment
of offenders, or in an agreement on a standard highway code) at
European level would be highly profitable. Moreover, the problem is
necessarily inter-disciplinary; its legal, social, public health, economic
and educational aspects require that several different groups of experts
must play their parts. Their contributions will not however be fully
effective unless they are seen and planned as elements of a single
operation. The Council of Europe should therefore include among its
aims the solution of certain broad problems on the urgency and importance of which a large number of Member Governments are agreed...'

The problem of social responsibility towards the old and the young is one
where again it has to be said that human wastage and suffering continue
because their elimination offers no immediate political profit. It has been
said that a man with no friends must be defended *because* he has no friends:
the same can be true of human causes on the highest, widest, and most
difficult scale. We must therefore applaud the fact that in the Council of
Europe at least, respect for the worth and dignity of the individual is a
permanent and continuing prime motive; that in Strasbourg at least
humanitarian considerations have a better chance of influencing political
action than anywhere else. Indeed they are often respected in Strasbourg
all the more because they are insufficiently respected elsewhere.

Mr Smithers' next point is appropriately practical:

'As in the case of economic problems, though probably in lesser degree
elsewhere, the Council of Europe should not attempt to be 'exclusive'
but should, on the contrary, examine very carefully in each case whether
there are other international bodies competent to carry out at least the
requisite studies preliminary to the main work. Two corollaries to this
inter-organisational task-sharing are however important.

'First, if the Committee of Ministers decides to transmit a suggestion
for study to another organisation, it should nonetheless reach its own
view as to (in the words of Article 15 of the Statute) "the action required
to further the aims of the Council of Europe" and should be satisfied
that this action can be taken or furthered by the other organisation.
Furthermore, as the comprehensive organisation specifically charged
with promoting wider European unity, the Council should continue to
follow the progress of the matter in order to satisfy itself that the interests of such unity are being adequately served. In this connection it must
be remembered that the argument: "If governmental delegation have
not arrived at agreement in one forum, they will not do so in another",
though often accepted as self-evident, is by no means necessarily true.

Differences of method, of membership and of structure can have a decisive importance.'

To some extent, this could again be seen as the beginning of a take-over bid—between the lines it does suggest that the Committee of Ministers of the Council of Europe should acquire and exercise a supervisory function in relation to other organisations. Nevertheless, if we bear in mind that this document is addressed primarily to Government departments, we can perhaps concede that a certain indication of determination is more likely to increase respect than diminish it, and to this extent was perhaps, after all, tactically wise.

Mr Smithers continued with an even harder point:

'It is necessary to examine critically the concept of duplication of work (between organisations). On the principle no problems arise. Where real duplication exists, it should be ended. Where there is a risk of duplication, it should be avoided. In practice however what at first sight may seem to be duplication often proves on closer examination to be more apparent than real. Some examples may make this clear. In application of the Treaty of Rome the Six have undertaken work on a number of subjects which are already on the agenda of the Council of Europe: duplication would occur only if the results which the Six are aiming at (including the machinery needed to ensure effective application of their decisions) were at least substantially the same as those that could be achieved in the larger framework...Finally, if what the Council of Europe seeks is a Convention or other legal instrument having binding force, whereas what, say, the Organisation for Economic Cooperation and Development or the European Conference of Ministers of Transport can prepare is a study or a recommendation to Governments, duplication is not necessarily involved.

'...if the risk of duplication is to be avoided, it is essential that constant close relations be maintained between the organisations. As a result of the Committee of Ministers' instruction to me in April 1964 to establish better liaison with the main European and international organisations the Secretariat of the Council has established much closer contact with the Secretariats of these latter and each side is now aware of what the other is doing and hopes to achieve. From these contacts I have learned not only that it is *quite wrong to assume that because a subject falls within the general competence of one organisation there is no scope for useful work on it in another, but that work undertaken in parallel by bodies having different methods and membership is often complementary and mutually useful.* Where one of the parties is the Council of Europe this is particularly striking.

K*

Unlike the majority of international organisations, the Council is
relatively ill-equipped to undertake technical studies. On the other hand
for the preparation of legal instruments giving form and force to the
joint conclusions of Governments it possesses *experience and a machinery
which at European level are unrivalled.*'

The headache lies in the implications of the fact that all this had to be said—
for as we shall see later, it was here no more than the gentlest of hints, and
what was actually here being described was a widespread confusion of
existing duplication. Mr Smithers' diplomatically necessary attempt to put
the best interpretation possible on a very bad situation has in fact forced
him into an immese understatement. This perhaps explains the uncompromising insistence of his next point, and all the more since he has already
emphasised the weaknesses of the Council of Europe as well as its potential
strength. Undermanned, ill-financed, hard to publicise, the Council of
Europe is nevertheless the 'unrivalled' method for 'the preparation of legal
instruments giving form and force to the joint conclusions of Governments'. Let us now watch how Mr Smithers goes on to address Governments directly, and note the key words that again keep coming into this
memorandum—'*coherent...*', '*concentration...*', '*balance...*', '*urgency...*'
What we are watching is as it were a photograph taken of a tide confused
but on the turn.

'It is imperative that the Programme of Work should ultimately form a
coherent whole. This first presentation already takes certain steps in that
direction, even though it is based on existing activities, all of which were
decided upon the basis of their individual merit rather than upon that
of the contribution they would make to the totality of the Council's
work. Thus the proposals for new activities and the attempt to indicate
priorities by means of completion-dates should lead eventually not only
to a concentration on problems of 'European' interest and urgency but
also to a better *balance* between the various sectors.

'In a Programme ranging over a very large area of European co-
operation it is obvious and understandable that particular proposals will
be differently regarded by Member Governments. To some they will
seem altogether consonant with their immediate national interest, to
others the same proposals may present short-term difficulties but potential advantages in the long term, to yet others they may be of doubtful
relevance to their national situation. The temptation in these circumstances may be for each Government to support those suggestions which
seem immediately advantageous to it and to reject the others.

'*The success of this project depends upon these temptations being resisted.*

For this there are at least three reasons. Firstly, the method which consists in striking out from the Programme the items which have little appeal for Government A, then for Government B, and so on, can lead only to a minimum overall achievement and to the disappearance of items possessing possibly substantial attractions for other Governments. Items should of course command the support of a sizeable number of Member States, otherwise they are of no practical interest; but this is not to say that reluctance or lack of interest on the part of some should be permitted to inhibit the others. Secondly, as has been pointed out, the draft Programme as it is now submitted to Governments already strives to move towards a certain balance, which it would be all too easy to upset. But an unbalanced Programme would hardly be better than no Programme at all, and is certainly not what the Committee of Ministers intended by its decision of 3 May 1965. Finally, one of the most valuable possibilities offered by the Council of Europe is that of a *more or less equal advance by all its Members* towards their common goal of closer unity. To take full advantage of this possibility, the usefulness of which has been heightened since the creation of the two economic groups (EEC and EFTA), implies a *readiness on the part of all to agree to activities being pursued which are of special interest only to some*. Application of this principle need not be carried to excess but the dangers of ignoring it are evident. It should moreover not be difficult for Governments to accept the Programme as a whole since their participation in specific activities will be a matter for their individual decision.'

While Governments are here being asked not to rock the boat, there follows immediately a gentle indication of how they could also help row the boat towards that destination of greater unity which all are concerned to reach. Mr Smithers now introduced the method of Partial Agreements, which we have already looked at earlier in Chapters Four and Five in relation to the Conventions of the Council. It is a method scarcely yet under way, and yet with great potential: it is, in fact, the method which by its flexibility is most sharply differentiated from that of the European Community in Brussels, and which most clearly demonstrates the complementary roles of the two organisations in relation to each other.

'The present system of Partial Agreements, as instituted by Statutory Resolution of the Committee of Ministers in 1951, is perhaps unnecessarily rigid and, in the light of experience, it may prove desirable to modify it. The Legal Directorate has been instructed to undertake a study of this point. The present Partial Agreements system does however enable countries to refrain from taking part financially and otherwise in projects which they consider of no interest to them or in which they do not wish or do not feel able to participate. To date, only very sparing use has been made of this procedure...abstention has been quite common: not one of the fifty Conventions and Agreements concluded under Council of Europe auspices is in force in all Member States, while cases of Governments not signing Conventions or not participating in the Committee of Experts instructed to draft them are frequent.

'In the future, however, this seems likely to change, in particular if the suggestions (below) are accepted as to a new organisation of committees of experts. Governments will find it easier to assess whether or not they wish to send delegates to one or another meeting, as the purpose of this meeting will be much more clear. Although as mentioned above, it is in principle desirable that all Governments shall participate in as many activities as possible, it is reasonable that if in specific cases they wish to abstain they shall be free to do so. Thus the fact that a proposal is not of direct interest to a Government need by no means constitute a reason for opposing its inclusion in the Programme.'

Mr Smithers then continued with a detailed exposition of the Programme sector by sector. While we shall examine the Programme under its various aims and sectors in the next chapter, we should here pick out some very suggestive passages—remembering always that they were designed to influence *opinion within Governments* on this entirely new project of an annual Work Programme making sense of *all* the Council of Europe's inter-governmental work.

On the aims themselves, Mr Smithers said:

'[They should] provide guidelines of real value to committees of experts and...enable parliamentary and public opinion to grasp the broad orientations of the Council's work...the statement of an aim in no way prejudges the manner or the means of attaining it. For example, the Committee of Ministers might decide at some future time to include among its aims the definition of a common European transport policy. The Council of Europe could doubtless itself contribute to establishing such a policy. But the essential instrument for preparing it would remain, the European Conference of Ministers of Transport, to which the Committee of Ministers should make known its wishes and expectations and lend any political and other support required...'

And on the exact technical status of the Programme:

'The Programme as a whole is cast in the form of a Ministerial Resolution referring to a list of aims and of project with dates attached, and giving instructions for their implementation to the Ministers' Deputies and to the Secretary General. The vote of this Resolution would signify the assent of Governments to a precise programme of inter-governmental work for the Council of Europe until modified by the next such document which will be presented to Ministers at their Spring Session 1967. The Resolution does not commit Governments to particular ways and means of executing the programme, nor to the consequential budgetary decisions. Execution of the programme is a *continuous process calling for continuous supervision:* this can be provided only by a governmental body meeting frequently and intimately acquainted with all aspects of the Council's work, a condition fulfilled by the Ministers' Deputies (i.e. permanent Government representatives in Strasbourg), assisted by the Secretary General. Budgetary decisions must be taken case by case...In the future the decision involved (for the Committee of Ministers) will be an annual revision of the Programme which will be submitted in time for its adoption at each Spring Session of the Committee of Ministers. This is also the moment when preparation by the Secretariat for the following year's draft Budget is normally beginning.'

And finally, picking up the suggestion above that a re-styling of committee methods would contribute to an increasingly useful application of the Partial Procedure method, Mr Smithers listed what he had in mind. It should here be remembered not only that the expert committees of the Council already numbered over sixty, but that this entire structure had grown over the years in an entirely *ad hoc* manner—each committee being created merely as and when required. It is no secret that in the preliminary work leading up to this first Work Programme one of the essential first steps was simply to make a list of what each Committee was doing—for previously no comprehensive survey had ever been made, and each of these Committees (recruited from the ablest expert talent available in Europe) were themselves persevering in their work without full knowledge of what work was simultaneously being done elsewhere in the same building. It was on the results of this survey that Mr Smithers' recommendations were made.

In a further passage on 'methods, structures and costs', Mr Smithers discusses the role and composition of 'plenary committees of senior government officials, usually styled committees of experts'. It may be as

well here to remind ourselves of the calibre of the work being undertaken by these committees. If we look merely at the headings under the
European Committee on Legal Co-operation, we find the following:

(a) Committee of Specialists for the comparative study of the laws of
European States.

(b) Committee of Experts for the preparation of a Convention concerning lost or stolen bearer securities.

(c) Committee of Experts on State immunity.

(d) Committee of Experts on the place of payment of foreign money
liabilities.

(e) Committee of Experts on the preparation of Digests of national
State practice in the field of public international law.

(f) Sub-Committee for the study of the privileges and immunities of
international organisations.

(g) Sub-Committee on fundamental legal concepts.

(h) Sub-Committee on the uniform interpretation of European treaties.

(i) Committee of Experts on the preparation of a European Convention concerning information on foreign law.

Any one of these nine activities is in itself a project of extraordinary
complexity—and this may perhaps illustrate the immensely larger complexity of what is here being so gently indicated in Mr Smithers' explanatory note to Governments. In conclusion, let us notice how Mr
Smithers summarises the entire matter in fifty words:

> 'The Programme is a statement of intention. When approved by the
> Committee of Ministers it will set out, in a single document, the list
> of targets, developing from year to year, in all the fields of its
> competence, which the Council of Europe proposes to reach in the near
> future...'

Seldom in public life do we hear even the shortest unmistakeable statement of intention. While such a declaration is always a comfort to hear
it is always a risk to make—and this statement of intention today stands
unequivocally on record, and brief as it is does give us a measuring-
stick for the present and future. 'In a *single* document', it says, 'developing
from year to year', it says, 'in *all* the fields of its competence', it says. This
at least is clear, and all the more when we remember the omnicompetence
of the Statute of the Council of Europe. And coming years will show
whether under successive Secretaries General this statement of intention
will continue to express a growing and harmonious accord between
both the currents of our time, and the record of achievement year by
year in Strasbourg.

We have here been watching the emergence of a new and recognisably European style in political technique. Mr Smithers' Explanatory Note shows the style of strategy and tactics that were necessary when this first project of an annual Work Programme was presented to the eighteen Governments—it is a formidable example of carefully graduated and successful persuasion on the all-European level. In the next chapter we shall see in detail how each Section of the Programme was defined and presented—here we are more concerned with some lessons on the larger scale revealed by this behind-the-scenes manipulation of men and affairs. As we have seen, it was between the lines very much in essentials a carefully understated exposition of five factors: men, money, motion, time and information—and these unified in terms of a *method*. And the method behind the method was, as we have seen, the prior establishment inside the Council of Europe Secretariat of a full-time Programme Unit— for it was only after the creation of this Programme Unit that it became possible to get a conscious grip on who within the Council was working on what, where, when, how, why, and for what purpose—and on who was paying, how, why, and again for what purpose.

Let us look at this last question: who is paying for what? If we consider that the cost of a four-day plenary meeting was (in 1965) 20,000 French francs, if we remember that this money is our own taxpayer's money contributed from all over Europe by decision of our Governments; that this one four-day meeting involves summoning and co-ordinating men of the highest ability and experience from all over Europe and perhaps elsewhere also; that this one meeting is convened to discuss items every one of which has its separate individual timetable and idio-syncrasies which require respect; that not only must the time and attention contributed by each invited committee-member be prevented from becoming merely a formally subsidised waste of time but must, on the contrary, prove to be an effective investment of that very personal experience and ability, that very limited time and money now in question —and further, that the work of just this one committee, at just this one meeting, must be dovetailed both in advance preparation and subsequent application with the endlessly ramifying work of many other men and women on many other equally complex items in many other committees and this not only in Strasbourg but in all the other cities and capitals of Europe as well—if we recall all this then perhaps we can begin to recognise the nature of the problems involved in managing a Work Programme for the Council of Europe—and of larger problems also, all relating to the unification of Europe through our day-to-day understanding and application of the European Idea. What are we watching here? Politics?

Not only that—we are watching an aspect of history itself on the move.

One characteristic of this tide of history is the emergence among us today of men who combine both a parliamentary and political personality with the now indispensable faculty of managerial ability on the larger all-European scale. And already at the national level there are an increasing number of men of this temper and cast of mind who are ready and waiting to assume these larger tasks just as soon as the context of events makes it possible—one example among very many is that of Lord Robens in Britain, Chairman of the National Coal Board. On the European level there are also examples of this phenomenon already at work— but inevitably there are only as many examples as there are places to be filled. And many of them are not widely known to the public—the trade-unionists of the Six are here an example, for already some among them are working very effectively indeed at the European level, yet still very quietly. This is becoming characteristic of all work—and this at all levels—of our present stage of European unification today, and is a managerial revolution new to our continent.

Earlier decades foreshadowed this. A famous example is that of M Paul-Henri Spaak's guidance of that phalanx of advancing experts who created the Rome Treaty. This was decisive in demonstrating by what *method* things needed could become things done. Nearly always the key is to be found in a judicious combination of new men and new methods— it is these new methods inside the process of European unification which are today evolving to the point where we can not only begin to see them clearly, but also recognise them for what they are—not only new, but characteristically European, and this in a new *style*. The indispensable men today emerging are indispensable not as individuals, but as a type, a phenomenon, a new adaptation of European political man. They tend to be men not only with that political aptness and intuition, ingenuity and skill which we are accustomed to see in public affairs—but men already instinctively able to govern and guide those structures of influence, authority and decision which are today themselves not merely emerging but already fast *outgrowing* our inherited and habitual party and national frameworks. These new areas of authority are themselves by their very nature especially vulnerable to criticism—for in the very nature of the way events themselves are today evolving, these new areas of authority must continue to spread and extend their influence not merely in reaction to events—but in advance of them. As Mr Jo Grimond was among the first to point out, there is a new type of political animal now active among us—and this is understandable, for whether we know it or not, already today in Europe we are tending very fast towards the creation of a new type of political habitat, and the present progress of the European Idea will increasingly demand that men of this calibre can come forward to fulfil this new and intensely challenging managerial function. This is already happening in ways not always immediately visible, and when visible not always immediately consistent. Men of this temper are new in our time and now that they are here power will accumulate increasingly around them: some among them will prove to be the great transformers of our century.

And yet, even with all this granted, it must also be said that these great transformers will themselves be essentially transitional—the events they transform are themselves a prior preparation for events yet larger, and these European political administrators represent what is still only a very early stage in what is here broadly termed the managerial revolution now under way in the politics of European unification. It has been said that every institution is but the lengthened shadow of one man—even in what appears to us a political jungle some of these men are already growing tall like trees, and we shall later be able to measure their height by the sheltering shadow of the institutions they will find themselves creating: the institutions of a truly unified and *long-enduring* Europe.

Yet while the soil from which they grow is rich, certainly, it is also stony. Some of the largest difficulties are underground and unseen: not immediately visible at all—great boulders of obstruction buried deep. We have here an example already to hand—Mr Smithers' Explanatory Note to Governments, at which we have already looked, though blandly persuasive, though an example in itself of this managerial revolution, was not so persuasive that it was easily accepted.

On 20 January 1966, Mr Smithers was forced to write a second Explanatory Note for the private information of Governments defending the mere inclusion in his Programme of the Section on Education, Culture and Science. We might well assume this was therefore a major matter— so it was, but not on any question concerned with the fundamentals of science, culture or education. It was not a question of any kind of 'What'— but a fundamental 'How', for while on the one hand the inclusion of this Section in the Programme was politically and psychologically essential, it could not on the other hand be denied that it was technically inappropriate.

What it came to was that the cultural wing of the Council of Europe (which, following Continental terminology, includes education and science under the word 'culture') had already just achieved a degree of organisational autonomy of its own, under the title of the *Council for*

Cultural Cooperation—or CCC. In his *first* Explanatory Note Mr Smithers
had already approached the cultural question in these words:

'It is not altogether easy to fit the sector, which, measured in terms of
staff and expenditure, is the largest of all those within the Council's
competence, into the framework of an overall programme of work,
for two main reasons...the CCC is itself a programming body,
specifically charged by the Committee of Ministers with "drawing
up proposals concerning the cultural policy of the Council of Europe"
and "formulating and implementing a new European cultural programme"...as recently as April 1965, the Ministers' Deputies formally
approved a policy statement drawn up by the CCC and setting out
in some detail the orientation of its future programme.

'The CCC's powers in this regard are however *limited* both by the
need for it to operate within the financial ceiling fixed by governmental grants to the Cultural Fund and by the fact that the Secretary
General...has the right to refer to the Committee of Ministers any
proposed decision which he considers incompatible with the aims of
the Council of Europe. More fundamentally, the activities of the CCC
*must of course be regarded as forming an integral and major part of the work
of the Council of Europe as a whole and hence must be appreciated, like any
other sector, in terms of the contribution they purport to make to the Council's
overall aim.* The determination of overall priorities for the Council's
work necessarily requires that close and critical attention be given to
its activities in the field of education, culture and science, which alone
absorb some 40 per cent of the entire budget for inter-governmental
committees and the staff serving them.

'The second cause of difficulty is that though a cultural programme
lends itself well to the formulation of general aims, it is often hard to
translate these into specific objectives...Governments might reasonably
expect a more exact formulation of the Council of Europe's present
and future projects in this sector. What appears to be needed is less a
change of subjects than a change of approach, in the direction of greater
precision and of a sense of greater urgency, expressed in a determination
to reach measurable results in a measurable time... (For example)
instead of being content to seek the improvement and expansion of
modern language teaching, the CCC should *set out clearly the sequence
of intermediate phases* by which member countries will endeavour to
arrive eventually at a stage where the European who cannot communicate with his fellow Europeans in a language other than his own is an
exception...national Ministries of Education have now to contend

with so many and grave domestic problems that often they cannot devote to it the time and resources which, from the European point of view, would be desirable...'

The lines of conflict are here becoming clear—for while on the one hand the CCC had already achieved Minsterial approval of at least the beginnings of a real cultural policy, and had also evolved its own programming methods, on the other hand the fact that it consumed 40 per cent of the Council's resources did mean that if its already increasing degree of autonomy continued unchecked, both the unity and the balance of the work of the Council of Europe as a whole could in years to come be threatened. It could, however, be argued that the very *structure* of the CCC demanded that it should be listed apart from the Work Programme of the Council of Europe—or even not listed at all within that context. Was the CCC to be recognised as an empire within an empire, or was it to be forced to pay tribute—on paper at least, in a form of words—and thereby accept the role merely of a proconsulate? This was the question—and it was predictable that the view of the Secretary General would be that the work of the CCC must be included within the Programme of Work, and not least for the very simple reason that if this was not done, then the Work Programme would from its beginning have already lost its most valuable attribute—that it was *complete*—and therefore worthy of engaging the earnest attention of the outer world.

Nevertheless, it came to the point where Mr Smithers was forced to admit in January 1966 that 'certain delegations'—which means certain Governments—were emphatically opposing his view, or, in other words, that certain Governments had felt themselves persuaded that they preferred to see full departmental justice done to the CCC even at the cost of thereby condoning a partial but damaging injustice being done to the public image of the Council of Europe as a whole.

Let us see exactly the words in which Mr Smithers defended his view in his second Explanatory Note:

'It was decided to include a chapter on Education, Culture and Science in the draft Programme submitted to the Committee of Ministers essentially because its omission would have led to a singularly misleading picture of the Council's total inter-governmental activities, of which of course our educational, cultural and scientific work forms an integral and most substantial part. Furthermore, it is useful that Governments should be able to see at a glance the list of existing and proposed work in this field, if only in order the better to assess whether

the proportion of resources devoted thereto is appropriate, having
regard both to the contribution this work makes to the fulfilment of
the Council's aims and to our commitments in other sectors of activity.

'I propose therefore to issue a revised list of educational, cultural and
scientific activities. This list, which, I repeat, should not in principle
call for decision by the Committee of Ministers will of course take
account of the conclusions reached by the CCC. *It will show all, and
only, those activities specifically approved by the CCC together with the new
proposals put forward by the permanent committees and by myself on which
the CCC has not yet ruled.* Though this list will be submitted primarily
for information it goes without saying that such comments and
suggestions as delegations may wish to put forward would be of
particular value at this time when through the Programme of Work
opportunity is offered for taking a critical look at the totality of the
Council's effort to achieve its Statutory aims...'

If it is useful for Governments to be able to 'see at a glance' what is being
done through Strasbourg—and this especially, perhaps, on cultural
matters, representing as they do the very soul of European unification—
it is certainly equally useful, perhaps more useful, for everyone else as
well, which includes not only 'interested' European opinion, but public
opinion in general. It is precisely this insistence by Mr Smithers on the
political importance of direct human communication that gives the Work
Programme both its individual character and its political effectiveness.
It is the very existence of the Work Programme in the form of a single
all-inclusive list which makes it potentially capable, by its very simplicity,
of changing attitudes far and wide on the work of all connected with
the aims of the Council of Europe. The reflex is essentially political—
this is the moment to recall it was made possible by the election of a
political Secretary General.

The section on Education, Culture and Science did thereafter go into
the Work Programme—for political, for structural, for symbolic reasons, and above all for this central reason that it is vital to communicate
what is going on in Europe today to as many people in Europe as possible.
And this incident is not the only example available today of the fact that
the more the men involved in the European political managerial revolution come to grapple with fast-evolving and increasingly complex
machineries—all handling new forms of power—so all the more can
we expect to find them seeking out and applying solutions that are not
only simple, but also human. For if these solutions do not display a deep,
sensitive and yet also tough understanding of human nature they will

not work—instead, they will break under that strain which the increasing complexity of human problems in Europe must impose upon them more and more. The example here quoted of an inter-Governmental struggle over the inclusion of one section in merely a first Work Programme of merely one European organisation is symbolic of yet larger problems still to come.

We have quoted so far only at the official level of actions taken, documents written—we have not yet indicated what we all know to be there: the harsh, abrasive struggles of human personality and purpose. Usually the fiercer the struggle the less the chance of those involved being able to record them, but we can here quote (with permission) part of a private letter written from Strasbourg in November 1965. The sentences we can quote are severely edited, and this letter must necessarily be anonymous. Nevertheless, even these sentences indicate more about the real problems inside the European Idea, and within the managerial revolution now accompanying this idea, than many pages of official records. For this is how these things not only happen, but are *felt* to happen by those who carry the daily burden of seeing that they do always continue to happen, and this regardless of ever-evolving difficulties.

'...for the last three months I have been working so concentratedly, and for the most part without guidance from on high, that I have given up private correspondence, even when I could persuade myself that it had at least business harmonics. Now the Programme of Work is out—or rather it will be sent to Governments on Tuesday. No one is going to recognise the amount of work that has been put into it, for it is now quite modest; very much more so than the first version which was submitted to the Secretary General, who promptly discarded it and then asked for something quite different, then rejected that. *The whole thing has been redrafted six times...*

'...As Mr Smithers insisted, it *is* useful to have listed, for the first time, all the Council of Europe's activities in a single document, with starting and finishing dates attached. For these current activities there are over 200; and by the end of 1967 the network of 50 Conventions will have grown to 60. Whether the Ministers will swallow the lot in December and May (for, to make the pill more palatable, we have bisected it) I do not know. My guess would be that they will accept 98 per cent, including the two things that really matter: (a) *permanent authorisation to the Secretary General to draw up the annual Programme*, thus bringing in a central planning and directing force where there was none before; (b) *agreeing that approximate finishing dates be attached to all our projects*, thus borrowing a valuable (if etiolated) leaf from the Treaty of Rome which will immensely strengthen the hand of the *Secretariat* vis-a-vis Committees of Experts. *This will accentuate the trend towards making the Secretary General the main motor of the Council of Europe*—for all that, under the Statute, he is not an "organ" of the Council of Europe and has only the slimmest powers. Which, completing the circle, may be of interest for the Conventions also—for all of these confer some additional functions (even if only of notifying ratifications, reservations etc.) and also occasionally new powers on the Secretary General. The interesting point is that these functions and powers are (or may be: legally it is a pretty point) independent of the Council of Europe as such. The Council of Europe could cease to exist but the Conventions would not cease to exist thereby, nor therefore the functions that they devolve upon the Secretary General of the Council of Europe. *Complicated...*

'...the Conventions...do not—on the whole—have habit-forming effects, at least as regards the people of Europe. I wish they did but, with some exceptions such as Human Rights, Establishment and perhaps the Social Charter, they do not. They may have such effects on Government Departments—my feeling is that, despite aberrations like the (British) 15 per cent surtax, few major national decisions are now taken without at least consultation with other Governments—but in respect of the poor sod in the street, the effects filter through at second or third level. And this matters because it means that people, and pressure groups, and non-governmental organisations rarely turn to Strasbourg—as they do turn to Brussels and its *décisions exécutoires*. A Strasbourg decision may in fact be as far-reaching as ones taken at Brussels, but, because it has to pass through the screen of national governments and/or Parliaments, it is not felt to be so. Is this important?

'I think so, because democracy in 1965 means, to a large extent, organised competing pressure groups, and so long as these continue to operate almost exclusively at national level, democracy *sur le plan européen* does not exist—despite Consultative Assemblies and the not negligible influence they can exert. One powerful pressure group of course remains: the European Civil Service. And one of the more interesting features of this year has been the greatly increased liaison and drawing together between the Secretariats of the Six, the Seven, and ourselves in particular.

'...of the more than two hundred items in the Programme *only some forty* are draft Conventions. Several are permanent activities—publications, Information and Research Centres, studies on work commissioned from non-governmental organisations, fellowships, comparative surveys of projected national legislation, art exhibitions, Film Prizes—which I find encouraging because these represent the *beginning of a recognised informatory or executive function at European level.* Others, particularly within the ex-Western European Union Partial Agreement, relate to *direct joint planning and agreement between Government Departments,* the Council of Europe serving mainly as framework and watch-dog. Thus, although the Council of Europe is indeed a Convention-making machine *par excellence* and although the whole Programme has been deliberately and explicitly orientated towards practical results of which the Conventions provide the most easily verifiable form—the Council devotes itself to many activities, other than drafting international legal instruments, and some of these are quite as useful. A too hopeful—indeed absurdly inflated—comparison might be made with a Government or National Ministry—though the time actually spent in preparing legislation is relatively small...

'...the Communities' techniques seem to me to point the way, and they have the other great advantage of being effective. So I, like them, would welcome their extension to other countries and other spheres (though not all would be suitable) and I would hope eventually for something similar within the Council of Europe...

'...I do agree that the aim—and the test—must be the rule of law...'

This letter indicates very truthfully part at least of the feeling in Strasbourg in 1965—truthfully, for it was scribbled without preparation or afterthought during the time when the first Work Programme of the Council of Europe was being designed and launched. Because it was written without the faintest thought of publication it is thus all the more valuable to publish. For this is how it really was—and with modifications this is still how it really is today. This is the sound of what the European Idea means to those who daily serve it: here is not only the raw, hard-working voice of history itself on the move but of that special form of history rare in any century—history in the process of conscious evolution towards the achievement of a defined purpose.

At the beginning of this chapter we saw at least some aspects of what we have come from, and during the course of this chapter we have also

seen at least some aspects of where we now are—today, in the 1970's.
But whither *are* we tending, and whither do we *wish* to tend? Let us
look again at that most powerful thinker, de Riencourt—and this time
not merely for the purpose of quoting a real warning, but for the larger
purpose of considering the extent to which there are possibilities open
to us today as we persevere in our determination to decide our own
evolution in Europe, our own destiny.

'Civilisation implies also the rise to supremacy of economic thinking
and the decline of truly creative Culture, whose conflicting ideas and
theories, stimulating when formulated, end up by causing the breakdown of a Culture's political and social structure because they are taken
too seriously. All the way from the post-Renaissance Wars of Religion
to Robespierre and Hitler there were tragic attempts to materialise
theoretical schemes, to impose abstract philosophies of life on one's
neighbours by all means, fair or foul, and fight to the bitter end
without thought of compromise. It takes many generations for men
to grow tired of philosophies and abstractions but this creeping fatigue
eventually overcomes intellectual curiosity and doctrinal proselytism.
And with exhaustion, comes a desire for the harmony of compromise,
for a constructive peace devoted to economic welfare rather than
cultural pursuits that always spill out into the political world, become
monstrously distorted, and end in bloody disaster. The age of Nazism's
monstrous Wagnerian drama comes to a close in a cataclysmic Twilight
of the Gods. From now on, culture will no longer be taken in dead
earnest but rather as a marginal activity that will not be allowed to
interfere with Civilisation's serious pursuit—the establishment of
security and economic well-being for as many human beings as
possible. It will be a secondary culture of Ciceros and Senecas growing
in the shade of the greatness of the original Culture...
'We shall put no obstacles in the path of the coming Caesars simply
by legislating against them; we would be attempting only to cure the
symptoms, not the profound disease. The problem is far more complex.
It is nothing less than the discovery of ways and means of reviving
our moribund Culture while retaining all the good and necessary
features of Civilisation. In other words, handing back to the creative
individual the functions and dignity which *society* has usurped. The
Caesars of the future, if they eventually materialise, will only be a
terrible symbol of something more terrible still: the death of our
Western soul—and the body would not be long in following it to
the grave of history...this might imply the destruction of the entire

human race as well. Advanced technology and fast superficial changes do not speed up or significantly alter the historical process; they merely make more certain that the next world conflagration will put an end to history altogether. Once again, what was an episodic drama in the past might be final tragedy tomorrow. It is up to us, who know better, to prevent this tragedy.'

It is thus that de Riencourt closes his book—*The Coming Caesars*—this is the last word of his argument. His warning on the final conflagration is not a warning we should blink, for we cannot all share Lord Gladwyn's assurance that the missiles will never be used—and it does require an effort of visualisation to see in real pictures what will happen if they are used. Just as no one should discuss the unification of Europe who has not contemplated the films of where we come from (or their equivalents in books, or human memories, or even merely the war museums) so also no one should discuss the question of whither we may be tending who has not directly faced the fact we may be tending towards the holocaust. The complement to Paul Rotha's film 'Mein Kampf' is Peter Watkin's film 'The War Game'. The possibility of nuclear confrontation is a permanent fact of our time; the possibility of instantaneous nuclear destruction is a permanent possibility.

Thus the warning—not only of sudden incineration but also of possible slow decay. Where is our hope? It is a question whether Europe's future is already determined, or whether Europe can show she has a real and creative will of her own. Determinism or determination? Decision or decadence? To what extent are we in Europe already condemned to imitate and serve the stable but sterile pattern of what de Riencourt calls 'civilisation'? To what extent are we condemned without hope of reprieve to abandon the creative but often unstable pattern of what he calls 'culture'? Could it be instead that the approaching unification of Europe will make possible something we do not yet fully anticipate: a new Renaissance in a new style and for a new purpose—not conforming to either of these past alternatives, but creating instead a synthesis or combination in itself new, necessarily unpredictable, and perhaps both stable and creative? If this is going to happen anywhere on the globe in these approaching decades, is it not most likely of all to occur in Europe?

And yet—'there is no Europe', said Kennedy. And it is true that his own first Inaugural told us where America then wished to tend: '...let us explore the stars, conquer the deserts, eradicate disease, tap the ocean depths and encourage the arts and commerce...' Criticise America as

we may, with whatever justification, where in Europe today can we
hear a voice of such vigour, a determination as fearlessly proclaimed?
What reason have we to hope we shall ourselves wake to a new Renaissance, and thereby astonish not only the world, but ourselves?

In May 1965 *Reader's Digest* published an article at exactly the same
time as the events we have been following in this chapter. It was by
Ernest Hause, and under the title DANTE: POET OF HOPE, written
in honour of the seven hundredth anniversary of the birth of Dante, he
said: '...writing in a time as fraught with strife as our own, the poet
sounded a trumpet call for order, peace and good citizenship. He envisaged a "United World" which makes him the first modern European...
His brilliant pamphlet, *On Monarchy*, condemned the cold war between
Emperor and Pope, which was splitting Europe asunder. Why should
the two not coexist, one holding spiritual, the other temporal sway?
Europe could thus be united under a single, just and enlightened government. All through his *Comedia* too, there runs a mighty current of world
politics and, to the end of his life, Dante raised his voice against injustice,
tyranny, and corruption in high places...Dante lived in a cruel age, and
the torments he describes are cruel (yet) the *Comedia* ends in a blaze of
glory...Today, the poet's message comes through as powerfully as ever.
Dante charts a course we may all try to follow—a journey to the depths
of our conscience and thence upwards to light and salvation. Virgil—
symbol of Reason—and Beatrice—symbol of Faith—will comfort us
along the way. Though Dante lived and laboured in a world that had
yet to emerge from the long shadow of the Dark Ages, there is in his
great work a foretaste of the bright new age that was to dawn upon the
world a few generations later: the age of humanism, of discovery, of
Renaissance. It is the individual, freed from the shackles of dark forces
that rises, triumphant, from the poet's work...in commemorating the
great Florentine...we also celebrate the birth of modern man.'

This was written at exactly the time when in Strasbourg the work of
the Council of Europe was acquiring its formula, title and principle—
for the title subsequently adopted for the Programme of Work whose
technical evolution we have been following was five words only—
'Man in a European Society'—a formula which when thus measured
against seven hundred years of European history acquires a new and
sudden stature. What reason have we to hope for a new and *European*
Renaissance? Why, the fact that we come from a past which contained
not only the cruelties of Dante's Inferno, but was the very world that
made his masterpiece possible. There are dynamic fires of the human
spirit burning today in our Continent, and just as they have burned for

many centuries so they will burn in the future, and in this certainty we can find fuel for our hope.

We are today living through the *pre*-history of the United States of Europe—and the 'Explanatory Notes to Governments' used as examples in this chapter are in their tone, style and strategic thinking—in their entirely personal determination and character—in their instinctive understanding how to handle certain men and certain matters, precisely because the issues are so large, themselves symbolic of this transitional stage. This, in a sentence, is the quiet suggestion of this chapter, and we shall see in the next chapters where it leads us. We may find it leading us to an adaptation—our own and surprising adaptation—of the mood expressed by Emerson:

> 'Now our day is come; we have been born out of the eternal silence; and now we will live—live for ourselves—and not as the pallbearers of a funeral, but as the upholders and creators of our age; and neither Greece nor Rome, nor the three Unities of Aristotle, nor the three Kings of Cologne, nor the College of Sorbonne, nor the Edinburgh Review is to command any longer...Now we are come, and will put our own interpretation on things, and moreover, our own things for interpretation...'

Whether we recognise it yet in Europe or not, our day will come. When it comes we shall have our own *European* interpretation to put on things, and our own European things for interpretation. Shadowing the hopes realised and the obstacles surmounted will come greater issues yet, and greater hopes and greater dangers too. For we have a European ship of state yet to build, and a ship that is not seaworthy cannot sail through storms.

CHAPTER NINE

'The Union Of Theory And Practice'

'The most serious mistake in the use of knowledge is the misplacing of its final end ... the benefit and use of man. ... Yet that which will most dignify and exalt knowledge is the union of theory and practice in a closer bond than has hitherto been known.'   FRANCIS BACON: *De Augmentis Scientiarum.*

THE EUROPEAN IDEA depends on creative duality: a successful and continuing combination of opposites—thought and action, theory and practice, imagination and realism, unity and diversity, pragmatism and philosophy. In the last two chapters we watched the introduction of the Council of Europe's inter-governmental Work Programme. Since its effect as a continuing initiative is designed to extend far into the future we should perhaps pause to notice that each year one day is set aside for contemplating the past, present and future of the European Idea—the Fifth of May. It is significant that Governments should have agreed on this—and as early as Europe Day 1966, Willy Spühler, Swiss Foreign Minister, made a speech which included the following: 'Today, for the second time, Europe Day is being observed in the Member countries of the Council of Europe. This day should strengthen in the peoples of this continent their feeling of fellowship, and lead them to measure the value of their collaboration.'

After carefully recalling the contribution of Sir Winston Churchill to the European Idea, and its progress in the years that followed, M. Spühler continued:

'When I say we should look beyond the European Economic Community and the European Free Trade Association, which are small economic groupings and only to some extent European, that brings me to speak of the Council of Europe, the only existing organisation which includes all Western Europe, and of which Switzerland became a full member three years ago. The Council of Europe proposes to realise a closer unity between its members in order to safeguard and promote those ideas and principles which are their common heritage and to forward their economic and social progress. The Council of Europe does not legislate. It does no more than adopt procedures for governmental co-operation. Its action can in principle be exercised in all fields except problems of national defence. Its organs—the Committee of Ministers and the Consultative Assembly —are formed, the one from representatives of member Governments, the other from the representatives of national Parliaments.

'In the political field, the Council of Europe seeks to realise the unification of Europe through the harmonisation of the national policies of member states. It also plays a considerable part in the legal, social and cultural fields. Fifty-four Conventions referring to a diversity of subjects have so far been created. They govern, in a co-ordinated way, particular aspects of international relations and are furthering the development of international law. In the wish to give their co-operation a precise form the Member states have undertaken by the elaboration of an inter-governmental Work Programme to draw up an inventory of those sectors where harmonisation between national policies can be successful.

'Since 5 May 1965, our country has ratified nine European Conventions and signed six more. Among these Conventions to which we have become party, the most important is the Convention for the Peaceful Settlement of Disputes. An agreement of this kind is in accord with a constant concern of Switzerland, who, even before her entry to the Council of Europe, has done her best to conclude bilateral treaties of conciliation and arbitration with the largest possible number of states. With the ratification of this multilateral European agreement, our relations with nine other European states are now regulated by uniform engagements.

'...The discretion with which the Council of Europe works guarantees the effective development of European co-operation. This construction advances step by step, perhaps without those spectacular developments which the impatient would like to see. Only the future will show us whether this pragmatic method is in fact the best formula for leading the states of our Continent towards

the unity of all Europe. It is in any case the formula which is closest
to our own aspirations.

'But this does not excuse us for all that from the obligation of
taking a position in affirming our wish to belong to a United Europe.
For it is our wish that the unity of Europe shall rest upon a federal
base. Such a structure appears to us the guarantee of our own survival.
Our country would be unfaithful to its principles, to its history, and
to its traditions if it refused to engage in this great debate...'

This speech was the first definitive Ministerial comment on the Council
of Europe's Work Programme to be addressed over radio and television
to the general public, and it came from a member of the Council's
Committee of Ministers within two days of Mr Smithers' first presentation of the Programme to the Assembly in Strasbourg. It is of special
interest that it was from Switzerland this immediate lead came on one
extremely difficult question—the relation of the methods of the Council
of Europe to the fundamental issue of a federal Europe—though it is
perhaps not surprising when we consider the Swiss experience of at least
one form of federalism. It is a question we shall be approaching in these
concluding chapters—and here we are already concerned with what Mr
Spuchler called 'an inventory of those sectors where harmonisation
between national policies can be successful', with the Council's first and
second annual Work Programmes, and thus with the origin of the
present entire series of Annual Programmes. They are each to some
extent a prototype showing how problems of immense diversity can be
handled at the all-European level—and as we shall see, they are so
designed that, like all the work of the Council of Europe (without any
official word being said) they do tend to contribute positively towards
the eventual creation of a federal Europe. In M. Spühler's speech the
two ideas of the method of the Council of Europe, and of building a
federal Europe, were placed very subtly in the closest juxtaposition.

The first comments from the Assembly itself were also indicative. In
the same Spring Session of 1966 the Chairman of the Committee of
Ministers, Mr Toncic-Sorinj, then Foreign Minister of Austria, threw out
some casually juxtaposed suggestions—that the Committee of Ministers
with its eighteen members should become the permanent meeting-place
of Foreign Ministers for discussion of political problems several times a
year within the Council of Europe; that the Work Programme con-
stituted in principle a comprehensive survey of what must be done;
that the realisation of this would have far-reaching effects in every
country of Europe; and above all, that it could achieve success only by

co-operation. Mr Toncic-Sorinj described the main task of the Council
of Europe as the ultimate unification of Europe—while decisive responsibility lay with the Governments, the Council of Europe was also the
only institution linking the EEC, EFTA, and other European countries
in addition. It was, he said, the Council's goal to work for the day when
there would no longer be competition or even merely co-existence
between these organisations—but *one united Europe*. Again the same tone
of suggestion is there—behind all the daily work of the Council of
Europe there is always a larger ultimate aim.

Sharper was the first comment from the floor of the Assembly by
Mr Hermod Lannung of Denmark, a most respected Parliamentarian
with long experience of the Council:

> '...The Council of Europe must also be congratulated on the elabora-
> tion of the Programme of inter-governmental work...this is a good
> example of combined efforts by the Assembly, which, as it often
> does, launched this idea, the Committee of Ministers who took it up,
> and the Secretary General, who worked on it and compiled the docu-
> ment which we have received from the Committees of Ministers
> and which we greatly welcome. Too often in the past, when we have
> been asked what the Council of Europe was doing, we have had to
> say that it stood for certain principles and tried to attain certain goals,
> but there is great virtue in being able to show people in black and
> white exactly what we are doing to translate those ideals and goals
> into facts.'

When we look at the Work Programme itself, it is at first glance no
more than a list of two hundred or more activities—present and planned—
and expressed in sentences with completion-dates added. These activities
are extraordinarily varied, and in some of its characteristics this list is
remarkably like the list of Conventions at which we looked in Chapters
Four and Five. To some extent it does appear a projection of both their
weakness and their strength. The Work Programme here primarily
under discussion is the *third* annual Programme, covering the twelve
months between May 1968 and May 1969—but we shall in this chapter
be referring both to this third programme, and to *both* the two preceding Work Programmes, those covering the years 1966/67 and
1967/68. It is rare in history to find complex subjects of human activity
consciously listed. It is rarer when they are listed not only consciously
but also conscientiously, not only for the record but for immediate
communication. The legal code of Hammurabi comes to us from the
Middle East across millenia only because it was a determined and

coherent *list*—and if today it is fashionable to laugh at codified accounts of what is happening, that is perhaps because we do not realise what we have. They look so simple we think they must be valueless—and yet if we look at the past, what would we not give to be able to lay our hands swiftly—to choose some odd examples—on the precise Work Programme of the French Encyclopedists, the Red Cross, the League of Nations, the Communist International, the Suffragette Movement—or, going right back, of the scholars directing work in the Great Library of Alexandria before it was destroyed by fire?

To come back to the present day, how often are we able to lay our hands on a single document giving us the Work Programme of a Trade Union, a Political Party, a Church, or a University? And yet in Strasbourg we have today exactly such a list—and this not at a sectional, limited, or even merely national level, but at the level of *Europe*—and in the context of an *Idea*.

For the theory and philosophy behind the Programme we need look no further than the speech of the Secretary General when presenting the first Work Programme to the Assembly of the Council of Europe on 3rd June 1966:

'The Assembly has before it...the inter-governmental Work Programme of the Council of Europe. That Programme is headed, *"Man in a European Society"*. The significance of the title is, first of all, that it envisages man himself and his needs in this age. Secondly, it envisages him not only as an individual, but also as a member of a European society with which the Assembly and the Council of Europe is deeply concerned...

'The development of modern technology based upon massive scientific progress has already altered the basis of society and has extended the horizons of the individual man, who now enjoys possibilities of a wider and richer range of experience than anything dreamed of by preceding generations. But the same process has created problems for society which are new, complex, diverse and increasingly numerous.

'Though having their origins in scientific and technological advances, many of these problems present themselves as juridical or social in character, while others are of a more material nature, for example in the public health field. A large proportion of them involve political considerations which may hamper individual Governments in their efforts to take practical action. Unless they are adequately dealt with by Governments, however, there is reason to fear that by an abuse of the great power over his environment which man has had conferred upon him, he may destroy the material and moral bases essential to the existence of life in society.

'The character of the problems now beginning to appear is such that only in the very largest States can the citizen look solely to his national Government to solve the larger part of them. In all other States affected by the development of technology man must look beyond the frontiers of his own land to a process of inter-governmental co-operation for a solution of many of the problems of life in the twentieth century.

'Because the States of Europe are relatively weak, yet technologically highly advanced, it is in Europe that these new problems of international co-operation first make their appearance and demand solutions by international action. In our Continent man finds himself not only a member of a nation State, but also a member of a community of European dimensions. His future well-being is intimately bound up with the wisdom and skill with which this wider society is to be managed.

'The inter-governmental Work Programme of the Council of Europe is an instrument in the hands of Governments for this purpose. By way of Conventions and commissions and joint measures, it offers the possibility of gradually evolving by inter-governmental action a structure of co-operation which will enable man in Europe so to live as to enjoy the full benefits of being a European.'

The structure is set out in the same speech. The programmed activities of the Council are listed under six *headings:* Economic, Legal, Social, Public Health, Environmental, Educational and Scientific. Under each of these headings are listed the activities in the following *categories:* first, work in progress, divided into permanent work, and work to be continued with approximate deadlines for completion—second, new work to be undertaken—third, activities that will be discontinued or scrapped—and fourth, work under study within the Secretariat. If we now multiply these six headings by the four categories we find the inter-governmental work of the Council of Europe programmed already under no less than twenty-four major and distinct classes. And there is also a fifth category: that of work successfully completed.

Even so simple a thing as a visible record of success can sometimes be an astonishing stimulus to further and increased—even accelerating—success. It does, however, have to be visible and this addition is no more than a logical extension of the principles of the Programme itself. It is

L

perhaps worth hoping that one small refinement could be added to future Programmes—that of giving an individual identification number to each activity and sub-activity, for there is at present no convenient shorthand or index-system for referring swiftly to separate activities, either individually or as a series.

More important are the conditions laid down for the inclusion of any activity—which is not easy to decide when the framework of politics-in-society here being managed extends from Iceland to Turkey, from the Mediterranean to the Arctic Circle. '...the Secretariat will determine whether there is sufficient interest in a given study; whether other organisations are already seized of it and if so in what way and for what purpose; whether, in its opinion, the Council is competent and equipped to deal with it and whether it fits appropriately into the Programme as a whole; and finally, if the results of all these enquiries appear to be positive, whether it would appear to be likely to command sufficient support from Member Governments to warrant its submission to the Committee of Ministers in a future programme.'

And the following warning appears, concerning work under study in the Secretariat. We are watching one aspect at least of what was in the previous chapter described as a managerial revolution: 'The publication of this list of subjects under study, which is not properly speaking a part of the Programme of Work, in no way commits the Governments of Member States and is *undertaken on the sole responsibility of the Secretary General.*'

We can also notice where these projects under study actually come from. The answer is potentially from any or all of us, and concealed both here and in the warning above, is the larger question of initiative— where it comes from, and who shall decide its fate. 'Most of these (pro-blems under study) have been brought to (the Secretariat's) attention by this Assembly, by individual Governments, by other international organisations, both public and private, and by individual persons in-terested in European problems.'

In fact the destiny of Europe is being—and will increasingly continue to be—determined for good or ill by those individual persons, whether in positions of authority or acting as private citizens, who are 'interested in European problems'. While not so long ago it was almost a luxury to display or prove an interest in European problems, it is now being acknowledged more readily as an increasing necessity—and will in time, perhaps sooner than we think, grow to be acknowledged as a civic *obligation*.

Nevertheless, this obligation is at present usually limited to the pro-fessionals—and unless we can do better ourselves, we are scarcely justified

in resenting this. The power of concealed decision in this Work Programme is firmly in the hands of the professionals—the Secretariat of the
Council of Europe. And that is to say, under the control in many ways—
though not all—of the Secretary General. With this in mind, we may
well ponder the following—indicating as it does possible lines for both
public and private debate, whether within the Secretariat, the Assembly,
the Committee of Ministers—or elsewhere—from within national
Governments to all interested groups, the general public, and the Press:

> 'While the Programme contains new items and excludes some which
> it has been decided to drop, it is largely an ordered presentation of work
> already sanctioned by Governments in previous years, before the
> establishment of the present framework. In the circumstances, it is
> understandable that the aims at the head of each chapter are sometimes
> not fully sustained by the list of projects appearing beneath them. It
> may also be thought that the Programme reveals that the balance
> of activities as between the various sectors is capable of improvement.
> But the procedures established by the Committee of Ministers do
> provide for a revised Programme of Work to be submitted to them
> each year at the Spring meeting. It will, therefore, be possible to
> adjust and develop the activities of the Council year by year until they
> fully sustain the aims set forth in the chapter headings and attain a
> satisfactory internal balance. This method of working will also enable
> the Council to take full account of the rapidly altering and developing
> needs of Europe, and to adjust its activities, if necessary, in the light
> of changes in the composition or relationships of other international
> organisations.'

This last sentence is a polite way of saying: let us consider now what
may happen in, to, and through the Council of Europe if the membership
of the European Economic Community should increase, and if the power-
relationship between the Council of Europe and the Community should
thus be forced to evolve new forms. This very large question we shall
examine in the next chapter: here let us notice that in this presentation
of the First Work Programme, all pivots on the *aims* at the head of
each of its chapters. This is also true of the second Work Programme a
year later—to the point where if the aims are fulfilled the programme
must become an annually renewed triumph—and also, whenever the *aims*
are changed, the entire purpose, orientation and character of the Programme is changed.

The original overall aim is defined in a Resolution of the Committee of

Ministers of 2nd May 1966, and indicates the method, style and attitude
in which the Programme was first officially launched on its voyage:

The Committee of Ministers,

1. RECALLING that the aim of the Council of Europe is to achieve a
greater unity between its Members for the purpose of safeguarding
and realising the ideals and principles which are their common heritage
and facilitating their economic and social progress and that this aim
shall be pursued through the organs of the Council by discussion of
questions of common concern and by agreements and common action
in economic, social, cultural, scientific, legal and administrative matters
and in the maintenance and further realisation of human rights and
fundamental freedoms;

2. NOTING with satisfaction that appreciable progress has already been
made towards this closer unity but aware that much remains to be done;

3. CONVINCED *that it is in the interest of Member States that the aims which
the Council of Europe proposes to achieve should be even more clearly defined,
together with the precise projects which the Council will undertake in
pursuit of these aims;*

4. DESIRING that the activities of the Council of Europe shall be carried
out in a spirit of maximum economy and efficiency;

5. HAVING INSTRUCTED the Secretary General at its 36th Session held
on 3 May, 1965 in Strasbourg to submit to it a draft overall programme for the inter-governmental work of the Council of Europe;

6. RECALLING its decision that this programme is to be a *continuing
process* carried out by the statutory organs of the Council of Europe in
accordance with Articles 10 and 15 of the Statute:

7. REFERRING to its Resolution (65) 23 particularly as regards its approval
of the form and broad lines of the draft Programme of Work presented
by the Secretary General and its decisions regarding work already in
progress;

8. CONSIDERING the Report of the Ministers' Deputies on new work to
be undertaken and work to be discontinued, at inter-governmental
level, drawn up in accordance with the observations of the Governments of Member States on the draft Programme and with the comments made by the Secretary General.

9. HAVING CONFIRMED the decisions taken by the Ministers' Deputies
as regards work in progress and taking note of Resolution (66) 24
on the structure and methods of work of inter-governmental committees;

10. OBSERVING that the subjects mentioned in Section IV of the various

chapters of the draft under the heading 'Work under study in the Secretariat', do not form part of the programme of work proper, have been included on the sole responsibility of the Secretary General and in no way commit the Governments of Member States;

i. DECIDES to approve the Programme of inter-governmental work of the Council of Europe as set out in the Appendix to this Resolution;

ii. INSTRUCTS the Ministers' Deputies to supervise the implementation of this programme;

iii. INSTRUCTS the Secretary General to report to it at its Spring Session 1967, and thereafter each year at the same time, on the execution of the Programme and also submit to it new proposals regarding the future inter-governmental work of the Council of Europe in the light of recommendations by the Consultative Assembly and of observations from Governments;

iv. ALSO INSTRUCTS the Secretary General to ensure that in the execution of the Programme of Work all duplication of the activities of the other international organisations concerned shall be avoided and to submit a report to the Deputies on ways and means of avoiding such duplication and promoting better inter-governmental co-operation;

v. INVITES the Consultative Assembly to express its views on the Programme of Work, its implementation and its future development.

Behind the carefully guarded complexity of this jargon, nearly everything has been officially granted that could be desired. The attitude of the Committee of Ministers is here in striking contrast to the attitude of the same Committee as we watched it in Chapters One and Two, during the early years of the Council of Europe. It should, however, also be pointed out that if the Ministers had realised in advance the full potential of what they were here so graciously granting, it is unlikely their attitude would have been exactly the same, or their decision as firmly and unequivocably positive.

Let us now look, one by one, at each of the Aims—we shall take as our example the Second Work Programme, that for 1967/68, and in each of these Aims we shall set in italics all additions to the text as it was in the First Work Programme of 1966/67. We shall thus be able already to see at a glance the exact nuances of those changes and evolutions that became possible during the first working year of the Programme's life.

Every one of these Aims is introduced under the same major title—'Man in a European Society'. First comes economics:

MAN IN A EUROPEAN SOCIETY: THE ECONOMIC STRUCTURE.

AIMS: To contribute to the reduction or elimination of obstacles to the free flow of goods, services and persons in Europe through the liberalisation and harmonisation of national laws and practices, *thus offering to Europeans full access to the resources of their continent and the maximum range of choice and opportunity.*

This attitude is necessarily sensitive, for in most people's minds the two ideas of economics and European unification tend to suggest perhaps too swiftly the European Economic Community only. This is the immediate and facile association—and as we saw in Chapter Six there are good reasons for this. The Community is certainly dominant in the economic field—but it is not yet representative of all Western Europe. And we can see here some of the complexities involved in any future co-ordination between the Council of Europe and the European Community—for as is carefully pointed out in this second Work Programme:

...the number of specialised organisations dealing with economic matters in Europe is already very considerable: the European Communities, the European Free Trade Association, the Organisation for Economic Co-operation and Development, the Economic Commission for Europe of the United Nations, to mention only a few...The Council's inter-governmental activities in economic matters are modest...(but) not unimportant...the Committee of Ministers has included as a permanent item on its agenda the question of the political aspects of European economic integration...a number of Council of Europe activities in other spheres have indirectly economic implications...this being a purely inter-governmental Programme, the economic work of the Consultative Assembly can find no place in it. This work is however both extensive and important. Each year the Assembly receives a progress report from most of the main economic organisations, many of which were indeed established following proposals emanating from it. These reports are scrutinised in committee, then publicly debated, then commented on in an official Resolution which is conveyed to the Organisation concerned. In this way the Assembly acts to some extent as the *parliamentary organ not only of the Council of Europe itself but of a large number of more specialised bodies...*

What we have here is an emergence of both supplementary and supervisory functions at several levels—and behind it a suggestion that it is nonsense to try and define exactly what has economic implications and what has not. This reflects an increasingly strong characteristic of the Europe of our time, when habitual distinctions between matters labelled 'economic', 'political', 'legal' or 'social' are becoming fast devalued by the interweaving interconnections of cause and effect which in daily practice we already take for granted—while simultaneously forgetting they will in time demand a new and more practical terminology.

MAN IN A EUROPEAN SOCIETY: HIS LEGAL AND ADMINISTRATIVE STATUS, HUMAN RIGHTS AND THE PREVENTION OF CRIME. (Here there are no additions)
AIMS: Harmonisation of national law with a view to the fulfilment of the statutory aims of the Council of Europe; establishment of a better legal order between Member States and the highest possible degree of equality before the law for citizens of a Member State on the territory of another State; consultation on impending legislation; joint preparation of laws; protection of human rights; common measures for the prevention of crime and the treatment of offenders.

As is appropriate for lawyers, the phrasing is here precise. There is here none of the careful blurring of the lines, or even the carefully contrived ambiguity of the previous statement of economic aims. As we saw in Chapters Four and Five, there is considerably more behind the legal aims of the Council of Europe than is usually formally admitted—however, there is here a repetition of the same—seemingly innocuous—phrase from the economic aims—'harmonisation of national laws' and when we realise that the words 'a better legal order' do in fact mean a European Community of Law, with all that implies, then we have again an indication of the direction in which all the legal work of the Council of Europe is quite consciously and deliberately tending.

This, however, is as far as the legal chapter goes in revealing its strategy. The list of activities includes many Conventions, but there is not yet any mention of any activity being undertaken on the *process* of Convention-making, though there is of the *interpretation* of Conventions once made. The introductory note to the chapter is discreetly departmental:

This long and important chapter brings together work done by several inter-governmental committees and covers legal work proper, criminological activities, questions of patents and trade marks, the legal aspects of broadcasting and television, and measures to improve the international protection of human rights...Legal work proper...falls to *the European Committee for Legal Co-operation*...on which the Consultative Assembly is also represented...*The European Committee on Crime Problems* has also an extensive programme...special attention has been given to juvenile delinquency and to road traffic offences: an attempt to standardise penalties for these latter will, it is hoped, contribute to making possible the European Highway Code on which the *European*

Conference of Ministers of Transport is now working...The ECCP is assisted by a high-ranking Advisory Scientific Council...owing to the co-existence of the European Convention for the Protection of Human Rights and Fundamental Freedoms...and the United Nations Covenants agreed last year (1966) *the Council's work in this sphere will be primarily concerned with preparing its contribution to International Human Rights Year*, 1968...

MAN IN A EUROPEAN SOCIETY: THE SOCIAL STRUCTURE *AND WELFARE*. AIMS: Harmonisation of national laws and practices with a view to the fulfilment of the statutory aims of the Council of Europe; gradual elimination of discrimination based on nationality; establishment of improved European social standards; practical action in favour of migrant workers and refugees.

The addition of the two words 'and welfare' to the chapter title was a Dutch suggestion—and, when we pause to think, it becomes clear that social structure is not necessarily the same thing as social welfare. This is a good moment to stress the concentration and brevity not only of these aims but of the activities listed under them. The one word 'social' for example, includes everything connected with the European Social Charter—which, as we saw in Chapter Three, is growing to mean a great deal. The 'elimination of discrimination' is again no small matter—in Britain alone, to name only one country, the permitted immigration of coloured people is already a tendentious political issue. While Americans would be likely to read this phrase primarily from the viewpoint of civil rights in terms of colour, it has in Europe further interpretations, which could become equally important. Discrimination of any kind is like vitriol thrown in the eyes of society—it causes pain, and it blinds the vision. When questions so large are involved, we may wonder why these aims— for all their virtue—need be so short. As with the Conventions of the Council, the answer has to be that the drafting of any text which must today gain the approval of eighteen European Governments, and which must yet be valid in both 'theory and practice' for the future, is not easy. While it is true that the shortest text is the hardest to draft, it is equally true that once successfully drafted then the shorter the text the greater the probability of its survival as an influence both in society as a whole and individual minds in particular. When we notice merely the two words added to the aim here quoted, we are already on the edge of the old question—which is mightier, the pen or the sword? Neither under Caesar nor under Charlemagne, neither under Bonaparte nor Hitler, has Europe ever been either completely or enduringly united—Europe has never been united by the sword. For short times, yes, and partially—but never more. The ultimate and full and enduring unification of Europe can become reality only by the open—and this will happen only when the definitive texts of the lawyers are finally signed by the statesmen.

These brief—deceptively brief—aims of the Council of Europe here quoted may thus lead further, evolve swifter, and survive longer, than we are perhaps yet ready to realise. This is true even of the apparently least sensational—as for example, the next, where after an entire year's work, one single word has finally been added.

MAN IN A EUROPEAN SOCIETY: HIS HEALTH AND HYGIENE.

AIMS: Uniformly high standards of health, hygiene and medical care, taking into account the impact upon man of modern society and techniques and making the most effective use of the resources of knowledge, *research*, experience and equipment at the disposal of member countries.

A glance at the activities under this heading is sobering—listing as it does so much that must be done, that scarcely anyone else is doing on the same scale or with the same method, and yet which is largely non-controversial in the sense of party or even national politics. Let us pick out as a single example a subject listed then as still under study: '*Mental health, in particular the problem of hospital treatment for the mentally sick.*' As all connected with this tragedy of our present society know, the suffering and statistics of those hospitalised for mental illness are staggering. It is perhaps the medical profession itself which would applaud quickest the value (and be quickest to point out the difficulty) of '*making the most effective use of the resources of knowledge, research experience and equipment at the disposal of member countries*'. Let anyone who doubts the urgency of both swift and massive action on a co-ordinated all-European scale take the trouble to visit any ward in almost any mental hospital in Europe. They may walk in doubting whether the problem is as grave as people say: they will walk out after half an hour not merely shocked, but wondering why the truth has even now scarcely begun to be told—and why those who *know* the full horror of the truth have *not* acted.

MAN IN A EUROPEAN SOCIETY: HIS PHYSICAL ENVIRONMENT AND RESOURCES.

AIMS: Investigation into and adoption of planned action to ensure that Europe's natural resources are *properly managed* and are not misused, wasted or destroyed, so that Europeans may enjoy a balanced and wholesome physical environment.

There is scarcely any need to point the moral of this for those millions

L*

who live, work and sleep under the oil and ash-laden skies of our cities.
Yet, as the addition suggests, it is worth looking also at the positive side
of the problem—for while Europe's natural resources and future attractiveness are today certainly being 'misused, wasted, or destroyed' on a giant
scale—the bill for resources lost through water pollution alone runs into
many millions in any currency—it is also true that when we consider
what could happen if there was a union of theory and practice on improving our environment and use of resources—when we look at the map of
all Western Europe just to start with, we can see only that our opportunity
is unprecedented. Even a mild project like the award of three European
Diplomas to the Peak District National Park in Britain, the Hautes Faunes
Nature Reserve in Belgium, and the Carmague Nature Reserve in
France, evoke landscapes to move our imagination. Even so, it is not
easy—the succinct item: 'Soil erosion and reafforestation in the Mediterranean area' could not, for example, be carried through—but was
relegated to become a mere study.

MAN IN A EUROPEAN SOCIETY: HIS FORMAL EDUCATION AND SCIENTIFIC
ATTAINMENTS, HIS CULTURAL DEVELOPMENT. (This, as we saw earlier, was
the cultural section to which several Governments raised objections—and
here it reappears somewhat uneasily and now under *two* separate headings,
each entirely new.)

1. HIS FORMAL EDUCATION AND SCIENTIFIC ATTAINMENTS.
    AIMS: To assist Governments to adjust their educational systems and
methods so as to fit their citizens for the Europe of twenty years hence,
especially through mutual aid, comparative surveys, the pooling of
experience and the co-operative organisation of research; to create
conditions permitting the progressive achievement of a real equivalence
of curricula, examinations and qualifications and allowing of the free
movement of students, academic staff and educational material; to
contribute to the provision in Member States, if need be on a joint
European basis, of adequate facilities for scientific and technological
research.

2. HIS CULTURAL DEVELOPMENT, YOUTH, NON-FORMAL EDUCATION AND
SPORT.
    AIMS: To preserve and develop Europe's cultural heritage, having regard
to its diversity and to the specific contribution of each country, and to
promote access to and appreciation of it; to make people aware of their
responsibilities as Europeans; to help to extend the new educational
opportunities now open to young Europeans after leaving school and to

sponsor the pursuit of the provision of appropriate facilities for physical activities and sport, especially through mutual aid, comparative surveys and the pooling of experience; to encourage the creative use of leisure in a civilisation where it is becoming increasingly wide-spread.

Behind these political and Civil Service formulae, we are here concerned with that mysterious imperative, which no civilisation can define, and without which no culture can live—the creative faculty, which as in Botticelli's painting, always means not only Venus arising, but the sea from which she is born—or, in ordinary words, all that makes life valuable, and all from which life springs.

This list of the activities of the Council of Europe in the educational, scientific and cultural realms does, nevertheless, mark out only some first seed-plots of the future, and contains only some few first seeds carefully planted. Even so there have been casualties—as with all chapters of the Work Programme of the Council of Europe it pays to notice what has been discontinued and abandoned—this, whatever the particular reasons, in fact for the far larger and primary reason that the resources allotted to the Council of Europe cannot today be stretched to include even one tenth part of all that *ought* to be done, and this, let it be repeated, for lack of resources from Governments.

On the positive side, however, let us note that if among some of those projects already under way there prove to be some which grow fruitful, then this is how they started. Culture, like oxygen, is both invisible and essential—and our attitudes to cultural questions can eventually have consequences beyond telling. 'When I hear the word "Culture",' said Goering, 'I reach for my revolver.' The consequences of that attitude were irredeemably damaging: but it exists even today—perhaps we should pause to examine our own attitudes. This is not of course to suggest that Governmental accountants are Hermann Goerings—or even Philistines—but that sometimes we do not care to admit how much we are losing merely by not caring.

This early evolution of the major headings in the Work Programme should be sufficient to indicate one aspect of the present turning-point in the evolution of the Council of Europe. In their unified diversity—even allowing for all its acknowledged imperfections—we can see something of what can happen when behind an initiative there is a method, behind the method an executive mechanism, and behind the mechanism a single individual mind carrying an indivisible responsibility. It is for the future to

show whether this initiative of an annual and all-inclusive inter-governmental Work Programme for the Council of Europe will or will not live
up to the Baconian standard, and continue to 'dignify and exalt knowledge' through the 'union of theory and practice in a closer bond than has
hitherto been known'. As things now are, it must depend on the attitude,
ability and determination of successive Secretaries General of the Council
of Europe. Yet the coin is as valid when reversed: it is equally true that the
continuing character of the Programme's evolution—its very reputation—
will have a decisive effect on the future character and evolution of the
office of Secretary General. An indecisive Secretary General—an ineffective Work Programme—either of these alone could break what is at
present a harmonious upward spiral of increasingly productive cause and
effect.

   Some characteristics of this spiral we can already identify. The first was
anticipated by Mr. Lannung, already quoted as saying the Programme was
suggested in the Assembly, accepted in the Committee of Ministers, and
worked out by the Secretary General. This raises the question of what in
Chapter Four we termed the 'first visible recorded move'—and here it
is not easy to identify. In the Work Programme itself it is stated to have
been an initiative of the Secretariat—and the Ministers might similarly
feel it an initiative of their own, for as we saw in Chapter Two, the seed
of the idea was part of an official document of the Committee of Ministers
certainly as early as 1954.

   Regardless of how we choose to allot the credit, it is clear from Mr
Lannung's words that even at the beginning of the Programme's history,
it was already recognised that the damaging and yet comprehensible
conflict between Ministers and Assembly which had for so long paralysed
the Council of Europe had at last been overcome—even if only partially,
and for the present. And there is a further nuance in what Mr Lannung,
with his immense experience of the Council, chose to praise. He is by
implication perhaps suggesting that the Work Programme is the monopoly of no one, yet can be used by everyone; that it has engaged the
interest of all yet without engaging their opposition; and that because all
can take credit, none need take offence. This attitude is all the more
valuable, all the better poised to meet any future storms, when we
remember that in Abraham Lincoln's words 'one single mind must be
master or there will be no decision on anything'. This is a truth directly
applicable to the Work Programme of the Council of Europe—the daily
responsibility as it is, and yet, we hope, the continuing pride and achievement of an unbroken succession of single minds—the Secretaries General
of the Council of Europe.

The characteristic we are here observing is that of a central hub to an increasingly expanding wheel of action at the inter-governmental level. If we express this negatively, we find that the Work Programme cannot be said to be the personal property of the Secretary General, for without the annually renewed approval of the Committee of Ministers the Programme is nothing. Nor can it be said to be the property of the Committee of Ministers for they could scarcely approve with equanimity a Programme that was provoking uproar in the Assembly—and without the extraordinarily complex preparatory work of the Programme Unit and the Secretariat as a whole they would have no Programme to approve. Nor can the Programme be said to be the property of the Assembly— which must perpetually manoeuvre between what the Secretariat suggests is possible and what the Ministers decide is permissible. The Secretary General thus has it always in his power to disappoint or anger the Assembly, to fail or disobey the Ministers; the Ministers have it always in their power to alienate the Assembly and inhibit or paralyse the Secretary General; while the Assembly have it always in their power to harass and oppose the Ministers on every point, large or small, sensible or trivial— and the Secretary General as well, and this not least because he is the most vulnerable. A great deal will therefore depend on the extent to which these destructive temptations are not indulged, even under great provocation. After all, it is at present true that all connected with the Council of Europe have excellent reason to feel they share an equal interest in the annual success of the Programme, the character of its evolution, and its value as it appears in the public mind—in a word, an equal share in its reputation.

The second characteristic is so obvious it can far too easily be ignored. This could be damaging, even dangerous—for it is a characteristic that should not be ignored, but exploited: if not exploited it can dwindle and disappear. The Work Programme is off to a good start: it has *momentum*.

This is perhaps not as simple as it sounds, when we remember what politics can be: a suspicious, hostile, super-sensitive and yet also supremely callous environment. The saying 'it is toughest at the top' is very true— the higher the level the tougher, the more cruel it can be—and the all-European level can be the most cruel of all. For the Work Programme of the Council of Europe to have been launched on the first years of its voyage with its sails so finely trimmed, with a great deal more canvas in the lockers to run aloft, and with its course so judiciously charted in anticipation both of winds predictable and winds that are not, is a matter for public congratulation.

The third characteristic may become increasingly important if maintained—for it has already been built carefully into the organisational structure of the Programme. It is simply that the Work Programme is to be renewed every year. Its annual and cyclic, predictable and repetitive character is pronounced. To resume our analogy, every year the next leg of the ship's course can be re-charted, its sails re-set—and if necessary its entire structure overhauled from keel to flag. In Mr Smithers' own words:

> '...The establishment of the Programme of Work will also initiate a yearly cycle in the work of the Council. This will begin in April or May, and will coincide with the meeting of the Committee of Ministers in Strasbourg, with the annual renewal of Parliamentary Delegations to the Consultative Assembly and with the election of its President and Officers, and finally with the start of preparation by the Secretariat of the draft budget for the ensuing year. Once the rhythm of events is established it will thus facilitate a close relationship between programming, and parliamentary and budgetary procedures...'

These three characteristics—that the Programme is the hub of a wheel, that it has momentum, and that it has an annual cyclic rhythm—deserve constant repetition, for the very good reason that if any one of these ceases to be true, then the Programme will thereby have been fundamentally damaged. It will have been damaged not merely as the Programme we now know, but in a much larger respect which has not yet been widely recognised—it will have been damaged in its capacity as a prototype, a first working model, a basis for action on a far wider scale. It is for this reason—that the Programme if preserved can lead to events yet larger again—that these characteristics must similarly be preserved. And this may not be easy, for each of these characteristics also indicates a danger.

First, if the Programme should be jolted off that central and therefore neutral ground of common value to all which it now occupies, central both to the inner circle of the organs of the Council, and to the outer circle of national Governments, parliaments and people, it must be thereby damaged, perhaps irretrievably. *The only way the Programme can survive is at that central point where it does itself resolve conflicting interests.* This cannot ever be easy when—to quote only two examples—the Economic chapter must involve complications with the European Community, and when the Cultural Chapters must involve quite different complications with the Holy See and the Government of a non-member Country: Spain—both of which take part in some of its activities. A glance through the list of activities will reveal repeated references to other organisations, other interests, other influences, all of which must be kept in perpetual and yet evolving equilibrium. The academic-cultural complex and the politico-economic complex—these are real forces in Europe today, and in successive Programmes it may become apparent that these or other groupings may be tending to acquire an influence which, if unchecked, could jolt the Programme off-centre and cause the wheel to swerve dangerously.

It will swerve all the more dangerously, of course, if its momentum has not been maintained. Each characteristic influences the others, and therefore all must be maintained. Yet already the danger of momentum decreasing is real. The election of a new Secretary General automatically means at least the possibility of a slowing down during the transitional period of a year or more during which he imposes his personality and policy. Or any impending and radical reorganisation of the processes of European unification following an enlargement of the European Community might well result in individual Government Departments adopting a wait-and-see attitude—that alone could seriously damage the momentum of the Programme. And because the Programme is admittedly not perfect, it is possible that the friction of concealed structural weaknesses could in time come to bear upon the moving parts of the Programme in such a way that its momentum does slow perceptibly. One of these weaknesses is perhaps already foreshadowed in these words from Mr Smithers' introduction to the Programme:

'Would it be possible, by granting substantially more budgetary resources to the Council, to do all the very urgent things which require to be done in order to bring about greater unity amongst our member States? The answer is, *not without a major change of method.* The problem is more than financial. For the method by which we work, that is to say one of relying upon committees of experts furnished by Governments themselves, places a substantial burden upon the expertise available in government departments and elsewhere. In the case of the smaller countries, which are the great majority in the Council of Europe, that is a very heavy burden indeed. There is therefore a limitation of personnel as well as funds, which could only be overcome if the Council were to employ substantially more of its own experts...'

It comes as a shock to realise that the demands of the Council of Europe have already reached a scale at which they will soon outstrip the manpower available from smaller states in expert fields. Yet statistically it should be no shock—with over sixty expert committees already serving the Council of Europe, this means in round figures it will not be long before a country like Ireland, Norway or Cyprus will be required to provide no less than,

shall we say, a full hundred experts for their representation in Strasbourg—
and this not on subjects where there is a reasonable number of experts at
home, but on *specialised* subjects where even a large country could well
have trouble recruiting more than a handful of adequately qualified men.

If we reverse our calculations, and suppose that countries provide
experts in proportion to their home population, we would have a situation
in which the arrival in Strasbourg, for attendance at all sixty or seventy
expert committees, of no fewer than two and a half Maltese all-purpose
experts would be a matter for applause, for Malta would thereby have
already over-fulfilled her quota. When expressed this way, the problem
becomes ludicrous—when expressed the other way, in terms of *required
expert man-hours per year per activity per country*, it becomes serious. And
we are still considering only part-time experts, asked to contribute merely
a few days, a few weeks per year. Where is the solution? It might well be
the creation of an all-European expert *corps d'élite*—and full time at that.
Or in other words, a new and radical evolution of what we may in time
be able to recognise publicly as a real European Civil Service. Either way,
the closer we look at the problem the more significant it becomes in
relation to what we are here considering—the danger to the Work
Programme of any slowing down of momentum.

Thirdly, there is the perpetual danger of what could happen if the yearly
rhythm should be broken. As we have seen above, the present rhythm is
ostensibly justified by its synchronisation with, for example, the renewal
of delegations to the Assembly or the Spring meeting of the Committee
of Ministers. But suppose these should themselves suddenly be changed—
that would not in itself justify the abandonment of the annual rhythm.
Any reliable administrative rhythm is better than none, but an annual
rhythm has the advantage of *not* being either a national or party-political
rhythm. It is the political anonymity of this metronomic rhythm that can
itself enable the Programme to defend, evolve, and increase its independent
political character at the European level—and yet it is the very anonymity
of this rhythm that could make it vulnerable. There is strong reason for
thinking that an annual rhythm is the best of all—that any tendency to
diminish this to nine or six months, or lengthen it to a two or three-year
rhythm should be resolutely resisted. Less than a year would mean great
administrative difficulty—longer than a year would mean a series of
agreed priorities speedily becoming quite out of kilter with events for lack
of the annual re-appraisal that is so strong a feature of the present Programme. Even worse would be the cessation of any regular rhythm to the
Work Programme—for without a predictable regularity in all its many
phases, its success itself becomes unpredictable—worst of all, it would

mean a loss of initiative in matters both small and also great. The annual systolic rhythm of the Programme is the pulse of its life, and any attempt to halt that rhythm is a thrust at its heart.

Let us hope these dangers never happen, and now more cheerfully regard another characteristic of the Programme which does not immediately force us to anticipate dangers—the fact that the Programme can be communicated to people. It is, in the form we now have it, a compressed document of 15,000 words. It can be given by hand to a stranger, it can be sent in the post to a friend. It is an example to other organisations, it can be sent to parliamentarians all round the world, it is a hand-book for speakers and teachers. If adequately distributed and publicised it can become for very many people a document of many-faceted interest, suggestion and example. Each one of us may find something in it, some particular emphasis, some particular item of work, that is for us especially new, interesting—and therefore a spur to our own most personal thought, speech and action.

This is not a small matter, for the relation between complex political power and simple communication of information is a fact today widely known, yet not widely understood. The communication value of the Council of Europe Work-Programme is that it is compendious yet brief. Its information-value can be measured. As Norbert Wiener tells us of the theory of messages: 'We may evaluate the amount of information (a message) carries by determining its probability in the *ensemble* of all possible messages, and then taking the negative logarithm of their probability.' While he most unkindly does not tell us precisely what a negative logarithm actually is, we can nevertheless grasp his meaning and paraphrase it as saying that there is sometimes political power in improbable simplicity.

The Work Programme is simple in form: that simplicity must be maintained, no matter how great the determination this may come to need. It is mathematically complex, politically labyrinthine, structurally new, and commandingly influential because all-inclusive—and this all-inclusiveness must be equally maintained, again no matter how great the determination this may come to need. It is this that gives the Programme both its impact and its prestige in the eyes of the outer world—for the less people know about what is happening in Strasbourg the more gratefully they can appreciate a document like the Work Programme, which, like a traveller's suitcase, contains everything needed on a journey and can be carried nevertheless in one hand. It is also paradoxically true that the *more* people know about the Council, the more they appreciate the way the suitcase has been packed, and their sudden unaccustomed freedom from the usually over-bulky impedimenta of their day-to-day political luggage. The Programme thus has also a Janus characteristic—it is a single focus for attention, yet also a multi-purpose medium of action. It is thus open to all European organisations, Governments, national, regional, sectional and local interests of every kind to make their voice heard on how the Work Programme can be improved, and how it should evolve. From hospital boards to farmers' lobbies, from lorry-drivers to research scientists, from Jean Monnet's Action Committee for a United States of Europe to the entire European Movement, the unity of the Programme opens the way to a diversity of constructive criticism and contributions. Yet as soon as this is widely realised—as soon as it is known that individual initiatives are not only welcome but *invited*—we can also confidently expect the Programme to come under precisely that complexity of pressures it was from the beginning designed to attract and justify. Its value invites this—and as we shall now see, this is already happening.

Let us first follow the reaction to the Work Programme in the Assembly. If we compare the first debate on the first Work Programme, held on 29 September 1966, with the debate on the European Social Charter held in the same assembly six years earlier and quoted in Chapter Three—and when we remember that *the entire debate on the Charter corresponds to merely one of the two hundred and more activities in the Work Programme of today*, we begin to see another aspect of the dramatic and fundamental change that has occurred between the workings of the Council of Europe as described in earlier chapters, and the Council we are able to describe today. For the same energies are now focussed today for the same aim as earlier, but now in a new dimension; there has been a sudden quantum jump in how and where these energies operate, and in attitudes behind them. The mere appearance of the first Work Programme forced the Assembly to respond immediately with an unprecedented mobilisation of its committee resources, as we see from the speech of M. Vos of the Netherlands, as he introduced the first draft opinion of the Assembly on the Programme:

> '...On 3rd May 1966...the decision in regard to the Programme had been taken by the Ministers, but...the Ministers invited the Consultative Assembly to express its views on the Programme of Work and on its implementation and future development. *We do not often get a communication from our Committee of Ministers and less frequently do we get an invitation, so here is a sign of some new collaboration between the Committee of Ministers and the Assembly.* After receiving this invitation the Assembly reacted in a specific way. It asked eight of our Committees and the Joint Working Party on regional planning to look at the

Programme of Work and to give an opinion in respect of the fields covered by their activities, not excluding remarks about the Programme of Work in a broader sense...The Bureau (Officers of the Assembly) then decided to set up an *ad hoc* Committee, consisting of the nine *Rapporteurs*, and to ask this *ad hoc* Committee to draw up a Resolution for discussion in this Assembly, taking into account the opinion formulated by the Committee...

'...For the first time, therefore, we can act as a parliamentary body with regard to the work done by the Committee of Ministers; and what is more, we are asked by the Ministers to do so...The Programme of Work...has its importance for the work of our Assembly but it has importance in other fields, too. For the first time the outside world gets a picture of what is going on in the Council of Europe with regard to intergovernmental work. We all hope that this may attract the attention of the outside world, as well as that of member countries and others.'

And from the Resolution M. Vos quoted as its key paragraph:

'...by presenting the Organisation's activities as an emergent whole, it provides a clearer picture for the outside world—not only for member countries, but for others as well, including *Eastern Europe*—thus increasing possibilities of contact and even of participation...*for third countries*, the Programme of Work constitutes a catalogue pointing to possible areas of collaboration...To an increasing degree, it should... also allow of the harmonisation of some of *the activities of the EEC and EFTA*, a long-standing concern of the Assembly.'

And M. Vos continued himself:

'...it is indispensable for Governments to undertake firmer commitments as regards the completion dates of certain Activities. (These) must not cease at the point where the Committee of Ministers adopts a European Convention or Agreement, or a Recommendation to Governments, *but should extend also to the implementation at national level of arrangements agreed at European level.* Governments should also see to it that such implementation is prompt and effective *at all levels of their respective national administrations.*

'...where the arrangements which have been agreed require ratification, it is important that Governments, assisted by national delegations to the Consultative Assembly, take pains to obtain such ratification with the minimum of delay. The fact that ratifications are so few and so belated constitutes one of the main weak points of the

Council of Europe's work and *jeopardises the efficiency of the Programme of Work.*

'...It should be recalled that the Programme of Work is not "closed" and the Assembly can always have new questions added, following the procedure laid down in the Statute...The Assembly, using its own methods, may make a useful contribution to the preliminary investigation of some new and useful subject, and attention may be directed to the very, very useful specialised conferences which are already taking place...We say that the Assembly, "through its *rapporteurs* and consulting experts, can document subjects on the agendas of its committees and working parties with a flexibility often lacking in Committees of Governmental Experts".

'...The Committee of Rapporteurs tried to formulate a programme for a new beginning of work between the Committees of Experts and the Assembly, a programme of work indicating and promoting new interdependence and collaboration between this Assembly and the Committee of Ministers *through the good offices of the Secretary General, who is the natural link between them.*

'...We suggest that the Assembly should *address itself to the Secretary General*...and "request the Secretary General to take into account all the observations, both general and particular, of the Assembly and its Committees when preparing the new Programme of Work which he intends to present to the Assembly during its Spring Session".

'*Addressing itself to the Committee of Ministers*, the Assembly should decide "to invite the Committee of Ministers also to take account of the Assembly's observations both when implementing the first programme and when finalising the next programme".'

An admirable speech—a most excellent lead to the Assembly as it prepares to evolve its own attitudes and policy towards the Programme. But what in fact is M. Vos saying? All success brings a shock-wave, and the mere launching of the Work Programme was already a major success. If we want to know what M. Vos is really saying we should notice the points of doubt implicit in his speech. To what extent should the Assembly be able to influence the Programme? Should it address itself to the Secretary General or to the Ministers? What can it do to prod Governments into effective implementation of the Programme? How should the Assembly co-ordinate its own procedures with those of the Committees of Experts? These and other questions are already being raised, and this in a speech not confined to congratulations but concerned with what the Assembly should do, and how. Could it be that here we are already watching the shock-wave at work, and that what we can now reasonably anticipate is a shock reaction from the Assembly, liable to be repeated every year as long as the Programme of Work proves itself an annually repeated success?

Let us follow these speeches further, bearing in mind the three suggestions made above—that the strength of the Work Programme is that it adopts a central position between Ministers, Secretariat and Assembly; that its great advantage is that it began with momentum; and that this momentum must be maintained according to a regular rhythm, preferably annual.

Mr Gustafson, Sweden.
    '...I am not the only one who asks whether this Programme of Work will weaken or strengthen the interest of our Assembly. In the Political Committee (of the Assembly) I have had reason to study this matter...the answer to this question depends on how the Assembly itself deals with the Programme...(it) could be an instrument for increasing the influence of the Assembly, and create a better balance between the Committee of Ministers and the Assembly...the Programme...can in no way restrict the initiative of the Assembly as the Assembly decides its own agenda...But what does the Programme do? What it does is impose a new discipline on each of the two main organs of the Council of Europe; on the Committee of Ministers as well as on the Assembly, and I think that is a good thing...If the Assembly confines itself to routine confirmation...and thus becomes a figurehead for the Programme...its influence might be diminished. *But the Assembly could increase its influence by fulfilling every year two functions...The Assembly should supervise the execution of the programme so that there is a real parliamentary control of the inter-governmental work... The Committee of Ministers in future should not escape as easily as it has sometimes done...The second task for the Assembly is to take initiatives for new subjects to be included in the programme in the following year, and this should be done every year...*More detailed information regarding the work of the Committees of Experts is needed.

    '...during this Part-Session we have seen how the subject of the Programme of Work has been pushed down to the bottom of the Agenda for two days in succession, and those who prepare the Agenda have thus given the impression that this question is of secondary importance and can be dealt with when we have some time left.

    'The Secretary General has attached much importance to this Programme of Work; the Ministers' Deputies have given much time to discussion of it, and the Committee of Ministers has taken it very seriously indeed...I sincerely hope that next year this item will be given a prominent place on the Agenda, a place which it really deserves. The Programme...presents the Council with an opportunity to engage in active and concretely-organised work which would transform the pious wishes contained in our Resolutions and Recommendations into reality. Let us make full use of it.'

Mr Silkin, United Kingdom.
    '...It is important that the document, both in form and layout, should be attractive, that it should be drawn up so as to appeal to and be understood by the public at large, so that the public of all the countries concerned understand what the Council of Europe is doing and intends to do in the future and are *clearly able to relate that work to the general theme of European unity*.
    '...In the last few days we have been debating a future Europe which, I think unanimously, we desire to see on a basis of unity, but... we have all realised that it is impossible to tell when that unity will be achieved...in terms of economic and political unity...in the meantime there is much that can be done to achieve a *social unity, a legislative unity*, a unity of the kind which will eventually draw us towards an economic and *political* unity.
    '...We believe that part of the attraction of this Programme to the general public in all the countries concerned will be the prospect of seeing concrete results within a period of time which can be seen and determined...we hope...that it will be possible for the Ministers to take a leaf from the biggest of the other European Communities and will set themselves and be able to follow a very rigorous timetable in the achievement of what they want to do...
    '...We want to see the work go forward so that...it will be possible within the framework of successive documents that are prepared on the same basis year by year to see the theme clearly more apparent, the theme of European unity.'

What we are here watching is the beginning of the counter shock-wave—a wave compounded of multiple concern, an underlying malaise derived from deeper concerns not yet openly or consciously expressed, tinged nevertheless with an immense admiration for what has been done—the whole adding up to a sudden concentration of attention on what the Programme really means. What are the principles at stake, where will be the future issues, of what nature will be the necessary points of compromise? Let us now look forward half a year to April 1967, and consider a most significant passage of arms in the Assembly between the Secretary General, defending his Programme, and Lord Gladwyn, speaking as a Member of the British Delegation.

Lord Gladwyn, United Kingdom.
'We are grateful to Mr Smithers for his statement and are deeply appreciative of his efforts and the reforms he has initiated, which are making the Council of Europe into a much more living reality.

'I suppose that we all take it for granted that, if the Communities are enlarged—if, that is to say, all the present potential applicants get in—there will be an Economic Community of at least ten, possibly eleven, or even twelve members. The intention is, I understand, in these circumstances, to have certain members of EFTA...as associated members of the Community.

'It is conceivable that, in a year or two, the membership of the EEC will be identical with the membership of the Council of Europe. In these circumstances—not certain but possible—would not Mr Smithers agree that the sensible thing would be to amalgamate the Council of Europe, the extended European Economic Community and Western European Union, to have at any rate one Parliamentary Assembly with perhaps the admirable present staff of the Council of Europe becoming, as it were, the social and cultural wing of the new and extended Community? Would not that be the kind of goal to which we should be heading? Is it not sensible to have it in mind?'

Mr Smithers.
'I think it is premature to cross these bridges in detail. Doubtless many people would agree with part of what Lord Gladwyn has said, but the problem is infinitely more complex. We have to take account of a number of other organisations and of future duties to be performed in Europe. I believe that these problems would best be pursued in detail when we are clear what the situation actually is with regard to enlargement (of the Community).'

Mr Edelman, United Kingdom.
'I join with Lord Gladwyn in congratulating Mr Smithers and his very hardworking Secretariat on this splendid Programme of Work. However, one point strikes me immediately even when merely dipping into the Programme at random. Many of these activities touch on those of other international organisations. For example, there is the harmonisation of laws governing labour contracts or the convening of a European Conference of Ministers of Labour and Social Affairs. These touch on the International Labour Organisation...

What machinery does Mr Smithers employ first of all to harmonise the activities contained in the Programme of Work with those of other international agencies?...to avoid unnecessary overlapping... avoid a proliferation of activity which does not serve any constructive purpose? Finally, I would like to say how much I appreciate the references of Mr Kyprianou to the question of an effective liaison between the Council of Europe and the United Nations, because that is directly relevant...'

Mr Smithers.
    'Mr Edelman's question can be answered in two parts. *First...it is the practice to invite to inter-governmental expert committees representatives of all those organisations which may have an interest in the particular field. Secondly, the Programme of Work is transmitted immediately to all other inter-governmental and indeed private international organisations which may have an interest in it and their comments are invited...*I believe, on examination, it will be found there is very little real duplication...(in) those items where the ILO might be thought to be competent... consultation has taken place...But the situation is not one that can simply be settled by Secretariats: it is more complicated than that. It depends on Governments giving to the representatives in the Council of Europe, the Committee of Ministers, the Ministers' Deputies and Expert Committees and to their representatives in other organisations the same instructions. As sometimes different government departments deal with different international organisations, this does not invariably occur...I think, if I may say so, my answer to Mr Edelman indicates that the question posed by Lord Gladwyn has very many complex aspects to it. Finally, I would like to say this: last year, governments instructed me to prepare a study on overlapping of international organisations and this study takes full account of U Thant's demand, now twice repeated, in his annual report, for a study by governments of the activities of international organisations in the light of their statutes. Our document is before governments and has been sent to other organisations...'

Sir Geoffrey de Freitas, President:
    'We are all most grateful to you, Mr Secretary General, for your very clear explanation. It was a most valuable statement.'

The significance of this sharply edged interchange is that Lord Gladwyn has put his finger on precisely that sensitive nub of doubt from which the malaise so apparent in the Assembly speeches springs—the entire future vocation and role of the Council of Europe. The very success of the Work Programme has made this question immediate and real—and the Secretary General has given the only answer then possible: that the question is premature and cannot yet be answered.

Is this really true? Let us go forward to the Autumn of 1967 and see what the Assembly had to say. On 27 September 1967, a report was tabled by M. Schultz (Rapporteur of the Assembly's Committee of Rapporteurs on the Work Programme) consisting both of a Draft Recommendation for the Assembly to adopt, and a supporting document giving the detailed opinion of each Rapporteur on each of the chapters of the Programme. This was the time when the application of Britain, Norway, Ireland and Sweden to join the European Community was being first presented—and debate on the Recommendation was postponed. Nevertheless, what it said was eloquent.

First let us look at the suggestions of each Assembly Committee on the relevant section of the Work Programme: the aims at the head of these sections are, of course, those already quoted earlier in this chapter.

The Economic Committee (*rapporteur* M. Czernetz, meeting in London) questioned the entire economic section. 'The aims and content...should be revised. This should either be extended to *include all activities relating to the harmonisation of national laws* in the economic field...or be incorporated in a *new chapter dealing with the effects of industrial and technical transformation on physical environment and conservation of natural resources.*'

The Legal Committee (meeting in Paris, *rapporteur* Mr Silkin). '...Last year (1966) the Committee expressed the hope that the Programme of Work would indeed become a "Council of Europe Plan for Europe", mapping out the broad lines of its future action. This hope still exists in 1967...the Legal Committee sees little sign of the co-ordination of activities under different chapters of the Work Programme...it may also be said that there often seems to be a lack of a common thread running through the activities of the Assembly's own Committees...the Programme of Work should be based upon a coherent definition of the place and task of the Council of Europe in the Europe of today and tomorrow. It does not contain any such definition...a minimum of a basic philosophy seems to be indispensable...It is true that the Programme of Work is still at its beginnings. But it is to be hoped that a serious attempt will be made to define such a basic philosophy.

'...certain circles in national administrations do not yet seem to be fully aware of the importance and possibilities of the Council of Europe as an instrument of technical collaboration. As far as its legal programme is concerned, the Council has a unique and unrivalled position in Europe and perhaps even in the world...

'...one of the alarming facts seems to be the very slow progress in the ratification of Council of Europe Conventions and the relatively limited effects which a number of these Conventions seem to have...On 31 March 1967, the Legal Committee heard a statement by M. Modinos, Deputy Secretary General, concerning the procedure and elaboration of European Conventions...On 24 May 1967, the Committee heard a statement by M. Golsong, Director of Legal Affairs, concerning...the decision-making process in the legal work of the Council...Accordingly, your Rapporteur would welcome consideration of the idea of establishing a *permanent European Law Commission under the auspices of the Council of Europe, with tasks and methods of an analogous character to that of the United Kingdom Law Commission*...

'...if certain critical remarks have been made in this Report on some aspects of the Programme of Work, this has been done in the positive and constructive spirit in which the Legal Committee wishes to contribute to the steady improvement of the Programme and of the programming mechanism and to the progressive establishment of a real "Council of Europe Plan for Europe".'

The Cultural Committee (meeting in Strasbourg, *rapporteur* M. Housiaux). '...because of the progress of industrial society, education and culture are no longer the privilege of a minority but concern the masses. The Europe that is gradually coming into being therefore needs powerful machinery for co-operation, the primary aim being the cultural advancement of all classes of society...The CCC should form this machinery, and its resources should be strengthened...by gradually moving more and more funds from the bilateral over to the multilateral sector.' The Committee advocated 'turning the European Conference of Cultural Ministers into a regular institution (which) should provide, at inter-governmental level, the political impetus now lacking'; that 'activities relating to the general problem of planning man's environment...should be concentrated in an operational programme'; that 'the Council of Europe should concentrate its activities increasingly on permanent education and cultural advancement'; and that there must be a European policy for youth.

The Committee on Science and Technology (meeting in Geneva, *rapporteur* Mr Kirk). The findings of the Committee were understandably aggressive and to the point, for the excellent reason that as yet there existed no Science and Technology chapter in the Work Programme. '...Can it be said that the CCC...is the appropriate framework for the necessary action?...*the fundamental necessity is to adopt a European policy in matters of science and technology whose framework is not restricted to any one of the international organisations.* [Present] co-operation...would be much more efficient and fruitful if it were organised and co-ordinated on the basis of a general plan...The humane sciences will have to be revolutionised if they are to make an effective and systematic contribution to finding a political solution to these problems.'

The Committee on Local Authorities (meeting in Paris, *rapporteur* M. Radius). 'The omission from the Programme of Work of any reference to man and his civic capacity in a municipal or a regional community, leaves a real gap...The Committee of Ministers' decision to set up a committee for co-operation on municipal and regional questions should open a new chapter in the inter-governmental activities of the Council of Europe...It is to be regretted that the...Programme makes no mention of the financial assistance provided by the Committee of Ministers for inter-municipal exchanges...*the basic units of society are...gaining in importance owing to the very fact of society's complexity*...In order to lay down... priorities, criteria should be drawn up on the basis of a firm intention and political decisions. The simple "inventory of current action" does nothing like lay down priorities, and is also not related to criteria established in advance. It would therefore appear that the Programme of Work in order to become a real 'Council of Europe Plan', as the Assembly desired in 1966, calls for a serious effort on the part of Governments, of the Secretariat and of the Assembly as well, to consider the true priorities in Europe and the functions that the Council of Europe can reasonably assume...The launching (of the Programme) deserves the unreserved support of the Assembly. The Committee on Local Authorities, however, would like the Programme to be bolder...The Assembly should be more closely associated with the drawing up of the Programme...This would have the...effect of making co-operation closer between the two bodies of the Council of Europe (i.e. the Assembly and the Ministers)...'

The Committee on Agriculture (meeting formally several times, *rapporteur* M. von Vittinghoff-Schell) congratulated the Second Work Programme on being better balanced than the First—gave a detailed commentary chapter by chapter through the whole Programme on those 'numerous and varied' activities within the competence of the Committee—advocated that 'the very important and urgent question of the social protection of self-employed farmers and their families' should be added to the Programme—noted that '...the only one of the Committee's proposals to be accepted by the Committee of Ministers in the new

Programme...is the inclusion...in the economic sector of the proposal relating to the International Centre for Advanced Mediterranean Agronomic Studies'. And the Committee concluded (there is here more than an echo of the same problems as seen in Chapter Three during the creation of the European Social Charter) that since from the agricultural point of view there was so very much that should be done, and yet could not yet be done, the root of the trouble was financial. 'Since the Work Programme is, as the Secretary General has said, "a piece of corporate management" by the Governments and the Assembly, it is up to the Assembly to help to secure an appropriate increase in the financial resources made available to the Council of Europe.'

The Committee on Population and Refugees (meeting in Paris, *rapporteur* Mme Jadot). The Committee welcomed the European Population Conference of 1966, deplored the fact that not all member countries contributed to the Council of Europe's European Resettlement Fund ('...a financial body which has given tangible proof of its effectiveness...'); emphasised its interest in 'certain new items in the Work Programme, namely: industrial safety for migrant workers, education of migrant workers' children, the present state of over-population in certain regions of Council of Europe member countries and the study of methods of compiling migration statistics,' and especially applauded 'the item concerning disaster relief...too often the Council of Europe has been unable to provide concrete assistance to victims of a disaster in a member country and to *prove thereby that collective solidarity is not an idle phrase.*'

The Committee then advocated—and strongly—four precise items. First, the *European Census*, an item of particular interest to all concerned with the future evolution and management of direct European elections: '...the Assembly, after observing that this question had scarcely been touched on by the first European Population Conference, asked for the synchronisation and standardisation of census-taking to be included (in the Programme) and for the second European Population Conference to pave the way for a European Agreement in this field...the synchronisation of census-taking was among the questions accepted jointly by the Committee of Ministers and the Assembly for inclusion in the...Work Programme. It would be paradoxical...if a question on which the two Council of Europe organs agreed should not be referred to a Conference of experts convened and financed by the Council...'

Secondly, the Committee urged yet again, here supported by the Social Committee of the Assembly—that a *European Conference of Ministers of Labour and Social Affairs* should be convened. This, as we shall see, became part of the agreed overall proposals of the Committee of Rapporteurs reporting, as a single body, on the Programme as a whole.

Thirdly, the Committee picked up sharply what might seem a minor point: '...as regards the pilot scheme for the vocational training of three hundred skilled workers, the Assembly cannot fail to be surprised at the tergiversations of the Committee of Ministers. That it is by nature complementary to the programme for the vocational training of student instructors which it has approved is obvious.'

Fourthly, on the Right of Asylum, the Committee stressed the weakness of a declaration which was 'no more than a token of good intentions *as opposed to a Convention giving legal form and force* to the recognition and exercise of the right of asylum'. This in fact touched on a most delicate and human matter—especially in relation to Eastern Europe—and amounted to a confrontation between the Secretary General, arguing, as the Committee admitted, that a declaration was the most Governments were likely to accept, and the Committee itself, arguing that only the legal force of a Convention would be adequate.

The Social Committee (meeting in Paris, *rapporteur* Mr Meyers) repeated its earlier suggestion that a *European Conference of Ministers of Social Affairs should be convened and also a second European Tripartite Conference.* This recalls the events described in Chapter Three—but the Committee went further, and commenting on the Programme as a whole, hoped that 'the chapter on co-operation in the social field be divided into main heads on main themes, reflecting the predominant considerations (living environment, working environment, leisure environment, social services, the social problems of various sections of the population, etc.) which would form the guide-lines of the Council of Europe's policy in the social field. This does not seem possible with the present sub-chapters and sections, where the problem of young workers, for example, appears in four different, unrelated places.'

On Assembly procedures, the Committee suggested a two-stage method—first, 'an opinion on the general plan of the Programme', and second an Assembly opinion on 'the actual contents of the Work Programme, not, of course, commenting...in detail but stating its view on the pattern of activities in the various technical fields'—and that 'the plenary debates (of the Assembly) should be attended and contributed to by a member...of the Committee of Ministers, so that the Assembly could subject the Council's inter-governmental activities to the same parliamentary scrutiny as the progress reports it periodically receives from other international organisations such as OECD, ILO and—in future, we hope—WHO...it would be paradoxical if the affairs of our own organisation were discussed less seriously and formally than those of other organisations whose...reports are more often than not presented and defended by a Minister or a responsible senior official...to ensure optimum conditions for such a debate, it is fundamentally important that the Assembly be kept properly informed...regularly sent the text not only of Conventions and Agreements but also of the recommendations to Governments which the Committee of Ministers adopts as a result of the work of the technical committee or groups of experts...

On the Ratification of Conventions, the Committee concluded it could not 'be content to let matters rest...it has been repeatedly stated that the conclusion of international treaties was one of the Council of Europe's purposes and one of the most effective means of action at its disposal. It would therefore be well for the Assembly to reconsider the whole matter in the near future...' And on the external relations of the Council, the Committee concluded with a '*request for a clear definition of the relationship between the Council of Europe and the other international organisations* so that—with a view to general rationalisation—the work of the Council can be properly compared', and a request 'that a position be taken up on the place and role of the non-governmental international organisations which have consultative status with the Council of Europe'.

These were the detailed opinions of the Assembly, Committee by Committee, on the *Second Work Programme*, chapter by chapter. The vigour and earnestness of these comments, whether adverse or congratulatory, leaves little doubt of the momentum of the Programme in the eyes of parliamentarians—and also little doubt how advantageous it would be to maintain its annual cyclic rhythm. It does, however, increase doubt on how long the Programme will in fact prove able to maintain its neutrally central position, carefully equidistant from the influence of Ministers, Secretariat, and Assembly. And it is clear that, because of both its weaknesses and its strength, the Programme is already coming under complex pressures, and that these pressures may result in its being radically modified and—let us hope—strengthened.

It will be noted that the comment of the Political Committee of the Assembly has not been mentioned. This is because the opinion of the Political Committee, and also the agreed overall opinion of all nine Rapporteurs meeting together as a single Committee on the Work Programmes (both with M. Schultz as Rapporteur) reacted to the emergence of the Work Programme in a way that only two years earlier could not have been anticipated at all, except perhaps by those who from the beginning had always secretly hoped that the Programme would prove to possess a catalytic power quite out of proportion to its apparent size. Yet even they may have been surprised—the title of the Draft Recommendation which M. Schultz tabled in September 1967 concerned nothing less than the Council of Europe as a whole, its functions, and its future—and this in a report designed for official publication and wide distribution.

Its tone is, first, one of overwhelming approval of the Work Programme as an initiative, and, secondly, a most timely and courageous determination to examine, question, and if possible clarify the very purpose and *raison d'être* of the Council of Europe as a whole. 'The Assembly can choose between two possibilities: it can either confine itself to polite generalities, or it can make a...thorough analysis of the Programme... which would not hesitate to penetrate to the heart of the problem by raising the question which underlies every undertaking and which concerned no more and no less than its finality'—or, in other words, the extent to which the Council of Europe—and its Work Programme—can justifiably claim the right to survive, a question already raised by implication, as we have seen, by Lord Gladwyn in the Assembly.

'The international scene has changed considerably', says the Report, 'since our Organisation was set up, and the Secretary General was the first to emphasise that fact in his remarkable speech in May 1965, and to try to draw the necessary conclusions.' (This is, of course, the speech reviewed in Chapter Seven, when Mr Smithers affirmed that the aims of the Council of Europe could be made so clear they could be written on the back of a post-card.) '...the transition from the "cold war" to co-existence, the advances made towards Eastern Europe and the passage from *détente* to *entente* have become part of a situation which must be faced up to without illusions by means of a reasonable policy. Is there any need to recall that this evolution has gone hand in hand with the decline of Europe as a world power? A tightening of the bonds between European countries has never been more necessary.'

And the Report continues: 'We must also take note of another change, less easily perceptible...that slow but irreversible appearance in international society of a tangible community spirit which has progressively changed the pattern of international relations (and) is an integral part of the progressive organisation of mankind on a world scale. If it seems inevitable it is nevertheless taking place in the face of enormous difficulties to the extent of *producing in certain circles a feeling of unease which sometimes blinds those concerned to its positive nature...the traditional structures and methods of international relations are proving inadequate*...no substitute has yet been found corresponding to needs which are certainly quite new but none-theless imperious. The crisis in the United Nations, concern about the function of regional organisations, the 'over-lapping' and rivalries between international organisations, the tensions between Ministries of Foreign Affairs and specialised Ministries involved in technical co-operation, the frequent misunderstandings between diplomats and international civil servants are all symptoms of a change, the cause of which must be clearly understood in order to avoid the irritation caused by its negative aspects. We are witnessing the re-shaping of relations between States which is certainly not taking place without stresses and strains, but which also marks the *transition to a new era in international relations*.

'It is against that background that attention must be paid to those who ask whether the Council of Europe is still equal to the task which it was once given or whether, on the contrary, as an instrument for international co-operation, it does not belong to a past age and should not therefore be dismantled like an obsolete machine which is no longer able to produce what was expected of it.'

This is the hard question—and perhaps one of the greatest compliments due to the emergence of the Programme of Work is that it has given the Assembly of the Council of Europe courage to face the question not only boldly, but openly in public print. 'A significant part of European opinion is asking that question. The astonishing lack of interest shown by the Press is a revealing symptom, but doubts as to the efficiency of the Organisation do not only exist outside. They are to be found in the minds of the very people who are supposed to use it, Parliaments and the Chancelleries of Governments.'

After the doubt, comes the conviction. 'It is also true, however, that some feel that the Council of Europe has an assured future. In their view *it is only now that the situation is favourable to its true potentialities*. They feel that thanks to its very general but unequivocal terms of reference *it has a function which it alone can perform* and which corresponds to a real present-day need on the part of the European States. We (the *rapporteurs*) are convinced that this view is the correct one...'

After stoutly insisting that the Statutory Aim of the Council of Europe stands, but that 'the experience of twenty years has revealed...the ingredients can now be seen in a different light', the suggested functions for the Council are defined as follows:

1. *The Council of Europe, a promoter of change:*
   '...Those who set up the Council hoped to stimulate...socio-economic

change by political means. It can now be seen that there has been a shift
of emphasis: rather than by political methods transformation is being
promoted through common action in economic, social, cultural, scientific, legal and administrative matters...the Council has left the diplomatic
scene to become a body for "technical co-operation". From being a
political alliance it has turned into an agency for "common development", as can be seen from its Work Programme and from the Assembly's
growing involvement in technical matters.'

2. *The Council of Europe, an agency for peace:*
  '...twenty years ago that mission was defined in a negative manner: by
excluding military questions. Since that time, the concept of peace has
evolved considerably...it has become dynamic, synonymous with a
sustained and systematic effort which is part of the general endeavour to
improve man's moral and material well-being so that it has been possible
to say that development is the new name for peace...
  '...international co-operation and peace are two aspects of the same
historical trend which leads to the consolidation and integration of the
community of mankind...
  '...*this cannot come from the traditional relations between sovereign States,
but will be the fruit of that multilateral technical co-operation* which is the new
feature of international society and reveals its superiority over traditional diplomatic methods through its capacity to transform existing
structures...
  '...the Council of Europe, as an agency of peace, has a genuine chance
of being useful at both the levels on which it operates.'

3. *The Council of Europe, a regional body:*
  '...It is now recognised that the success of a world-wide international
organisation is inconceivable without the existence...the intermediary
and mediating action, of regional organisations representing the geographical, ethnic and cultural characteristics of the different parts of the
world and those who live there.
  '...international, technical and multilateral co-operation can be pursued
more easily by regional groupings. *The day when U Thant expounded this
new doctrine in the Consultative Assembly was a decisive date in the history
of the Council of Europe*...these responsibilities must be shouldered by
"Europe" as a whole for the simple reason that no one European State
can assume them on its own...we can readily see if we look at the existing
European organisations one by one, *that the Council of Europe alone can
claim to represent our continent.*'

M

4. *The Council of Europe, the trustee of Western Humanism:*

'Let us not forget that the Council of Europe is the institution which gave birth to the European Convention on Human Rights and is where that Convention is implemented. Its existence is indissolubly linked with the concept of man's inalienable dignity and liberty which is the heritage of Western Humanism. *The responsibilities that this entails are the glory and pride of our organisation.*

'Western Humanism is Europe's contribution to the world. It is the driving force behind the astonishing process of change which marks our age, finding its ultimate motivation in the will to emancipate man from material contingencies and to bring about his intellectual and moral self-fulfilment...

'...we know that scientific and technological development may well turn against man himself. It is here that the Council of Europe, the guardian of human rights, must face up to its responsibilities: while promoting the process of change, it must see that change serves man and does not bring him into servitude.

'A Work Programme on the theme "Man in a European Society" implies the application of a *humanism of development.*

'Humanism too is subject to change. The fascinating adventure of mankind is also paving the way for the humanism of the Twenty-First century, which...will appear under new forms. It is not enough to codify the achievements of the past. *We must project an attractive vision of man's destiny into the future.*'

5. *The Council of Europe's fundamental function: prepare the future.*

'...the Council of Europe has undergone a strange metamorphosis during the past twenty years. From a diplomatic alliance it has become an agency for technical co-operation, *from the warden of "human rights" it has become the workshop of a humanism of development*...our Organisation stands today as a regional organisation for the peaceful development of a society in evolution. Its basic task is to prepare the Europe of tomorrow in a changing world by promoting economic, social and cultural development.

'The Work Programme has had the merit—and this should be em- phasised—of indicating the right approach...we would suggest that the Council of Europe's function should consist in stimulating and promoting the socio-economic process by providing member States with the services necessary and indispensable to them for their own development... *The Council will be useful to the extent in which it renders services which no other organisation can offer and which no single State can find at home with the same ease.* These services can be varied; information, enquiries, comparisons of ideas and experiences, not to mention the preparation of appropriate legislation and the carrying out of operational programmes...'

6. *Provision for systematic forecasting.*

'What do we know of Europe in the year 2000? In order to answer the question "what will be the society of tomorrow?", we must above all decide what we want it to be...we must now determine the "kind of life" we are aspiring to...we find ourselves confronted with alternatives which involve our deepest convictions concerning man's destiny.

'*Should not the main service to be provided by the Council of Europe consist in a systematic endeavour to forecast, indeed to anticipate the future, based on technical and scientific studies and revealing the major cultural and social options of tomorrow?*

'It must be acknowledged that Europe lacks a body where an overall view can be defined and discussed in a long-term perspective. By directing its work towards a systematic study of future living conditions in the European community in order to determine their evolutionary trends, the Council of Europe could become the body where possible and desirable model "futures" are worked out, the instrument which national legislators and administrations so badly need to make the necessary choices. *The Council of Europe is better placed than any other organisation to put the future of Europe as a whole on the drawing-board.*'

Thus the theory—what of the practice? Does the Report have any practical suggestions? Its key suggestions are three—and each raises larger problems, at which we shall be looking in the next chapter. These suggestions are—first that since the functions described above cannot possibly be fully fulfilled with 'the Council's present resources and working methods', then Governments must 'decide to provide the Council with the appropriate resources' and 'instruments of thought and research'. This of course involves the question of a *political* decision by Governments—and possibly an across-the-board decision involving not only the functions of the Council of Europe, but much more besides.

Secondly, that since the implications of the Work Programme are in fact evolving so far and so fast, it is essential that 'technical co-operation must be placed under the responsibility of the competent (Conferences of) Ministers'. This again implies a very large *political* decision.

Thirdly, that if the day-to-day handling of the Work Programme at the Ministerial level could in fact be transferred to a much more sophisticated structure of European Conferences of Specialised Ministers, then this could result in freeing the Council of Europe's own single Committee of Ministers from an immensely heavy burden—thus permitting them to resume their original and finer function: *that of becoming the only all-European Conference of Foreign Ministers.*

This chapter ends by suggesting far larger questions than those it has answered. There is a reason for this. During this chapter we have done no more than look at some aspects of the Council of Europe's Work Programme—yet in doing that, we have of course been studying a quite extraordinary aspect of the European Idea itself at work in practice: seen as it were in cross-section. If this is not enough to illustrate the complexity of the European Idea in our time, let us assemble a deliberately higgledy-piggledy list of our *contemporary* activities as documented in the second Work Programme of the Council of Europe, and ask what this list would reveal about ourselves, our struggles, our attainments, our weaknesses, and our growing hopes, if viewed, say, by a historian peering back from the year AD 3000?

...revision of administrative arrangements for the health control of sea, air, and land traffic...haemoglobin: establishment of a European standard... systematic development of a the European research potential, mainly through existing centres for confrontation and research: commissioned survey on research facilities available in member countries in different key-sectors, e.g. molecular biology, radio-chemistry...University curricula—chemistry, biology, physics, geography, history, economics, social sciences, education, mathematics... European Consular Convention...international classification of patents of invention...co-ordination of criminological research...right of asylum, preparation of a draft Declaration...harmonisation of fundamental legal concepts...social services for migrant workers: preparation of a Recommendation to Governments...social problems of the aged and future action on their behalf, preparation of a Recommendation to Governments...preparation of the European Demographic Conference...examination of international social Conventions...industrial safety and health...European Pharmacopoeia...comparative study of national nature conservation legislation...documentation centre for education in Europe...free movement of academic personnel...cultural identity card...participation in the civic education campaign sponsored by the European Cultural Centre (Geneva)...implementation of the European Convention on Establishment and European Social Charter...laws governing investment trusts...alignment of laws on restrictive business practices...harmonisation in the field of company law...harmonisation of European food health laws...study of means of promoting the uniform interpretation of European treaties...social aspects of regional development policy (urban areas)...human relations in industry: preparation of a report...Council of Cultural Co-operation project for Turkish teachers...training, recruitment and status of teachers in adult education: pilot survey in six countries...sending of youth experts to Greece and Cyprus...meetings between practising lawyers from all member countries of the Council of Europe... immunities of persons taking part in proceedings before the European Commission and Court of Human Rights: preparation of a draft protocol...survey of existing translations into the languages of Member States of the principal codes or other legislative instruments in force in Member States of the Council of Europe...adoption of children: preparation of a Convention...Social Policy Information Bulletin... European Young Workers Statute...exchange of information in the fields of 1) epidemiological and demographic studies and immunisation programmes, 2) cancer...international transport of animals...comparative study and possible harmonisation of the European Convention on Human Rights, the United Nations draft Covenants and possibly other regional Conventions...exchange of young workers: examination of the practical effects of existing agreements with a view to the possible preparation of a European programme...

How this would be judged one thousand years from now we cannot today even venture to guess—for this is the *pot-pourri* of the European Idea in our time, and we are too close to believe we can ourselves accurately judge either the Idea or our own reaction to it. Nevertheless, the European Idea is an *Idea*—and our observer in the year three thousand might well notice carefully that we in our time were at least beginning to evolve the intellectual tools necessary to a conscious shaping of our history.

If we now consider the Work Programme of the Council of Europe within the context of the European Idea, and the European Idea within the context of the evolution of human thought itself, and measure all this against the multiple intervening issues touched on in this chapter—then we are forced to admit we are now confronting large questions. We have looked at some aspects of the European Idea in practice; we have glimpsed some aspects at least of the theory—yet the true *union* of theory and practice awaits us still in the future, and still depends entirely upon our uniting inspiration and hard work in coming decades. All this combined should be enough to make us face these questions, for we have a European ship of state yet to build, and a ship that is not seaworthy cannot sail through storms.

CHAPTER TEN

'Let Us Be Quite Sober'

'Still, let us not be over sanguine of a speedy, final triumph. Let us be quite sober.'
ABRAHAM LINCOLN, in a letter to J. C. Conkling, 26 August, 1863

THE EUROPEAN IDEA includes a motive and a meaning, a mandate and
also a mystery. It includes also a great hope: for we must be bold enough
to believe that some day all the people of Europe will rejoice in their
unity. In the last three chapters we have been looking at the Council of
Europe's Work Programme—we watched it grow from an idea to an
active political process, we heard voices in the Assembly suggesting it
should be seen as forerunner to a yet larger 'Plan for Europe'. We saw
something of the motive and meaning in the European Idea, and by
the end of the previous chapter we were being led to realise the mandate
forced on us by the necessity inherent in the European Idea. And yet the
mystery still remains, and many questions are not yet answered.

In this chapter we shall look at some of these yet larger questions.
When we look at the European Idea as it manifests today, one of its
most striking characteristics is negative. It is an absence of something—
a void not yet filled, a silence waiting for something to be said. The
silence is on the federalist necessity—the void is that which a federal
structure must fill—the absence is that of a daily federal context within
which the real work of a European Renaissance can grow. Nearly all
our present difficulties arise from the fact we are not yet able to work
in a federal environment—the mandate imposed on us is the creation
of this environment, and it is understandable that lacking this federal

structure as we do, we find power, responsibility and ideas—structures, functions and initiatives—distributed across Europe today in a tangled confusion of deceptive and extraordinary ways. It is a paradox of the European Idea that those who claim most to represent movement towards unity are themselves sometimes least united. One example among many is the dichotomy, even tension, today existing between the Council of Europe in Strasbourg, and the European Community in Brussels.

This seldom appears on the surface. But here is Mr Harold Wilson, who became on 24 January, 1967 the first British Prime Minister to address the Assembly of the Council of Europe. Shortly before the British application to join the Community was presented, and on his way to encounter President de Gaulle in Paris, Mr Wilson said:

'...We mean business...because the interests of Europe as a whole—wider Europe no less than those of western, northern and southern Europe—will be served, as equally our own separate (British) interests will be served, by creating a greater and more powerful economic community...The concept of a powerful Atlantic alliance can be realised only when Europe is able to put forth her full economic strength so that we can...speak from strength to our Atlantic partners...

'...Britain's loyalty to...the Atlantic Alliance...must never mean subservience. Still less must it mean an industrial helotry under which we in Europe produce only the conventional apparatus of a modern economy while becoming increasingly dependent on American business for the sophisticated apparatus which will call the tune in the seventies and eighties.

'...Let us not be defeatist about Europe's technological contribution compared with that of the United States...What would the American industrial economy look like today without jet aircraft, directly based on a British invention...antibodies...the electronic revolution based on the British development of radar; indeed the entire nuclear superstructure which could never have been created except on the basic research of Rutherford and other British scientists?

'All right, this is blowing trumpets, and why not? What is wrong with too many of us in Europe is that we seem to have lost that art...'

This is good solid scientific stuff—so far this is the Brussels wavelength. What, then, of the Strasbourg tone—the human note—the higher and wider appeal? '*High Heaven rejects the lore*', said Mr Wilson, quoting Wordsworth, '*of nicely calculated less or more*'...He spoke of:

'...removing tension and creating a wider unity embracing *all Europe, east and west*, and, looking outwards still more widely...to the only war we seek, the war on want and hunger, to what we can contribute in our own distinctive (European) way to solving the problems of racial tension...they can be overcome if all of us, while treading our way through the complicated economic and political issues involved, can keep our eyes firmly fixed on the vision we have proclaimed...

'Those of us entrusted with the responsibilities of government have the challenging duty...of leading an impatient generation. It is a generation impatient of the mumblings, bumblings, and fumblings of what has too often passed for statesmanship...this new generation will write the next chapters in (our) history—it will condemn beyond any power of ours to defend or excuse, the failure to seize what so many of us can clearly see is now a swirling, urgent tide in man's affairs...'

As suggested in earlier chapters, it is the force of this tide that piles up great log-jams of difficulty—and the intractability of these log-jams contributes towards the present psychological crisis in the politics of Europe. National politics are no longer felt to be effective—and European institutional politics are still too far removed from us, too indirect, too complex for us to feel they are yet effective. It would, for example, be widely agreed that for Brussels and Strasbourg to come to a public understanding, agreement, or joint declaration on aims, methods, and timing would be a giant step forward, and yet also that this would require an imagination and skill in leadership which today we must soberly agree is rare. Yet why is this?

First, it is today still difficult for either Brussels or Strasbourg to define their real *aims* publicly—or to some extent even privately. As we saw in Chapter Six, the real aim of at least the Brussels Commission of the Community is the creation of a federal Europe—yet this is seldom alluded to in the Press, and as we saw, cannot be proved by quoting official speeches, but only by scrutinising public information bulletins. And in Strasbourg, as we have seen, the strategy is to prepare for what is widely admitted can only be a federal Europe but without openly saying so—and this in a multitude of different ways which on the surface do not reveal their inner intention.

Secondly, the *methods* open to Strasbourg and Brussels are defined by their founding treaties. The Community rests on the Treaty of Rome, the Council of Europe rests on its founding Statute—and this will continue until either or both is amended or superseded. The plans of the Community can be termed locked plans, proceeding with great difficulty and caution along carefully laid railway-tracks, to agreed time-tables, and through fields of action meticulously fenced with detailed definitions. This is the inflexible method: perhaps later it will change. And the Council of Europe must continue to work within its Statute, which, though weakened by its veto on defence, and lacking the sterner inherent discipline of the Treaty of Rome, is in many ways open-ended, flexible, and undefined. And perhaps this also will change—as we have seen there is an undeniable strengthening of discipline growing out of the Council's annual Work Programme.

The third reason is that it is naturally difficult to achieve agreement between an organisation extending to six countries only, and an organisation already extending to eighteen. The span of difference is great—yet we cannot admit it is so great that it need be insuperable. It has been demonstrated in Strasbourg that all-European action is possible in many immediate ways, and that opinion in Strasbourg would genuinely welcome with the greatest interest and enthusiasm a real co-ordination between Strasbourg and Brussels. The will and wish exists on the one side—can we honestly claim it exists on the other?

The sober truth at present is that we can not. There is no proof of genuine interest within the Community outwards towards the wider and more subtle methods being pioneered today in Strasbourg. There is even evidence of hostility. It is a fact that only shortly after the announcement of the *first* Work Programme, already in Brussels a gentle whisper was to be heard that what was being planned in Strasbourg was 'too ambitious'. In summer 1966, Mr Martin Vasey—then a news correspondent of *Agence Europe* in Luxembourg—reported in an article contributed to *Carillon* (the alumni journal of the College of Europe in Bruges, now published under the editorship of Mr John Lambert as *Agenor*) that the Work Programme could 'do little to solve the basic economic and political divisions of Europe, as long as the European Economic Community's participation in the Programme is subject to a general proviso guaranteeing complete freedom of action to develop its own common policies whatever is decided in Strasbourg. *Spokesmen of the Six never tire of explaining that the aims and methods of the Community are different in kind from those of the Council of Europe.*'

How, therefore, are we to regard this dichotomy between two great institutions, both dedicated to the same aim? Even this dichotomy in the Strasbourg-Brussels relationship is quoted only as example—for there are others equally visible in Europe today, and more serious examples

M*

may unexpectedly arise to confront us. If this non-alignment, this tension, this refusal to admit openly that both are on the same side of the barricades and likely to find themselves confronting the same enemies— if this continues, then who is to take the lead, and who is to give way? If each side believes it is fighting on the side of the angels, who then should conciliate, conform and concede? And when one, or the other, or both sides have done this, have they betrayed or have they saved their cause, and who is to judge their action? It is astonishing we should have to ask these questions of institutions already working at the European level and in the interests of Europe—but this is how it is happening. When we consider the difficulties of the environment in which these institutions work, and realise that solutions will be achieved only through the action of key individuals, we can recall the following words by John F. Kennedy in his *Profiles in Courage*. They are today no longer applicable merely in America, but also to Europe—and this at both national *and* European level:

'Today the challenge of political courage looms larger than ever before...our everyday life is becoming so saturated with the tremendous power of mass-communications that any unpopular or unorthodox course arouses a storm of protests...Our political life is becoming so expensive, so mechanised and dominated by professional politicians and public relations men that the idealist who dreams of independent statesmanship is rudely awakened by the necessities of election and accomplishment. Of course it would be much easier if we could all continue to think in traditional political patterns...to move and vote in platoons...We shall need compromises in the days ahead, to be sure, but these will be or should be, compromises of issues not of principles. We can compromise our political positions but not ourselves. We can resolve the clash of interests without conceding our ideals, and even the necessity for the right kind of compromise does not eliminate the need for those idealists and reformers who keep our compromises moving ahead, who prevent situations from meeting the description supplied by Shaw: "*Smirched with compromise, rotted with opportunism, mildewed by expedience, stretched out of shape with wire-pulling and putrefied with permeation.*" Compromise need not mean cowardice...it is frequently the compromisers and conciliators who are faced with the severest tests of political courage...'

Much of this can be translated already into the European idiom— certainly too much to allow us to remain entirely acquiescent and comfortable as we regard the condition of our time, the characteristics of what is happening—and far more important, what is *not yet* happening. Already it is in Europe, more than in America, that an uncompromising insistence on the carrying through of creative compromise is becoming more and more essential for our successful political evolution. Already it is in Europe, more than in America, that we must somehow learn to 'resolve the clash of interests without conceding our ideals'. Could there in fact be any shorter, firmer word on the European Idea in general— and on what is here our chosen example—the sadly strained relations between the European Community and the Council of Europe.

Let us see for ourselves the extent to which this American idiom is appropriate to the European context. The fundamental difference between the European and American context—as has been repeatedly suggested in this book—is that in *Europe* there is a great debate yet to come; a debate never yet fully opened; a debate whose imminence is present in the minds of many of our public men; a debate on which the future of Europe may well turn, and a debate which must itself indisputably turn on points of principle. It is the federalist debate: *not* on how to solve the separate and manifold questions of European unification, but on the paramount necessity of establishing a method of government itself capable of solving these questions. It is the debate on whether we are prepared to accept great change in order to reap great success. And it is the debate whose importance President de Gaulle proved himself great enough to understand in advance of many of his contemporaries— but tragically not great enough to confront in such a way as to invite the respect of generations to come. And it is of course the debate which Mr George Brown did dare to mention, and most skilfully, in his closing words as Foreign Secretary to the Labour Party Conference in Scarborough in October 1967, and this on television to the general public. But in what context was the question raised? If we look again at our chosen example, the relationship between the European Community and the Council of Europe, the fact remains that a federal statement of aims by the Council of Europe could not command the unanimous support of Governments and we cannot expect it. Similarly, a federalist statement of aims by the Commission of the Community in Brussels— although already revealed in black and white as we saw in Chapter Six— would, if pressed forward by the spokesmen of the Commission in daily political action, most seriously weaken the work of the Commission through the opposition it would provoke and enrage.

We thus have two organisations the tendency of whose action is indisputably towards the eventual creation of a federal system and yet neither of which can yet say so. When we consider all the other organisations

involved in the unification of Europe today—and in a context of
over three hundred million people—this amounts to groups of political
engineers all trying to handle these turbulent political currents of our
time with an astounding assortment of methods. Some of these methods
are limited, ancient, proved and safe. Some are so powerful they could
be explosive. Some are at present only exploratory, limited to pilot
schemes and first endeavours. We have all this happening without the
different groups being connected to each other by what is now becoming
self-evidently indispensable—a single, interconnecting political grid-
system—all-purpose and yet serving a single end—and designed to
maintain a daily balance and equilibrium, a perpetually fluid movement
and flow of political energy from place to place, and from level to level
as varying political and human needs arise. This grid-system corresponds
to that eventual trans-European federal structure whose absence is the
root-cause of our difficulties today, and whose creation—regardless of
difficulties—is our duty.

Our present skeletal grid-system, which does now partially exist in our
contemporary phase of European unification, does therefore demand
strengthening at certain levels. If we consider the levels of power now
already involved we find that the European Community is operating at
a level we can term *ultra*-political, while the Council of Europe is operating on power-frequencies which include among others what we can
term *sub*-political and also *supra*-political. There are phases of activity
on both sides which do not yet correlate with each other—and also
many which happily do. The overall unifying grid of established political
connections, structures, and working mechanisms is of course still
missing because the necessary cross-connections have not yet been
authorised by Governments. In the meantime the dilemma of the
engineers is that since they cannot gain political permission to construct
the unifying grid, they are forced to continue building their isolated
power-houses of different types fulfilling different functions by different
means, knowing that ultimately the existence of these power-houses—
their very inconsistency and incoherence—will make the necessity of
constructing a unifying and interconnecting political grid-system self-
evident—and not merely to Governments, but to public opinion.

In the meantime, however, observing as they must the difficulties
around them, driven as they are to accept that narrowly defined latitude
for building which they at present enjoy in partial, limited, insufficient
and unco-ordinated ways, they nevertheless continue with their work
while simultaneously preserving what amounts to a professional con-
spiracy of silence. We can reasonably ask: how long will it be possible

for this combination of purposeful confusion and deliberate silence to continue? How long, in fact, will our political leaders feel themselves free to indulge the luxury of permitting it to continue? For the confusion is increasing, the contradictions are becoming more apparent, and the institutional disorder of action at the European level must sooner or later become a matter of comment in the Press, and concern among the public.

On the positive side, however, let us notice those levels at which the Council of Europe's inter-governmental Programme of Work and the policies and programmes of the European Community do at present communicate with each other. First, through the members of the Council of Europe's Committee of Ministers, who include representatives of the Member Governments of the Community. Second, through those parliamentarians of the Six who also sit in the Council of Europe's eighteen-nation Consultative Assembly. Third, through the contacts which continue all through the year between the Secretariats in Brussels and Strasbourg, officially and privately. These connections already exist, but only in terms of a *power-structure* across Europe which is inconsistent and incomplete, fluid and evolving—and this within a society itself in a condition of flux, turmoil, and uncertainty. For those who have power today this is alarming—for those who have not, it is increasingly perplexing. And for the general public this means there must come a time of wrenching loyalties, leading as we must hope to widening and enlarged loyalties. For the decisions which will have to be faced in coming decades, though guided as they may be by statesmen, must in the end be endorsed democratically by the people as a whole, and willingly, in full knowledge of what we are doing. If not so endorsed in the beginning, these decisions must in the end be ineffective.

If we look at some of the more subtle characteristics of this evolving power-structure, half-hidden as they are by the simultaneous evolution of our society as a whole, we see that one difficulty of any agreed plan or programme between the Council of Europe and the Community is that while on the one hand it would open the door to agreed action, on the other hand it would simultaneously close the door to all alternative lines of action. A firm decision in one direction must foreclose freedom of action in other directions. This is most true of all with controversial decisions where the stakes are high: we can understand that this unwillingness to foreclose future options can weigh against irrevocable decisions on either side. This is of course all the more true if the number of organisations involved increases to three, or four, or even more.

Any real reform at this all-European level must overcome that in-built inertia common to all organisations—their self-defensive insistence on maintaining at least the *status quo*. There is also the difficulty that each agreed plan of action—once in operation—automatically creates a centre of power which locks into a continuing framework of events all those men and women responsible for its continuing existence. These centres of power are themselves no more than precise and limited groups of people working together for precise and approved purposes. These groups—whether in Strasbourg, Brussels, or anywhere else in Europe— are above all human, and it is because they are entirely human and not merely automatons limited to obeying directives, that we must consider their human and individual characteristics before all else.

Thus no matter how theoretically welcome the parallel or complementary aims of another group at work in the same field may be, it is true that if the success of that second group begins to interact with the success of the first group, then the men and women in the first group will react profoundly—intellectually *and* emotionally, consciously *and* subconsciously. As we know from daily life, it is an inevitable fact that hostility, jealousy, envy, and at the worst, quietly effective stabbing in the back, occurs most often not between friends and enemies, but between friends already working on the same side—for they are closest to each other. Symptoms of this evil are already visible, and causing damage all the more dangerous for not being acknowledged.

We are the first generation in history to confront the day-to-day difficulty of managing the process of European unification—and while this is a source of pride, it is also an unprecedented predicament. If we succeed, we shall become the only generation to have experienced this, but we are today far more impressed by the fact that the answers to our problems are unknown than by the thought that our opportunity may later be judged to have been unique. When we contemplate events on the European scale, it is precisely because we are facing events on an unprecedented scale that we do not always immediately recognise the nature of those human difficulties which, at a more familiar level, we take for granted.

There is a fundamental difference between political organisations which possess their own centre of decision—and those that do not. Thus for example, Western European Union (the defence organisation linking the Six and Britain) today lacks a centre of decision. The Council of Europe is, on the contrary, in the form of its Work Programme, and in its legal sanctions as applied to multilateral conventions, now starting to evolve one, as we saw in earlier chapters. These two organisations are thus fundamentally different—not merely in what they do but in how they do it, and this even though on the surface they may appear similar in that both are organisations for solving problems at the European level.

The decisive point in the evolution of these centres of decision is that moment at which they cease to be dependent upon decisions taken by national Governments *solely in terms of separated national interests*. The Commission of the European Community is on the verge of passing this transitional point, this watershed, this European political Rubicon—but it has not passed it yet since, as the whole of Europe knows, it is still dependent on the absence of a veto by any single Member Government. Similarly, in the Council of Europe in Strasbourg, the progress of the Intergovernmental Work Programme is still subject to the unanimous approval of all eighteen Member Governments, but is acquiring a momentum which may carry it over this key transitional point.

We can thus distinguish between European organisations still wrapped in the cocoons of their early transitional stages, and those which will soon have emerged with ability to move and act at the genuine European level. It is understandable that the difficulties of the Council of Europe and of the European Community have resulted in each concentrating on making progress along its own line, and at its own special level—and this without co-ordination between the two having yet been properly achieved. How then, when, and in what form will emerge that indispensable master-programme that must come into being to unite the activities not only of these two organisations, but of all those organisations already possessing centres of decision and all serving the common aim of genuine European unification?

No master-programme of this nature yet exists. Its creation has scarcely even been attempted. And yet action on this scale must occur if the European Idea is to enter an advanced stage of evolution. And even though a movement towards action on this scale is already discernible in the proposal voiced in the Assembly that the Council of Europe's Work Programme should logically be expanded to become a true 'Plan for Europe', in Strasbourg this thinking is at present still limited to those levels of action where the Council of Europe has already established predominance. And as we know from Brussels, an extended master-programme reaching out beyond the present fields of competence of the European Community as defined under treaty, while it may not be absent from the thinking of leaders within the Community, is not yet at the forefront of that thinking —and has certainly not yet achieved public discussion. And even to the extent where it may be active in private thinking and discussion, at present even this advance planning is still limited to those areas where the

action of the Community has already established predominance. These
two strata of initiative are not yet combined. Nor are they extended to
those many other increasing areas of activity at present still the prerogative of yet other organisations. There is as yet no composite plan—even
on paper—which combines into a coherent whole and sets forth plainly
in simple words the many separate Work Programmes of all these
institutions and groupings. These Programmes are today very much in
existence (we have only to compare, for example, the organisation and
projected work of the three European Space Agencies—ELDO, ESRO
and CETS)—but they are not yet adequately co-ordinated at all with
each other. While the previous diversity of initiative which brought
these groupings into existence and carried them forward was admirable,
less admirable is our present hesitation to make the larger and more
difficult *political* decisions now needed to endow these groupings with
their real and deserved heritage—a unified framework within which to
evolve yet further.

It has to be stressed that not only have these plans and programmes
and activities not yet been dovetailed, but many of them have not been
made public—or even readily available to circles of informed opinion.
Thus it is scarcely possible yet for objective comparisons to be quickly
and accurately made on the wider European scale. This alone does much
to impede—if not prevent—that very formulation of press and public
opinion which would itself facilitate and accelerate the necessary political
decisions.

It can be argued that no such master-plan will ever be possible. It can
be argued that the men responsible are right not to publish exactly what
they are doing for public comparison. It is the plausibility of these arguments, and the strength of the interests which combine in their support,
which demand that these arguments be all the more resolutely opposed.
One of the most formidable aspects of the Council of Europe's Work
Programme and one which displays very considerable political courage,
is that it does oppose both these attitudes and these arguments—and
resolutely.

Resolution is certainly needed. It can be plausibly argued that the
problem here is merely mechanical and therefore merely mechanical
advances will be adequate—or that co-ordination can continue most
admirably merely by means of increasingly complicated structures of yet
more and more co-ordinating committees—or that the creation of what
was earlier described as a trans-European grid-system in politics can be
approached solely by the use of engineering methods. This can all be
argued: but is not this exactly what we have to combat—this

complacency, this lack of imagination, this instinctive tendency to lines
of least resistance? We have to supersede these attitudes. We hope to
do so by combining both human inventiveness with a determined
political will to act.

There will be those, and they are not few, who will refuse to take this
view, and continue to argue stubbornly that action at the level of an
all-European master-programme is not possible. Yet can they prove it
is not possible? Can they even prove there is no need for us to think in
this way about the future of our own continent? Surely not. It is in fact
very hard to demonstrate that the European Idea will have any further
meaning at all if we do not succeed in viewing the next essential stage of
European unification from at least a higher vantage point than we do
now.

The work of the Brussels Commission of the European Community
has already proved itself beyond dispute to be a political invention whose
method is capable of far wider application than at present. Simultaneously
the Work Programme of the Council of Europe in Strasbourg is already
fast proving itself a trial prototype of what a real all-European, all-
organisational, and all-level Work Programme could be—and is thus
also a method capable of far wider application. If this can be agreed,
can we not make the yet larger jump and agree that the two methods
combined could result in a single all-European and all-purpose method
whose potentiality we do not yet fully realise, but the need for whose
creation we can no longer honestly deny?

It may of course be objected—and here we have the final and last-
ditch argument—that the American model shows no exact parallel, either
to the kind of work being done through Brussels, or through Strasbourg.
Yet this is again because America began her evolution within a federal
context, and all her evolving activities were from the start already en-
closed within a party-political federal structure. Our own difficulty in
arriving at a federal structure in Europe—our own disadvantage in first
having to struggle for long years through the mud before we can begin
our true progress along the hard high road—itself gives us an unexpected
advantage derived precisely from our difficulty.

We have our chance today in Europe—our unprecedented chance—
of creating new levels of constructive individual action, new forms of
social organisation, and new methods of political endeavour which will
not only be our own original European creation but also at first un-
paralleled in any other region of the globe. Every one of these will at
first anticipate and hasten—and later supplement and enrich—our future

European federal structure, and in ways which neither Africa nor Russia, the United States or South-East Asia, China or Latin-America will prove able at once even to emulate. There is no disadvantage from which advantage cannot be drawn, and it is the absence of a federal structure in Europe today, combined with the intensity of our semi-conscious struggle towards such a federal structure, that opens to us, in most unexpected and yet welcome ways, new dimensions of achievement in science, technology, law, ethics, education, social standards, art, culture, politics— and above all, *new dimensions of responsibility towards mankind as a whole*, and this in ways we may not in this century yet be fully able to anticipate.

We are in Europe so rich in human capacity, yet still completely in-experienced in its truly European use and application. One of our greatest psychological stumbling-blocks is that we still react today too completely to what we see around us at any time as the facts of European unification. We forget too quickly the forces that are bringing these facts into exist-ence. For the facts are transitional—today's crisis becomes so swiftly tomorrow's historical footnote—whereas the historical forces which bring them into existence are continuing.

As we have seen during this book, the triumph of the Council of Europe has been that the facts of its work have continually and sur-prisingly changed, whereas the long-term logic of its purpose has not changed at all. The triumph of the European Community has been that the facts of its work each year also change dramatically, yet never the logic of its purpose. We have not, however, yet reached the stage of ever knowing in advance the order in which the elements in the European equation will eventually fall into place and assume their proper relation-ship to each other. We cannot yet calculate the unexpected permutations that will combine to form our European political landscape tomorrow. We can rely only on being prepared for the unexpected, on attempting to anticipate it as best we may, and on adapting to it as fast as we can when it comes. That is to say, we must be equally prepared in one or ten years to find ourselves having to approach the whole process of European unification within an entirely *military*, or an entirely *monetary*, or an entirely *social*, or an entirely *trans-European party-political, legal, or con-stitutional* context. We do not know the levels at which we shall be working, we do not know the directions in which our efforts will have to be aimed. We cannot tell whether European political union will precede or follow direct European elections—or whether an effective and lasting re-ordering of European organisations will precede or follow an enlargement of the European Community—or whether an organic link between the Community and the Council of Europe will precede or follow the extension of the Council of Europe's Work-Programme method and technique to other organisations—or whether any real testing of the principles of the European Convention on Human Rights will precede or follow the emergence of a European Parliament (whether small or large) with real legislative power. We cannot tell whether an extension of European unification towards Eastern Europe will precede or follow the establishment of majority voting inside the Community's Council of Ministers—or whether the creation of a European Reserve Currency will precede or follow agreement on the unification of European national currencies—or whether indeed a number of these possibilities will accompany each other simultaneously, while others drop out of view and others arise to surprise us.

Thus our entire thinking has, on the one hand, to be so firmly founded that it remains valid and unchanging through every possible permutation of circumstances—and on the other hand, we have to ensure that it is always so flexible that no matter what permutations of events arise, it continues to make sense. This is therefore the moment at which we should look soberly at seven propositions first suggested in Chapter Six. They were there introduced briefly but optimistically: let us now review them from a deliberately cynical, negative and even hostile viewpoint—emphasising difficulties, and not hesitating to shine a spotlight into the shadows.

1. *That the European Idea implies a European Federal Government.*

Here the most serious objection is that a massive and unprecedented transference of power and responsibility is involved. This question is consistently avoided today—and one reason for silence is the sheer size of the transference of power that will be necessary. Furthermore, it will be unexpectedly complex—for it will involve a transference of power not merely upwards, but also down. The dynamic of the European Idea demands that any danger of top-heavy over-centralisation of power must be counter-balanced by an equal distribution of power outwards at lower levels. Only these two processes together can provide a stable basis for further evolution. If either of these processes alone appears to us sufficiently disturbing, the prospect of the two occurring simultaneously must be more so. Yet this is how it will have to be done.

A second sober objection is that the creation of a European Federal Government may take a very long time. Shall we see it by the year 2000? Noone today can tell. By accepting this as our aim, we thereby consciously embark upon a troubled and perplexing time of continuing crisis and danger which may endure for decades. If this time of tension endures too long, then our spirits may weaken and final success may be lost. On the other hand, if for unexpected reasons it should suddenly become possible to bring this aim very much closer, this in itself can result in a most delicate and complex process being brought too speedily to a conclusion in such a way that the structure thereby created may not later be able to stand against larger and unanticipated pressures.

It is human to fear the unknown, the unfamiliar—and while the mere novelty of a project should be no cause for opposition, it is true that confidence can grow only after we have proved by our own experience our capacity for dealing with what was previously unfamiliar. The problems of political evolution involved in the creation of a European Federal Government are not merely vast—they are still totally unfamiliar. We simply do not yet know what life in a truly unified Europe will be like. While the creation of the American Federal Government offers a psychological parallel, and is a proof that even our fear of the unfamiliar can be overcome by the bold and energetic example of a few convinced men, nevertheless the American example is not a model directly applicable in either structure or scale. Our problem in Europe today is many times larger—we shall have to overcome it in Europe not only for the first time, but in our own way. It is not only a problem of creating entirely new structures of power, it is even more a human problem—that of learning to accept for a long time a continuously difficult process of political evolution.

Most difficult of all must be the adjustment of large populations towards entirely new attitudes on accountability in politics—towards where we expect responsibility to centre, and the forms in which we expect to see it. This is one of the reasons why so much attention is paid in Strasbourg to the Assembly of Local Government Authorities, itself a creation of the Council of Europe. It cannot be repeated too often: the creation of a European Federal Government demands radical adjustment of our attitudes at all levels of government and throughout Europe. Yet apart from initiatives of this kind through Brussels and other organisations as well as in Strasbourg, real work towards a smooth and necessary transference of increasing responsibility to local, regional and municipal authorities, together with preparation of the necessary legislative and constitutional adjustments that this will demand, has scarcely yet begun, and must be soberly admitted to be an area of extreme difficulty. As the European Idea makes progress at higher levels so this lower level will force itself all the more on our attention, and reveal itself not merely as the essential counter-balance, but as an area that at first sight must also appear increasingly labyrinthine.

If we now look at what will in time become the middle level of our politics—that is to say, at what we know today as the *national* level—we find that we are at present in a position where decision-making at the European level—whether in Brussels, Strasbourg or anywhere else—does certainly take place all the time, but the communication of these decisions to the European citizen is still usually done solely by national authorities. We thus have an anomalous situation in which a Minister in a national Parliament can be criticised face-to-face for a European decision involving his Department but without that criticism being either justified or effective. Alternatively, if criticism is addressed to where the decision was actually made—directly to the European level—while this may be entirely justified there is still at present no effective mechanism whereby pressure can be brought to bear. The necessary structures of European political accountability at the top are entirely missing, responsibilities are unclear, and the men involved cannot be brought personally to account.

In a different sense, this same problem is also to be seen at the local level. In many countries of Western Europe today there is increasing dissatisfaction with the attitudes of local and regional authorities towards their national governments. Where this dissatisfaction has either a marked ethnic or geographical *raison d'être* it is potentially all the more powerful and enduring. It is thus permissible to hope that in time real attention will be given to creating a direct link between local authorities and European authorities. The creation of this link, however, will again involve such radical and unprecedented political inventiveness that again the more we contemplate this necessity the more we may well hesitate.

These objections, these warnings, are themselves however merely some among many already apparent in the immediate future. What of the distant future? What of the situation when our aim is achieved, what if a European Federal Government is seen to be coming into existence? What do we fear? On the one hand we have good reason to fear the emergence of a tyranny or dictatorship—no matter how veiled, complex, or subtle its forms may be. It is already being asked today whether the European Convention on Human Rights is in fact structurally strong enough to withstand possible attack in years to come by anti-democratic forces—whether of the Right, or of the Left. This is merely one sign of the pressures we can anticipate.

On the other hand we have equally good reason to fear that a form of European Federal Government may come into existence which assumes responsibility and engages our hopes, and yet does not—or will not—exercise those necessary forms of power, through appropriate

methods, which will be indispensable to ensure success. We have equal
reason to fear a Federal Government that is too strong, and a Federal
Government that is too weak. We are forced again to the dilemma
posed by Abraham Lincoln in a Message to Congress on 4 July 1861:
'*Must a government of necessity be too strong for the liberties of its own people,
or too weak to maintain its own existence?*' There is no escape whatever
from this question. We are approaching a time when the European Idea
itself may well come to be expressed as a continuing confrontation with
this question. In the decades to come we shall find ourselves forced to
answer this question not merely through structures of government but
by the good will we accord them, not merely in easy times but in times
of grave emergency, and not merely within the terms dictated by twentieth-century European unification but within a context of global evolution which itself must increasingly influence the values against which we
must measure the efforts of our own Europe.

This dilemma is merely one of the sober objections that can be advanced
against any acceptance of this first Proposition. Most of these objections
are themselves founded upon a hidden quality not to be ignored when we
contemplate the present and future process of European unification, but
on the contrary to be valued for what it is rapidly becoming—a deadly
sin. This is meant in the political sense that this quality is potentially
deadly to the European Idea—for while the question of the creation of a
European Federal Government can never be answered until it is first
clearly posed, it is also true that when it is posed, this deadly quality can
gain sudden strength—for it is fear.

2. *That a European Federal Government implies an unbroken succession of
individual minds carrying all-European responsibility.*

The most serious objection here is very human—it is that we naturally
hesitate to entrust so much power to any single human being. Is it
necessary? Is there not some easier way? Our dilemma here is that posed
in Plato's *Republic*, but we have to solve it without accepting his solution
for we cannot construct Europe by relying on the emergence of philo-
sopher-kings—on the contrary we have so to construct Europe that we
can rely upon an unbroken succession of entirely ordinary men. And it is
already too late for us to seek some easier way—concentration of political
power at the European level in individual minds is already happening in an
increasing numbers of ways. This process is now irreversible and we
cannot possibly go back: it is already later than we think.

Furthermore, it is an objection that we have here to fear not merely
individual weakness in places of high authority, not merely individual

ambition, or individual blindness—for it is the combination of these dangers with the creation of a European Federal Government that can lead to incalculable consequences. It can be objected that since a truly united Europe must make decisions possible at whose scale, scope and consequences we may well blench, than at least these decisions should not be entrusted to fallible individuals—that this is a risk we dare not run. If the power-structures necessary to guarantee the continuing unity of Europe must be so vast, does this not bring in question the entire desirability of the European Idea?

Dare we entrust the policies of a unified Europe to an unbroken succession of single minds—no matter how dedicated, gifted or worthy— when a truly unified Europe can mean a unified Europe swept by a unified wave of social unrest, or committed perhaps to a Middle East or African war as America is today committed to Vietnam, or carrying the real responsibility for her own defence and thereby committed to an exercise of responsibility that could mean the destruction of mankind? It can mean a Europe where regional insurrection is possible. It can mean a Europe where even minor mishandling of critical decisions can result in widespread and temporarily irredeemable misery. It can mean a Europe where problems of the morality of power and of the public good can come unexpectedly upon us in a context where the political forces at work may not be at all the same as we know them today—and this before any of us are properly ready.

It is entirely possible that any combination of these and other dangers can result in evils that are worse, both in kind and degree, than those we experience today in a Europe not yet united. It has to be said that a truly united Europe makes entirely possible—perhaps even makes unavoidable— crises on an all-European scale and with all-European consequences and in ways which public discussion today has scarcely yet even begun to contemplate. We have to face the question: are crises on this giant scale, involving not merely ten or fifty millions of people, but two and even three hundred millions, to be entrusted for their safe solution to an unbroken succession of individual minds?

How many among us know even our own minds as yet on this matter? How many among us can steadily contemplate these questions? The objections here briefly indicated are merely some among many more than can be advanced against this second Proposition, and again there is inherent in them a quality potentially deadly to the European Idea. It is the deadly political sin of short-sightedness, the deliberate adoption of blinkers. If not recognised in time and corrected, it can become a blindness not merely of one or two individuals among us, but of millions.

3. *That the two preceding propositions both imply European direct democratic elections.*

Here the most sober objection is that we face a dilemma at present insoluble. Much depends on the efficacy and speed with which we establish a European franchise—but it can at once be objected that we cannot hope to have direct European elections until both our people and our national governments are ready. It can equally be objected that neither our people nor our governments can be ready until they have had direct experience of these elections for several years. The same objection is strong at the party-political level—either trans-European political parties must evolve as they are now most slowly and painfully doing both within the Community and the Assembly of the Council of Europe but without exercising a true mandate—or the mandate must become real through direct elections before the parties are sufficiently evolved. We can express this another way by saying either the progress of European unification must continue *without* direct democratic participation—or that this progress must be *delayed* until after the keystone of the arch has been finally fitted into position. It can be objected that European elections must wait until *after* Europe is united: it can equally be objected that it is a mockery to talk of creating a democratic union of Europe if the only way this can be done is by a deliberate postponement of the democratic principle.

The second sober objection is that there is at present no seriously declared political will towards the establishment of direct democratic elections. Europe today has not yet dared to recognise the truth of what Thomas Jefferson meant when he said 'I know no safe depository of the ultimate powers of society but the people themselves...' The most that can be said is that in Brussels and Strasbourg the principle has not been abandoned. The 1967 report of the Brussels Commission on the four national candidatures for membership of the Community was careful to include the phrase '...election of the Parliament by universal suffrage...' but this was in the context of a paragraph devoted to objectives difficult to achieve while the Community still works under the rule of unanimity.

Direct elections may be the keystone of the arch—it may be this alone that will hold the entire European Idea together in years to come—this may be the quite unconscious aim towards which all our present progress is tending—but there is today no determined campaign to argue the matter, or to convince people it is important, or to encourage and hold their enthusiastic support. There is today not one Government in Western Europe prepared even to express an opinion on direct European elections —there is scarcely even a national political party prepared to include direct European elections in its programme. Like both the two preceding

propositions, we have here a third which at the top provokes silence—
and among the mass of our people an uneasy puzzlement and growing
frustration—and that because of the silence at the top.

There are exceptions. Individual voices there are, and group movements
also. M. Pierre Pflimlin, former President of the Assembly of the Council
of Europe, has faced the issue in his book *Europe Communautaire*. The
European Movement through its various national branches has not neglected to mention the matter. And adherents of M. Spinelli have never
ceased to maintain a propagandist influence, limited though this has been
by lack both of private resources and an informed public response. There
was even a time shortly before the defeat of the European Defence Community when direct European elections seemed just round the corner—
yet the corner was not turned, Europe went another way, and today,
even in vocal European circles, it can well be objected that it is after all
no more than realistic to leave the matter where it now is—gathering dust
on a shelf hidden from view somewhere deep inside a most curious
political limbo.

This in turn has allowed the opponents of a genuinely European electoral
will to maintain a silence born of contempt. The strongest objection to
this third proposition is that this contempt is well founded—for after all,
if the question is not even being adequately urged, it can scarcely invite
respect—and its opponents will naturally profit by being careful never to
oppose it. There was a time when even President de Gaulle proved
himself sufficiently impressed by the approaching inevitability of the issue
to display on the one hand a cunning mock-welcome for the 'explicit
decision of an immense mass of Europeans' while cynically suggesting
that this opinion could be satisfied with irregular referendums, rather than
regular elections. That was the beginning of another great debate, but that
time has passed, the debate did not continue, and since on the federalist
side the question has been allowed to lapse, it cannot be denied that we
have today the entire process of essential and preparatory public education
to begin all over again. This in turn can lead to a more subtle objection—
for if the process has yet to begin, and if it will be so difficult, then it can
be argued that it would be most unwise to rely too much upon it, or to
permit it to monopolise too much of our political energy—that it would
be wiser, in fact, to seek entirely different roads and quietly forget about
the European rights and obligations of the European voter.

It can be objected either that the European voter is not yet ready to
assume any responsibility at all—or, alternatively, that he or she does not
yet exist. It can certainly be objected that even if, for the sake of argument,
a potential European electorate may exist at the level of an inarticulate

366

Done this dayDone this day

willingness—of a general feeling that given the chance we would all try to play our part—it is nevertheless true that this electorate is not yet ready at all in terms of education, experience, or even basic information upon European issues.

It is also true there has been no prolonged or adequate discussion of this in the Press, and there has been no determination on the part of those who control the Press media and television to keep this matter in public view merely as part of their journalistic duty to the public—and this not in even the briefest and most occasional form, not even merely as a public service. This is entirely understandable as long as they take their cue for silence from the political leaders in front—we have for once a real example of the dumb following the blind, and at the tail of the queue we have that most miserable spectacle: the bewildered European citizen, going he knows not where for reasons he knows not why.

It can further be objected that neither national parties, powerful national interests of all kinds, national governments, and least of all national Civil Services, are yet either prepared or even theoretically willing to confront the problem. Perhaps we are unrealistic in hoping for any real enthusiasm by these men or institutions at the prospect of what will amount to a fundamental transmutation of their public and private political power. This phenonomen was seen at work at the time of the founding of the Council of Europe in the days of Ernest Bevin—we have today the same phenomenon again approaching, but now on an immensely larger scale.

It is for these reasons that the advocates of European direct democratic elections have always said there must be a planned transitional period of five or ten or more years, during which membership of a genuine European Parliament with real legislative powers whether of the Six, the Ten, or more countries besides, would during the first stage be composed of representatives nominated by national parliaments—and in the second stage by an arrangement whereby a proportion of representatives would be directly elected by *European suffrage*, and the remaining proportion nominated as before by national Parliaments, and that only in the third stage would all be directly elected—*as Europeans, for Europe, and by Europeans.*

Yet even this can happen only as the result of a carefully implemented plan in all the countries concerned, and this demands a prior political decision on the largest scale. Since Governments are not yet ready to make this decision, and since they are under no popular pressure to do so, the result is, as Dr Roy Pryce has also pointed out, that 'the ordinary voter as such still remains imprisoned within a purely national framework of power'. The difference here between the voter and national administrations today is that Governments and Civil Services at least *know* they are imprisoned—whereas the voter does not realise it yet at all. Thus when we say that the European voter must be educated to demand his European Franchise, or that those holding power within national frameworks must be encouraged to welcome adjustment to the unfamiliar exercise of new and wider forms of power *within a trans-European democratic structure*, and this with regard to the interests of Europe as a whole as well as their own special interests in particular, and in a social environment itself evolving very fast indeed—it can be objected most convincingly that Europe today is not yet ready.

Does this mean we must continue to trust only the politicians because we dare not yet trust our people? It seems as if many in public office adhere to this view—and after all, if we again take a deliberately sobering example, it can seem plausible that if a time should come when we find ourselves concerned with the construction of a credibly autonomous European defence structure—with, in fact, the creation of a genuinely European command and control system for nuclear defence, that this could seem to be best done if not at the mercy of the voter. This is the extreme example involving life and death. There are many more which may well come much sooner upon us, and though they may not involve so much danger, they may well involve even more difficulty, and are thus all the more vulnerable to the same objection.

There is another quite different objection—it may be we shall have to choose between work towards a genuinely democratic structure embracing Western Europe—and work towards increased co-operation with Eastern Europe. Can we expect autocratic regimes to the East to look kindly on the birth of a genuinely democratic European electoral will in the West? For while this electoral will may at first well be hesitant and erratic, it is also likely that once it has discovered the full range of its opportunity, it will become increasingly vigorous, outspoken, and powerful. Above all it will be new and therefore disconcerting—and we may indeed here have to face a serious choice with far-reaching consequences.

We must be clear on the sheer size of this issue. It involves a radical and at present quite unprepared adjustment of all present structures of power, and this by means of an action itself entirely unprecedented. We are dealing here with the long-term future of three hundred million people— this excluding Eastern Europe—and while transformations of this scale have happened before in history, as in Russia and China, *they have never yet been achieved democratically.* In Chapter Two we saw how the first proposal for a European Coal and Steel Community faced one of its greatest obstacles when no one could prove in advance that the project could be either launched or successfully carried through: the same objection is valid on European direct elections—but now on a scale immensely larger, on a principle yet more important, and on a question directly involving the individual citizen. It is very likely the entire matter will come to hinge on the evolving attitudes of national political parties. And if we review all the objections here mentioned but now in purely party political terms, they become all the more serious, all the more intimidating.

As far as national parties alone are concerned, one immediate test is already approaching. For when in years to come a decision on political union in Europe confronts those Governments directly concerned, it will be an immediate question whether their decision on structures of authority at the top will or will not be complemented by a decision on the method of electoral mandate that accompanies, justifies, and sustains those structures.

We are thus approaching the dilemma earlier suggested: are we to rely upon creating a politically united Europe *without* reference to a directly expressed European electoral will—or are we to rely upon the emergence of this will *prior* to an established framework of political union? The time-tables here must necessarily be so intricate, and the difficulties of achieving even preliminary agreement by governments, parliaments and people must necessarily be so difficult, that it can again be seriously objected it would be wiser not to compound these complications by seeking to achieve all at once, and that in terms of the practical management of affairs by those responsible at the top it would be only realistic to allow any idea of direct European elections to be swept from the board and indefinitely postponed.

Where then is the deadly political sin we shall have to recognise and combat if this third proposition is to become reality? It is the entirely human emotion of jealousy—jealousy by individuals towards other individuals, jealousy by particular group-interests towards other group-interests, jealousy by existing institutions of power towards new institutions of power. It would not be human, for example, for politicians accustomed entirely to national frameworks of authority not to feel jealousy, self-righteous resentment and even bitter hostility towards one of the most obviously predictable results of direct European elections— the emergence of a new breed of politician, the European politician elected entirely for European questions, representing a newly designed form of constituency, and basing his day-to-day political action on a new mandate within a new context. It is not possible to look upon politics always in terms of policies alone—personalities also are important, and when the struggle for power between personalities reaches the scale of a struggle between what may well come to appear an Old Guard and a New Guard, then the consequencies of jealousy alone can become so powerful a political sin as to influence the future of all of us. Jealousy is a corrosive quality and works silently—it can eat painfully into the joints of action—and the more the European Idea progresses, all the more must we watch to see that this is not permitted to impede and damage a process so incomparably larger than the interests of any single individual or group among us.

4. *That the first three propositions together demand unceasing and increasing support, both popular and governmental, for the maintenance, strengthening, and improvement of the Community principle and method.*

It can be immediately objected this proposition is not relevant to countries outside the Community. Or that the increasing accumulation of technocratic power at present concentrating in Brussels is not adequate reason for an unceasing support of the Community principle and method—or that if the progress of the Community encounters delay or difficulty that this in itself is not an added reason for our increasing support. It can be objected that as long as the Community lacks a popular mandate it is scarcely justified in asking for popular support—or that governments can scarcely be required to support without question from mere principle the growth and extension of a political structure which is not only incomplete, ill-balanced, and uncontrolled in the parliamentary sense—but also quite openly designed to supersede and transform many of the functions of these governments. Or that the Community principle and method have nevertheless already gathered sufficient momentum during this decade not to need any further increased effort for their maintenance—or that there is no urgent reason why the Community should be strengthened—or that the fundamental problems involved in any improvement of the Community method and principle are so difficult they are better postponed.

An even more serious objection concerns our own attitudes and loyalty. It still requires a rare enthusiasm and conviction to believe not merely in theory but in hard practice that the hypothetical future should dictate our loyalties rather than the tangible present—that loyalty to the abstract idea of a future united Europe should precede the creation of that unity. How can we be loyal to what has not yet happened, and how can we be asked to place that loyalty foremost among our attitudes today? We are all accustomed to the concept—and in some countries have been so trained for centuries—'My country, right or wrong'. It can be soberly objected that the time has not yet come for us to require people to act from an enlargement of that attitude, so that it says 'Our Europe, right or wrong' — and many would argue such an intensity of loyalty must itself be undesirable. For the implications of this fourth proposition are that individuals and groups throughout Western Europe, whether already citizens of the Community or not, are under an obligation imposed on them by events to support the Community principle and method even when this can mean damage to their particular interests, even when this loyalty cannot be shown to be justified in immediate terms, and appears to be based solely upon an entirely arguable conviction that the idea of the Community is more important than all its present disadvantages, and that support for the Community is always justified from principle alone.

These questions are not hypothetical. When the miners of the Borinage rioted in the streets against the Belgian Government for obeying the wishes of the Coal and Steel Community, and when recently the French small farmers demonstrated against their threatened loss of livelihood following the implementation of the Common Market agricultural policy by the French Government, the method of the Community was thereby impeded, and its principle directly opposed. These are but forerunners of the real tensions that can come to test our loyalties to a far more dangerous and dramatic extent in years to come—though it can be argued that incidents of this nature contain no larger meaning and can be safely disregarded. It can be objected that when—to mention merely one more example—Professor Hallstein visited Rome during the meeting there of the Heads of Government of the Six in 1967, shortly after his dismissal at French insistence from the Presidency of the Commission of the European Community, and when Italian students then greeted him with placards saying WE WANT HALLSTEIN—LONG LIVE THE EUROPEAN NATION that this was no more than an unrealistic and unthinking outbreak of youthful fervour, and in no way indicated the emergence of any larger loyalty to which each of us in time must sooner or later declare our personal attitude.

Even more serious is the objection that may be loudly voiced whenever countries increasingly committed to seek admission to the Community find their applications either vetoed, blocked or postponed. This is the objection which says that a setback should be met with a diminution of political will rather than an increase, and that a temporary denial of membership of the Community thereby justifies subsequent policies whose tendency must be to make future applications even more difficult— as for example by a diversion of energies towards long-term reliance on strengthening EFTA or even by a precipitate attempt to seek a cure-all for present ills through premature construction of an Atlantic or any other

grouping. This is the objection that betrays a fundamental uncertainty on
what long-term aims should be, a willingness to opt for lines of least
resistance, and indeed sometimes an absence of any coherent and continuing conviction in *any* direction.

The objection is valid, however, to the extent that every failure and
delay in enlarging the Community must pose immediate and dramatic
problems for those countries concerned. It is asking a great deal for opinion
in those countries to remain resolutely committed to the support of that
very Community from which they are being excluded. There is a test
here not only of whether some of us even possess long-term aims but also
of whether we are capable of enlarging our loyalties in advance of events,
and of maintaining a will to create those events.

It is already envisaged in Ankara that a time will eventually come when
Turkey will become a full member of the Community. This intention
reveals a long-term steadfastness of political will in Turkish governmental
circles which, if it is to be successful, will have to be maintained—
regardless of all controversy and convulsion that may in the meantime
arise—for perhaps ten, twenty or twenty-five years. It is reasonable
to object that this is entirely unrealistic; that Turkey would be wiser
to settle for what she can immediately see. This is an extreme example of what applies also to Norway and Ireland, Britain and Denmark—and also to the neutral countries: Switzerland, Finland, Austria
—and in a different sense even to countries like Spain and Portugal.
If these countries continue to be excluded from the Community would
they not be wiser to settle, each in their separate way, for some second-
best solution which has the advantage of being in immediate reach?

These objections—and the many more that could be added—are all
serious, and there is inherent in them again a deadly political sin. This time
it is double and two-edged. Each of its aspects tends to reinforce the
other. Both have already damaged the European Idea immeasurably, and
are the cause of many of our present difficulties—the one is weakness of
will, the other narrowness of loyalty. For weakness of political will always
accentuates our tendency to withdraw into rigid and previously established frameworks of loyalty; while a refusal to enlarge loyalties in advance
of events always results in the sapping of political will. If the two together
continue to dominate our attitudes, the damage they will cause in years
to come will continue to increase and be ever more dangerous.

*5. That the Community principle and method must also always be complemented
by improved, widening and coherently organised inter-governmental co-operation*

The immediate objection to this proposition is that if taken to an extreme it undermines the previous proposition. As suggested in Chapter Six, the element still missing in support of the previous fourth proposition is popular opinion—it is missing even more in this fifth proposition. And there are further objections, for if energy is divided between action in support of the Community, and action in support of wider and better inter-governmental co-operation, it can well happen that both levels of political activity do continue but without the two being linked, and even with the divergence between the two levels increasing.

Thus it is possible to envisage that a deadlock on enlargement of the Community could result in an immediate and determined emphasis on inter-governmental co-operation—as for example, in science and technology—to the extent that the fundamental principle of the Community, and above all its inherent federalist aim, suffers a severe setback to its public credit and prestige. It is even possible that really successful inter-governmental co-operation—if not so designed that it complements the work of the Community—could result in our entire long-term aim, as represented in Propositions One, Two, and Three, vanishing from our political agenda for a decade or longer.

Alternatively, it is equally possible that an enlargement of the Community could so monopolise our political priorities and enthusiasm that the more subtle and far-reaching achievements already coming into our grasp at the level of widespread and all-European inter-governmental co-operation could vanish from our agenda. To some extent it can happen that what has been termed the 'Matthew Principle' can come into operation at these and also other levels of European co-operation—the principle that '*to those that have shall be given, and from those that have not shall be taken away even that which they have*'. The larger the scale of events in Europe, the more this principle can be seen at work. There is a real warning here on the dangers of imbalance between unco-ordinated levels and dimensions of action when we regard—as we must—the European Idea as a continuing and inter-related whole where every part affects every other, and there the whole affects every part.

We have already seen in the previous three chapters the potential demonstrated in Strasbourg for improved, widening and coherently organised inter-governmental co-operation. We have seen that the idea of a Plan for Europe is already being actively voiced in the Assembly. It can nevertheless be paradoxically objected that even this cannot become possible until after a great deal more is done as well—and some aspects of what has to be done are reflected in the following London *Daily Telegraph* report in May 1967, by Walter Farr in his 'European Notebook'.

A LOOK INTO THE 'TIROIR'

'Moves at the Rome summit to merge the Common Market Commission with the corresponding bodies in the Coal and Steel and Euratom communities have revived interest in a plan supported by Mr Selwyn Lloyd ten years ago for merging the whole of the European institutions—official, Parliamentary and Ministerial—into a single system.

Known, like so many European plans as 'the grand design', it would mean the telescoping of the four 'rival' Parliamentary Assemblies, those for the Council of Europe (18 member-States), Western European Union (British plus the Six), the European Free Trade Association (7) and the European Parliament of the Six into one Parliamentary body.

MPs of the 18 countries in the Council of Europe would all sit together when Council matters such as cultural co-operation between Western and Eastern Europe were being discussed. For debates on WEU, EFTA, and the Common Market the Parliament would be reduced so that it consisted only of MPs from their member States.

Similarly the decision-making Ministerial Councils of the four organisations could, if Britain joins the Six, be partially or in some cases totally merged.

The plan provides that there should be Parliamentary and Ministerial committees, each dealing with specific fields of European integration, including economics, culture, finance, technology (including armaments), energy, foreign affairs and defence.

This is known as the *tiroir* (drawer) system. Member States would be able to fit themselves into whichever *tiroirs* suit them. For instance Sweden, which is a member of the Council of Europe only, would, because of her neutral policies, be linked only with the economic, financial, technological and cultural *tiroirs*. Britain, if she joined the Market, would be in all of them and sit in all the Assembly debates.

It is suggested that the *tiroir* system could best be constructed round the WEU Ministerial, official and Parliamentary institutions since they are already linked with NATO and include an Armaments Committee. WEU Ministerial Council meetings are also already becoming a useful forum for helping to co-ordinate the policies of Britain and the Six towards Eastern Europe.'

The central priority here is given to defence, but the implicit criticism is valid—our present confusion at the organisational level of European unification is undeniable. The preliminary mapping out of fields of activity for present and future work has scarcely begun. An agreed and continuing

N

division of labour between different organisations, whether private, public, inter-governmental, or Community has all yet to be achieved—the present allocation of money and manpower to different organisations is not done in terms of any previously agreed purpose or method—and the consequence of all this is duplication of work in some fields, and a complete absence of work in others. And it can be objected that the distinction suggested in this fifth proposition between inter-governmental and Community work is perhaps over-simplified, perhaps not central at all—and that there are other aspects of our present confusion to which our attention might be better directed first.

Thus when we consider the military work done through WEU within the framework of NATO; the regional work of the Council of Europe and its inter-relationship with the European work of the United Nations; the differing levels and intensities of economic work today being done in Europe through EFTA and the Common Market; the Specialised Ministerial Conferences mentioned in the previous chapter—or the increasingly complex work now being done towards technical, scientific, and aero-space co-operation by many varieties of political and industrial groupings at different levels—then this fifth proposition can seem much less satisfactory as a guide to our thinking on the differentiation and co-ordination of functions in the unification of Europe than a straight-forward, all-embracing, and mechanically attractive re-arrangement of those organisations already existing. The *tiroir* system does at least have the advantage—if successful—of providing a once-for-all solution to every present conflict of priorities.

It can also be objected that the adoption of a mere principle as a starting-point for consideration of any complex problem in politics often means a willingness to reject short-cuts, and to embark instead on a long, slow, arduous process of gradual implementation—whereas the achievement of an agreed, simple, and all-inclusive political decision by all Governments concerned would be much more impressive, and perhaps also more effective. And if circumstances should so evolve that such a decision should become possible without prior decision being necessary on the deeper and more fundamental questions of principle, then the objection becomes even stronger: such a success we would all applaud.

It can further be objected that the word 'must' in this proposition is either premature or unrealistic—for it suggests the two levels of inter-governmental and Community work progressing not merely har-moniously, but with each method actively complementing the other. This is not at all how things are today—and it cannot begin to happen until there is both a working agreement to make it possible, and an unwavering spirit of loyalty to a common aim in order to make it continue to happen. No organic link yet exists between the two organisations and their two levels of action—and, as we have seen during this chapter, the difficulties of creating this link are formidable. And this link is merely one part of what has been referred to earlier as a political grid-system unifying all levels of power and social organisation in Europe—even the *tiroir* system is no more than a part of the whole. It can therefore be objected that this fifth proposition is premature, in that it can be read as pre-supposing a far greater advance towards political union than is yet achieved.

And there is always the human element present—the larger the scale of events the more influential become individual strengths and weaknesses. Every organisation tends to fight for its own survival, every group of men with power tends to fight to preserve that power, every establish-ed and continuing interest tends to fight to defend its interest, and the replacement of these men, groups, interests and organisations by new ones does not change or diminish the problem, for it will always re-appear. It could therefore even be said that this proposition is not strong enough—for behind all this discussion of how better to reshape the processes of European unification there is again a deadly political sin concealed, and the more the European Idea proceeds the more damaging the effects of this political sin can become. It is that of selfishly limited ambition—that is to say, ambition inadequate to the higher ideal which would transform it with honour into a motive worthy of enthusiastic and pro-longed applause, both by us today and by those who will come after us.

6. *That this inter-governmental co-operation must not only support the Com-munity but also be simultaneously expanded beyond the Community circle of influence outwards to all Europe.*

As with the last proposition, the immediate and most sober objection here is that this sixth proposition attempts to combine aims which are not necessarily in the same political dimension, and which could become incompatible. It does in fact advocate a deliberate division of energies. If the preceding fifth proposition is read as applying—for the sake of argument—only to Western Europe and within the eighteen countries of the Council of Europe, or even only within the Six of the Community—and even if the fifth proposition can be fulfilled, it remains true that the combination of what is already admittedly an immensely complex human and political operation with the extension of this work towards Eastern Europe may impose a demand upon our own human capacities which we cannot yet fulfil.

Alternatively, it can be argued that if the extension of all this work should prove even more constructive and encouraging than at present we have reason to hope, then this must inevitably result in a diminution of energy which would otherwise have been devoted to the stabilisation of our firm political base in Western Europe—that base on which the future of European unification indisputably depends.

As suggested under Proposition Three, the very success of co-operation and communication with Eastern Europe could, as an unexpected by-product, result in a tacit and tactical go-slow on advances in Western Europe towards both political union and direct elections. It can further-more be argued that a decisive breakthrough in Western Europe towards either political union or direct European elections could produce, again as a by-product, a similar go-slow on energy directed towards Eastern Europe. And it can be objected that until governments have made up their minds on the *tiroir* problem, and until the processes of integration in Western Europe achieve new forms, then the extension of these activities to Eastern Europe can but double and compound the duplication, over-lapping and sheer wastage of work today so marked in the West. If an all-level co-ordination of work, even if only at first within the Six countries of the Community, is not yet possible, how can we seriously expect a satisfactory extension of this same work at a number of very varying and complex levels to a geographical area at least four times as large, and at least four times as complicated—and with much of it in Eastern Europe still on the far side of what we can term 'The Human Rights Divide'.

Thus it can be said that the creation of political coherence in Western Europe must create political problems for co-operation with Eastern Europe. Co-operation extending from Eastern Europe *westwards* is to a considerable degree a product of the respect there felt for the proved strength and attractiveness of growing unification in the West. It is of course also a product of increasing awareness in the East of potential common advantage and interests, but nevertheless these attitudes of respect, admiration and the hope of deriving advantage must sooner or later come to be balanced against the price to be paid when a commitment to co-operation imperceptibly tends more and more to become a commit-ment to common political aims. All these pressures are already at work, at varying levels, and in an unco-ordinated way, and it can be soberly objected that this sixth proposition does demand far too much.

And it can also be objected that if this proposition came to be successful only at the cost of diverting energy to a single level of action—whether *sub*-political or *supra*-political or even *ultra*-political, then this failure to achieve a harmoniously balanced advance at all levels of society will in itself contradict the real intention of the proposition. The proposition as worded is careful—it advocates no more than that this inter-governmental influence should be 'expanded' beyond the Community outwards to the whole of Europe. But the implication is that this shall be pursued actively, and the further implication is that it shall be successful, and the most sober and serious objection of all is that which can arise out of the very success of, shall we say, a real and all-embracing trans-European Code of Co-operation. For if the effective extension of inter-governmental co-operation to Eastern Europe is intended to occur in harmony with our own western democratic ideal of respect for the individual and for human rights—then a time must surely come when this harmony will be challenged. The very success of extended co-operation with Eastern Europe could lead to fierce argument that it is not worth achieving mere co-operation if we must ourselves pay the price of weakening our own principles, and that in fact if we do not therefore go slow, we shall be throwing away our priceless heritage for a mess of doubtless very profitable pottage.

It is noticeable that co-operation with Eastern Europe is today discussed in terms of increased East-West trade; of a political *détente* between Eastern and Western systems; of a method of progressing tactfully towards the ultimate reunification of the German people and the settlement of the Oder-Neisse question, and above all the dissipation of military tensions created by the present confrontation between NATO and the Warsaw Pact. An extension of inter-governmental co-operation can certainly contribute to all of these, but is it to these that our real and highest aims are limited? We have to admit that to the extent this proposition is already coming into operation, it is doing so without either agreed policies or even principles behind it. It can even be objected to this proposition that its very success, if improperly motivated, can endanger all other six propositions here suggested. The political deadly sin here inherent is very clear; it is the everlasting temptation to compromise future principle for the sake of immediate practical benefit.

7. *That our ultimate aim, to be achieved by a harmonious combination of a steadily strengthened Community with a steadily widening inter-governmental co-operation, must be a European Federal Government not merely of Western Europe only, but for all Europe, for all time, and founded on the perpetual defence and extension of human rights.*

Here the most deadly objection, which must be met if any of these propositions are to stand, is that if this seventh proposition is not taken literally it need not be taken seriously at all. Alternatively, if it is taken absolutely seriously then it imposes on us an inflexibility of purpose which, it can well be objected, is unrealistic.

The key words which distinguish this proposition from the first proposition are of course *'for all Europe, for all time, and founded on the perpetual defence and extension of human rights'*. This is an all-or-nothing position. It is necessary only to demonstrate that it is not all, to prove it is in fact nothing. And the immediate objections to the argument that such an absolutism of aim is essential or even appropriate, are of course legion. Is not this aim too long-term, too demanding, too grandiose, too complex, too abstract, too unobtainable? Can it not be argued we do not yet need to think about all this? Can it not be reasonably said that the present evolution of European integration is quite sufficiently difficult for us to postpone either official or personal decisions of attitude on where in fact we intend we go, or the reasons for which we are today seeking to unite Europe? Is it in fact even reasonable to ask people to work now— and this sometimes at the cost of considerable personal or communal sacrifice—for a long-term future which we in our time may well never see, and of whose eventual success we have at this moment no proof?

More subtle is the objection that even if it is agreed that this proposition as an *aim* does possess that simplicity which would, if accepted, at least bring consistency and coherence into both our motives and our actions, as an *aim* it is in fact too sophisticated and ambitious for it to be able to command not merely a majority of official and public opinion today, but even a convincing proportion. Thus even if its theoretical value is entirely admitted despite all objections, nevertheless can it not indeed be argued that it is at this present time quite unrealistic in any practical sense? It can be objected that even if we admit 'without a vision the people perish', it does in sober fact make a great deal of difference whether the people see a vision they have reason to hope they shall themselves personally experience. Even if it is further granted, merely for the sake of argument, that Thomas Paine was right when he said 'such is the irresistible nature of truth that all it asks is the liberty of appearing', can this not be answered very simply with the immediate and obvious objection that in fact, when all is said and done, this proposition does *not* represent the truth of what our real aim should be in Europe? It can even be objected that we have no need of any single, central and consciously understood idea to govern and guide the historical evolution of what today we call the process of European unification.

The inherent political sin here is simple. It is the quality of political equivocation on the moral criteria that govern both our individual and collective political action. This is the rock that lurks below the sea of every political endeavour. If encountered unawares it can sink the stoutest ship. It is quite sufficiently edged to pierce and shatter the most noble ideals of the European Idea as we know it, and on this alone all can founder.

These are but some of the objections that can be advanced against each and all of these seven propositions. These objections are not all consistent with each other—but then they do not need to be, for they represent no more than various alternative possible viewpoints. Critical objections need not be consistent, but positive advocacy should at least make the attempt.

On the more positive side, it is justifiable to say that our entire present progress towards European unification is no more than a preliminary stage, and that since we are today living through what will later be seen as the pre-history of a united Europe, we should not be unduly surprised by the difficulties that surround us. The creation of a federalist Europe is the publicly avowed objective not of the majority of our political leaders at all, but of a small—though quietly and steadily increasing—proportion only. Our present progress towards the real unification of Europe is a process being carried forward by a determined minority in trust for the future, and until we have passed the critical turning-point when that trust can be handed over to its true holders—until the moment when a European electorate can express our genuine European will on all European questions—*our primary duty must be to uphold the European-minded among our leaders to the utmost of our ability*, while giving thanks also that our difficulties are not far greater than they are.

This is an optimistic attitude—and now that we have looked at both some positive as well as negative aspects of the European Idea, we should also make a further effort to achieve a positive and practical summary of what can perhaps be done in the years now approaching. Let us therefore limit ourselves to the immediately possible. Let us confine ourselves to that strictly limited realm of questioning with which this chapter began— our chosen and symbolic example of the power-relationship between the Council of Europe in Strasbourg and the European Community in Brussels.

It will have been noticed that the *tiroir* solution, while designed as a contribution to the creation of an effective political grid-system introducing order into the present condition of European unification, does also bear a remarkable similarity to the ill-fated Eden Memorandum quoted at the end of Chapter Two. Both were a little too good to be true, both glossed over the immensely difficult prior political decisions which these proposals required before they could succeed, and in the Eden Memorandum at least, the timing was badly chosen. While we must continue to hope that a 'Grand Design' on the scale of the *tiroir* system, aiming at transforming the European scene by means only of a reorganisation of existing organisations, may become possible—it may perhaps be more helpful, perhaps even wiser, if we here limit our attention to one combination only among the very many elements here involved.

When we focus solely on the relations between Brussels and Strasbourg, what we are doing is seeking to establish some form of coherent link between two organisations which represent on the one hand an intensification and unique defence of the Community method and principle, and on the other hand an intensification and unique defence of a much wider inter-governmental method and principle. The one is limited to the narrower frame of the Six, the other is extended to the widest frame now open to us, the Eighteen countries of the Council of Europe. And as we all know, there is often a secret and subtle relationship between extreme opposites. We shall perhaps not be wrong if we seek first to attempt a reconciliation between these two theoretically irreconcilable extremes, rather than attempt to base our progress upon other organisational combinations which press for our attention. As has been pointed out earlier, a considerable proportion of the Council of Europe's fields of activity are not covered at all by the Rome Treaty. What is to happen to these if the Community *is* enlarged? It is possible that as the geographical range of the Community extends, so the competence of its founding Treaties should also be extended to match its progress—but not only would this be enormously difficult in political terms, but it is extremely hard to demonstrate convincingly that the Community method and principle would be immediately applicable to every field of European unification. It is thus alternatively possible that Governments might think it safer to decide that certain of these specific tasks should be allotted exclusively to the Council of Europe on the basis not only of its twenty years' experience but of its very wide membership. This would, however, require a very clear understanding that once this decision had been made, then the Community would thereafter stay out of these fields—and it is precisely on this undertaking that agreement could founder.

Three possible points of conflict and difficulty now become clear. It must first be said that at present governments have not yet demonstrated they are capable of this kind of thinking and action. If they were, this would all have already been done in earlier years, and it has not been done. Secondly, because it is probable that the immediate human reaction within any enlarged Community would be to follow up its geographical extension by a complementary but not necessarily justified attempt to extend the Community's sphere of competence beyond that framework which is either legally or structurally yet possible or appropriate. Thirdly, because it is also a fact that the Council of Europe has today acquired a new and very striking emphasis in its work.

Not only is it dedicated to an ever-increasing legal structure unifying all-European action through all its Member states, but it has nevertheless succeeded—and here it is almost alone among European organisations— in maintaining the *moral* emphasis of its work on the one entirely central and admirable principle on which every one of us can agree—the benefit of this work to *man, the individual man, the entirely solitary and unprotected European private citizen*. Only in Strasbourg can it today be said that first attention is given to the consequences of high-level political action on the ordinary individual. And just as in Chapter Five we looked at the Conventions of the Council of Europe through the puzzled, but cynical, and yet nevertheless hopeful eyes of our Citizen of Novara, so in other fields of political action it is primarily in Strasbourg that our Citizen may not only himself feel most at home, but will also be deliberately and con- sciously made most welcome. It is precisely this humanitarian orientation and accepted vocation of the Council of Europe which is both least known and most precious—it deserves not only to be recognised and defended, but to be deliberately strengthened and itself expanded, and this by means both of governmental action, and also popular support.

These are merely some among the many possible questions that will arise concerning the Strasbourg-Brussels relationship if the Community is expanded. And while it could be said in the past that the danger threat- ening Strasbourg was that of being crushed between the upper mill- stone of an amorphous Atlantic grouping and the lower millstone of the tightly concentrated Six, today this is likely to be replaced by a larger danger if the Community is successfully enlarged—that of the Council of Europe now being crushed between the lower millstone of a Community extending to ten or more countries, and the upper millstone of an equally amorphous pan-Europeanism seeking to extend effective co-operation well beyond even the present range of work now being pioneered in Strasbourg. And it is entirely possible that these difficulties may well be further compounded by difficulties not yet at all widely anticipated.

We cannot yet tell at all what the policy of an enlarged Community towards Eastern Europe will in fact prove to be—or what would happen if the Eastern European countries themselves seized the initiative by constructing their own counterpart to Western European unification and created, shall we say, a Council of Eastern Europe—or, at a different level, if the work of the Specialised Ministerial Conferences in Western

Europe should find themselves unexpectedly successful in engaging the active participation of Ministers from East European Governments. We are here dealing not merely in questions, but in compound uncertainties.

If the Community is *not* enlarged many of these uncertainties will become even more important. Let us suppose that enlargement of the Community is blocked for a number of years. Let us suppose we must continue to work within the present three-to-one ratio of the Six and the Eighteen. If this is going to be our continuing predicament, then the special claims of Strasbourg to our increasing attention will continue to be central to any consideration of the Strasbourg-Brussels relationship—that is to say, that the Council of Europe represents *par excellence* the humanitarian approach to the European Idea; that it is the widest grouping of democratic European countries now in existence for active purposes (as can well be seen through the work of its Assembly); and that the turning-point in its evolution recently achieved through the successful launching of its inter-governmental Work Programme, 'Man in a European Society', itself provides a new and so far irreplaceable feature of the European scene. We have looked at some of the causes and attributes of these characteristics in previous chapters, and during the last five years the impetus, mood, and practical advances demonstrated in Strasbourg have come to assume such dimensions that the Council of Europe can today present, with entire justification, an entirely new claim to our attention and respect.

What does this mean in practical terms for the immediate future? What is required is to find a formula for using and strengthening the Community method of the Six in Brussels (which is to say, amongst a relatively small number of European States) while simultaneously combining this with the rapidly improving inter-governmental method in Strasbourg (operating as it does among a far larger number of European States) and doing this in such a way, as already suggested in Proposition Five, that the two methods complement each other. For Strasbourg at least this involves finding a working formula and solution that is not merely structurally or mechanically complex, but in its decisions on values must be seen as extremely subtle. The problem is difficult to solve because the nature of the problem is elusive. In other words, for Strasbourg at least it is not merely a question of preserving its present activities in certain fields, or of defending merely the social or cultural or legal work now going forward in Strasbourg, but far more a question of *preserving and intensifying the humanitarian values and the political ethos of the Council of Europe*—whether in these fields today, or in other fields tomorrow. It is essential that this distinction between levels of political value shall be constantly emphasised and publicised.

The same of course is equally true of the Community. It would be equally unjust to talk merely of its work in terms of its form, rather than of its spirit. It is thus important that those protagonists of real co-operation between Brussels and Strasbourg shall force the battle on to that ground where it becomes most realistic—the common ground which does exist between the direct progress taking place in Brussels towards an embryonic federal structure within the member countries of the Six, and direct progress in Strasbourg in the wider frame of the Eighteen towards the governmental and public acceptance of a new *attitude*—that of regarding the European Idea from the single, unified and morally splendid formula expressed in the words 'Man in a European Society'.

If sufficient pressure can be mounted to convince both Governments and concerned public opinion that these two related aims can be effectively combined, then the first great and necessary point will have been gained: that of an approach to the problem based on agreed *principle*. It will be essential to gain this first point if the Community is enlarged, yet it will be even more important to gain it if the Community should not be enlarged. Either way, it must be agreed it is not yet likely that all the countries of Western Europe will become members of the Community within, shall we say, the next ten or even twenty years. It is also probably true that a premature attempt to extend the Community mechanism to all Western Europe could mean the breakdown of the Community, and that the burden of incorporating so many new and still unco-ordinated elements into what is, after all, a strong yet delicate mechanism in Brussels would be far too heavy. Whether the Community is enlarged or not, means have to be found whereby both the progress of non-member states towards European unification, and the co-ordination of this progress with the work simultaneously proceeding within the Community, can both be assured—and also increased. This has to be achieved in every field possible—which includes those fields of action where a full and direct application of the Community principle and method are not yet appropriate.

The second essential point to be gained is that this increased co-ordination between Brussels and Strasbourg should not be delayed. As has been suggested earlier, there are at least three possible lines along which progress could be made—first, through the creation of a *European Civil Service;* second by evolving a two-level formula that would enable very much closer co-operation in practical ways between the Council of Ministers of the Community and the Committee of Ministers of the

Council of Europe, and also between the European Parliament of the
Six and the eighteen-nation Assembly of the Council of Europe; and
thirdly by seeking a *direct agreement or Treaty of Association linking the two
organisations, and defining agreed guidelines for the future on aims, methods and
spheres of competence.* This argument against delay, and in favour of
progress along one or more of the lines here suggested, becomes all the
stronger if a real enlargement of the Community is itself delayed. If it
becomes clear that for the immediate present the Community method and
principle must remain limited to its present Six members, it must
become equally clear that during this time it will be all the more important
—indeed essential—to make possible a steady intensification of work
towards European unification on the wider all-European scale in all ways
possible. It is not too much to say that this work may then have to be
constructed wholly through the Council of Europe—for any lesser
solution is likely to be proved inadequate to its aim.

It must here be admitted that while there is in Strasbourg immense
respect for the Community method and principle, there is however still
missing that genuinely helpful spirit of confidence and enthusiasm that
would be created by the successful establishment of an organic link
between the two organisations. It must also be admitted that while there
is in Brussels a growing if reluctant respect for the Council of Europe
principle and method, there is also an absence of enthusiasm, sometimes
even of interest, in the wider Europe which Strasbourg alone represents
and serves. Both attitudes are understandable: the problem is to enable
both attitudes to be superseded by something very much better. The
present existing arrangements between Strasbourg and Brussels are still
limited to a Protocol to the Treaty establishing the Coal and Steel
Community, and an out-of-date agreement concluded between the
Council of Europe and the Commission of the Community—and while
each in their time were admirable, there are few who would not admit
they are now obsolete and inadequate.

Two of the possible alternatives here suggested—that of a structural
co-ordination of Ministers, Parliamentarians and Secretariats on both
sides—or of a joint declaration or *Treaty of Association* agreed by governments and making no structural change but seeking rather to define
future aims and methods, are very different. While the creation of a real
organic link by structural means would be a decisive step forward, it is also
likely to prove extremely difficult to achieve. Alternatively, the creation
of a link by means only of a document of state which does at least demar-
cate fields of interests, and does present to the public a common front
uniting both organisations might prove less effective, but could also be

perhaps easier to achieve. From the point of view of Strasbourg, the next few years are likely to impose a precise challenge to leaders of opinion within the Council of Europe, and primarily to the Secretary General and his office. It has been suggested in Chapter Seven that the election of a new Secretary General in 1969—and of a new President of the Consultative Assembly—is likely to be of profound importance for the future of the European Idea as represented in Strasbourg. Yet the dilemma we can here anticipate is that in Strasbourg two alternative lines of advance suggest themselves. First, the question we have already discussed: the creation of a real link between the Council of Europe and the Community—and secondly, the effective intensification and extension of the inter-governmental method of the Council of Europe's Work Programme both through Western Europe and also towards the countries of the East. If these two objectives can be achieved simultaneously, then the ideal of the European Idea will have been admirably served, and the positive consequences will be influential and lasting. But, if we consider this dilemma soberly, it must be admitted that a choice may have to be made in Strasbourg between these two possible lines of advance. One of them is likely to gain priority over the other, and we cannot yet tell which it will be.

We have already noted in earlier chapters how the powers of political initiative, strategic suggestion, tactical leadership and above all personal and executive example and influence are coming now to be centred more and more in the office of Secretary General. In coming years it may be here we shall have to look for the resolution of these and other dilemmas; that it will be on the Secretary General himself, rather than on individual Governments, European parliamentary opinion, or national depart-mental advice that the responsibility will rest—and that the outcome of events may be determined by the extent to which this responsibility is not only accepted within the Private Office of the Secretary General itself, but also recognised by others and therefore given every possible support and assistance. On the combination of these two responses depends the continuing translation through Strasbourg of the European Idea into effective and continually increasing political action.

During this book it has perhaps become clear that the progress of the European Idea has displayed an astonishing capacity both to disconcert its critics and to confound its prophets. And as has been suggested yet again during this chapter, a primary characteristic of the European Idea is that it results in complex and continuing permutations of ever-changing difficulty. With every succeeding year we are forced to view the European

Idea from a changed viewpoint. It is constantly evolving, and always capable of surprising us yet again—and this not least because it possesses, as earlier chapters have attempted to suggest in many ways, a subtle and powerful inner characteristic which we can term—to borrow a phrase from the scientists—*auto-catalytic*. It possesses an inherent power to feed, perpetuate and intensify its own capacity to evolve. And when we examine our seven suggested propositions in terms of objections to them, it becomes clear that at any time the European Idea is always capable of provoking many temporarily entirely justified objections. Yet not only has the Council of Europe passed a turning-point in its evolution during the last five years but because of this fact it now approaches a yet larger possible crisis on its future orientation, character and form.

The emphasis of previous chapters, and particularly this chapter, has thus been on difficulty—let us face the truth of some even harder questions. At the human level we do not yet know what we shall allow to happen to the qualities of happiness and hope as the European Idea progresses. We do not yet know if we shall be able to overcome the horrors and paralysis that can come upon us through weariness, fatalism, fear or dishonesty. We cannot yet say what we will permit to happen to the rule of law as the European Idea becomes, as it must, and if not by one way then by another, the European Fact. Not one of us can say what will happen when the politics of Spain, Great Britain, Ireland, Scandinavia, Finland, and many more countries as well, to say nothing of the Six countries at present constituting the European Community, do struggle to achieve their only true context of meaning: that of politics at the all-European level, and in terms of a recognised, evolving and accepted community of both interest and action. Not one of us can say what will happen not merely in politics but in ethics, morals, myth, religion or science when the best in our past combines and fuses—just as sand and lead fuse into the finest and most translucent glass—to make the best in our future. Not one of us can say what will happen when the powers of decision in Europe develop new modes, or what issues will be forced upon us when the structure of an eventual *European Constitution*, the expression of a real and direct *European electoral will*, the decisions of a *European juridical authority* armed with sufficiently powerful sanctions, and above all the actions of a *European Federal Government*, founded upon the perpetual defence and extension of human rights and the dignity of the individual European citizen, all become a determining part of the fabric of our daily lives.

Least of all can any one of us today say what will become possible when we learn to welcome as common sense that the destiny of our united Europe is, and as a matter of course, entrusted to an unbroken succession of individual minds, not only over decades but over a century and more—and this as a process designed from the start to continue in perpetuity until it can itself become an integral part of something even greater. Not one of us can even say that Europe will find the way to a destiny worthy of her name, or that Europe will qualify to show the world that responsible and morally inspired leadership which the world has good reason to expect from Europe at her best, if this responsibility is not so entrusted.

We are thus forced into a position where our very difficulty must drive us forward. And if not one of us can truly prophesy what will happen, the duty weighs all the more heavily upon each of us of examining what we individually believe *ought* to happen—and of examining ever more carefully what we can each contribute towards making it happen. We must each recognise what may happen if we do not so contribute.

It is not too much to say that the very difficulty of European integration can be overcome only by a sufficient number of individuals resolutely adopting an open and declared position on the future of Europe. This is therefore the moment to summarise the attitude expressed in this book— and since every chapter in this book has ended with the same unchanging sentence, this is perhaps the point at which the thinking behind it should be explained so that the reasons for its choice may contribute to its value. The image used is not idly chosen: it has an ancient and honourable history, and has many applications—as we can see from the Epistle of St James: 'Behold also the ships, which though they be so great, and are driven of fierce winds, yet are they turned about with a very small helm...' In politics this image has the added value that it is capable of expressing accurately and simply very complex meanings, and its very familiarity gives it both an enduring and an endearing quality.

The fundamental argument of this book can thus be best expressed by saying that we have in Europe today a European ship of state to build, launch, and navigate—that this is a matter of the utmost public urgency to all our millions of people. While it is certainly possible to create a partially united Europe without a Federal Government, this partial solution will inevitably prove itself inadequate to our hopes and needs, even a trap, a cul-de-sac that can divert and nullify even our very best efforts—and this perhaps for decades. It is not only in the highest and best interest of each of us now, but above all in the highest and best interest of those who will come after us tomorrow, to work now towards first the creation—and thereafter the resolute maintenance—of an independent, autonomous, and constitutionally harmonious Federal Government for all Europe and for all time.

Our European ship of state is already building but our shipyard is still disordered. Some day this ship of state must set sail across the unknown sea of our future, but the charts of this future have scarcely yet been drawn and our course is not yet agreed. Our ship has therefore so to be built and manned that it can sail not only across unknown seas—not merely without shipwreck—but cheerfully and in a spirit of high adventure.

How can any of us feel safe in a ship that was not built *from the start* to survive, not merely the predictable storms of a season, but the unpredictable storms of tumultuous centuries? Who among us today will dare to say that our European ship need not be so built—or designed for any but a proudly united and free people? It is our responsibility to consider most soberly, not only our duty to ourselves and the present, but equally our duty to the future and to all the many millions of others who will come after us. For we are not building a ship to be rowed—now or ever— by galley-slaves: we are building a ship for free people only, and this for always.

Let us face a harder question still. Let us admit that while it is certainly possible that our European ship of state—our Federal Government of Europe—may prove impossible to build satisfactorily without grim and even bloody civic conflict at some time and at some place in Europe, and while we must therefore pray that it can be built without such conflict, nevertheless we must in full awareness of the difficulties which our own determination may bring upon us, all agree that our ship must nevertheless be so built and launched that its crew can thereafter at any time surmount—and this without irreparable consequences—both internecine conflict on the voyage and all storms that may come, no matter their form, no matter their suddenness or strength. For it cannot be denied that the ocean of endeavour today opening out for Europe is both vast and unknown; that if storms come those storms will be great and terrifying; and that once embarked on the voyage we shall not be able to turn back. The safety of our voyage will later prove to have been determined to a decisive degree by the design and construction of our ship—and thus the *future* of Europe depends *today* on our resolving now that our ship shall—regardless of difficulties—be so designed, so constructed, so launched and so navigated that it shall prove seaworthy through storm and whirlwind—through every known and unknown danger of the future.

CHART SHOWING THE DEPOSIT
OF RATIFICATIONS OF COUNCIL OF EUROPE
CONVENTIONS AND AGREEMENTS [1]

TITLES OF CONVENTIONS AND AGREEMENTS

1.* Statute of the Council of Europe (including amendments and additions) (1949-1963).

2. General Agreement on Privileges and Immunities of the Council of Europe (including the Supplementary Agreement and the four Protocols) (1949-1961).

3.* Special Agreement relating to the Seat of the Council of Europe (1949).

4.* Supplementary Agreement to the General Agreement on Privileges and Immunities of the Council of Europe (1950).

5. Convention for the Protection of Human Rights and Fundamental Freedoms (including the first Protocol) (1950-1952).

    5. (i) Declaration regarding Article 25 of the Convention for the Protection of Human Rights and Fundamental Freedom (Right of Individual Petition).

    5. (ii) Declaration regarding Article 46 of the Convention for the Protection of Human Rights and Fundamental Freedoms (Jurisdiction of the Court).

6.* Amendments to the Statute (May 1951).

7.* Amendment to the Statute (December 1951).

8.* Statute of the Council of Europe incorporating Amendments and Texts of a Statutory Character adopted in May and August 1951.

9. Protocol to the Convention for the Protection of Human Rights and Fundamental Freedoms (1952).

10. Protocol to the General Agreement on Privileges and Immunities of the Council of Europe (1952).

11.* Amendment to the Statute of the Council of Europe (1953).

12. European Interim Agreement on Social Security Schemes relating to Old Age, Invalidity and Survivors, and Protocol thereto (1953).

13. European Interim Agreement on Social Security other than Schemes for Old Age, Invalidity and Survivors, and Protocol thereto (1953).

14. European Convention on Social and Medical Assistance, and Protocol thereto (1953).

15. European Convention on the Equivalence of Diplomas leading to Admission to Universities (1953).

16. European Convention relating to the Formalities required for Patent Applications (1953).

17. European Convention on the International Classification of Patents for Invention (including Annex as amended) (1954-1961).

18. European Cultural Convention (1954).

19. European Convention on Establishment (1955).

20. Agreement on the Exchange of War Cripples between Member Countries of the Council of Europe with a view to Medical Treatment (1955).

21. European Convention on the Equivalence of Periods of University Study (1956).

22. Second Protocol to the General Agreement on Privileges and Immunities of the Council of Europe (1956).

---

1. The conventions and agreements in this chart, which is of a merely informative character, are not numbered in the chronological order of signature used in the Publications Catalogue of the Council (European Treaty Series).

Situation as on 15 May 1968.

23. European Convention for the Peaceful Settlement of Disputes (1957).

24. European Convention on Extradition (1957).

25. European Agreement on Regulations governing the Movement of Persons between Member States of the Council of Europe (1957).

26. European Agreement on the Exchange of Therapeutic Substances of Human Origin (1958).

27. European Agreement concerning Programme Exchanges by means of Television Films (1958).

28. Third Protocol to the General Agreement on Privileges and Immunities of the Council of Europe (1959).

29. European Convention on Compulsory Insurance against Civil Liability in respect of Motor Vehicles (1959).

30. European Convention on Mutual Assistance in Criminal Matters (1959).

31. European Agreement on the Abolition of Visas for Refugees (1959).

32. European Convention on the Academic Recognition of University Qualifications (1959).

33. Agreement on the Temporary Importation, free of duty, of Medical, Surgical and Laboratory Equipment for use on free loan in Hospitals and other Medical Institutions for purposes of Diagnosis or Treatment (1960).

34. European Agreement on the Protection of Television Broadcasts (1960).

35. European Social Charter (1961).

36. Fourth Protocol to the General Agreement on Privileges and Immunities of the Council of Europe (1961).

37. European Agreement on Travel by Young Persons on Collective Passports between the Member Countries of the Council of Europe (1961).

38. European Agreement on Mutual Assistance in the matter of Special Medical Treatments and Climatic Facilities (1962).

39. European Agreement on the Exchange of Blood-Grouping Reagents (1962).

40. Agreement between the Member States of the Council of Europe on the issue to Military and Civilian War-Disabled of an International Book of Vouchers for the repair of Prosthetic and Orthopaedic Appliances (1962).

41. Convention on the Liability of Hotel-keepers concerning the Property of their Guests (1962).

42. Agreement relating to Application of the European Convention on International Commercial Arbitration (1962).

43. Convention on the Reduction of Cases of Multiple Nationality and on Military Obligations in Cases of Multiple Nationality (1963).

44. Protocol No. 2 of the Convention on the Protection of Human Rights and Fundamental Freedoms, conferring upon the European Court of Human Rights competence to give advisory opinions (1963).

45. Protocol No. 3 to the Convention on the Protection of Human Rights and Fundamental Freedoms amending Articles 29, 30 and 34 of the Convention (1963).

46. Protocol No. 4 to the Convention for the Protection of Human Rights and Fundamental Freedoms, securing certain rights and freedoms other than those already included in the Convention and in the first Protocol thereto (1963).

47. Convention on the Unification of Certain Points of Substantive Law on Patents for Invention (1963).

48. European Code of Social Security, and Protocol to the European Code of Social Security (1964).

49. Protocol to the European Convention on the Equivalence of Diplomas Leading to Admission to Universities (1964).

50. Convention on the elaboration of a European Pharmacopoeia (1964).

51. European Convention on the Supervision of conditionally - sentenced or conditionally released Offenders (1964).

52. European Convention on the Punishment of Road Traffic Offences (1964).

53. European Agreement for the Prevention of Broadcasts transmitted from Stations outside National Territories (1965).

54. Protocol to the European Agreement on the Protection of Television Broadcasts (1965).

55. Protocol No. 5 to the Convention for the Protection of Human Rights and Fundamental Freedoms, amending Articles 22 and 40 of the Convention (1966).

56. European Convention providing a uniform Law on arbitration (1966).

57. European Convention on Establishment of Companies (1966)
58. European Convention on the Adoption of Children (1967).
59. European Agreement on the Instruction and Education of Nurses (1967).
60. European Convention on Foreign Money Liabilities (1967).
61. European Convention on Consular Functions (1967).
    61 (i) Protocol concerning the Protection of Refugees.
    61 (ii) Protocol in respect of Civil Aircraft.
62. European Convention on Information on Foreign Law (1968).
63. European Convention on the Abolition of legalisation of Documents executed by Diplomatic Agents or Consular Officers (1968).
64. European Agreement on the restriction of the use of certain Detergents in washing and cleaning Products (1968).
65. European Convention for the Protection of Animals during International Transport (1968).
66. European Convention on the Protection of the Archaeological Heritage (1969).
67. European Agreement relating to persons participating in proceedings of the European Commission and Court of Human Rights (1969).

KEY

 Not signed.

 Signed, but not ratified (or no declaration has been made in the case of 5 (i) and (ii)).

 16.IX.1969   Dated the State has signed at a date later than that on which it was opened for signature.

White spaces with a date — opposite the name of a country — show the date of deposit of the ratification except in columns 5 (i) and 5 (ii).

EXPLANATION OF SYMBOLS AND LETTERS

(*) Ratification by all Members which have ratified the Agreement.

(**) Ratification by all Contracting Parties to the Convention.

(a) Entered into force on 11.VII.1956.

(b) Not a Member of the Fund.

(c) Dates from which the time-limits indicated in the declarations began to run.

(e) Declarations made under Articles 25 and 46 of the Convention also apply to Articles 1 to 4 of Protocol No. 4.

(f) Declaration made under Article 25 of the Convention also applies to Articles 1 to 4 of Protocol No. 4.

(g) Not a Member of the Pharmacopoeia.

(h) Spain adhered to this Convention on 21.III.1962.

(i) Accessions to this Convention.
Spain   4.VII.1957.
Holy See   10.XII.1962.

(j) Accessions to this Convention: South Africa 28.XI.1957, Israel 29.IV.1966: Spain 28.VI.1967.

(k) Accessions to this Convention:
Australia   7.III.1958 (entry into force, 24.V.1958).
Israel   18.IV.1966 (entry into force, 16.X.1966).
Spain   1.IX.1967 (entry into force, 1.IX.1967).

(l) Entry into force: 21.I.1964.

(m) Entry into force: 1.XII.1961.
This Agreement applies solely to the nationals of the other Contracting Parties.

(n) Entry into force: 1.I.1961.

(x) Israel adhered to both these Conventions on 27.IX.1967.

INDEX

Adenauer, K., 65, 195, 202

Agence Europe, 349

Agriculture, Committee on, 335–6

Alsace, suitability of for European capital, 35, 36

America, 11; supports EDC, 65; European dependence on, 199; partnership with Europe, 215–16; vigour of, 301–2; federal structure of, 357, 360

Austria, 86, 371; delegates of in Council of Europe, 15, 306; applies for associate membership of European Community, 205

Beesley, H., views on European franchise, 232; comments on Work Programme, 264–6

Belgium, 86; joins Council of Europe, 10, 15, 40; joins ECSC, 52, 54

Benvenuti, L., Secretary General, 1956, 240–1, 242

Bevin, E., 12; vision of Europe, 21, 22, 42, 43, 53, 66, 67, 366

Bidault, M., at Council of Europe, 12, 45, 46

Blum, L., at Council of Europe, 12, 14

Boothby, Lord, federalist approach of, 46

Brentano, H. von, 64–5

Briand Memorandum, 17

Britain, 371; joins Council of Europe, 10, 15, 40; opts out of ECSC, 51–4, 198; vetoes reform in Assembly, 63; rejects EDC, 66–72; ratifies Convention on Human Rights, 146; accepts Social Charter, 89, 114; applies for membership of European Community, 205, 206; de Gaulle's attitude to, 223, 333, 347; immigration problems of, 316

British Commonwealth countries, 87

Brown, G., European views of, 233, 351

Brugmans, Professor H., European views of, 7–9, 14, 26, 95–6; *History of European Civilisation*, 16

Brussels, 37; headquarters for European Economic Community, 201, 203;

Brussels Commission combines EEC, Euratom, and ECSC, 208–9, 222, 251; relationship of Commission with Council of Europe, 251, 252, 287, 347, 348–59, 364, 379–84

Brussels Pact, 11, 42, 48

Carter, Horsfall, *Speaking European*, 13, 60

Cassimatis, M., federalist approach of, 46, 47

Churchill, Sir W., 7; vision of United States of Europe, 10, 34, 47, 229, 230, 239, 304; Zurich speech of, 16, 196; at Council of Europe, 26, 39, 41; calls for European Army, 49–50, 57, 59, 63, 64–5; becomes Prime Minister, 67; proposes summit with Russia, 73

Common Market, see European Economic Community

Compulsory Insurance of Motor Vehicles, Convention on, 163

Consular Functions, Convention on, 167

Consultative Assembly, 25; deadlock with Committee of Ministers, 27, 34, 42, 44, 48, 57, 61; character of, 39–40; federalist nature of, 58–61, 62; Specialised Authorities created, 60, 62; need for leadership in, 148; debates on Work Programme, 306–7, 326–38; Working Party on Relations with National Parliaments, 148–9

Coudenhove-Kalergi, Count, 17

Council of Europe, 1949, Statute of, 10, 11, 14, 23–31; 197, 348–9; federalists versus functionalists, 45–6, 59–60; overlaps with European Economic Community, 222; aims of, 24, 267; weaknesses, 26–31; Hemicycle of, 41, 49, 90, 96; change in, 69–70, 270, 319, 358; works on Social Charter, 90–5; unavowed federalist aims of, 226–8, 351; lack of effective political rôle, 249–50, 255; policy towards non-member states, 258, 261–2; promotes unity among members, 263, 266, 282; lack of information centre, 271–3, 280;

effect of national elections on conventions, 277, 278; need for experts, 324; relationship with Brussels Community, 140, 331, 347, 348–88, *pass*; future of, 340–3. *See also* Council of Europe, Conventions of, Experts, Committees of, Ministers, Committee of, Secretariat, Work Programme, and committees under their titles

Council of Europe, Conventions of, 2; interaction of, 114; characteristics of, 121–3, 173–81; provision for, 125–6, 144; types of, 126–7; first records of, 128–30; proposal for action, 130–2; polarisation of individual initiative, 132–4; polarisation of conflict, 134–7; emergence of compromise, 137–42; casual and uncoordinated appearance of, 156; need for support of governments, 157; consistency of, 161; aims, 162–4; legal programme of, 165–8, 170–1, 220; problems of ratification, 144–7, 149, 169, 171–2, 151, 152, 305, 327; Partial Agreement method, 172–3, 253–4, 334; classification of, 181–7

Cultural Co-operation, Council for, 293–6, 334

Crime Problems, European Committee on, 315

Cripps, Sir S., 52–3

Curtis, D., Deputy Secretary General of Council of Europe, 241, 242

Daily Telegraph, The, Russell's letter to, 164–5; article on European Community, 217; Hartley's article in, 222–3; Farr's article in, 373

de Gasperi, A., at Council of Europe, 12, 14; founder member of European Community, 202

de Gaulle, General, political concepts of, 18, 365; votes for in presidential election, 124, 125; impedes Community decisions, 208, 213, 217, 222, 223–4, 225–6, 228, 252, 351; opposes British entry, 248, 249

Dehousse, F., 93, 95; candidature of, 244–6; votes for, 248

Del Bo, Dino, 204

de Madariaga, S., 12

Denmark, joins Council of Europe, 10, 15, 40; accepts Social Charter, 89; negotiates with European Community, 205, 206

de Riencourt, 261; *The Coming Caesars,* 300–1

de Rougemont, Denis, 14; *Twenty-one centuries of Europe,* 16

Directorate of Information of the Council of Europe, 166–8

East African Commonwealth countries, 206

Eastern Europe, possible co-operation with, 234, 235, 327, 359, 376

Eccles, D., 135

Economic Questions, Committee on, 135, 333

Edelman, M., views on Work Programme, 331–3

Eden, Sir A., 67, 71; announces British non-participation in EDC, 68; establishes WEU, 73–4

Eden Plan, 70–1, 379

Eisenhower, General, 30, 65; Supreme Commander of NATO, 63

Establishment, Convention on, 1955, 138–9, 140, 170, 177, 183, 186

European Atomic Energy Community, creation of, 200, 202

European Blood Bank, creation of, 162

European Coal and Steel Community, 1, 60, 65, 66; creation of, 49–58, 158, 194; High Authority of, 198, 199, 204; achievements of, 200; pattern for European Economic Community, 201; possible fusion with other Communities, 373

European Companies, Convention on, 183

European Defence Community, 64–73; collapse of, 72–3, 75, 199, 364, 365

European Economic Community, 1, 70; headquarters of, 37; articles on direct elections, 1960, 108–9; Commission's handbook on, 1964, 194–209, 221; federal structure and aims of, 201, 203, 226–8, 287; relationship with Council of Europe, 348–59, 379–84; fusion with two other Communities, 207, 373; Hallstein's speech on, 209–15; legal aspect of, 218–22; overlaps with Council of Europe, 222, 307; need for change, 224; stages in development of, 205–6; economic basis of, 251, 314; possible expansion of, 311, 331, 370–1

European Free Trade Association, 197, 214, 235, 251, 258, 259, 287, 374;

European Free Trade Association—*cont.*
linked with Council of Europe, 307;
tiroir plan, 373
European Parliament, 207, 373
European Patents Office, idea for, 130,
135
European Payments Union, 54, 196
European Social Charter, 2, 88, 186;
criticism of, 161; Council works on,
90–5; articles of, 103–7; implementation, 106, 114, 169; preamble of,
109–10; terms, 110–13; ratification,
113–14; polarisation of conflict in
drafting of, 135–6; debate on, 326
European Space Agencies, 356
Europe, different aspects of geography
of, 189–238
Europe Day, 1966, 304
Experts, Committees of, 114, 115, 131,
132, 139, 167, 328
Extradition Convention, 130–1, 133

Farr, W., 'European Notebook', 372–3
Federal Government of Europe, arguments for, 6, 229–38, 359–88 *pass*
Finland, possible co-operation with, 234,
253, 371
France, joins Council of Europe, 10, 15,
40; fears Germany, 50; joins ECSC,
52, 54; supports then rejects EDC, 64,
72–3; fails to ratify Human Rights
Convention, 84, 153; vetoes Britain's
application, 206
Freitas, Sir G. de, writes to *The Economist*, 235–6; President of the Council
of Europe, 332

Gaudet, M., defines Community law,
219–21
General Agreement on Tariffs and
Trade, 214
Germany, delegates of in Council of
Europe, 15, 40; joins ECSC, 54;
Soviet Zone of, 64; and EDC, 64–5;
fear of, 50–1, 72; accepts Social
Charter, 99, 114; becomes member of
European Community, 201, 202, 253
Gladwyn, Lord, 34; Common Market
Campaign of, 45; European views of,
231, 301; views of on Council of
Europe, 331, 332, 339
Golsong, M., Director of Legal Affairs,
334

Greece, delegates of in Council of
Europe, 15, 40

Hague Congress, 1948, 12–13, 14, 15, 19,
129; purpose of, 20, 21, 22, 56–7,
196–7
Hallstein, Professor W., 7, 202; President
of the Common Market Commission,
208; gives fourteenth Sir Daniel
Stevenson Memorial Lecture, 209–17,
218; methods of, 252, 253
Heath, E., 52
Hertenstein Declaration, 16–17
Holland, joins Council of Europe, 10;
joins ECSC, 52, 53, 54; policy over
pirate radio, 150
Human Rights Building, Strasbourg, 82,
83
Human Rights and Fundamental Freedoms, European Convention on,
1950, 2, 31–3, 34, 76–88, 118–19, 316,
359; articles of, 77–80; elements in,
83–8, 186; evolution of, 136; not
ratified by France, 153; pressures on,
361
Human Rights, Commission of, 80, 83,
177
Human Rights, European Court of, 8,
134; jurisdiction of, 79, 80–3

International Labour Organisation, 122,
331, 332, 337
Ireland, joins Council of Europe, 10, 15,
40; accepts Social Charter, 89, 114;
applies for membership of European
Community, 205, 333
Israel, fosters connection with Council
of Europe, 192; negotiates with
European Community, 206
Italy, joins Council of Europe, 10, 15,
40; joins ECSC, 52, 54; member of
European Community, 253

John XXIII, appeal for Human Rights, 86
Joint Legal Services of European Execu-
tives, 221
Justice, European Community Court of,
1951, 131, 207, 220, 221
Justice, Conference of Ministers in
Rome, 1962, 165–6

Kennedy, President, 205, 207; Trade Expansion Program of, 205; *Profiles in
Courage*, 350

Kennedy Round, 222
Kormoss, Dr L. B. F., 191

La Malfa Proposals, 61–2
Lannung, H., 307, 320
Lecanuet, J., 124, 125, 231
Legal Cooperation, European Committee on, 167, 315, 333
Legal Service of European Executives, 219
Legalisation of Documents, Convention on Abolition of, 167
Liabilities of Hotel Keepers, Convention on, 163
Lincoln, A., Deputy Secretary General, 1955, 242
Lindsay, K., 12, 27, 41
Local Government Authorities, Assembly of, 360; committee on, 335
Luxembourg, joins Council of Europe, 10, 15, 40; headquarters of ECSC, 37, 52, 54

Mackay, R. W. G., 12; *Towards the United States of Europe*, 13, 19, 88–9; letter of to *The Times*, 28–30; at Council of Europe, 45, 46, 47, 60–1; criticises British attitude, 52–3
Mackay Protocol, 28–30, 31, 61, 62
Macmillan, H., federalist sympathies of, 45, 46
Mancholt, S., 202
Marchall, L., Secretary General, 1953–6, 241
Maxwell-Fyfe, Sir D., letter of to *The Times*, 28–30, 61; federalist approach of, 46, 146; speaks in Consultative Assembly, 67–8
Messina, the Six meet at, 200
Ministers, Committee of, 25; deadlock with Consultative Assembly, 27, 34, 42, 44, 48, 57, 61, 197, 255, 320; chairman of, 39; power of veto, 187; appoints Committee on the Revision of the Statute, 61–3; submits candidates for position of Secretary General, 241; contacts other organisations, 285; must approve Work Programmes, 290; Resolution of May, 1966, 311–13
Mitterand, F., 124, 125
Modinos, P., Deputy Secretary General, 82–3, 242, 252; background of, 246, 247; votes for, 248

Mollet, Guy, 47, 196
Molter, M., rapporteur of Draft of Social Charter, 96, 98, 101, 102–7
Monnet, J., 12; assists in Schuman Plan, 50–1, 52, 54–7, 194, 198, 202; Action Committee for a United States of Europe, 326
Morrison, H., 67

National Youth Committee, 264
Netherlands, *See* Holland
Nigeria, 206
North Atlantic Treaty Organisation, 11, 14, 42, 48, 49–50, 63, 70, 74, 240, 374; possible rôle for, 235; links with European Communities, 373
Norway, 86; delegates of in Council of Europe, 15, 40; accepts European Social Charter, 89, 114; applies for membership of European Community, 205, 333
Nutting, A., 66; *Europe will not wait*, 23, 43, 65; presents Eden Plan, 70

Organisation for European Economic Cooperation (OEEC), 29, 30, 63, 196, 215, 260; replaced by OECD, 282
Organisation for Economic Cooperation and Development (OECD), 215, 282; work of, 285; progress reports from, 337

Paris, J–C., Secretary General, 1949–53, 41, 241
Partial Agreements system, 287–9
Peaceful Settlement of Disputes, Convention on, 131, 133–4, 186, 305
Pflimlin, P., President of Consultative Assembly, 248, 365
Pinder, J., *Europe against de Gaulle*, 32
Pirate Radio Stations, Convention on, 163, 164
Pleven, R., 64
Population and Refugees, Committee on, 336–7
Portugal, exclusion from Council of Europe, 24, 137, 262; possible co-operation with, 234, 235
Programme of the Section on Education, Culture and Science, 293–6
Programme of Work, *see* Work Programme
Pryce, R., *The Political Future of the European Movement*, 13, 366–7

Radio Caroline, 150; takes case to European Commission for Human Rights, 177
Radio Veronica, 150
Radius, R., President of Social Committee, 96–8
Rey, J., President of the Brussels Commission, 209, 252
Reynaud, P., 12, 135
Robens, Lord, 292
Robertson, Dr A. H., *The Council of Europe*, 15–16, 88, 94, 136, 249–50
Rome, Treaty of, 1957, creates European Community, 140, 202, 220, 267, 348–9. *See also* European Economic Community and European Atomic Energy Commission
Royal Institute of International Affairs (Chatham House), 209–14
Russell, C., letter to *The Daily Telegraph*, 164–5

Saar, delegates of in Council of Europe, 15, 40
St James's Palace, London, 11; Statute of Council of Europe signed at, 25
Schmitt, Professor, *The Path to European Union*, 40, 41, 43–4, 48, 54–5
Schuijt, M., drafts Social Charter, 96, 98–102, 161
Schulz, M., 333, 338, 339
Schuman, F. L., *International Politics*, 14, 16
Schuman, R., 49, 50; supports Monnet plan, 57–8; Declaration of, 1950, 14, 49, 197–8. *See also* European Coal and Steel Community
Science and Technology, Committee on, 334–5
Secretariat of Council of Europe, responsible for Work Programme, 251, 254, 271, 311, 320
Secretary General of Council of Europe, 2, 25; checks implementation of Social Charter, 114; powers of, 129–30, 385; election of, 239, 241–4, 323; responsibilities in Work Programme, 310, 311, 312, 313, 320; links different departments, 328; circulates conventions, 145, 146
Silkin, Lord, 330, 333
Smithers, P., background as candidate for position of Secretary General, 247; election of, 248–9; his views on

European unity, 250–64; introduces Work Programme, 254, 259–60, 264, 267, 269–70, 306, 308–9, 323; explanatory memorandum to member governments, 274–90, 291, 293, 295, 303; in debate on Work Programme, 331, 332
Social Committee of the Assembly, works on Social Charter, 92, 93, 95; sub-committee of, 114, 115
Social Security Code, application of, 170
Spaak, P-H., at Council of Europe, 12, 14, 29, 39, 44, 45, 47–8, 68; resignation of, 63, 69, 73, 245; founder member of European Community, 196, 200, 202, 292; Secretary General of NATO, 240
Spain, 371; exclusion from Council of Europe, 24, 137, 253, 262, 322; possible co-operation with, 235
Spühler, W., comments on Work Programme, 304–6
State Immunity, Convention on, 167
Stewart, M., ideas of on European co-operation, 234–5
Strasbourg, choice of for Council, 12, 26, 34–8; letter from on work of Council, 297–9
Sweden, delegates from in Council of Europe, 15, 40; accepts Social Charter, 89, 114; applies for associate membership of European Community, 205, 333
Switzerland, delegates from in Council of Europe, 15, 305, 306; applies for associate membership of European Community, 205

Tiroir system, 373, 376, 380
Transport, European Conference of Ministers on, 285, 288, 315–16
Tripartite Conference, 1958, 94–5; states necessary ratifications, 105, 106
Turkey, delegates in Council of Europe, 40; becomes associate with European Community, 206, 234

United Kingdom, *see* Britain
United Nations, members of, 263; Covenants, 1966, 316

Vos, M., comments on Work Programme, 326, 327–8

Wahl, Professor, 134
War Cripples, Agreement on exchange of, 163
Warsaw Pact, 377
Western European Union, 47, 69, 74, 206, 331; lacks centre of decision, 354; possible fusion with EEC, 373; work of, 374
Wilson, H., addresses Council of Europe, 347–8
Work Programme, 73, 129; necessity for, 254, 259–60, 264, 267, 269–97, 299, 306; programme unit set up, 356–7; draft for, 273; discontinued projects, 279, 280; selection of work, 281; approach to European unification, 282–4; need for support from member states, 269–70, 287, 343, 355; cost of, 291; varied activities of, 307–10, 313–19; First Work Programme, 1966/67, 277, 313–14; debate on, 326–38; Second Work Programme, 1967/68, 313–19; participation of whole Council in, 320, 321, 354; European nature of, 304, 357, 382, 385; momentum of, 321–2, 323–4, 329, 338; annual renewal of, 322, 324–5, 329, 338, 349; communication value of, 325; report on, 338–43; relationship with EEC, 353
Work Programme, committee of rapporteurs on, 328, 333, 338–45

Yugoslavia, exclusion from Council of Europe, 24, 137

Zurcher, Professor A. J., *The Struggle to Unite Europe*, 176
Zurich, Churchill's speech at, 16